THE ONE MEDIATOR, THE SAINTS, AND MARY

THE ONE MEDIATOR, THE SAINTS, AND MARY

Lutherans and Catholics in Dialogue VIII

Edited by
H. George Anderson
J. Francis Stafford
Joseph A. Burgess

Augsburg ■ Minneapolis

Joseph Andrew Sittler 1904–1987
Jerome D. Quinn 1927–1988
Carl J. Peter 1932–1991
Fred Kramer 1902–1991
✠ T. Austin Murphy 1911–1991
Ut Omnes Unum Sint

THE ONE MEDIATOR, THE SAINTS, AND MARY
Lutherans and Catholics in Dialogue VIII

Cover design: Judy Swanson

Library of Congress Cataloging-in-Publication Data

The One Mediator, the Saints, and Mary / edited by H. George Anderson, J. Francis Stafford, Joseph A. Burgess.
p. cm.—(Lutherans and Catholics in dialogue : 8)
Includes bibliographical references.
ISBN 0-8066-2579-1 (alk. paper)
1. Lutheran Church—Relations—Catholic Church. 2. Catholic Church—Relations—Lutheran Church. 3. Jesus Christ—Person and offices. 4. Christian saints. 5. Mary, Blessed Virgin, Saint—Theology. I. Anderson, H. George (Hugh George), 1932– II. Stafford, J. Francis, 1932– III. Burgess, Joseph A. IV. Series.
BX8063.7.C3064 1992
235′.2—dc20 91-40822
CIP

The paper used in this publication meets the minimum requirements of American National Standard for Information Sciences—Permanence of Paper for Printed Library Materials, ANSI Z329.48-1984. ∞™

Manufactured in the U.S.A. AF 9-2579

96 95 94 93 92 1 2 3 4 5 6 7 8 9 10

Contents

Abbreviations

AAS	*Acta Apostolicae Sedis*
AB	Anchor Bible
Ap	Apology of the Augsburg Confession
A.V.S.	*Acta Synodalia Sacrosancti Concilii Vaticani Secundi* (Rome: Typis Polyglottis Vaticanis, 1971–)
BAGD	*A Greek-English Lexicon of the New Testament and Other Early Christian Literature,* Walter Bauer's 5th ed., tr. and ed. by F. W. Gingrich and R. W. Danker (Chicago: University of Chicago Press, 1979)
BC	*The Book of Concord. The Confessions of the Evangelical Lutheran Church* (tr. and ed. T. Tappert; Philadelphia: Fortress, 1959)
BS	*Die Bekenntnisschriften der lutherischen Kirche*
c.	circa
CA	*Confessio Augustana* (Augsburg Confession)
CCL	*Corpus Christianorum, Series latina* (Turnhout: Brepols, 1953–)
C.O.D.	*Conciliorum Oecumenicorum Decreta* (ed. G. Alberigo et al.; Freiburg: Herder, 1962)
CPG	*Clavis Patrum Graecorum* (5 vols.; ed. M. Geerard; Turnhout: Brepols, 1974–87)
CR	*Corpus Reformatorum* (28 vols.; ed. C. G. Bretschneider and H.E. Bindseil; Halle and Braunschweig: C. A. Schwetschke, 1834-1860)

CS	Common Statement
CSCO	*Corpus scriptorum christianorum orientalium* (Louvain: Secretariat du Corpus SCO, 1903–)
CSEL	*Corpus scriptorum ecclesiasticorum latinorum* (Vienna: Academia Litterarum Caesarae Vindobonensis, etc., 1866–1926)
C.T.	*Concilium Tridentinum: Diariorum, Actorum, Epistularum, Tractatuum Nova Collectio* (ed. Societas Görresiana; Freiburg: Herder, 1931)
d.	died
DS	*Enchiridion Symbolorum* (33d ed.; ed. H. Denzinger and A. Schönmetzer)
DV	*Dei Verbum*
ER	*Encyclopedia of Religion* (16 vols.; ed. M. Eliade; New York: Macmillan, 1987)
EWNT	*Exegetisches Wörterbuch zum Neuen Testament* (ed. H. Balz and G. Schneider; Stuttgart: Kohlhammer, 1(1980)–3(1983)
FC Ep	Formula of Concord, Epitome
FC SD	Formula of Concord, Solid Declaration
GCS	*Die Griechischen Christlichen Schriftsteller der ersten drei Jahrhunderte* (Berlin: Akademie Verlag; and Leipzig: Hinrichs, 1897–1941)
G.K.T.	Hubert Jedin, *Geschichte des Konzils von Trient: Dritte Tagungsperiode und Abschluss;* 1: *Frankreich und der neue Anfang in Trient bis zum Tode der Legaten Gonzaga und Seripando.* 2: *Uberwindung der Krise durch Morone, Schliessung und Bestätigung* (Freiburg-Basel-Vienna: Herder, 1975)
JB	Jerusalem Bible
JBC	*Jerome Biblical Commentary* (Englewood Cliffs NJ: Prentice Hall, 1968)
LBW	*Lutheran Book of Worship* (Minneapolis: Augsburg, 1978)
LCL	*Loeb Classical Library*
LG	*Lumen Gentium*
L/RC 6	*Teaching Authority and Infallibility in the Church* (Lutherans and Catholics in Dialogue 6; ed. P. C. Empie, T. A. Murphy, and J. A. Burgess; Minneapolis: Augsburg, 1980)
L/RC 7	*Justification by Faith* (Lutherans and Catholics in Dialogue 7; ed. H. G. Anderson, T. A. Murphy, and J. A. Burgess; Minneapolis: Augsburg, 1985)

LThK	*Lexikon für Theologie und Kirche* (2d ed.; Freiburg: Herder, 1(1957)–10 (1965)
LW	*Luther's Works* (general ed. J. Pelikan and H. Lehmann; St. Louis: Concordia Publishing House; and Philadelphia: Fortress 1(1958)–55 (1986)
LWp	*Lutheran Worship* (St. Louis: Concordia Publishing House, 1982)
Mary in the New Testament	*Mary in the New Testament. A Collaborative Assessment by Protestant and Roman Catholic Scholars* (ed. R. E. Brown, K. P. Donfried, J. A. Fitzmyer, and J. Reumann; Philadelphia: Fortress; and New York: Paulist, 1978)
NAB	New American Bible
NABRNT	New American Bible Revised New Testament
NIDNTT	*New International Dictionary of New Testament Theology* (Grand Rapids MI: Zondervan 1(1975)–3 (1978)
NJBC	*New Jerome Biblical Commentary* (Englewood Cliffs NJ: Prentice Hall, 1990)
PG	*Patrologiae cursus completus, Series graeca* (ed. J. P. Migne; 167 vol. and 2 index vol.; Paris, 1857–66, 1928, 1936)
PL	*Patrologiae cursus completus, Series latina* (ed. J. P. Migne; 221 vol. and 5 supplementary vol.; Paris, 1841–64, 1958–70)
RSV	Revised Standard Version
SA	Smalcald Articles
SC	*Sources chrétiennes* (Paris: du Cerf, 1942–)
S. T.	*Summa theologiae*
TRE	*Theologische Realenzyklopädie* (Berlin, New York: de Gruyter, 1977–)
TDNT	*Theological Dictionary of the New Testament* (ed. G. Kittel; tr. and ed. G. Bromiley; Grand Rapids MI: Eerdmans, 1(1964)–10 (1976)
TWNT	*Theologisches Wörterbuch zum Neuen Testament* (ed. G. Kittel; Stuttgart: Kohlhammer, 1(1933)–10, 2 (1979)
WA	Martin Luther, *Werke* (Kritische Gesamtausgabe; "Weimarer Ausgabe"; Weimar: Böhlau, 1883–)
WA TR	WA Tischreden
§	Sections of "The One Mediator, the Saints, and Mary," pp. 19-132 of this volume.

Preface

From 1983 to 1990 the Lutheran/Roman Catholic dialogue in the United States of America discussed the topic "The One Mediator, the Saints, and Mary." This, the eighth round of theological dialogue, has tested the doctrinal implications of the fundamental affirmation and material convergences of the seventh round, the topic of which was "Justification by Faith." For the most part the Confessio Augustana article on the intercessory role of the saints and the Roman Catholic dogmas of the Immaculate Conception and of the Assumption served as the background for the theologians' discussions. In testing the rule contained in the common christological affirmation of the seventh round, the dialogue has made an earnest search for further areas of convergence. At the same time the members of the dialogue acknowledge that there are remaining doctrinal differences between Lutherans and Roman Catholics concerning Christ, the One Mediator, the Saints, and Mary. Considerable research into the long history of these doctrinal and pastoral issues has accompanied and undergirded our discussions. Unquestionably we have come to a better appreciation and understanding of the doctrines and practices of Lutherans and Roman Catholics over the past four centuries. The articulation of the "resulting divergences" and "church-uniting convergences" has more than warranted our seven years of prayer and dialogue on this topic.

At the beginning of the eighth round in 1984, Bishop T. Austin Murphy of Baltimore, the Catholic co-chairman, indicated his desire to resign. He had held the position of co-chairman since the beginning of the dialogue in 1965. For his nineteen years of formal commitment to the ecumenical enterprise, both Lutherans and Roman Catholics are grateful.

We also wish to acknowledge the generosity of the Lutheran and Roman Catholic theologians who have participated in these discussions. When the history of the ecumenical movement is written, the extraordinary contributions and gifts of these men and women will be seen as pivotal for the realization of Christian unity.

We now submit this document to the authorities, theologians, pastors, and people of our supporting churches for their reflection and judgment. We await their reaction to our findings and recommendations toward unity.

Co-chairmen:

✠ J. FRANCIS STAFFORD
Archbishop of Denver

H. GEORGE ANDERSON
President, Luther College

Chronological Listing of Sessions and Papers

Session 37: Milwaukee WI, September 16–19, 1983

Robert B. Eno, S.S., "How Much Pluralism . . ." (unpublished).

Kenneth Hagen, "Lyra and Luther on Luke 1:26-55" (unpublished).

Kilian McDonnell, O.S.B., "Extended Memo on the Veneration of the Saints" (unpublished).

Session 38: Seguin TX, February 23–26, 1984

Eric W. Gritsch, "Luther and the Veneration of Mary" (incorporated into his essay in this volume).

Kenneth Hagen, "CA 21 and the *Confutatio, de cultu sanctorum*" (unpublished).

Session 39: Cincinnati OH, September 20–23, 1984

Robert B. Eno, S.S., "Mary and Her Role in Patristic Theology" (published in this volume; the section on Augustine's Mariology is republished from *idem, St. Augustine and the Saints* [The Saint Augustine Lecture for 1985; Philadelphia: Villanova University Press, 1989] 87–94).

Karlfried Froehlich, "Mary in the Hymns of Martin Luther" (unpublished).

Carl Peter, "The Eschatology of *Lumen Gentium*: Beyond in Both Directions" (published in revised form as "The Last Things and *Lumen Gentium*," *Chicago Studies* 24(1985) 225–37; published in this volume with sections from the version in *Chicago Studies*).

Elizabeth A. Johnson, C.S.J., "Roman Catholic Documents Concerning Mary since Vatican II" (unpublished).

Session 40: Marriottsville MD, February 21–24, 1985

Joseph A. Fitzmyer, S.J., "Biblical Data on the Veneration of Holy People" (published in this volume).

Robert B. Eno, S.S., "The Cult of the Saints in the Fourth and Fifth Centuries" (published *idem, St. Augustine and the Saints* [The Saint Augustine Lecture for 1985; Philadelphia: Villanova University Press, 1989] 29–48).

Georges Tavard, A.A., "Saints and Angels in Jeanne d'Arc's Piety" (unpublished).

Robert Bertram, "Mary and the Saints as an Issue in the Lutheran Confessions" (unpublished).

Gerhard Forde, "What Is a Saint? Notes on a Lutheran View" (unpublished).

Avery Dulles, S.J., "Karl Rahner on the Mediation of the Saints" (unpublished).

John Frederick Johnson, "Mary and the Saints in Contemporary Lutheran Worship: An Overview" (published in this volume).

Frederick M. Jelly, O.P. "Biblical Texts Used by Aquinas for His Theology of the Saints in Glory" (unpublished).

Session 41: Techny IL, September 19–22, 1985

John Frederick Johnson, "Anselm on the Virgin Birth: A Reflection on Mary" (unpublished).

Joseph A. Burgess and Elizabeth A. Johnson, C.S.J., "A Glossary of Terms with Comments" (unpublished).

Joseph A. Burgess, "Three Reflections" (unpublished).

Karlfried Froehlich, "The *Libri Carolini* and the Lessons of the Iconoclastic Controversy" (published in this volume).

Carl Peter, "*Quodlibetum* on the Church's Treasures (*Thesauri Ecclesiae*)" (published as "The Church's Treasures [*Thesauri Ecclesiae*] Then and Now," *Theological Studies* 47[1986] 251–72, and incorporated into his essay on the Council of Trent in this volume).

Avery Dulles, S.J., "Karl Rahner's Mariology" (unpublished).

Kilian McDonnell, O.S.B., "*Lex Orandi, Lex Credendi*, and Mary" (published in this volume).

Session 42: Burlingame CA, February 20–23, 1986

Robert B. Eno, S.S., "Pre-Constantinian Roots of Devotion to the Saints" (incorporated by *idem* into the volume, *St. Augustine and the Saints* ([The Saint Augustine Lecture for 1985; Philadelphia: Villanova University Press, 1989]).

Kilian McDonnell, O.S.B., "The Liturgical Veneration of the Saints: A Note" (unpublished).

Gerhard Forde, "Could Invocation of the Saints Be Considered an Adiaphoron?" (published in this volume).

Karlfried Froehlich, "Modern Liturgical Movements, the Saints, and Mary in Protestantism (Germany only)" (unpublished).

Robert Bertram, "A Constructive Lutheran Theology of the Saints" (unpublished).

Carl Peter, "The Council of Trent and the Communion of Saints: A Long Footnote" (incorporated into his essay on the Council of Trent in this volume).

George Tavard, A.A., "Bonaventure and John Duns Scotus on the Virgin Mary" (on Bonaventure: published as *idem, The Forthbringer of God. St. Bonaventure on the Virgin Mary* [Chicago: Franciscan Herald Press, 1989]; on John Duns Scotus: incorporated into his essay in this volume).

Frederick M. Jelly, O.P. "Mary in the Theology of Thomas Aquinas" (unpublished).

Session 43: Wheeling WV, September 18–21, 1986

Frederick M. Jelly, O.P., "Misplaced Mediation of Mary and the Saints in Medieval Popular Piety" (unpublished).

John Frederick Johnson, "Mary and the Saints, Use and Abuse: A Critique" (unpublished).

John Reumann, "How Do We Interpret 1 Timothy 2:1-5?" (published in this volume).

Gerhard Forde, "Nature, Creation, and Grace: Some Preliminary Observations for Discussion" (unpublished).

Carl Peter, "Nature as Presupposing, Perfecting, and Not Destroying Nature" (unpublished).

Robert B. Eno, S.S., "The Fathers and the Cleansing Fire" (published in the *Irish Theological Quarterly* 53[1987] 184–202).

Session 44: Tampa FL, February 19–22, 1987

Elizabeth A. Johnson, C.S.J., "Mary as Mediatrix" (published in this volume).

Frederick M. Jelly, O.P., "The Roman Catholic Dogma of Mary's Immaculate Conception" (published in this volume).

Avery Dulles, S.J., "The Dogma of the Assumption" (published in this volume).

Eric W. Gritsch, "Lutheran Reactions to the Marian Dogmas of 1854 and 1950" (incorporated into his essay in this volume).

Robert Bertram, "Luther on the Unique Mediatorship of Christ" (published in this volume).

Session 45: Chicago IL, September 17–20, 1987

Session 46: Orlando FL, February 18–21, 1988

Session 47: Dayton OH, September 22–25, 1988

Session 48: Lantana FL, February 16–19, 1989

Session 49: New Orleans LA, September 21–24, 1989

Session 50: Lantana FL, February 15–18, 1990

COMMON STATEMENT

THE ONE MEDIATOR, THE SAINTS, AND MARY

Introduction

(1) From its outset in 1965 the theological dialogue between Lutherans and Roman Catholics in the United States has concerned itself with doctrines that have united or separated their churches from one another since the sixteenth century. The degree of consensus or convergence that exists on the Nicene Creed, Baptism, the Eucharist, the Ministry, Papal Primacy, and Teaching Authority and Infallibility has been expressed in summaries and joint statements[1] that have become important for relations between our churches and for wider ecumenical discussions.

(2) In 1983 the dialogue completed a common statement on "Justification by Faith," published with background papers in 1985.[2] We agreed "that the good news of what God has done for us in Jesus Christ is the source and center of all Christian life and of the existence and work of the church" (§4). We shared an affirmation that "our entire hope of justification and salvation rests on Christ Jesus and on the gospel . . ." so that "we do not place our ultimate trust in anything other than God's promise and saving work in Christ" (§§4, 157). We asked our churches and Christians of all traditions to study our declaration together and find in it (§§161–64) an invitation to "the good news of God's justifying action in Jesus Christ" that "stands at the center of Christian faith and life" (§§2, 165).

(3) In setting forth our material convergences on this doctrine and an "incomplete convergence on the use" of it as "a criterion

of authenticity for the church's proclamation and practice" (§§150–60), we indicated need for further dialogue (§154), testing the use of this critical principle. A number of possible test issues were noted, including ecclesiastical structures, means of grace, papacy, infallibility, and teachings on Mary and the saints (§§117–20).

(4) In light of the sole mediatorship of Christ, which was termed "the correlative" of the principle of justification by faith (§117), the present statement focuses on the saints and Mary, which became a divisive subject in the Reformation period. We shall begin in Part One, on issues and perspectives, with (I) the problem in the sixteenth century. Next we shall turn to (II) the perspectives of our two traditions on the crucial issues. Then (III) we shall reexamine the problem in the present context, which has changed in some ways from the situation in the sixteenth century. We shall here indicate dimensions of the problem and some resulting divergences, investigate whether they need to be church-dividing, propose church-uniting convergences, and draw a conclusion. In support of these convergences and the steps which we ask our churches to consider, Part Two provides foundations from (I) Scripture, which is normative for both our traditions; (II) the second to the sixteenth centuries, where historical studies show the complexity of the issues; and (III) subsequent periods, including the Second Vatican Council. These foundations undergird the proposals at the conclusion of Part One.

(5) In many instances we are dealing not only with doctrines but also Catholic and Lutheran thought structures as well as expressions of worship and piety. It should be noted, however, that the dialogue did not discuss in any depth, nor do we attempt here to report on, present-day matters of popular and folk religion, aspects in comparative religion or the history of world religions, feminist questions, or a total systematic theology of the saints and Mary. Amid these immense and much debated areas we have dealt only with issues that have divided our churches since the sixteenth century and seem still to be divisive.

PART ONE: ISSUES AND PERSPECTIVES

I

The Problem in the Sixteenth Century

(6) Late medieval piety was marked by a great emphasis on the intercession of deceased saints and in particular by an intensification of confidence in the power of Mary. The steadily increasing number of saints invoked to remedy human needs and ills, and the long-accustomed role of Mary as mediator between the faithful and Christ, obscured the traditional theological distinction between adoration (*latria*) and veneration (*dulia*).[3] In 1517, when Martin Luther called for an academic disputation on the use of indulgences and their relationship to the sacrament of penance, the cult of the saints and Mary became a related issue.

(7) In 1517–18 Luther had assessed and found seriously wanting a number of practices and institutions that he encountered in the church of his day. His criticism focused on: a) sacramental confession-absolution; b) indulgences; c) the papacy with its powers of binding-loosing; and d) purgatory as well as prayer for the dead. What concerned him with each of these was the role people thought it played in the forgiveness of post-baptismal sin.

(8) To be specific, the constitution *Omnis Utriusque* of the Fourth Lateran Council (1215) required Christian adults to confess their sins once a year to their parish priest so as to obtain God's forgiveness.[4] But even after one had received absolution in this manner, the obligation remained to perform works of satisfaction for the sins that had been forgiven; indeed, theologians taught that this was an integral part of the sacrament of penance. Here, however, the church could help by mitigating or eliminating the penalties which sins, though forgiven, still deserved in divine justice.

The church did this by having recourse to and applying the superabundant merits of Christ and the saints (indulgences). For the use of this treasure, which was to benefit the whole church, the pope, as Christ's vicar, and bishops were responsible. Those who both needed and could profit from such help included the deceased as well as the living (purgatory and prayer for the dead).[5]

(9) Luther regarded the system of which these elements were parts as claiming to bring the forgiveness that could come only from Christ. His attitude to the saints and Mary was guided by this christocentric view of life which was expressed in the fundamental affirmation of justification by faith alone. Luther had gained this christocentric view in an intense struggle for the biblical meaning of penance and a rethinking of the soteriological implications of the trinitarian dogma, focusing on the incarnation of Christ.[6] Having been steeped in the cult of the saints during his formative years, Luther and other Reformers, notably Andreas Karlstadt, began to criticize the cult.[7] They said that it caused people to have greater confidence in the merits of deceased saints than in Christ. Some Reformers, like Martin Bucer, called for the removal of all Saints' Days in the liturgical calendar, but Luther advocated a more moderate stance towards the saints and Mary.[8]

(10) None of Luther's early opponents sensed his concerns about penance more keenly than did the Dominican theologian Thomas de Vio (Cajetan).[9] In his reaction to Luther in 1518 he understood Luther to a) deny that indulgences derive their efficacy from the fact that in granting them the church mediates the merits of Christ and the saints to assist the baptized in making satisfaction before God after the forgiveness of sins and b) maintain that through indulgences the church relies on the promised power of the keys (Matthew 16:19) so as to loose bonds that it has imposed for infractions of its own (rather than divine) laws. Cajetan countered by saying that these positions were at odds with the presentation of indulgences in the bull *Unigenitus* of Pope Clement VI. And such documents rank right after the authority of the Scriptures.[10]

(11) More was involved here than a Scholastic's appeal to authority. Cajetan set himself to answering each of Luther's various arguments against indulgences as applying the merits of Christ and the saints. But by introducing papal teaching, he was asking Luther to trust in the church and its self-understanding with regard to the forgiveness of sin and its consequences—this on the basis of Matthew 16:19 (the power of the keys).

(12) There was a difference between the two with regard to trust. What Luther distrusted while holding to the promise of Matthew 16:19, Cajetan trusted and urged him likewise to trust on the basis of that same promise. Should the church be trusted to mediate God's forgiveness, both of sin and its consequences? Here they disagreed. The association of the saints' merits with those of Christ figured centrally in the disagreement.[11]

(13) In the bull *Exsurge Domine* of 1520 views taken from Luther's recent writings were condemned. Those views had to do with the same practices and institutions that Luther had criticized in 1517–18. Forty-one propositions were cited without the contexts in which they had originally appeared. The censures ranged from "heretical" to "seductive of the simple-minded" and "at odds with catholic truth."[12] Which censure or censures applied to which proposition and why each was rejected were not indicated, nor was official clarification forthcoming. After Luther's excommunication in 1521 things remained in that state. For further papal and conciliar teaching one had to wait until Pope Paul III convoked the Council of Trent, which met for the first time in 1545.

(14) Luther's rejection of the cult of the saints and Mary was based on the contention that such practice is not based on divine command and detracts from trust in Christ alone. He declared that instead of relying on deceased saints, whose world is hidden and mysterious, baptized Christians should follow the command of Scripture to care for the weak and needy in the world; these need more attention than the deceased saints.[13] Luther was convinced that the practice of invoking the saints only continued the medieval tendency to transform Christ the "kindly Mediator" into a "dreaded Judge" who is to be placated by the intercession of the saints and Mary, and by a multitude of other rites.[14] Departed saints may be remembered, but invoking them is to be omitted from liturgical celebrations.

(15) Luther's attitude toward deceased saints and Mary was centered in his concept of example. Some Christians, now departed, exemplified bold faith while on earth through their words and deeds. To Luther, the most prominent saints were biblical figures like John the Baptist and Paul and later church teachers like, most notably, Ambrose, Augustine, and Bernard. John Hus was to him also a prominent saint because God had endowed him with great gifts to renew Christianity.[15]

(16) Although Luther was critical of some collected legends of saints, he advocated the use of other legends for edification, such

as Jacob of Voragine's *Golden Legend* (*Legenda aurea*), which contained stories about exemplary saints like Bernard, whom Luther "venerated."[16] He also chose to honor Henry von Zutphen, the first Lutheran martyr, executed in Brussels in 1524, and told his story in the style of ancient martyrologies.[17] He also encouraged one of his students, George Major, to publish a revised version of the *Lives of the Fathers* (*Vitae Patrum*) and, in a preface, recommended it as edifying literature.[18] He thus continued the hagiographic tradition in this sense, but he stressed its exclusively edifying and pedagogical character: Deceased saints may be venerated as examples of faith in Christ, "the saint of saints," from whom all holiness flows.[19] But because all of them have become righteous through Christ alone, no saint is holier than another, according to Luther.

(17) Since little had been defined dogmatically about Mary, Luther felt free to develop his own views on the basis of Scripture and tradition. He accepted the dogma of Mary as "God-bearer" (*theotokos*) and affirmed her perpetual virginity; he called her Immaculate Conception "a pious and pleasing thought."[20] Consistent with his christocentric stance, Luther contended that such notions should not become official doctrines. He affirmed some festivals involving Mary on a scriptural basis, but rejected two: the Assumption and the Immaculate Conception.[21]

(18) According to Luther, Mary embodied God's unmerited grace which was evidenced in the *Magnificat* (Luke 1:46-55), and as such she typified the church. He contended that the church, like Mary's virginity, would never be destroyed, no matter what the opposition and persecution.[22] Luther affirmed Mary's Assumption into heaven, but considered her Assumption no different than that of others like Abraham, Isaac, and Jacob, who had been promised life with God forever. Thus, according to Luther, Mary points only to Christ, whose ascension would be dishonored if she were invoked.[23]

(19) Luther's hymns, when they refer to Mary, do so in the language of a Marian piety reflecting his views. It is a part of an incarnational Christology informed by biblical and patristic tradition which focuses on the exaltation of Christ and on theTrinity.[24] "Christ alone should be invoked as our Mediator."[25]

(20) The first Lutheran constitutions and liturgies (*Kirchenordnungen*) were normed by Luther's doctrinal concern that neither the saints nor Mary is to be invoked because Christ is the only Mediator and Scripture is silent about such invocation. Saints may be honored as mirroring the grace and mercy of God, but Christ alone is the Mediator who represents the faithful (1 John 2:1; Rom

8:34).[26] Statements such as these represent a significant contribution in the West toward a dogmatic clarification of the veneration of the saints.[27]

(21) When Emperor Charles V invited the princes and representatives of free cities in the empire to discuss their religious differences at the Diet of Augsburg in 1530, Elector Frederick of Saxony asked the Wittenberg theologians to prepare an account of the beliefs and practices in the churches of his land. Philipp Melanchthon was asked by Luther and other leaders of the reform movement to draft what has become known as the Augsburg Confession, which consisted of two parts: "chief articles of faith," and "articles about matters in dispute, in which an account is given of the abuses which have been corrected." CA 21 is the final article of the first part, and it served as the platform for doctrinal dialogue on "the cult of the saints." It reads (German text):

> It is also taught among us that the saints should be kept in remembrance so that our faith may be strengthened when we see what grace they received and how they were sustained by faith. Moreover, their good works are to be an example for us, each of us in his own calling. So His Imperial Majesty may in salutary and godly fashion imitate the example of David in making war on the Turk, for both are incumbents of a royal office which demands the defense and protection of their subjects. However, it cannot be proved from the Scriptures that we are to invoke saints or seek help from them. "For there is one mediator between God and men, Christ Jesus" (1 Tim. 2:5), who is the only saviour, the only high priest, advocate, and intercessor before God (Rom 8:34). He alone has promised to hear our prayers. Moreover, according to the Scriptures, the highest form of divine service is sincerely to seek and call upon this same Jesus Christ in every time of need. "If anyone sins, we have an advocate with the Father, Jesus Christ the righteous" (1 John 2:1).[28]

(22) A Catholic response to the Augsburg Confession was mandated not by the pope in Rome but by the emperor in Augsburg. This initiated a drafting process which in turn included revisions that were made because Charles V desired a less polemical tone. The final text, the *Confutation*, was forthcoming on August 3, 1530.[29] Never having received papal or conciliar approval and lacking the status of official teaching in the Catholic Church, it remains to this day what it was at the time of its composition, the work of a group

of theologians speaking in their own name at the Diet. That did not, however, keep it from exerting a great deal of influence.

(23) Charles V not only maintained that the *Confutation* was a refutation of the Augsburg Confession; he expected the Lutheran party at the Diet to acknowledge this. In addition to being denied a copy of the text (which they had heard read), the Lutherans took offense at the harshness of its tone and were apprehensive as a result of the negative stance it took with regard to a number of their own positions.

(24) In its response to CA 21 the *Confutation* expresses surprise at the lack of vigilance on the part of the princes. They have tolerated an error, namely, that the memory of the saints may be cultivated to promote imitation of their faith and good works but not for the purpose of invoking them and seeking their help. The civil authorities should have done something to keep this view from being spread and acted on in their territories. Given that the church has repeatedly condemned the position in question—so the *Confutation* states bluntly[30]—CA 21 is to be completely rejected. The princes are urged to be of one mind with the church. In particular, as regards the veneration and intercession of the saints, they should believe and confess what the Christian people everywhere believe and confess and what was observed in all the churches even at the time of Augustine. For to the widespread cult of the saints he attested when he wrote:

> The Christian people celebrate with religious solemnity the memory of the martyrs so as to imitate the latter as well as to be associated with their merits and helped by their prayers.[31]

(25) Since CA 21 had appealed to Scripture, the *Confutation* did likewise. If God will honor those who minister to Jesus (John 12:26), why should not mortals do so as well? And it did not stop with veneration; it went on to intercession. Job (42:10) had his request granted when he prayed for his friends. Will not the God who acceded to Job's petition do likewise when the Virgin Mary makes intercession? And if one objects that Job prayed while yet alive, in Baruch (3:4) God is asked to hear now the prayer of the dead of Israel. So the dead do pray for us. To that the Old Testament attests in its presentations of Onias and Jeremiah in the Second Book of Maccabees (15:12-14). That angels pray for us one learns from the Scriptures (Zech 1:12ff; Job 33:23ff; Rev 5:8, 8:3). If angels do this, why deny that saints do so as well? Christ is indeed the sole Mediator of redemption (1 Tim 2:5; 1 John 2:1), but there are many

mediators who make intercession. For Moses was a mediator (Deut 5:5) and prayed for the children of Israel (Exod 17:4; 32:11-13, 30ff) as Paul would later for those sailing with him (Acts 27:23ff). That same Paul asks the Romans (Rom 15:30), the Corinthians (2 Cor 1:11), and the Colossians (Col 4:3) to pray for him, and prayer was made in the church without stopping for Peter when he was in prison (Acts 12:5). The saints in heaven are Christ's members (1 Cor 12:12, 27; Eph 5:30); their wills are conformed to his; they see their head pray for us; who can doubt that they do what they see Christ doing?[32]

(26) The *Confutation* thus defended both the veneration and the invocation of the saints. Asserting that Christ is the sole Mediator of redemption, it proposed Mary and the saints as "mediators of intercession."[33] It did not regard invocation as contrary to Scripture but as having a biblical basis. At the same time it did not criticize aberrations in this form of Christian piety. What the *Confutation* did was to call for trust in the church's understanding of itself as a body whose members (deceased as well as living) are empowered by Christ their head to help one another.

(27) Melanchthon responded to the *Confutation's* criticism of CA 21 in the Apology of the Augsburg Confession (1531). The honor of the saints, he repeated, is in no way denied by Lutherans. "Honoring the saints" includes: 1) giving thanks to God for them as examples of God's mercy and of faithfulness; 2) being strengthened in one's faith by God's grace in their lives; and 3) imitating their faith, love, and other virtues. Melanchthon readily conceded that angels and living saints in the church universal on earth and in heaven intercede for believers.[34] What he denounces is the step from intercession to invocation. "Scripture does not teach us to invoke the saints or to ask their help."[35] Invocation of the saints, he submits, has no command or example or promise in the canonical Scriptures and therefore no certainty. In fact, it is a relative novelty not attested in the early church before Pope Gregory the Great (590–604).[36] The Confutators make matters worse by introducing the notion of the merits of the saints being applied to other Christians, thus making the saints propitiators instead of intercessors when they claim that there is "one Mediator of redemption" (*unus mediator redemptionis*) and there are "many mediators of intercession" (*multi mediatores intercessionis*).[37] But a propitiator must have a clear promise that God will hear prayers through him and that his merits will be accepted to make satisfaction for others. Christ

has both promises, the saints have neither, despite theological statements to the contrary and the formulae of the liturgy. The saints are not authorized by God to act as mediators of redemption, nor is Mary so authorized. As the Mother of God she is worthy of the highest honors, prays for the church, and is an example of faith and humble obedience. But she never claimed to have the authority which later teaching applied to her when it contrasted her mildness to the image of Christ as the dreaded judge. Such authority belongs to Christ alone. Christians have no grounds for trusting that the saints' merits are transferrable to others.[38] Equally erroneous in Melanchthon's eyes is the notion of specialization among saints, each providing special help for those who call on them. Such teaching is dangerous, indeed pagan.[39] Seeking help and trusting in other mediators besides Christ leads to the collapse of trust and diminishes knowledge of Christ. Melanchthon draws on historical experience for this central assertion: First, there was simple commemoration of the saints in the ancient prayers; then came the invocation of saints with all its abuses, that were worse than pagan practices, especially in the superstition surrounding images, undergirded by preposterous and fabricated legends. Melanchthon notes that these abuses are not only present in popular piety and practice, but are aided and abetted by the teachers of the church, including the Confutators who do not use their knowledge of doctrine to expose these manifest abuses. To require, as the *Confutation* suggests, the invocation of the saints is tantamount to requiring abuses, and temporal authorities need to exercise their God-given responsibility to protect the consciences of the faithful from abusive ecclesiastical requirements and to defend those who teach sound doctrine.[40]

(28) When Pope Paul III called a General Council to meet in Mantua in 1537, Elector John of Saxony instructed Luther to prepare a statement indicating the articles of faith in which concessions might be made for the sake of peace and the articles in which no concessions could be made. Luther quickly produced a statement as his theological testament in case he should die, since he had become severely ill. The statement was submitted for adoption by the Smalcald League, an alliance of princes, at its meeting at Smalcald on February 8, 1537. Though present, Luther was unable to participate in the discussions because of illness. The statement was never adopted by the league. But many of the clergy attending the meeting signed what became known as the *Smalcald Articles*, which became part of the *Book of Concord* in 1580.[41]

(29) In the section on "the invocation of the saints," Luther charged that their invocation is in conflict with the chief article, justification by faith, and undermines knowledge of Christ. He also repeated the warning of the *Augsburg Confession* that the invocation of the saints is not commanded in Scripture because "we have everything a thousandfold better in Christ."[42] Luther conceded that the saints in heaven "perhaps" (*vielleicht, fortassis*) pray for those on earth, but it does not follow that the saints in heaven should be invoked. "If such idolatrous honor is withdrawn from angels and dead saints," Luther contended, "the honor that remains will do no harm and will quickly be forgotten."[43]

(30) In 1541 Emperor Charles V persuaded Rome and leading Protestant Reformers to discuss their theological differences during the meetings of the Diet of Regensburg. A papal delegation, led by the papal legates Gasparo Contarini and Giovanni Morone, and a Protestant team, headed by Philipp Melanchthon, discussed the cult of the saints in the context of the doctrine of justification. But both sides were unable to move beyond the positions of the *Confutation* and of CA 21. Catholics asserted the legitimacy of the invocation of the saints as an authentic ecclesiastical tradition; Lutherans opposed the practice because it obscures the sole mediatorship of Christ.[44]

(31) In 1563 a response to the Reformation critique of the cult of saints was forthcoming in the form of conciliar teaching. At the very close of the Council of Trent three decrees were approved dealing with purgatory; the invocation, veneration, and relics of the saints as well as sacred images; and indulgences.[45] Each was written with the intention of providing a mandate for the correction of abuses. For none of these decrees was there time to formulate more than a brief *doctrinal* exposition. The majority of the Council members wished to bring the proceedings to a close. Lengthy debate was out of the question. But to propose no teaching at all on what had been such neuralgic issues would leave the impression that nothing could be said on behalf of the practices in question. What is more, there was general agreement that these practices needed reform.

(32) In dealing with justification, the Council had already described the defective character of the saints' holiness in this life (Mary excluded, they were not exempt from venial sin). Because it felt more was needed, it went on to approve a decree dealing with the invocation, veneration, and relics of the saints as well as

with sacred images. The points emphasized in that decree would later be very influential.[46]

(33) The decree expressed concern about the need to teach the Christian people that the saints reigning with Christ pray to God on our behalf. The faithful should be instructed that it is good and useful to invoke the saints as well as to have recourse to their prayers and help in obtaining God's benefits through our one Redeemer and Savior, Jesus Christ. Conversely it is ungodly (*impie sentire*) to deny that saints are to be invoked or to assert that: a) they do not pray for human beings; b) calling on them to pray for our individual needs is idolatry; c) such invocation is at odds with honoring the one Mediator, Jesus Christ; and d) it is foolish to beseech with voice and heart those who reign in heaven.[47]

(34) Attention is then directed to a closely related issue—relics. Because of the doctrines of the Mystical Body, the indwelling of the Holy Spirit, and the hope of future resurrection, the bodies of the martyrs and other saints are to be venerated. In this way, many favors come from God.[48]

(35) As for religious art, the decree stipulates that images of Christ, Mary, and the saints are to be retained in churches. But the grounds for this do not lie in a belief that: a) there is any divinity or power in those images; b) anything is to be sought from them; or c) trust and reliance are to be placed in them as pagans once looked to idols and put their hope in them. Rather, the honor paid to such images is referred to those imaged. Not an innovation, this is said to be the position of earlier councils and in particular that of Nicea II (787) in its struggle with the Iconoclasts. Through images and paintings, people are taught and confirmed in the articles of faith. They are challenged by the benefits and duties that come from Christ as well as by the miracles God works through the saints and the salutary example of the saints. They are encouraged to thank, love, and adore God; to cultivate piety; and to live their lives in imitation of the saints.[49]

(36) As for abuses, they are to be eliminated. There are to be no images that portray what is dogmatically false or that offer the occasion of dangerous error to the unsophisticated. God cannot be represented so as to be seen by human eyes; people should not be left to think otherwise. In all these matters superstition and avarice are to be eliminated as well as anything that is sexually suggestive. Holiness befits God's house. Celebrations of saints' feasts and the veneration of relics should not be times of revelry. As for the future, episcopal oversight and approval are required if it is a question of

introducing sacred images departing from the customary or of acknowledging new miracles or relics.[50]

(37) Pastoral care is to be exercised by bishops both in teaching about the solidarity of Christ's members (living and deceased) as well as in the elimination of abuses. That was the Council's prescription for what was needed in the cult of the saints. This was to become an important part of the agenda of the Counter Reformation.

(38) The Lutheran position remained what Luther had asserted in the SA of 1537.[51] Lutheran response to the Council of Trent is summarized in the massive work of Martin Chemnitz, *Examination of the Council of Trent* (1565–73), which rejects the Tridentine teachings on the invocation of the saints and Mary. Chemnitz contends that neither Scripture nor tradition, as viewed by Luther and the CA, supports such teachings.[52] Normative Lutheran teachings, collated in the *Book of Concord* in 1580, are based on the CA, Ap, and SA, which affirm commemorative veneration of the saints and Mary, but reject any invocation of them. Mary is honored as "the Mother of God" (*mater Dei*) and as "the most blessed virgin" (*laudatissima virgo*) in the context of Christology.[53] One of Luther's disciples, Ludwig Rabus (1524–92), attempted to preserve the intention of the Lutheran Confessions by creating the first massive Lutheran martyrology, portraying saints as models of Christian witness.[54]

II

Perspectives on Critical Issues

(39) In the sixteenth century Lutherans and Catholics were at odds as to whether veneration and invocation of Mary and other saints in heaven detracted from the trust, confidence, and hope that should be put in Christ the one Mediator. Today the problem has not vanished. Its continuing character will be clear if one considers how different the perspectives of our two faith communities can still be on the matter. Such a systematic analysis will help to show how and why each community is consistent in holding the position it does on the saints and Mary.

A. Lutheran Perspectives

(40) Lutherans prefer to address the complex problem and series of issues narrated above, first of all, in a positive way.

a. They are convinced that Jesus Christ, crucified once for all, is the one Mediator between God and humanity and so is all-sufficient to save.

b. They believe that Jesus Christ as the Risen and Exalted One intercedes for us at God's right hand (Rom 8:34) and that, since we are justified by faith, we have access to God (Rom 5:1-2); we are enjoined therefore to speak in prayer directly to God through Christ.

c. If Lutherans use the term "mediation" at all with reference to the communication of God's grace to us, they speak of it especially in terms of the work of the Spirit and the ministry of word and sacraments as means of grace.

d. Lutherans, following the New Testament, regard all justified believers in Christ as saints and view sanctification both as God's gift, along with justification, through baptism and faith, and as a way of living in a holy manner according to God's will.

e. Lutherans have been willing to speak of the advance not only of the gospel in the world but also of believers in faith (Phil 1:12,25), and of reflecting or even beholding the glory of God and being transformed or conformed through baptism and the Spirit to the divine image (2 Cor 3:18; 4:6; Rom 8:29), but they are always aware that such advance or conformation is accomplished only by a gracious activity which exposes the depth of sin at the same time as it works to combat such sin. Lutherans have therefore preferred to speak in terms of the "*simul*" of justification/sanctification and sin (*simul justus et peccator*) when describing Christian life, lest growth in grace be confused with human paradigms of progress or human accomplishment. Such growth in grace, for Lutherans, does not come to consummation in this life, but only when the promise which inspires such growth is completely fulfilled in Christ's return.

f. For believers "on the way" in Christ, Lutherans have spoken positively of the exemplary nature of saints, living or dead, and of Mary.

g. In speaking of the Christian dead, Lutherans trust the witness of Scripture and the hope of the resurrection, but do not find scriptural support for encouraging or requiring the invocation of saints who have died or of Mary to intercede for us. Prayer, Lutherans have insisted, must come from faith and faith must rest on promise. Since Scripture makes no explicit promise in this regard, the practice can have no sure basis (Ap 21:10) and could trouble consciences if required.

(41) In many of these interrelated areas Lutherans have had also to respond in the negative to assertions by Catholics that Lutherans regard as unwarranted. Such responses are the reverse side of the positive position presented above and stem ultimately from the criteriological function of the doctrine of justification by faith. In some cases specific differences appear with regard to the extension of the meaning of biblical passages under the church's magisterium. In this way there is a difference over ecclesial authority, in relation to Scripture, for making doctrinal assertions. Lutherans have found the emphasis on "many mediators of intercession" in the *Confutation* confusing and seeming to detract from the unique role of Jesus Christ. Furthermore, the origins and unofficial standing of the *Confutation* add to Lutheran uncertainty about the gravity of this emphasis.

(42) The crucial issue in this dialogue for Lutherans therefore remains that of the sole mediatorship of Christ over against the invocation of the saints and Mary. Although Lutherans do not deny that deceased and living saints join together in praising God—indeed this is affirmed in some eucharistic and other liturgical celebrations—they have difficulties with the customary definition of invocation when it applies to someone other than Christ, namely, as the practice of calling on someone and asking for something for one's benefit. Lutherans believe such practice detracts from the sole mediatorship of Christ because it seems to assume or to imply that Mary and certain deceased saints are somehow more accessible or benevolent than Christ. That is why Lutherans appeal to the doctrine of justification as the norm by which the practice of invoking saints and Mary needs to be judged. Lutherans continue to ask why it is useful, or indeed necessary, to place one's trust not only in Christ but in the saints and in Mary as well. Justifying faith rests on the sufficiency of Christ, who alone is to be trusted as the Mediator through whom God, in the Holy Spirit, pours out the gracious gift of salvation. Thus Lutherans could ask, "Granted that blessed Mary prays for the church, does she receive souls in death, does she overcome death, does she give life? What does Christ do if blessed Mary does all this?" (Ap 21:27).

(43) From a Lutheran perspective the crucial issue here is the nature of Christ's mediation itself. It should be noted that the term "mediator" does not figure prominently in Lutheran Christology. Even though the 1 Tim 2:5 passage is cited in CA 21, the emphasis is clearly on the fact that however Christ's saving work is described, he is the *only one* who does it. So CA 21 cites the 1 Timothy passage to emphasize that Christ is the *one* "Mediator," but is quick to add other titles as well that relate to the issues at hand: Christ is "the *only* Savior, the *only* High Priest, Advocate, and Intercessor." The emphasis is quite obviously not on the concept of mediation as such but on the uniqueness of Christ's work for us before God over against the question of the invocation of saints. As with all christological titles, the meaning and use of "Mediator" is determined by what actually happens in Christ and not by previously given usage. The point is that Christ establishes himself as the one and only "Mediator" through his own person and work. This must be borne in mind in discussions such as the present one where the term gains a prominence not usual in Lutheran theology.

(44) Consequently, we can here put the question sharply: What sort of mediation is it of which Christ is the sole agent? In the

Lutheran view, Christ's mediation is such that his life, death, and resurrection authorize and institute a speaking and doing (word and sacrament) through which he *himself* is imparted to create faith. The act of salvation is not, as the word suggests, that of a "go-between" who imparts some "thing" or prior timelessly existing divine favor or "grace."[55] He gives himself. He *is* what and who is to be given, and the proclamation of his life, death, and resurrection *is* the giving. His self-giving is such that it can be perpetuated only in the proclamation in word and sacrament. Thus it reaches its goal only in the proclamation of the victory achieved in the concrete event of the cross and the resurrection. Christ enters the world of sin and death, becomes a curse for us, and the outcome hangs in the balance. If the victory is not won, if there is no resurrection, sin and death win the battle and there is no mediation because there is nothing to be proclaimed. Since, however, Christ is raised, he alone is to be proclaimed, and only through faith in him can one stand in the judgment. The only mediation there is occurs in the speaking, the promising, and the sacramental giving engendered by the event itself. For Lutherans Christ alone engenders such speaking and doing, and Christ alone is therefore not only the sole Mediator, but the one who is mediated.

(45) It goes almost without saying, therefore, that the sole mediatorship of Christ does not exclude but rather impels to further "mediation" in the sense of a transmitting through word and sacrament. But Lutherans rarely speak of "mediation" in this connection and prefer rather to speak of the ministry of word and sacrament, the actual doing of the deed in the living present. They confess that this ministry was instituted by God for the sake of the gospel, to instill faith in Christ, the sole source of salvation. Salvation is thus "mediated" or communicated through the gospel, preached and heard as well as sacramentally enacted. Thus the word and the sacraments are sometimes spoken of as "means" (*Mittel, instrumenta*) through which the Holy Spirit gives faith to those who receive the gospel (CA 5). Ministry is thus service impelled by the sole mediatorship of Christ. One may be said to "cooperate" with God when one obeys the commission of the risen Christ to serve as his ambassador and declare him to be the Lord. In other words, one "cooperates" with God when one lives and acts in the belief that Christ alone is the sole mediator, trusting that we are saved *sola fide, sola gratia*.

(46) The differing "thought structures" referred to in our dialogue on justification[56] no doubt affect views on mediation and subsequent attitudes toward the practice of invoking saints and Mary.

Lutherans fear that a "transformationist model" tends to understand mediation too much as the distribution of "transforming grace" from the "treasury" of the superabundant merits of Christ and the saints through exemplary or properly authorized "intermediaries." The result is to extend mediation ecclesiologically via sacramental ordination, episcopacy, and perhaps speaking of the church as sacrament here on earth and the activity of saints and Mary on behalf of the faithful in heaven. Lutherans, however, think about mediation more in christological than ecclesiological terms: Christ gives himself in word and sacrament, thus continuing to be present to those who receive him in faith through the power of the Holy Spirit. Those who, through the power of the Spirit, in faith receive Christ in word and sacrament experience "mediation" of salvation. Thus Christ himself is the mediation. He takes our sin and gives us his righteousness. In such a view any suggestion that the righteousness of the saints somehow avails before God, even if such righteousness is acquired by the power of grace, will appear to question Christ's sole mediatorship and become cause for turmoil of conscience. Nevertheless, in the Lutheran view, deceased saints may still be exemplary models of faith in Christ alone, but they are not perceived as mediators additional to the Christ communicated in the gospel.

(47) The Lutheran Reformation called for a redefinition of the term "saint" in the light of the gospel of justification by faith alone. A saint is one who is justified by faith alone and who consequently lives and acts on that basis, one who claims and desires nothing for self but lives in the light of divine grace. Implicit in this view of sainthood is a critique of what Lutherans understood to be a theology of merit and the idea that saints were those who because of meritorious service enjoyed the immediate beatific vision and so could share their merits or be invoked. Lutherans held that saints are those who, being justified by faith, are freed to turn their attention toward the living saints, the neighbor, the naked, hungry, thirsty, and poor. Saints who do this in conspicuous fashion are celebrated and held up as examples and encouragement for the life of faith in this world. In other words, they are not viewed as gaining extraordinary status in the afterlife according to a scale of merit, but rather simply as prominent examples of the obedience and perseverance of faith in suffering and trial. This issues in a somewhat different understanding of the "communion of saints." Saints are those who because of faith participate in the sufferings and the joys of brothers and sisters here on earth, identifying with their

burdens in order to free them from such burdens. Saints, therefore, are respected and venerated when their example in the life of faith on earth is followed, not when they are invoked for aid after death or when their merits or works are in some way substituted for the shortcomings of "less-saintly" Christians. The critique of the system of merit means that Lutherans have been more concerned about saints as examples for the service of the living than as possible intercessors beyond death. Lutherans have generally held that since the life of the departed is hidden from us, no affirmations of faith can be based thereon and that attention should be turned to the service of the living.

(48) Lutherans therefore continue to adhere to the Lutheran Confessions, which hold that we should thank God for deceased saints as examples of divine mercy, that they should be viewed as models of faith, and that they should be honored and imitated.[57] Some Lutherans concede that "perhaps" the saints in the church triumphant intercede on behalf of the saints in the church militant.[58] Other Lutherans grant that blessed Mary prays for the church.[59] All remain suspicious of invoking deceased saints, even though Catholics insist that, in a "rightly ordered faith," the practice—though sometimes abused—does not conflict with the sole mediatorship of Christ. Lutherans contend that such an extension of Christ's mediation has no scriptural mandate, provides insufficient spiritual certainty, and tends to encourage abuse in the church's devotional life.

(49) With regard to Mary, Lutherans affirm her as the "God-bearer" (*theotokos*) and hold her in high esteem as the most praiseworthy of all the saints. In this sense Mary is to Lutherans a symbolic prototype of the church: she is obedient to the mandate of the Holy Spirit, humble in her great calling, and the embodiment of the unmerited grace of God. Luther and Lutherans continue to affirm that she gloried neither in her virginity nor in her humility, but only in the gracious regard God had for her.[60] The Marian dogmas affirming her Immaculate Conception (1854) and her bodily Assumption (1950) have saddened Lutherans because these dogmas have no scriptural basis and were promulgated as infallible truths without consultation with other Christians. Lutherans feel compelled to object to both the method used and the assertions made in these papal definitions because they represent a doctrinal development reflecting specifically Catholic concerns rather than ecumenical ones.[61] Lutherans have, however, preserved and recovered some cherished aspects of Marian devotion, based on the

"Magnificat" (Luke 1:46-55): The prophetic proclamation pointing to the power of the unmerited grace of God.

(50) The Lutheran critique of the invocation of the saints and of Mary must be viewed in the light of a Lutheran emphasis on the sanctified life as the proper response to Christ, the sole Mediator of salvation. Lutherans believe that proper praise and glory are given to the work of the one Redeemer when the saving mercies of the justifying God are reflected in a life of obedient, loving service. Lutherans hold, furthermore, that faith does not mean individualism, but rather a being born anew into the communion of believers, the body of Christ which is the church. As members of the church, believers participate by grace in the divine trinitarian life—in a "mystical union" (*unio mystica*) that anticipates the full future glory of Christ "beheld with an unveiled face" (2 Cor 3:18; cf 5:1-10 and Rom 8:20-30 in the context of 8:18-39). By the work of the Holy Spirit the ministry of word and sacraments "mediates" the present Christ, to whom the faithful respond with worship, with good works, and with other fruits of the Holy Spirit. Growth in grace, knowledge, love, and hope are the unfailing consequence of justifying faith. The interim between Christ's first coming in Israel and his final return at the end of time is filled with the advance of the gospel and, through the power of the Holy Spirit, response to it. All of Christian life is nurtured and sustained by the Christ who is "mediated" through the gospel and the Holy Spirit.[62] Thus Lutherans speak of God's solidarity (oneness) with creatures, of God "for us" (*pro nobis*) in Christ, and of unmerited salvation "outside us" (*extra nos*).

(51) At several points above the Lutheran emphasis on Scripture and a hesitancy to extend its meaning on the basis of the church's magisterium have been apparent. An example is the citation of James 5:16 with reference to the invocation of saints. The context is discussion of "the prayer of faith." The assurance that "the prayer of a righteous person avails much when set in operation (by God)" or ". . . in its effects" is not extended by the passage itself to deceased justified or holy ones. Similarly with 2 Thess 1:10[63] God "who is wonderful in his saints," which possibly refers to angels, is in context a reference to the *parousia*, not the invocation of the dead. Such uses of Scripture do not provide the clear basis Lutherans would require to move beyond the Confessional writings.

B. Catholic Perspectives

(52) "Christ the Light of the Nations" was the theme with which the Second Vatican Council introduced and set the tone for its

teaching about the church. It did so in *Lumen Gentium*,[64] where doctrine about the Lord Jesus and the salvation that Christ brings in the Holy Spirit is determinative for doctrine regarding the church. To be sure, as a result of a deliberate choice made by the council, its treatments of Mary (chapter 8) and other believers who are now in heaven (e.g., the apostles and Christ's martyrs: chapter 7 and esp. §§49–50) are found in the same document, which deals with God's people and church on earth.[65] But in context this people and church have already been presented (chapters 1 and 2) as tracing their historical reality and identity to the eternal mystery of the Father's will to save human beings through the Son in the Holy Spirit. Both the incarnation and the mystical body are intimately connected aspects of that same trinitarian mystery of salvation. Each involves faith on the part of human beings, as well as the works that are its fruit. But whether these gifts are found in the Lord's mother, her kinswoman Elizabeth, Anna, Stephen, Paul, or later disciples, their reality and effectiveness result entirely from the unique mediation of Jesus Christ.

(53) But what does it mean to speak of Christ as Mediator? And as for Mary and other disciples of her day or later, how do their faith and its fruits relate to the salvation of which he alone is Mediator? Like other Christians, Catholics ought to regard the answer to the first of these questions as determining the reply to the second.

(54) In answering the first, it is important to recall at the outset that language is being stretched when the term *Mediator* is used of Christ. The starting point is the practice of describing a person as mediating when he or she stands in between two others (whether the latter be individuals or groups) with the purpose of setting up or changing a relationship between them. An essential feature of this conventional usage is that all parties involved are human beings.

(55) The New Testament and later Christian tradition employed the term to describe Jesus in the relationship between human beings and the God whom he called Father. The intent behind this usage was to point to the historical figure who unites in himself the natures of God and humanity and who by his work in the flesh reconciles to God the alienated human family. Clearly some elements that were involved when the mediation was exclusively between human beings could not survive in this theological version. Thus in the New Testament Jesus Christ is not Mediator in the sense that on his initiative something was done which caused both God and

human beings to change their stance toward one another. To be more specific, his suffering and death did not require an otherwise unwilling God to be compassionate by granting sinners forgiveness and new life. Everything that Jesus accomplished as Mediator came about because God from eternity chose to love the human race and to save it only through and because of Jesus. Led in his humanity by God's prevenient grace, which was poured out upon him without measure, he freely returned the Father's love, becoming "obedient unto death, even death on a cross" (Phil 2:8). "Therefore," in view of his activity as Mediator, Jesus was exalted as risen Lord and unique head. He is called sole mediator because no justification, sanctification, grace, or merit can come about except through him and as merited by him.

(56) If the term "mediation" is applied to exemplary believers, angels, priests, or others, this is only in a derivative sense, insofar as the one Mediator chooses to work through them as instruments or channels. Included in the Mediator's role is the empowering of apostles, prophets, preachers, teachers, and other kinds of disciples for the benefit of those who need to be apprised of God's grace toward all because of Jesus and who must be helped if they are to respond in faith, hope, and charity. But how do the roles of those others relate to his? They neither add to it nor detract from it. They make it real throughout the ages, result from it, and draw on it as an unsurpassable source.

(57) Here recourse to an important text of the Second Vatican Council may be helpful. In chapter 8 of *Lumen Gentium* the subject is Mary, who is described as being invoked in the church under the titles of Advocate (*Advocata*), Aid (*Auxiliatrix*), Helper (*Adjutrix*), and Mediatrix (*Mediatrix*). After noting this, the council adds immediately that the dignity and efficacy of Christ the one Mediator are not thereby threatened. As grounds for this it submits that no creature can ever be numbered along with (*connumerari potest*) the incarnate Word, the Redeemer. There is no standard of measurement common to Creator and creature. Nevertheless, it goes on, the priesthood of Christ is shared in (*participatur*) both by ordained ministers and by all the baptized. Similarly there is but one divine goodness; nevertheless, it is really diffused (*realiter diffunditur*) in creatures in diverse ways. Then, after the introduction of the analogies of Christ's priesthood and God's goodness, the council moves to make an application:

> So also the sole mediation of the Redeemer does not exclude but rather gives rise to a cooperation (*cooperationem*) that varies on

> the part of creatures and that is but a sharing (*participatam*) from this one source (*ex unico fonte*).[66]

As Christ's priesthood is shared and God's goodness is really diffused, so Christ's mediation gives rise to derived cooperation on the part of others.

(58) The council thus singled out a role that Mary exercises at present and in the same context of *Lumen Gentium* described that role as intercession. In saying, then, that Mary is invoked in the church, it meant that her assistance (or intercession) is sought by disciples in need on earth. And concerned to allay the suspicion that this compromises Christ's mediation, it compared her heavenly role at present with the cooperation that it regarded as the hallmark of Christian discipleship on earth. But what does the latter entail?

(59) The New Testament presents individuals who were empowered by God to carry out roles engaging a freedom born of grace and resulting in others being touched by divine favor (e.g. Luke 1:44-45 for Mary and the as-yet unborn John; Acts 16:13-15 for Paul's preaching and Lydia's believing). These are instances of what *Lumen Gentium* would later describe as cooperation that is both derived from and totally dependent on the one Mediator, Jesus Christ. But the question must still be posed: If faith and its fruits involved cooperation on Mary's part as well as on the part of Paul, if that same faith and its fruits have similar implications for other disciples, how is that cooperation to be understood?

(60) In Catholic teaching it implies that from eternity the Father chooses to save for Christ's sake and in a way that involves the free agency of human beings. By grace the latter conform their wills to the divine and so like Christ seek for others the good which it is God's pleasure to offer. A life of faith despite adversity, service to one's neighbor with no hope of recompense, unselfish prayer for one's sisters and brothers in Christ—these are examples of such involvement or cooperation. They are effective because: a) the Father grants salvation in the Holy Spirit thanks solely to Jesus Christ; b) the efficacy of this one Mediator is so great as to enable disciples to share freely and actively in his saving work; and c) given the incommensurability of the infinite and the finite, that sharing does not reduce either the Mediator to being a partial source of forgiveness and new life or his disciples' role to doing nothing at all in this regard. As a result, even and especially when they are in spiritual need, followers of Christ can turn for help to sisters and brothers in the Lord who are expected to respond because they

are empowered by grace to be of assistance. Seen in this light, reservations regarding Christ's having commissioned disciples to help fellow wayfarers toward salvation would be a limitation of his mediation. Catholic teaching has these presuppositions when it uses *cooperation* to describe the roles of disciples in relation to their Lord's accomplishments.

(61) It is Christology that is decisive. The human obedience of the word incarnate was at once the result of grace and the source of grace for others.[67] Because this is so, the cooperative roles that Jesus Christ gives to his disciples on earth through the centuries are the fruit of his mediation and contribute to others' reception of the grace he mediates. At times those roles are described as a kind of "derived mediation." But this means only that the New Testament makes Jesus Christ the Mediator in the sense that he alone can and does accomplish the whole of salvation, without his disciples thereby doing nothing of salvific importance. Their cooperation results from his mediation, which transforms sinners into ministers so that it is not simply their human words but rather God's word in theirs that reaches hearers who come to believe (1 Thess 2:12-14). Because of his mediation disciples are enabled to suffer with him as a prelude to being glorified with him (Rom 8:17-18); like Paul they are legates on behalf of Christ, with God, as it were, exhorting through them (2 Cor 5:19-20). In the one Spirit they have been baptized into one body where each member lives not merely to share in what happens to others but to meet the needs of other members (1 Cor 12:12-28). Because of this solidarity Christians can accept responsibility for one another: by prayer, by recalling for one another God's promises and claims, by shouldering the burdens of neighbors, by correction as well as example, and by associating themselves with the sufferings of their crucified Lord and Head in works of penance flowing from faith. This is what it means for the Mediator to empower disciples: their total dependence involves sharing actively and freely in his saving work—doing more than nothing on behalf of others in need of salvation.[68]

(62) Hopes and fears enter into Catholics' assessment of the "derived mediation" or creaturely cooperation through which Christ's saving grace reaches human beings. They fear that without it Christ's unique mediation will be made fruitless and sterile. This threat appears realistic to them if every form of piety and worship, function, office, every meaning, truth claim, and type of witness are liable to be suspected of being a pretender seeking to displace

the Lord unless it has explicit biblical foundations. This could happen if justification by faith alone were to be made the *sole* norm for judging all churchly discourse and practice. They hope to avoid this and to give God what is God's by stressing the truth of the manifold cooperation to which Christ's mediation gives rise as his grace is brought to those in need.

(63) This dialogue has led to a better understanding of the fears and hopes of Lutherans. They too fear that Christ's unique mediation will be made fruitless and sterile. They fear this especially with regard to what has been called "derived mediation" or creaturely cooperation. Christ has been and is still today displaced at times by forms of piety and worship, offices and functions, meanings, truth claims, and types of witness. Each of these may call for trust that is misplaced because it is grounded in no divine promise or guarantee. Hope in Christ as Mediator requires criticism of "derived mediation"; prime candidates for such criticism are the cult of Mary and canonized saints in Catholic teaching and piety.

(64) Catholics can learn from Lutheran hopes and fears. Even so, Catholics may rightly maintain that the possibility of abuse does not warrant abolition of a teaching or practice. They freely recognize that ethnic, racial, and cultural factors enter into the expression of piety with regard to Mary and canonized saints as well as into its criticism. They know that piety in this form is deeply rooted in the lives of ever so many Catholics throughout the world. But although not all that can be described as an abuse in this matter is so in fact, still where real abuses are found, efforts must be made to direct the piety in question toward Christ the one Mediator. This may at times involve support of church leaders when the latter attempt to determine whether alleged apparitions of Mary or a canonized saint are authentic, only to be characterized as lacking faith for so doing.

(65) Perhaps a further point is worth considering. The two sets of hopes and fears described above and associated with Catholics and Lutherans may express different but not incompatible reactions to the mystery of the coexistence of the triune God and responsible human agents.[69]

(66) Of course Mary and many other of God's holy ones are no longer on earth. But the love of God in Jesus Christ is stronger than death (Rom 8:38-39). And Catholic teaching promotes confidence that death is not strong enough to keep those united with Christ in heaven from continuing to pray for others yet *in via* and from being called on by those others for just that prayer.

(67) The New Testament commends petitions on behalf of all human beings. But it also encourages Christians to turn to their fellow disciples for help and prayer on their behalf. That turning is in no way in conflict with the mediation of Christ, in whom there is ever so much more to be found than in any of his followers. In similar fashion Catholics are not deterred from turning to Mary or other sisters and brothers now in heaven for help and prayer. This is not in their view an affront to Christ or a meaningless gesture. Indeed, in this recourse they are encouraged by the conviction that the prayers of disciples now in heaven will proceed from a charity heightened by personal experience and awareness of the serious plight of wayfarers. One way, among others, of avoiding misdirection of such prayer and consequent abuses in the Catholic Church was by establishing and from time to time reforming the process of beatification and canonization. Neither beatification nor canonization conflicts with the Catholic teaching that all who are justified are holy people and saints. Similarly neither implies that only those beatified and canonized are in heaven now while earthly history continues. Furthermore, neither means that canonized saints have merits which make God bound to do what they request on behalf of clients on earth. But both do account at least in part for the fact that the term *saint* in Catholic parlance more often than not means one recognized by the church as in heaven and so one who can be turned to with trust as a true disciple of Christ.

(68) One may be unable to explain in detail or with apodictic certainty how Mary and canonized saints in heaven know the needs for which they are to pray when asked to by a disciple on earth.[70] Still in their cases as with Paul (Phil 1:23) the end of life on earth led to something much better: being with Christ. Like the repentant thief, they are in paradise today with the Lord, who has entered his kingdom (Luke 23:42-43). They are, however, still his disciples and as such imitate what their Lord does as he makes intercession for us with God (Heb 7:25; Rom 8:34).

(69) From a Catholic point of view, then, honoring Mary and the saints, imitating their example, and calling on them for help can be ways of attesting vividly to the unique mediation of Jesus Christ as well as to the truth of the gospel.

III

The Problem Reexamined

A. Dimensions of the Problem

(70) The problem faced by our dialogue on the one Mediator and the questions about mediation is a complex one. Both our churches are committed to Jesus Christ as Lord, hope, and goal of their existence. Both recognize the importance of the canonical Scriptures, Christian tradition, the ministry of word and sacrament, ecclesial community, and the examples of Christian saints past and present. Both agree on the unique mediatorship of Christ (*solus Christus*) and the justification for sinners (*sola gratia*) that Christ provides; they use this doctrine "as a criterion of authenticity"[71] for the church's practice with regard to the saints and Mary. The problem, however, is how to affirm the unique mediatorship of Christ so that all the "mediations" in his church not only do not detract from, but communicate and extol, his sole mediatorship. However, the very fact that we have come to agree on this form of the question and especially on the priorities that question reflects is for us a cause for joy.

(71) In earlier statements this dialogue has discussed Baptism, the Eucharist, the Ordained Ministry, Papal Primacy, Teaching Authority, and Justification by Faith. In each of these areas, and especially in connection with justification by faith, we have encountered differences related to one aspect of mediation, that is, how Christ's saving work is communicated. We think that we have found further clarity and convergence on that basic issue.

(72) Among the repercussions of this problem of how the Mediator's saving work is communicated are specifically questions about the roles of the saints, including Mary, and about intercession

and invocation of the saints and Mary. Both our churches affirm that the risen Christ, through the Holy Spirit, continues to effect salvation in and through the church. Both speak of human sinfulness, the importance of Christ's cross and resurrection, the word of God, and sacraments. Both allow for human agency in proclamation, witnessing, ministry, and the response of faith. It can be said, however, that there is a contrast in our respective understandings of continuity and discontinuity. That "God's word saves by being declared" introduces, into the Lutheran understanding of the life of faith, discontinuity between the old and the new, between the bound will and the liberated will, and between the gravity of sin and the grace of justification, so that the justified are *simul iusti et peccatores*.[72] In contrast, Catholic theology stresses "transformation or perfecting of the old," including an element of continuity as well as of renewal.[73] The contrast can also be seen in "another critical principle," urged by Catholics, alongside of justification by faith, namely, "to recognize God's grace where it is at work," including its renewing effects already present.[74] The contrast is exhibited in the fact that Catholics tend to use mediation language for the action of human ministers, as well as for the saints and Mary, whereas Lutherans tend to reserve such language for Christ the one Mediator. These differing emphases have had important consequences for piety and devotion. At issue has been how the saints and Mary function in mediation.

(73) The difficult questions in the present round of the dialogue are tied to the criteriological use of justification and of the continuity of grace at work. We have also been aware, however, of a number of further questions, some of which have been touched on in previous rounds of dialogue, some in this round, and others not yet in depth. For example, how should the church and its tradition be subject to Scripture and influence the interpretation of Scripture? Does doctrine develop, and if so, how does one ascertain the legitimacy of such developments? What is the value of the *lex orandi* and of the *sensus fidelium* as sources of dogma? What is the teaching authority and, more specifically, the teaching authority of the hierarchy, particularly the pope? How does the church deal with distortions and abuses as it responds to the call for continuous conversion to the gospel? However, we do not think that these issues have to be dealt with before any real progress can be made on substantive questions concerning Mary and the saints. On the contrary, we dare to hope that the advances which this present round of the dialogue reflects may in time shed light on these other issues as well.

B. Resulting Divergences

(74) In Section II we have alluded to differences in the ways our two traditions understand the very concept of mediation and apply it to Christ as the one Mediator. Questions can arise, especially about the role of the humanity of Christ in the work of redemption, including the relationship between the two natures in Christ and the sharing of attributes (*communicatio idiomatum*). In what sense does he take on our sins and "become sin" for us (cf. 2 Cor 5:21; Gal 3:13)? How does Christ function as head with respect to his body, the church? Christology and ecclesiology are themes that must constantly be kept in mind.

(75) The present round of discussion raises questions about the relationship between Christians living on earth and those who have passed beyond the veil of death, and more specifically the relationship with those regarded as saints in heaven, among whom Mary holds a special place in the official Confessions or teaching of both our churches. In this regard we have identified four divergences.

1. The Term "Saint"

(76) The first divergence concerns the meaning of the basic term "saint" or "holy one" (*hagios, sanctus*). As applied to human beings, it can be used in at least four senses: (1) All those who have been justified by the grace of Christ, whether living or dead; (2) those who, having been thus justified on earth, have entered into eternal life; (3) particular figures, especially biblical personages, who are examples of holiness; and (4) those of any age or nation whom the church, either through custom or formal canonization, has singled out as members of the church triumphant so that they may be commemorated in public worship. Lutherans tend on the whole to use the term "saint" in its wider, biblical meaning, as including all the justified, whether on earth or in heaven, whereas Catholics tend to use the term in a narrower sense to mean those in heaven, especially those officially "canonized" and proposed as models of holiness.

2. Intercession of Saints

(77) An initial question regarding the prayer of saints in heaven for the sake of others (intercession) has to do with our knowledge about the condition of the Christian dead. Do they now live with

Christ and, if so, are they aware of the situation and needs of people still on earth? If these questions are answered in the negative, it is more difficult to claim an intercessory role for them and to justify calling upon their help in our prayers.

(78) The Catholic magisterium teaches that some of the deceased are already glorified, beholding "clearly the triune God as he is" (*LG* 49).[75] As biblical grounds for the intercession of saints, the Confutation referred to texts such as Baruch 3:4, 2 Macc 15:12-14, and Rev 5:8 and 8:3-4, but the exegetical difficulties are today recognized. For their confidence in the prayers of the saints in heaven Catholics rely not simply on biblical texts but also, as stated elsewhere,[76] on the sense of the faithful, on ancient and approved liturgical prayers, on the explicit teaching of popes and councils, and on theological reasoning from the biblical data. Thus the dispute comes down in great part to the sources of Christian doctrine and the principles of interpretation.

(79) Lutherans point to the paucity of information provided by Holy Scripture concerning the state of the dead between their death and the end-time. Like Catholics, Lutherans confess that God gives life to the dead in Christ. Lutherans grant that the saints in heaven and Mary intercede for the church in general (Ap 21:9) or at least perhaps do so (SA 2:2:26), but in neither alternative do they find any decisive ground for affirming that the departed are aware of prayers addressed to them (Ap 21:9, 12, 27; SA 2:2:26).

3. Invocation

(80) Sharper differences arise concerning the invocation of saints: Should Christians be encouraged or required to ask their prayers and help either in general terms or for certain specific favors? Catholics hold that the practice of invocation is encouraged by the church, which is to be trusted. More specifically, they argue that the invocation of saints, although not explicitly commanded in Scripture, is not forbidden and seems to be a legitimate extension of the biblically approved practice of asking for the intercession of those living on earth (e.g., Rom 15:30-32; 2 Cor 1:11; Col 4:3) and the special value attributed in Scripture to the prayer of the righteous (Jas 5:16). The legitimacy of the extension, to be sure, depends on the conviction that those who die in close union with Christ are taken up into eternal life and become outstanding members of the communion of saints. Relying in part on materials that have come to light since the sixteenth century, Catholics point out that the

practice goes back to the early centuries and was taught by a number of church fathers in the East and West prior to Gregory I.[77]

(81) The invocation of saints, in the Catholic view, does not attribute to them the power that belongs to God alone because the saints are not addressed as saviors or redeemers but simply as intercessors, in much the same way that fellow human beings on earth are addressed when one asks them to pray for some intention. Far from detracting from the work of Christ, the practice, they believe, provides increased awareness of his work, for Christ is glorified in his saints (cf. *LG* 48 and 50). Prayer to God and invocation of the saints do not stand in a competitive relationship, but in turning to the saints as intercessors one places trust ultimately in God and in Christ to whom all prayer is ultimately directed. No benefits are conferred by the saints that are not conferred by Christ himself. Although Catholics are encouraged to pray directly to God, they may also draw profit from asking the intercession of the saints, in whom God's grace was so effective when they still lived on earth.

(82) In certain periods of history and certain parts of the world the practices of invoking the saints and treasuring their relics were adversely affected by popular superstitions that have somewhat obscured the role of Christ as sole Mediator of redemption. Church authorities have a responsibility to be vigilant in preventing superstition, to the extent that they can effectively control popular religion. In the present ecumenical climate many Catholics would agree that if Christ is faithfully preached, abuses will gradually recede.

(83) Lutherans oppose the invocation of saints, particularly for help on specific issues, on the twofold ground that it leads to uncertainty in prayer and detracts from the sole mediatorship of Christ. In support of the first objection they assert that the invocation of saints is not commanded or recommended in the canonical Scriptures and therefore rests upon no biblical promise. For the second objection the Lutheran contention has been and is that invocation attributed to the saints honor and power that belong to God alone; that it obscures the word of Christ; and that it transfers to the creature the trust that should be placed in no one other than God.

4. Marian Doctrine

(84) In relation to the theme of the present dialogue, the central question about Mary has to do with her mediatory role. Inspired

by the doctrine of the divine motherhood[78] and by biblical texts such as John 2:1-11, Catholic spiritual writers have attributed exceptional power to Mary's intercession with her son. Medieval authors such as Bernard of Clairvaux and Bernardine of Siena viewed her as "mediator with the Mediator." A number of modern popes, such as Pius IX, Leo XIII, Pius X, and John Paul II, in devotional instructions, have applied to Mary the title "Mediatrix." But movements to define the doctrine of Mary as "Mediatrix of all graces" have thus far met with no encouragement from Rome. While noting that Mary is invoked *in* the church as Mediatrix, Vatican II chose deliberately to use this formula rather than assert that she is so invoked *by* the Church (cf. *LG* 62).[79] Without necessarily repudiating the poetic language of hymnody and devotion, many contemporary Catholics hold that it is theologically inappropriate to speak of Mary as Mediatrix because "Mediatrix" is so easily misunderstood in ways that weaken the doctrine of Christ as "sole Mediator."

(85) Lutherans, while conceding that Mary "prays for the church" and is "worthy of the highest honors," have consistently denied that she, or other saints, should be regarded as mediators or propitiators, on the ground that reliance on their merits would detract from the sole mediatorship of Christ. They particularly object to the practice of extolling the mercy of Mary as though Christ were "not a propitiator but only a terrible judge and avenger" (Ap 21:28).

(86) The most difficult areas regarding Mary are undoubtedly the two dogmas defined in the Roman Catholic Church since the sixteenth century: the Immaculate Conception and the Assumption. As regards the former, Catholics point out that Mary was in a true sense redeemed by Christ and that her "preservative redemption" is in fact the supreme instance of his redemptive work. The dogma emphasizes the absolute prevenience of grace, inasmuch as Mary was redeemed without prior merits of her own "in view of the merits of Jesus Christ."[80] The definition was an assertion of papal authority but it was preceded by centuries of increasing agreement among Catholic theologians and among the Catholic people, by numerous petitions for the definition, and by a virtually unanimous consensus of the episcopate in response to the consultation undertaken by Pius IX.[81] The lack of ecumenical consultation in the definition of the Immaculate Conception may today seem regrettable, but such consultation was rarely practiced by popes or councils for their doctrinal decisions prior to Vatican Council II.

(87) Luther himself professed the Immaculate Conception as a pleasing thought though not as an article of faith (and indeed the

belief had not attained dogmatic status at that time). The Lutheran Confessions are silent about it. Lutherans overwhelmingly rejected the dogma as defined in 1854. Their objections are based on the normative Confessional assertion that all descendants of Adam and Eve except Christ are "conceived and born in sin" (CA 2:1); that there are no positive biblical testimonies to Mary's exemption from original sin; and that the definition itself was an unwarranted assertion of papal authority, one made after consulting only Roman Catholics.

(88) The dogma of the Assumption (1950) gives rise to similar divergences. Catholics generally agree that neither the Immaculate Conception nor the Assumption is taught as such in Scripture or in early patristic tradition. They see these dogmas as having a limited grounding in certain biblical teachings, such as Mary's being "highly favored" by God and her unique maternal relationship to Jesus. Beyond this, many theologians appeal to various biblical types and figures of Mary as developed in the tradition. These have included the typology of Mary as the "second Eve" and the interpretation of her as the "woman clothed with the sun" in Revelation 12. Modern authors, including Pius XII in his bull of 1950, see a nexus between the Immaculate Conception and the Assumption: it was appropriate for Mary, being preserved from original sin, to be exempted from subjection to the power of death and corruption.[82]

(89) Luther preached on the Assumption and held that not only Mary but several other biblical figures were already taken up into the life of glory. There were early Lutheran pastors who affirmed the Assumption as both evangelical and Lutheran.[83] The Lutheran Confessions do not refer to the Assumption of Mary. Generally Lutherans reject the doctrine as lacking support in the Scriptures and in the early patristic tradition.[84] Like the dogma of the Immaculate Conception, the 1950 promulgation lacked ecumenical consultation.

C. Need the Divergences Be Church-Dividing?

(90) The goal of ecumenical dialogue is not to eliminate all differences, but to make certain that the remaining differences are consonant with a fundamental consensus in the apostolic faith and therefore legitimate or at least tolerable. Reconciliation is a process admitting of many degrees, leading up to full fellowship in faith,

in sacramental worship, and in a structured ecclesial life.[85] It is therefore important to ascertain what bearing the differences disclosed in the present round of the dialogue have on the kinds of fellowship just mentioned.

1. The Term "Saint"

(91) The difference of usage of the term "saint" in our two traditions can make for some difficulty of communication but is not of itself church-divisive, since neither church actually rejects the usage of the other. Lutherans, although they commonly use the term "saint" to include all justified believers, do accord certain individuals, biblical or postbiblical, the title of "saint" and sometimes commemorate such individuals on particular days in their liturgical calendar and name churches or religious groups in their honor. While Catholics tend to reserve the title of saint to particular individuals whose eminent holiness is certified to them by the church, they also use the term in a much broader sense, to include all who have entered into the joy of eternal life, as in the feast of All Saints, or all who are justified and live by their faith in Christ.

2. Intercession of Saints

(92) The discrepancy between Catholic and Lutheran teaching on the intercession of saints is not the decisive one. Lutherans do not deny the Catholic doctrine, but question its biblical basis and its certainty. They assert that Christ prays for us, as do saints on earth and perhaps in heaven. Catholic doctrine affirms the intercession of the saints in heaven. This intercession is seen as a presupposition for the doctrine of invocation, which has held a greater place in the controversy. Intercession as a church-dividing issue, therefore, can best be treated below under invocation.

3. Invocation

(93) The question of church-divisiveness may be engaged by considering three more specific questions: Does the Catholic Church require its members to invoke saints? Could Lutherans live in union with a church in which this practice was encouraged but not imposed? Could the Catholic Church live in union with Lutherans who preach Christ as sole Mediator with the conviction that the invocation of saints will thereby recede?

(94) The most formal statement of the Catholic Church on the invocation of saints comes from the Council of Trent, which, in its

positive teaching, affirmed that it is good and useful to invoke saints and to have recourse to their prayers and help in obtaining God's benefits through Jesus Christ, "who alone is our Savior and Redeemer."[86] But neither Trent nor any other council or pope has imposed upon the individual Catholic the obligation of venerating saints or of invoking them. Vatican II in *Lumen Gentium* described it as "supremely fitting" (*summopere decet*) to invoke the saints and have recourse to their prayers (*LG* 50).

(95) Although it seems clear that no one is obliged to invoke the saints in private prayer, the question of public prayer is more complex. In the eucharistic liturgies (canons) of the Catholic Church, including those approved by Paul VI, all prayers are addressed to God—none to the saints, even Mary. The invocation of the saints is rare in the official prayers of the church, but it does occur in the first of the penitential rites of the Eucharist and in the Litany of the Saints, which is used in the Easter Vigil and in the rites of baptism and ordination. Mary is, of course, invoked in many approved nonliturgical prayers, such as the second part of the angelic salutation (the "Hail Mary"). Precisely because the church regards the invocation of the saints and Mary as "good and beneficial," the individual Catholic is strongly encouraged to make use of, and participate in, such prayers. Many Catholics continue to respond to this encouragement with enthusiasm. But there is no reason for thinking that a person who refrained from personally invoking saints would forfeit full communion with the Catholic Church. This freedom now enjoyed by Catholics would certainly be enjoyed also by Lutherans should a greater degree of communion between the respective churches be achieved.

(96) In response to the second question above in paragraph 93, it may be noted that in the sixteenth century Lutherans asked for freedom to abstain from the invocation of saints and freedom to preach the doctrine of justification by faith so as to protest against the practice and the abuses which that practice had occasioned. Melanchthon objected to the *Confutation* on the grounds that it presented the invocation of departed saints as "necessary" and condemned the Lutherans because they "do not *require* the invocation of saints" (Ap 21:1; emphasis added). But Melanchthon and others did not refuse to be in communion with a church that did not require them to invoke saints.

(97) This dialogue has not reached agreement on the substantive issue whether invocation of saints is legitimate and beneficial. Catholics deny that the practice in and of itself is idolatrous or injurious

to the honor of Christ the one Mediator, even though the practice must be protected against abuses. The Catholics of this dialogue recognize that abuses have occurred and that the doctrine of the sole mediatorship of Christ provides one critical principle for identifying abuses. Other critical norms are given in official Catholic teaching, notably in the apostolic exhortation of Paul VI, *Marialis Cultus*.[87] The Lutherans of this dialogue are of the opinion that the practice is not church-dividing provided that the sole mediatorship of Christ is clearly safeguarded and that in any closer future fellowship members would be free to refrain from the practice.

(98) In response to the third question raised in paragraph 93 above, Catholics could enter into a fellowship where there would be freedom for Lutherans to proclaim the one Mediator, with their particular conviction that the invocation of the saints would thereby recede. Catholics could live in such a fellowship with the understanding that their own tradition of worship would be respected and not impugned as idolatrous.

4. Marian Doctrine

(99) With regard to the mediatory role of Mary, our dialogue has not revealed any tendency on the part of Catholics to look upon Mary as a propitiator or to consider that her mercy is anything but an expression and reflection of the mercy of Christ himself. Catholics today do not commonly speak of Mary's heavenly "mediation," if they use the term at all, except to express her intercessory role with her son. Understood in this way, the heavenly mediation of Mary differs only in degree from what we have dealt with under the headings of the intercession and invocation of saints.[88]

(100) In an earlier round of our dialogue we have already discussed the disagreements between Lutherans and Catholics on the two modern Catholic Marian dogmas, the Immaculate Conception and the Assumption. In our discussions of teaching authority and infallibility in the church the Catholics were asked to what extent the nonacceptance of these two Marian dogmas (as well as the dogma of papal infallibility) would preclude communion and unity. The Catholic members took the position that disagreements regarding these particular dogmas did not "*of themselves* exclude all Eucharistic sharing between the churches."[89] In other words, if there were sufficient doctrinal agreement on other matters (including, for example, the ordained ministry), it might be possible to have limited eucharistic sharing even beyond what is now permitted by

canon law.[90] But the Catholics added that in such a relationship of incomplete ecclesial communion Lutherans and Catholics could not ignore the remaining differences. They would have to pray and study these disputed questions and "search for a more shared understanding of the Word of God as it applies to Mary."[91] The Catholic members of the dialogue reassert this position today.

(101) From the Lutheran side, one may recall the honor and devotion paid to the Mother of God by Luther himself, including his own attitude to the Immaculate Conception and the Assumption, which he accepted in some form. The Lutheran Confessions offer high praise for Mary as foremost of all the saints. When confronted with contemporary abuses, however, the Confessions warn of "idolatry" with regard to the saints (LC Ten Commandments 21; *BC* 367; SA 2:2:26; *BC* 297) and express the fear that Mary "in popular estimation . . . has completely replaced Christ" (Ap 21:28; *BC* 232–33). Lutheran reactions, where voiced, to the dogmas about Mary's Immaculate Conception (1854) and Assumption (1950) were negative. The statements of the Second Vatican Council, however, demonstrate that the sole mediatorship of Christ can be asserted and the role of Mary further interpreted by Roman Catholics in ways that old Lutheran fears can be diminished. The Lutherans of this dialogue are of the opinion that, as long as the sole mediatorship of Christ is clearly safeguarded, these two Marian dogmas need not divide our churches provided that in a closer future fellowship Lutherans as members would be free not to accept these dogmas. But the link between the problem of infallibility and these theological assertions about Mary makes full agreement unattainable at the present time.

(102) In the greater fellowship we envisage between our churches, continuing efforts would have to be made together to apply hermeneutical principles to the Marian dogmas.[92] Lutherans and Catholics would have to try to see together how far decisions since the separation have been stamped with a certain particularization in thought and language, and how they could be reread in the context of the whole tradition and with a deeper understanding of Scripture. In this way it might be possible to transcend differences regarding the definitions of 1854 and 1950 without doing violence to the essential content. Unless and until such agreed reinterpretations can be achieved, the two Marian dogmas must be acknowledged as an obstacle to full fellowship between our churches, though they need not prevent a significant advance in the relationship that already exists.

D. Church-Uniting Convergences

(103) Although such divergences continue, Lutherans and Catholics in this dialogue can propose together a number of convergences pertinent to our topic which we commend for consideration within our churches and beyond them:

1. We reiterate the basic affirmation that "our entire hope of justification and salvation rests on Christ Jesus and the gospel whereby the good news of God's merciful action in Christ is made known; we do not place our ultimate trust in anything other than God's promise and saving work in Christ" (L/RC 7:4, 157).

2. We now further assert together that Jesus Christ is the sole Mediator in God's plan of salvation (1 Tim 2:5). Christ's saving work and role in God's design thus determine not only the content of the gospel and its communication but also all Christian life, including our own and that of Mary and the saints who are now in heaven.

3. As Christ prayed in the days of his flesh (Heb 5:7) for those whom God had given him (John 17), the risen Christ continues an intercessory role for us at the right hand of God (Rom 8:34; 1 John 2:1; Heb 7:25).

4. The Holy Spirit both intercedes for us with God (Rom 8:26-27) and is God's advocate with us (John 14:16-17; 15:26; 16:7-15).

5. The grace of Christ the Mediator is mediated to us as ongoing communication of the gospel, through the Spirit, in the ministry of word and sacrament.

6. The Holy Spirit acts in those who minister, as, through the means of grace, sinners are brought to faith, justified, and sanctified in Christ.

7. One specific result of the gospel's communication is thus sanctification or holiness, a gift from God through Christ, experienced by faith, in the Holy Spirit. Granted in baptism, holiness is confirmed, preserved, and deepened by word and sacrament.

8. The term "saint" is used in both our traditions for all those justified by the grace of Christ, and, to one degree or another, for certain individuals among them, marked by holiness, who live the life of faith in devotion toward God and love toward the neighbor in exemplary ways, calling forth praise to God.

9. All those sanctified, together with the One who sanctifies (Heb 2:11), constitute a communion of saints in Jesus Christ.

10. The fellowship of those sanctified, the "holy ones" or saints, includes believers both living and dead. There is thus a solidarity of the church throughout the world with the church triumphant.

11. It is in this community of saints that we are promised through Christ forgiveness, communion with God, and eternal life.

12. This fellowship included the hope of resurrection, Christ being "the first fruits of those who have fallen asleep" (1 Cor 15:20).

13. In the fellowship of living and departed saints, believers are inspired by others, as examples of God's grace, to greater faith, to good works, and to thanksgiving for one another.

14. Christians honor saints in at least three ways: by thanking God for them; by having faith strengthened as a result of the saints' response to God's grace; and by imitating in various situations their faith and other virtues.

15. Among the saints who have played a role in God's plan of salvation for humanity, Mary, who bore Christ, is in particular to be honored, as "God-bearer" (*theotokos*) and as the pure, holy, and "most blessed Virgin" (*laudatissima virgo*).

16. Prayer to God—as doxology and thanksgiving; as confession of sin; as petition and intercession; and as submission to God's will—has divine command and promise and is an integral part of the Christian life (Luke 18:1; Rom 12:12; 1 Tim 2:1; John 16:23).

17. Saints on earth ask one another to pray to God for each other through Christ. They are neither commanded nor forbidden to ask departed saints to pray for them.

18. Devotion to the saints and Mary should not be practiced in ways that detract from the ultimate trust that is to be placed in Christ alone as Mediator.

19. Doctrine (*lex credendi*), on the one hand, and liturgy and devotion (*lex orandi*), on the other, belong together and shape each other. While each of our traditions has put that relationship differently at various times and under changing circumstances, what is normative in both our traditions is that doctrine and worship together should promote the unique mediatorship of Christ. Both our traditions are characterized as liturgical churches with concern for piety and devotion.

E. Next Steps

(104) Building upon our prior consensus about Jesus Christ and the gospel as the source and center of all Christian life, we have in this round of dialogue come to a deeper appreciation of the unique mediatorship of Jesus Christ and its normative role with regard to the issues before us. His sole mediatorship is the ground

of our common hope and of the communion of all the faithful, living and dead, in the new life of grace. While united by these bonds, our churches are still separated by differing views on matters such as the invocation of saints and the Immaculate Conception and Assumption of Mary. Notwithstanding these differences, our churches would make greater progress toward fellowship by taking two further steps within the framework of common study and dialogue:

1. if Lutheran churches could acknowledge that the Catholic teaching about the saints and Mary as set forth in the documents of Vatican Council II (cf. §§ 192-201) does not promote idolatrous belief or practice and is not opposed to the gospel (cf. § 101); and

2. if the Catholic Church could acknowledge that, in a closer but still incomplete fellowship, Lutherans, focusing on Christ the one Mediator, as set forth in Scripture, would not be obliged to invoke the saints or to affirm the two Marian dogmas (cf. §§ 100, 102).

(105) These steps put difficult questions to both our churches, but we believe them to be realistic in view of all that we have said about the existing convergences and the possibilities of dealing with unsurmounted divergences. The steps are further supported, we believe, by the biblical and historical foundations to which we now turn.

PART TWO: BIBLICAL AND HISTORICAL FOUNDATIONS

I

Scripture on Christ, the Saints, and Mary

(106) The sixteenth-century problem concerning the saints and Mary and the resulting issues between Catholics and Lutherans rest on a long, generally shared history over many prior centuries. The scriptural witness at the outset of Christianity provides a starting point on these subjects in both our traditions. Because of the normative nature of Scripture for Lutherans and Catholics, its teachings can point toward and support agreements and convergences. Anything said about saints or "holy ones" in the Bible must be viewed in the framework provided by the scriptural depiction of the holy God who redeems and creates a people, first in Israel and then through Jesus Christ.

(107) The Old Testament presents as the One God a Lord who had brought Israel out of Egypt and who entered into a covenantal relationship with a people who were to be God's "own possession among all people" and a "holy nation" (Exod 19:4-6). This God, the Holy One, had elected Israel out of love (Deut 7:6-8; 26:18-19) and both promised to dwell in the midst of this people (Exod 29:45-46; Deut. 16:6, 11) and called for them to be holy, consecrated to God's will (Lev 11:44-45; 19:2).

(108) In the New Testament, faith finds its center in Christ Jesus who died for our sins and whom God raised from the dead and exalted. God is his "holy Father" (John 17:11), who through the gospel calls Jew and Gentile out of all peoples and tongues and nations into his own kingdom, in Christ (1 Thess 2:12; Rev 5:9; 14:6). The God who calls is holy; those called and elect are a holy

nation and are to be holy in their conduct (1 Pet 1:15-16; cf. 1:2; 2:9). They are washed (baptized), sanctified, and justified (1 Cor 6:11); they are God's own possession (1 Pet 2:9).

(109) For the New Testament period one can speak of a "communion of saints" (*koinōnia tōn hagiōn, communio sanctorum*), to use a later creedal phrase.[93] For those who believe in Jesus Christ have fellowship with the Father and the Son (1 Cor 1:9; 10:16; 1 John 1:3), participation in the Spirit (Phil 2:1; cf. 2 Cor 13:14) and in Christ's sufferings with the hope of the resurrection (Phil 3:10), and have fellowship also with one another (1 John 1:7). Since Christ who died lives now at God's right hand, this communion extends beyond earthly life. A variety of images are employed in the New Testament to suggest the present state of the dead in Christ; these images will be discussed below.

A. Christ the Mediator

(110) For this fellowship Jesus the Christ is the pioneer and perfecter of faith (Heb 12:2), the One who sanctifies and around whom those who are sanctified gather (Heb 2:10-12), the Holy One (Acts 3:14; 4:27, 30) through whom forgiveness of sins is proclaimed and by whom God exonerates (Acts 13:35-39; Rom 8:29-30, 33-34). The risen Christ intercedes for us (Rom 8:34; Heb 7:25). Among the many titles in the New Testament honoring Jesus Christ for what he is and what he did, one played a particular role in Lutheran-Catholic debate of the sixteenth century—"Mediator."

(111) The Hebrew Scriptures mention intermediaries who act on behalf of Yahweh. These include God's "messengers" (the *mal'āk YHWH*, "the angel of the Lord," and "angels" generally), the spirit, wisdom, and the word. At times the latter figures are personified, even hypostatized in developing Judaism. Priests, prophets, and kings sometimes play intermediary roles in passing on God's will to his people. In particular, Moses, especially at the sea (Exod 14:15-18) and at the mountain (Exod 19:3-6; 24:4-8), carries out such an intermediary function. He is aware of himself as God's archetypal prophet or mouthpiece (Deut 18:15) and is even commissioned to "consecrate" Aaron and his sons to serve as Yahweh's "priesthood" for his people (Exod 28:3, 41, 43; 29:1-44). In yet another way Moses serves in an intermediary role when he "besought the Lord his God" on behalf of the Hebrews who had sacrificed to the golden calf (Exod 32:11). Still other prophets and priests served in a similar

intermediary role; in particular, Jeremiah and Ezekiel "addressed the word of the Lord" to Judah or to the exiles (Jer 1:1-3; Ezek 1:1-3). Again, in another sense an intermediary role was played by the Servant of Yahweh when he "made intercession for transgressors" (Isa 53:12). Thus, "though the word [mediator] is not used, mediatorship is at the heart of OT religion."[94]

(112) The Greek word *mesitēs*, "mediator," which occurs six times in the New Testament, is found in the Septuagint only at Job 9:33. The Hebrew of this verse reads: "There is no arbitrator (*môkîah*) between us, [who] will set his hand upon us both." In the Septuagint this is expanded: "Would that there were a mediator for us, even a judge, who also listens in the midst of us" (*eithe ēn ho mesitēs hēmōn kai elenchōn, kai diakouōn ana meson amphoterōn*). Here the Septuagint has introduced a contemporary term for an "umpire, arbitrator, mediator," attested in secular Hellenistic Greek, where it served to express mediation between human and divine beings in many religions.[95] In Job 9:33, Job begins to depict the God in whom he trusts as an "arbitrator," as he will eventually depict him also as his "witness" (*ʿēd*, 16:18) and his "Redeemer" (*gō'ēl*, 19:25; cf. Job 33:23).

(113) Against such a background of intermediaries in the religion of Israel, the New Testament affirmation of Jesus as "the mediator (*mesitēs*) between God and the human race" must be understood. The term occurs in 1 Timothy 2:5 in a creedal passage, possibly derived from liturgy or catechesis,

> For there is one God.
> There is also one mediator between God
> and the human race,
> Christ Jesus, himself human,
> who gave himself as ransom for all.
> (NABRNT, 1 Tim 2:5-6a)

The death of Jesus is testimony (v. 6b) to God's will that all human beings be saved and is the truth (vv. 4, 7) which Paul proclaims. Other New Testament passages speak similarly of Christ's mediation: "the Mediator of a better/ new covenant" (Heb 8:6; 9:15; 12:24) or even "the 'surety' (*engyos*) of a better covenant" (7:22). Jesus is not only the Mediator of a better covenant, enacted on better promises (Heb 8:6), but is now also the sole Mediator between God and human beings. 1 Timothy 2:5 asserts the unique mediatorship of Christ; in him alone, not in Moses (the intermediary between God and Israel, Exod 19:3-6; 24:4-8; Deut 5:27; cf. Gal 3:19-20) or angels

(Gal. 3:19; Acts 7:53) or anyone else, is salvation to be found (Acts 4:12).

(114) When the New Testament uses *mesitēs* or *mesiteuein*, it denotes what God has accomplished for human beings through Christ. It is primarily a movement from God to us. The New Testament, however, also portrays Christ Jesus as an intermediary in other senses: he intercedes (*entygchanein*) on our behalf with his heavenly Father (Rom 8:34; Heb 7:25; 9:24); "we have an advocate (*paraklēton*) with the Father, Jesus Christ the righteous" (1 John 2:1). In this case the movement is from human beings to the Father through Christ; though an intermediary role is expressed, it is not called "mediation" in the New Testament. Similarly the Spirit functions in both ways, from God to us, and to God on our behalf, the Spirit interceding "for the saints according to the will of God" (Rom 8:27), but *mesitēs* and its cognates are never used of the Spirit (cf. Rom 5:5; 8:26-27; John 14:16-17, 26 *[paraklētos]*).

(115) The exact context in which 1 Timothy 2:5-6 (cited above in section 113) is found is important and a matter of some dispute. The reference to the one Mediator occurs in an exhortation to prayers of various sorts "for all human beings" (2:1) and "for kings and all who are in high positions, that we may lead a quiet and peaceable life, godly and respectful in every way" (2:2 RSV; NABRNT "a quiet and tranquil life in all devotion and dignity"). The passage later speaks about the conduct of men at prayer (2:8) and of women in dress, adornment, and deeds (2:9ff.). There is dispute over the word "this" in v. 2, "This is good, and it is acceptable in the sight of God. . . ."

a. One view runs thus. Although v. 3, "this is good and pleasing to God our Savior," may seem at first to refer to that immediately preceding purpose clause ("that we may lead a quiet and tranquil life . . ."), in the larger context the demonstrative "this" undoubtedly refers to the prayers "for all human beings" (including kings and other authorities), whom "God wishes to be saved" (v. 4). Thus the author exhorts Christians to address their supplications to God that all "may come to the knowledge of the truth" that God is one and that there is "one mediator between God and the human race, Christ Jesus, himself human, who gave himself as a ransom for all" (2:5). Thus the truth of the unique mediatorship of Christ is affirmed in a context in which Christians themselves are urged to supplicate God for the salvation of all. The apostle sees himself as a herald of this truth: "a teacher of the Gentiles in faith and truth" (2:7).

b. The alternative holds that when v. 3 says "this is good and pleasing to God . . . ," the reference is to the prayers in v. 2b ("that we may lead a quiet and tranquil life"), in the spirit of Jer 29:7 (prayer for the welfare of Babylon). If one takes the reference in the word "this" more broadly and claims that what is "acceptable to God" is the prayers of Christians for everyone (2:1), that all come to "knowledge of the truth" about salvation (2:4), then that interpretation calls for certain distinctions: first, between Christ's unique self-giving as ransom for all and Christians' intercessions. The way to knowledge of the truth is the apostolic preaching (v. 7). It requires, second, a distinction between prayers "for everyone" (v. 1) to come to the knowledge of the truth (4b, in relation to the divine will and work to save them) and prayers "for kings and all in authority" that we may live at peace (v. 2). The prayers and supplications for the peace and quiet of the civil and social world of Christians are thus not directly for the conversion of pagan rulers and others.[96]

c. At issue between Lutherans and Catholics have been later theological extensions of themes in this passage with regard to intercession and "mediation" by Christians in relation to Christ as the one Mediator. Aspects of this issue have been seen in Part One, above.

(116) 1 Timothy 2:1 employs a variety of terms for praying: "supplications, prayers, intercessions, and thanksgivings" (*deēseis, proseuchas, enteuxeis, eucharistias*).[97] For our concerns it is important to note that, just as the New Testament speaks of Christ interceding for us with the Father, so it also recognized that Christians can intercede for others (1 Tim 2:1, *enteuxeis*, otherwise only at 1 Tim 4:5, "prayer"). The New Testament, using various other terms, frequently urges Christians to pray, especially for one another (Eph 6:18; Col 4:3; 1 Thess 5:17), even if some limits are suggested (John 17:9; 1 John 5:16). The term "intercessions" occurs in the RSV only at 1 Tim 1:5, with the verb only at Heb 7:25 (*entygchanein*, of Christ; see [114] above) and Isa. 53:12 (hiphil of *pagaᶜ*, of the Servant). "Invocation" is reflected in RSV only in the verb at 1 Pet 1:17 (invoke God as Father; Greek *epikaleisthai*, "call upon").[98]

(117) Through his mediatorial death and resurrection Jesus accomplished salvation for human beings and guarantees it. In the Pauline letters there are many ways of expressing this mediation.[99] We may single out two of these here. In the context of his discussion of justification, Paul depicts God setting forth Christ Jesus "as an expiation by his blood, to be received by faith" (Rom 3:25). In 2

Cor 5:18-21 Paul speaks of how God "reconciled us to himself through Christ and gave us the ministry of reconciliation" (v. 18). In (or through) Christ God was reconciling the world to himself, not counting their transgressions against them (v. 19, cf. 21). "To us" God entrusted "the message of reconciliation" (v. 19). "We, therefore, are ambassadors for Christ, God making his appeal through us; on behalf of Christ we make our appeal, 'Be reconciled to God' " (v. 20). "For our sake" God made Christ "to be sin who knows no sin, so that in him we might become the righteousness of God" (v. 21). In such ways Paul portrays the mediating role of Christ Jesus in the justification and salvation of human beings and the role of Christ's ambassadors in a ministry of reconciliation (v. 18), with a message of reconciliation (v. 20).

(118) Colossians 1:24 occurs in a passage about reconciliation through Christ (1:22) and Paul as minister and preacher of it (1:23). In the history of interpretation 1:24b has had an important role in that it helped open the way to medieval ideas of a treasury of merits to which saints, by their sufferings, contributed, for the redemption of others. The passage deals with how Paul, by his preaching, proclaims Christ, whose cross reconciles those hostile and estranged (1:21-23, 25-29). In his sufferings during the course of his missionary ministry, the apostle says, "I am filling up what is lacking in the afflictions of Christ on behalf of his body, which is the church" (NABRNT). Interpretations are numerous, among them the claim that something is lacking in the vicarious sufferings by Christ himself, which is being supplied by Paul (and subsequently others). Hence the view arose that the sufferings of Christ and the saints combine to form the *thesaurus ecclesiae*, each contributing a share. Such "merits" were the target of Reformation critique, though Col 1:24 itself does not enter into the discussion in the *Confutation* or the *Book of Concord*.

(119) Today Catholics and Lutherans can agree that, however the details of 1:24 are understood, there is no disparagement in the passage of the unique mediation by Christ through the cross. Nor does the "filling up" contradict the reconciliation wrought by God through Christ "in his body of flesh" and solely "by his death," a reconciliation of which the author regards himself a"minister" (1:22-23). One likely interpretation finds here an expression of the sufferings that Paul vicariously endures for the "saints" or the church, sufferings which unite them or it with Christ; the author supplies, in his preaching and suffering, what may still be lacking in the share of sufferings that all are called on to endure in proclaiming

of the word of God (cf. 2 Cor 1:4-6). Another interpretation is that Col 1:24 reflects an idea found at least in later Jewish apocalyptic texts, of a quota of "woes of the messiah"[100] that must be met.

B. The "Holy Ones"

(120) It is within the biblical framework of God, Christ, and the believing community of those justified and redeemed that a fuller understanding of "saints" and of Mary must be unfolded. In this discussion the unique mediatorship of Christ himself is assumed and agreed upon.

1. Holy Ones or Saints in General

(121) God, the Creator of all things, made a covenant with and gave the law to Israel as his chosen people. The Israelites were called to be dedicated to God's service as "a holy people," *ʿam gādôš* (Greek *ethnos hagion*, Exod 19:6; cf. Lev 19:2).

(122) Not only was Israel as a whole so characterized, but it was inspired by the example and memory of saintly forebears: the "righteous" Noah, "blameless in his generation" (Gen 6:9); Abraham, reckoned as righteous because of his faith (Gen 15:6); the patriarchs Isaac and Jacob; Moses and the judges; kings and prophets. Individuals within this people were further characterized as "holy" because of their dedication to Yahweh or his temple service: Elisha (2 Kgs 4:9), the Levites (2 Chr 35:3), the Nazirite (Num 6:5). In this way the holiness of Yahweh was reflected in his people.

(123) It was also reflected in the heavenly court of angels, often called "holy ones": "Yahweh, your God, will come, and all his holy ones with him" (Zech 14:5; cf. Deut 33:2; Job 5:1). They were associated with Israel's cult (Ps 89:5, 7 [-Hebrew Ps 6, 8]) and were believed to assist the people (Dan 10:11-13; 12:1).

(124) In time there emerged in Judaism itself, especially as notions about the afterlife (resurrection, immortality) developed, the remembrance and veneration of holy ancestors. Though Ecclesiastes pessimistically comments, "There is no remembrance of bygone human beings" (1:11), Sirach records his famous eulogy of Israel's ancestors (44:1–50:24). For him they were "men of piety" (44:1), whose "righteous deeds have not been forgotten" (44:10). That eulogy singles out Moses as "equal in glory to the holy ones" (45:2), records about Elisha that "in his life he performed wonders, and after his death marvelous deeds" (48:14), and utters a prayer for

the Minor Prophets, "May their bones return to life from their resting-place" (49:10).

(125) This honoring of the saints of old led to the building of "tombs of the prophets" and "monuments of the righteous" (Matt 23:29). This was a manifestation of popular religion among Palestinian Jews in the last two pre-Christian centuries. It provided, in particular, special honor for those who suffered or died because of their Jewish faith in times of persecution. Thus were venerated the aged scribe Eleazar (2 Macc 6:18-31) and the seven sons of a Jewish mother, tortured and killed because of their refusal to eat pork (2 Macc 7:1-42). These stories, further embellished in 4 Macc 5:4–6:30; 8:3–17:10, even record the epitaph: "Here lie an aged priest, a woman full of years, and her seven sons. Through the violence of a tyrant bent on destroying the Hebrew nation, they vindicated the rights of our people, looking unto God and enduring torments even unto death" (17:9-10).[101]

(126) The term "holy" was applied to Christian disciples in earthly life, now regarded as God's people in an extended sense. 1 Peter 1:15-16 explicitly quotes Lev 11:44-45 or 19:2 and applies it to Christians. For Paul "saints" becomes the common designation of Christians to whom he writes (Rom. 1:7; 15:25; 1 Cor 1:2; 2 Cor 1:1; Phil 1:1). This designation is a mark of their calling, a destiny envisaged also by John 17:17, 19.

(127) Though Paul never calls himself *hagios*, "holy," he does recommend to his Christian readers at times that they "be imitators" of him, as he is "of Christ" (1 Cor 11:1; cf. Phil 3:17; 1 Thess 1:6). He is also aware of the Thessalonians as an example (*typos*) for all believers in Macedonia and Achaia.

(128) "Saints" is a title extended even to those who had fallen asleep and were raised at the time of Jesus' death and appeared in Jerusalem after his resurrection (Matt 27:52-53).

(129) The Epistle to the Hebrews, having defined faith as "the reality of things hoped for, the proof of things that one cannot see" (11:1), goes on to praise Old Testament figures famous for such faith, those who because of it received divine approval (Abel, Enoch, Noah, Abraham, Sarah, Isaac, etc.). "All these, though well attested by their faith, did not receive what was promised, since God had foreseen something better for us, that apart from us they should not be made perfect" (11:39-40). They become, however, "a cloud of witnesses" that surround us (12:1), and the author of Hebrews thus hints at a solidarity existing between his Christian readers and such people of faith in times gone by. Christian leaders

are commended as "those who addressed to you the word of God; contemplate the outcome of their lives and imitate their faith" (13:7).

(130) The Book of Revelation makes use of apocalyptic devices to honor Christians who have died for their faith. They "have come forth from the great tribulation, having washed their robes and made them white in the blood of the Lamb" (8:14). Numberless, from every nation, tribe, people, and tongue, clothed in white, they stand before the enthroned Lamb, for their salvation has been achieved by the Lamb (14:1-12). A beatitude is uttered over them, "Blessed (*makarioi*) are the dead who die in the Lord from now on . . . that they may rest from their struggles, for their deeds follow them" (14:13). Thus a Christian author has not only adopted a traditional Jewish literary genre, but has also continued the Jewish practice of honoring "saints" who have died for the faith. As was suggested by Heb. 12:1, "the cloud of witnesses" (see [129] above), the author of Revelation implies a corporate relationship of those already put to death for the word of God with others still to suffer that fate. The souls under the altar are told to wait a little longer "until the number of their fellow servants and brethren be filled up, those who were going to be killed as they themselves had been" (6:9-11; cf. Rev 18:20, 24).

(131) The later Pauline letters, however, reflect an ambiguity in the veneration of holy ones, especially when by this is meant "the worship of angels" (Col 2:18). False teaching in Asia Minor churches seemed to exalt "principalities and powers" (2:15; cf. Eph 1:20-23) and to impugn the role of the cosmic Christ, now seated at God's right hand "in the heavenly places, far above every rule, authority, power, or dominion—and above whatever name can be named" (1:21). All these God has put under the risen Christ's feet and "made him the head over all for the church" (1:22). As in other New Testament writings, these letters were insisting that faith in Christ, as the perfect image of the Father (Col 1:15) and the only Redeemer, must be the touchstone of belief and worship among the people of the new Israel.

(132) Just as Old Testament passages speak at times of individual holy persons and recall their faith, so in the New Testament individuals are singled out as holy ones; for example, in the Epistle to the Hebrews (chap. 11, of Old Testament figures). Thus Elizabeth and Zechariah, "upright in God's sight, living blamelessly according to all the commandments and requirements of the Lord" (Luke 1:6); John the Baptist (Luke 1:15); Simeon, "upright and devout," with whom the Holy Spirit was (2:25); Anna, "worshiping day and night

with fasting and prayer" (2:37); Joseph of Arimathea, "a disciple of Jesus" (John 19:38), "a good and upright man" (Luke 23:50); and, after Jesus' resurrection, Stephen, "full of faith and the holy Spirit" (Acts 6:5), "full of grace and power" (6:8). Though none of these persons is explicitly proposed in the New Testament for imitation or special reverence, their exemplary character serves to glorify God and his Christ, with whom they are associated.

2. Deceased "Holy Ones"

(133) What of the saints who have departed from this life? The Augsburg Confession cites 1 Tim 2:5 in a context that states, "It cannot be proved from the Scriptures that we are to invoke saints and seek help from them" (21:1). The Apology (21:9; *BC* 230) insists "there is no passage in Scripture about the dead praying, except for the dream recorded in the Second Book of Maccabees (15:14)," a reference to how Judas Maccabeus encouraged his troops by reporting a vision he had had. In it, Onias the high priest prayed for the Jews, and Jeremiah, the prophet who had died over four hundred years before, appeared and gave Judas a golden sword, thus endorsing self-defense by the Jews on the Sabbath. The *Confutation* also cited Baruch 3:4, "O Lord, Almighty, God of Israel, hear now the prayer of the dead of Israel . . . ," with the comment, "Therefore the dead also pray for us." Underlying any discussion here is the question of the state of Christian (and Jewish) holy ones who have died. If they are not yet raised to life or not yet purged from their sins or they simply "sleep," how can they pray for us? But if they already reign in glory, ought not one invoke them to make petitions for us, with Christ as they are? Lutherans have raised the first question, and Catholics have stressed the second. Our views rest on the same biblical data. We also share certain common influences in the history of the development of the many views that exist on the present status of the dead in Christ. These views sometimes cut across Confessional lines.[102]

(134) For the most part, the Old Testament Scriptures envision after death, at best, a diminished existence, cut off from God, in Sheol, a place of gloom and silence (though not of punishment) in the netherworld (Ps 94:17; 88:10-12; Job 10:21-22; 30:23). Yet Israel's strong sense of divine justice looked at times toward a future righteous balancing of inequities in life, and Israel's long experience of God's redemptive power brought assertions about God's hand reaching even to Sheol (Amos 9:2; Ps 139:8). It is often difficult to

tell whether certain verses refer to a real resurrection of individuals who have experienced physical death or to a corporate restoration of the nation.[103] While Ezek 37:1-14; Isa 26:19; 53:10-12; 26:19; and Hos 6:2-3 have all been taken to refer to resurrection of the dead, Dan. 12:2-3 is the clearest reference. Here, as elsewhere, there is an apocalyptic setting about what will happen "at that time," i.e., on the day of the Lord. Since the state of the dead is often described as "sleep" (Job 14:10-12; Dan 12:2; Jer 51:39, 57), resurrection is "awakening," especially for the righteous (Ps 16:10-11; Isa 26:9-19). Occasionally there is reference to a "double resurrection," of both good and bad, "some to everlasting life, and some to . . . everlasting contempt" (Dan 12:2).

(135) In the literature of Judaism,[104] often in writings that Protestants count as Apocrypha and the Council of Trent included in its canon, there are further statements of expectation about an afterlife. These are sometimes put in terms of resurrection. In contrast to gloomy pictures of Hades (Sir 14:16; 17:27-28; 22:11; cf. 46:19), there is hope for vindication (cf. Wis 3:7, in light of Dan 12:1-3) and resurrection (Sir 46:12a). The Maccabean martyrs cherished the hope of being raised, but their oppressors would not be raised (2 Macc 7:9, 14; 2 Esdras [Vulgate 4th Esdras] 7:32-38, 47). Benediction 2 in the synagogue prayer *Sh^emoneh ʿEsreh* says of God, "Thou quickenest the dead." The Mishnah later denied any share in the world to come to the person "who says that there is no resurrection of the dead [prescribed in the Law]."[105] But not all Jews agreed on the resurrection hope. As is well known, the Sadducees are depicted in the New Testament as denying it, but the Pharisees as embracing it (Mark 12:18 par.; Acts 23:8). The 2 Maccabees 12 passage, about Judas Maccabeus "taking account of the resurrection" (v. 43), suggests that some Jews thought that those who fell in battle would not rise; others thought that they would but that "atonement for the dead" was proper.[106] The invocation at Baruch 3:4, that God hear "the prayer of the dead of Israel," likely, however, refers to Israelites in exile in Babylonia or is a mistranslation in the Greek.[107] The evidence in the Dead Sea scrolls from Qumran about a belief in an afterlife is ambiguous.[108] Sometimes hope for an afterlife was expressed in terms of immortality. The latter view is derived from the body-soul dichotomy of Greek thought (Wis 3:1, 4; Philo *Abr.* 258; Josephus, *Jewish Wars* 3.8.5 = 3.372–75; and rabbinic references).[109]

(136) In the Gospels Jesus affirms the resurrection hope.[110] His announcement of God's imminent kingdom and the overcoming

of Satan (Matt 12:28 par. Luke 11:28; cf. Luke 10:18 and the healing miracles, including raisings of the dead; and Matt 11:5 par. Luke 7:22) was joined with references to judgment (Matt 12:41-42 par. Luke 11:31-32; Matt 10:28) and apocalyptic expectations about the coming day of the Lord (Matt 8:11-12 par. Luke 13:28-29; Mark 13 par.). In the dispute with the Sadducees (Mark 12:18-27 par.) Jesus answered their question about the resurrection with the claim that by God's power the dead are raised, for God is "the God of the living." A bodily existence is involved in the "life" and "kingdom" one enters (Mark 9:43, 45, 47 par.); so also with the Old Testament patriarchs (Matt 8:11 par.). Jesus' own expectation of vindication for himself included being raised up (Mark 8:31; 9:31; 10:34 par.), and, for the Twelve, exaltation in the "new world" (Matt. 19:28 par. Luke 22:28-30).

(137) It is Jesus' own resurrection that is the real starting point for New Testament development of teachings about life after death. The testimony that "God raised Jesus from the dead" (1 Thess 1:10; 1 Cor 15:15) or "Christ has been raised/is risen" (1 Cor 15:4) or, more rarely, "Jesus rose" (1 Thess 4:14) meant, to those attuned to the Pharisaic-eschatological hope, God's victory over death, promise of the new age soon to come, and expectations of resurrection/life/the kingdom of God for Jesus' followers. In particular, the fact that Jesus was raised made him the "first fruits" (1 Cor 15:20) pointing to the full harvest that would follow for his disciples.[111]

(138) "Resurrection" is to be distinguished from mere "resuscitation" out of death, where someone was brought back to natural, terrestrial life for a time.[112] The New Testament vocabulary for resurrection resulting in eternal life involves terms meaning "raise (up), cause to stand on one's feet, awaken" (*anistēmi, egeirō*), but also "make alive" (*zōopoieō*), "live" (*zaō*), and even "be vindicated, justified" (*dikaioō*; 1 Tim 3:15).[113]

(139) The connection between Christ's resurrection and that of believers is clearly made in Paul's letters: because we believe Jesus died and rose, so too will God raise us up (1 Thess 4:14, 16-17) and make us alive (1 Cor 15:20-21), through the "Spirit which dwells in" justified believers (Rom 8:11). To present this hope and its implications Paul employed a variety of images in 1 Thess 4:13–5:11; 1 Cor 15; 2 Cor 5:1-10; Phil 1:19-26, and elsewhere, some of them cast in apocalyptic terms. Paul "hoped for, preached, and defended a personal 'resurrection from the dead' not as a radically new creation out of nothing but as a making alive and transformation of the dead, earthly 'body,' i.e., the personal, bodily existence" of the individual believer.[114] There is continuity (not *creatio*

ex nihilo), but only by God's creative power can resurrection come about. The "spiritual body" (*sōma pneumatikon*, 1 Cor 15:44)—with the "image" of Christ, the last Adam and life-giving spirit, vv. 45, 49—is Paul's term to preserve both aspects, continuity and newness. Such divine action is necessitated because of the reign of sin over all human beings, so that all persons do sin, with death coming in sin's wake (1 Cor 15:21-22; Rom 5:12-21, cf. 3:9, 20, 23). Involved in the human situation is "eternal" death (Rom 6:16, 21, 23), not merely that we are "dead in sins" (Rom 7:13, cf. vv. 9-11; Eph 2:1) but also death at the end, as the "last enemy" (1 Cor 15:26); from all this, Christ rescues (1 Cor 15:54-56). In the face of those who would stress present salvation alone, Paul had reservations, for there is a future aspect for the believer. Yet Paul can apply resurrection, new-life language to existence now in Christ (2 Cor 5:17) or for the (eschatological) "acceptance" of Israel, which is termed "life from the dead" (Rom 11:15).

(140) The other New Testament writings exhibit in varying degrees the present and the future sides of redemption. The Fourth Gospel especially stresses the former, as do Colossians and Ephesians; the Pastoral Epistles and to a considerable extent Luke-Acts, the latter side. But a certain balance is maintained throughout.[115] From Luke's depiction of the risen Christ as "flesh and bones" (Luke 24:39) was to develop the later phrase in the Apostles' Creed, "resurrection of the *flesh*," a terminology impossible for Paul (cf. 1 Cor 15:50) and a departure from usual New Testament phraseology, "resurrection of or from *the dead*."[116] The judgment aspect is frequently connected with a future resurrection.[117]

(141) As to when Christians arise, find life, or live, three general ways of speaking can be distinguished, each with scriptural support.[118] These three ways do not necessarily exclude one another. In subsequent centuries there have been various combinations of the three with each other and with the ideas of resurrection and immortality.

a. One way holds that the promised life with God begins immediately after an individual's death, with judgment either at that moment or later.[119] Paul writes, for example, of his desire "to depart and be with Christ" (Phil 1:23; cf. 2 Cor 5:1-10, with mention of "the judgment seat of Christ"). Sayings in Luke support such an expectation ("today you will be with me in Paradise," 23:43; cf. the analogy to Christ, 24:26; Acts 2:32-33). John's Gospel insists that the person who believes in Jesus shall, upon dying, live and never die (11:25). Rev 6:9-11 pictures the "souls" of the slain to be "under the altar" and waiting for the Lord to judge. This view offers great personal consolation: each receives life at his or her own death. It preserves the future aspect in that all is not attained in this life. But it weakens the corporate nature of the New Testament view of the resurrection.

b. Another way is that there will be a general resurrection and judgment at the last day and that, until then, the dead "sleep" or "rest" (cf., e.g., Dan 12, esp. vv. 2-4, 9, 13; or 1 Thess 4:14-18).[120] The strengths of this view include its corporate emphasis on the people of God coming into eternal life together and a realism about the fact that all is not yet fulfilled and cannot be till all the redeemed live together in God's kingdom. A weakness is the tendency toward apocalyptic scenarios about what happens step by step at the parousia. The future aspect may divert attention from life now in God's world and from awareness of the salvation already achieved in Christ's cross and resurrection.

c. A third way sees the new life of the resurrection to be already present, now, during the believer's days on earth.[121] John's Gospel most clearly presents such a realized eschatology: the believer "does not come into judgment, but has passed from death to life" (5:24-27; 6:35-51). According to Paul, newness of life is available "in Christ," through Jesus our Lord "who was put to death for our transgressions and raised for our justification" (Rom 4:25–5:2; cf. also Eph 2:5-7; and the hymnic excerpt 5:14, probably connected with baptism, "Awake, O sleeper, and arise from the dead, and Christ shall give you light").[122] This view brings the resurrection life vividly into the present. Its eschatology, however, when one-sided, can lead to the heresy of those "who have swerved from the truth by holding that the resurrection is past already" (2 Tim 2:18; cf. 1 Cor 15).

(142) These New Testament ways of speaking, using "rise/find life/live," though multivalent, involve for believers the hope of a personal resurrection and a post-mortem, post-parousia eternal life. This life of God's new age will be bodily (though the new body will be "spiritual"), corporate with others, and with Jesus, before God. It is not the result of possessing an "immortal soul,"[123] although a saying of Jesus once refers to "those who kill the body but cannot kill the soul" (Matt 10:28).[124] This life will be a renewed spiritual existence given by God, which is called in 1 Corinthians "donning immortality" (15:53-54). It involves more than escape from death, for there is also deliverance from sin. Resurrection of the dead is, like justification, dependent on God's promise and

saving work in Christ. At times the resurrection hope is depicted as a future fulfillment for all together, at times as individual, and on occasion as already impinging on existence as life now.

3. Mary

(143) Against the biblical background about saints in general one has to view the treatment of Mary in the New Testament.[125] Though there may immediately come to mind the words put on her lips by Luke, "From now on all generations will count me blessed" (1:48), that verse must not be torn from its context, for it has to be seen against the various ways in which Mary is pictured in the New Testament.

(144) Whereas "God" is mentioned in every book of the New Testament, and also "Jesus" (Christ)—except for 3 John, Mary is named only in the Synoptic Gospels and Acts. In the Johannine Gospel she is referred to as "the mother of Jesus" or "his mother" (2:1, 3, 5, 12; 19:25-26). In the other twenty-two books indirect allusion to her may appear in Gal. 4:4-5 and Rev. 12:1-17; otherwise no mention is made of her. These other New Testament writings are concerned either with early Christian exhortation, with *ad hoc* problems, or with an interpretation of the Christ-event and its meaning for humanity; thus mention of her would be uncalled for. Most attention has been devoted to her in the Gospels of Matthew, Luke, and John, whereas she is mentioned but twice in Mark (3:20-35; 6:3) and once in Acts (1:14). Although other terms of praise are used for Mary in the NT, as we shall see, yet at no place in the NT is she called "holy, saint" (*hagia*) or "upright, righteous" (*dikaia*).

(145) In Mark, usually deemed the first Gospel to be written and a source for Matthew and Luke, Mary is mentioned in two passages. (a) Mark 3:20-35 is a literary unit in which vv. 20-22 are related to vv. 31-35.[126] Verses 31-35 clearly concern Jesus' "mother and his brothers" and are understood by commentators to explain "his own" (*hoi par' autou*) in v. 21. Hence the NAB and the RSV (1971 edition of the New Testament) render v. 21 as "his family" (cf. NABRNT, "his relatives"). This means that Jesus' mother and brothers, who have heard about him, have come out to take him in hand because "he is beside himself" (v. 21).[127] Later, when they stand outside the house crowded with those listening to him and ask for him, Jesus substitutes a spiritual family for his physical, natural family: "Whoever does the will of God is my brother, and sister, and mother." (b) In Mark 6:1-6a Jesus in "his own country" astonishes people in the synagogue: "Where did he get all this? . . . Is

not this the carpenter, the son of Mary, and brother of James, Joses, Judas, and Simon?" Jesus comments: "A prophet is not without honor except in his own country, and among his own relatives, and in his own house." Thus Mary shares in the misunderstanding of Jesus that his own disciples manifest frequently in the Marcan Gospel.[128] In these Marcan passages, though Mary has a carpenter son, she is not said to be part of his spiritual family nor one who understands him or honors him as a prophet.

(146) In the Matthean Gospel two passages parallel the Marcan episodes just discussed. (a) In 12:46-50 those who constitute Jesus' spiritual family are his "disciples," not his physically related mother and brothers. A difference is detected in the omission by Matthew of reference to "his own" who consider him to be "beside himself." (b) In 13:53-58 Matthew omits in v. 57 Mark's reference to "his own relatives," and Jesus is now said to be not "the carpenter" but "the son of the carpenter," and his mother "is called Mary." In these ways the Matthean form of these episodes tones down the negative picture of Mary in Mark (reducing it at least to neutrality).

(147) A more pronounced role that accounts for this shift in emphasis is given to Mary in the opening infancy narrative in Matthew. Like other women mentioned in the genealogy of Jesus (1:1-17), Mary is seen as an instrument of divine providence in the messianic plan of God; of her is "begotten Jesus, who is called the Christ." Her virginal conception of him is, according to some source critics, taken over from a pre-Matthean source and clearly set forth in 1:18-25 (*virginitas ante partum*). In chapter 2 she plays little part aside from v. 11; she is referred to in the phrase "the child and his mother" in vv. 13, 14, 20, and 21. Thus Matthew's opening presentation of Mary singles her out and sets the tone for presenting a less negative picture of her in her two appearances during Jesus' ministry (see §146).

(148) Luke presents the most extensive portrait of Mary in his Gospel and Acts. Though she does not appear in the genealogy (3:23-38) and plays no part in the accounts of his ministry, death, and resurrection, she is indirectly referred to in two episodes (that correspond to the Marcan passages). In the account of the rejection of Jesus at Nazareth (4:16-30), those who listen to him ask, "Is not this the son of Joseph?" (4:22); all reference to the carpenter, to Mary, and to his brothers and sisters disappears. Jesus' own remark about the reception of a prophet becomes merely, "No prophet is acceptable in his own country" (4:24), with all reference to relatives

and house suppressed. Again, whereas Mark and Matthew portrayed Jesus substituting a spiritual family for his physical, natural family, the Lucan Jesus depicts it otherwise: "My mother and my brothers are those who hear the word of God and do it" (8:21).

(149) In still another episode, peculiar to Luke, a woman moved by Jesus' preaching during his ministry utters a beatitude over the mother who bore him and nursed him. Jesus himself counters with a beatitude of his own: "Blessed, rather, are those who hear the word of God and keep it" (11:27-28). Though his reply has often been taken as a corrective (= "No, rather"), it is more likely intended as a modification (= "Yes, but even more"). Thus 11:28 may be related to 8:21. In such episodes of the ministry Luke has sketched Mary far more positively than either Mark or Matthew has done.

(150) Mary's portrait in the Lucan Gospel is most emphatically painted in the infancy narrative. The announcements of the births of John and Jesus and the accounts of their birth, circumcision, and manifestation set forth their origins in antithetical, step-parallelism, which enhances the role of Jesus over John. If John is born by heaven's intervention to barren parents, Jesus is so born to a virgin, Mary. If John is to be great before the Lord and go before him in the power and spirit of Elijah, Jesus will be "great," the heir to David's throne, and Son of God. Mary herself is *kecharitōmenē*, "highly favored woman," chosen by God to bear this extraordinary child through "the power of the Most High"; and to this singular election she responds with her obedient *fiat* (1:26-38; contrast Zechariah's disbelief [1:20]).

(151) In the visitation scene (1:39-56) she is recognized by Elizabeth as "the mother of my Lord" (1:43) and pronounced both "blest" (*eulogēmenē*) in her motherhood and "blessed" (*makaria*) because of her faith in the fulfillment of what has been said to her by the Lord (1:42b, 45). Mary answers with her Magnificat, praising God who "has done great things" for her and who works mightily in behalf of the hungry and those of low degree. In the course of it she explains why "from now on all generations will count me blessed" (*makariousin*, 1:48).

(152) Mary gives birth to Jesus in Bethlehem, where she has gone with Joseph who, as a member of the house of David, is to be registered in the census. There her newborn child is identified by a heavenly chorus as "Savior, Messiah, and Lord" (2:11). Mary is said by the evangelist to have "kept all these things in her heart" (2:19, 51), pondering over them. She is depicted in the oracle of

Simeon as one through whose soul "a sword shall pierce" (2:35), because her child is "marked for the fall and rise of many in Israel." The implications of that ominous pronouncement over Mary herself are spelled out, when Jesus as a twelve-year-old is taken to Jerusalem for the Passover and remains behind in the temple when his parents start off for home in Nazareth. When they return and find him, Mary complains, "Child, why have you treated us like this? Look, your father and I have been terribly worried and have been searching for you." Jesus replies, "Why are you searching for me? Did you not know that I had to be in my Father's house?" (2:48-49). Thus the sword of discerning judgment pierces Mary's soul as she begins to learn what sort of son she has borne; her physical motherhood has to yield to another relationship. And Luke depicts that as discipleship, for in Acts 1:14 he portrays her sitting in the upper room in Jerusalem after the passion and death of her son, along with "the women" and "his brothers," praying and awaiting "the promise of the Father" (Luke 24:49; cf. Acts 1:4). In this lengthy Lucan treatment of Mary she is extolled for her motherhood and faith, but tested in her devotion and comprehension.

(153) Mary's role is differently developed in the Fourth Gospel, which has no infancy narrative, never names her, and has no parallels to the Marcan ministry episodes. She appears as "the mother of Jesus" in two episodes peculiar to this Gospel, at the wedding of Cana (2:1-12) and at the foot of the cross (19:25-27). Indirect reference may be made to her in 1:13; 6:42; 7:41-43; 8:41. At Cana Mary indirectly requests of Jesus an intervention to relieve an embarrassing situation, the failure of the wine supply at a joyous wedding celebration. The episode has a primary christological purpose in that the miracle reveals Jesus' power and him as a source of help in time of trouble; what he does is an example of the "greater things" of which he himself spoke in 1:50, and it "manifests his glory" (2:11). But Mary plays an important role in raising the question about the wine and in giving directions to the waiters (vv. 3, 5). She is depicted, it might seem, as having confidence in her son but as initially misunderstanding his "hour" or role (v. 4). Yet he acquiesces to her persistence and supplies the wine. The passage has given rise to various interpretations, some affirming Mary's "intercessory" role, others not.

(154) Mary's trust, despite her lack of comprehension, eventually leads to a more profound understanding and solid faith. She remains with Jesus (unlike his brothers, 7:5) and at length appears with other women at the foot of the cross (19:25-27), at "the hour"

when he is glorified (17:1). There she becomes a model for those who believe in him. The dying Jesus is then presented as concerned about his mother and entrusts her to the care of the beloved disciple, who has not deserted Jesus (like the other disciples), but who becomes the witness par excellence of Jesus' ministry and death, and who guarantees his community's understanding of Jesus. Mary and this disciple thus symbolize the community of believing disciples that the crucified and dying Jesus leaves behind, the kind of community that comes into being in the post-resurrectional or Pentecostal period in other traditions. The new mother-son relationship proclaimed by the dying Jesus reflects the replacement of his natural family by a new family of disciples. As in the Lucan writings, the mother of Jesus thus meets the criterion of the spiritual, eschatological family of Jesus. Mary's role is a symbol for other Christians.

(155) Overall, in the New Testament writings, there is a variety of portraits of Mary. Though Mark's picture of her is somewhat negative, Matthew's is less so, Luke changes the picture more dramatically, and John is most positive. As the tradition about her develops from this New Testament matrix, there is a rich and imaginative unfolding of a new body of doctrine in the second and following centuries.[129]

II

From the Second to the Sixteenth Century

(156) The development in Christian history of the biblical themes sketched in the preceding sections was not only indebted to Jewish sources but was also affected by the common culture of the Greco-Roman world into which the young church carried its message. Recent scholarship has emphasized the fact that the early Christian movement established its own theology and lifestyle in close interaction with the thought forms, conventions, and customs of contemporary people.[130] While the Christian faith shaped much of the ideological and cultural framework of the West from the fourth century on, Christianity itself had not been impervious to the influence of its environment. There can be no doubt, for instance, that the doctrinal formulations of Christology in the early centuries owed much to the dialogue with the popular philosophies of the time, especially Stoicism, Platonism, and various Gnostic systems. A comparable contact with the religious thought of the age must be assumed in the evolution of Christian ideas about mediators and the unique mediatorship of Christ. The belief in angelic and demonic powers between heaven and earth was part of the fundamental convictions of most people, both Jews and pagans, and the idea of a redeemer revealing knowledge from the divine realm to humans and bringing salvation to believers formed the core of the teaching of a number of cults and cultic associations.

(157) Similarly, Christian convictions and practices regarding holy people and martyrs were shaped in an environment which had its own saints. After the Maccabean revolt with its heroes and martyrs, Jewish popular piety intensified the cult of biblical figures and other

reputed saints at their tombs, where their memory was celebrated and their intercession sought despite official hesitation. In the Hellenistic world after Alexander the Great (356–323 B.C.), the classical hero worship at local sanctuaries of mythical demigods, kings, or founders had given rise to an official ruler cult which under the Roman Empire became an emperor cult and was extended by Caligula (37–41 A.D.) and especially Domitian (81–96 A.D.) to the living emperor, finding expression in elaborate symbols and rituals.[131] Veneration of the emperor's image by decoration or coronation, solemn procession, prostration, and other worship gestures customary in the East became an important part of public ceremonial throughout the Empire. Since Augustus, temples and shrines were erected in the emperor's honor, encouraging devotional exercises similar to those which characterized the shrines of popular healing deities such as Asclepios and Sarapis. These practices included pilgrimages, sacrifices, prayers, oracles, votive gifts, incubation (sleeping in the holy precinct in expectation of dreams, revelations, healings), and traffic in charms, amulets, and other mementos. While the civic ritual of the emperor cult and of local deities was resolutely rejected by Christians, nevertheless, parallel devotional phenomena developed in their own cult of martyrs and saints. This paradox is a sign not so much of deliberate borrowing or unconscious imitation but of participation in the religious expressions of an age in which, in the final analysis, both sides gave and received.[132] In the history of the first Christian centuries the task of sorting out what was truly compatible with the centrality of Christ and the uniqueness of his mediatorship in the beliefs and practices surrounding other mediators proved endless. A book such as the *Shepherd of Hermas*, written in Rome in the middle of the second century, shows some of the difficulties.[133] Here, Christology borrows from angelology, and Christ, the Son of God, is associated with heavenly figures such as the Shepherd, the Angel of Repentance, and other angelic spirits and powers.

(158) Of great importance for all subsequent development in this area was the firm insistence of the New Testament on the resurrection of Jesus and of all Christians, even though the term "resurrection" allowed for different ways of reading the biblical data in light of popular convictions about death and the afterlife. The canonical and apocryphal Acts of the Apostles speak of the difficulties encountered by Paul and the early Christian missionaries when they preached the resurrection.[134] The second century seems to have been the age of debates over the resurrection, especially

with Gnostics, who, in the perception of many Christians, tried to interpret away the reality of the message.[135] In the later creeds of the church a special accent fell on the "resurrection of the dead and the life of the world to come" (Creed of Nicaea-Constantinople) or, in an ancient phrase fervently defended by Tertullian, "the resurrection of the flesh" (Apostles' Creed), perhaps because of such denials of the promised future life. Internal disputes are recorded in the third century when Christians in Arabia, apparently seeking to preserve aspects of the biblical witness against a doctrine of the soul's immortality, argued that the human soul dies with the body and will be raised together with it. Eusebius testifies that Origen of Alexandria (c. 185–253/54) was instrumental in having this view rejected.[136] While Origen's own theories about the fate of souls in a cyclical process of salvation remained under suspicion and were censured by the Emperor Justinian in 543,[137] it seems quite clear that by his time the teaching of the immortality of the soul, understood in one way or another, had come to be a widely held, if not the dominant view in Christian theology, often combined, but sometimes also in tension with, the basic assertion of the resurrection of the dead.

(159) For the early generations of Christians the question of the afterlife of those who have died and of their interim state until the general resurrection received added actuality through the persecutions and the ensuing martyrdoms. In the late first century, conviction about the destiny of martyrs after their death is documented in a context where the primary concern is to offer an example that may be imitated. Corinthian Christians, plagued by strife, contention, and envy, are told in the First Letter of Clement that peace will not be restored to their church without faith and the endurance of suffering on their part. They are given Old Testament examples from which they are to draw this conclusion. To the same end they are asked to consider what they may learn from the great Christian "athletes" of their own generation, specifically from the apostles Peter and Paul. Because of jealousy Peter suffered many tribulations; in this way he gave his witness and "went to the glorious place which was his due" (1 Clement 5:4). Paul, too, suffered as a result of jealousy and strife. A herald in the East and West, he gained renown for his faith, teaching righteousness to the entire world. Having witnessed before rulers, he passed from this life and went "to the holy place," thus providing the most sterling example of endurance (5:5-7). Finally the Corinthians are reminded of a great host of other Christians (perhaps the *multitudo ingens* that

Tacitus says Nero persecuted [*Annales* 15:44]) who were victims of jealousy and became great examples in their endurance of torture (6:1).

(160) Early in the second century Ignatius of Antioch shows his own conviction about what lies in store for him after martyrdom in Rome. He expresses his desire to be killed by the wild beasts quickly so that he may "get to Jesus Christ" (Rom 1:2; 5:3). In line with New Testament texts that suggest an existence with the risen Christ immediately after death for specific believers (1 Thess 4:15-17; Luke 23:43), especially those who suffered for his sake (Phil 1:23; Acts 7:54-60; Rev 6:9-11; cf. Luke 16:19-31), it became a common Christian conviction that the martyr's reward included the immediate transition to eternal life with Christ. The Acts of the Martyrs are replete with indications that this very hope emboldened persecuted Christians to face martyrdom with calm.[138]

(161) As the martyrs seemed to join the "great cloud of witnesses" above (Heb 12:1), their remembrance celebrated in rituals such as memorial meals on the anniversary of their martyrdom (*dies natalis*), gatherings and graffiti at their place of burial, and the erection of funerary monuments assigned them a special place in the body of Christ; their intercession in heaven for those who were left behind was thought to be especially powerful.[139] The earliest mention of a memorial cult at the resting place of the bones of a Christian martyr is found in the *Martyrdom of Polycarp* (18:1-3), written shortly after the middle of the second century. Respect for, and veneration of, the saints, burial in the vicinity of their tombs, pilgrimages to the places where they had lived and died or were buried, and adoption of a saint as "patron" of a church or town were practices endorsed and even recommended by some church fathers.[140] Similar to the conviction of many pagans, the belief that these saints can and do perform miracles on behalf of their devotees was not uncommon. There was less clarity about the fate of other deceased Christians in the interim state. But since Christians believed that all who died in Christ would eventually share in his resurrection, their funerary art could portray the dead as praying in heaven with the community of saints on earth. In the imagination of many, these "souls in peace" formed a great crowd around the martyrs, ascetics, virgins, and widows who were honored for the special holiness of their lives. Thus the understanding of the church of the "saints" (cf. Rom 1:7; 1 Cor 1:2; 2 Cor 1:1, etc.) was not limited to those fighting here on earth under the banner of Christ, but included

those perfected by their death in Christ, a church triumphant such as the visions of Rev 7 describe it.

(162) Early references to Mary, the Mother of Jesus, outside the New Testament are rare. They include, however, several remarks in the letters of Ignatius of Antioch which, in an antidocetic argument, point to the mystery of Jesus' birth by the Virgin.[141] The first clear signs of an independent biographical interest in the person of Mary appear in the literature of the late second century. This interest in the Mother did not develop in competition with the central theological affirmations about the person and work of Christ, but as its natural complement. As the imagination of Christian authors tried to fill what could be perceived as gaps in the accounts of the life of Jesus, apocryphal writings made their appearance, inventing new details, especially in relation to his birth and infancy and the days between his death, resurrection, and ascension. Curiosity about the childhood of Jesus spawned legendary tales which tended to heighten the miraculous nature of his birth. Foremost among them was the so-called *Protevangelium of James*, written during the late second century, a fanciful account of Jesus' birth and its prehistory which promoted a high ideal of Christian asceticism by presenting an exalted picture of Mary the Virgin, her noble origins, her early life, and her extraordinary personal sanctity.[142] The interest in the days after Good Friday and Easter directed attention to the eschatological perspective of Christ's ultimate victory over death by describing his descent into the underworld and his triumphal ascent into heaven. The extracanonical traditions were often linked to secret wisdom presumably communicated to the Apostles and Mary by the risen Lord.[143] Such literature had a considerable impact on popular piety and devotional practices in regard to Mary and the Christian dead. As the apocryphal writings often painted a docetic picture of Christ, magnifying his divine character at the expense of his humanity, the human ties between Mary and her son became important in the theological defense of Christ's coming as a true incarnation: being fully divine, the Word of God was also fully human as the son of a human Mary.

(163) It was the task of the bishops and other Christian leaders to teach the truth of the gospel by making sure that such developments and the piety which accompanied them remained subject to the unique, sufficient, and universal mediation of Christ. They were not always equal to the task. Bishops did try to curb the use of noncanonical gospels, acts, and apocalypses; together with many

other similar books, the *Protevangelium* is expressly denounced as "apocryphal," i.e., inauthentic, by the so-called Gelasian Decree (end of the fourth century).[144] But while some early leaders such as Tertullian advocated rigorous standards in rejecting pagan ways and customs, others encouraged "baptizing" all kinds of practices and writings for use among Christians. To check this syncretism and resist the constant pressure of popular piety, which was pursuing goals and interests of its own, would have required a practical and spiritual authority which was beyond the modest means of the average local leadership in the churches. Thus it is easy to discover a great deal of ambiguity about the doctrinal issues involved in the popular devotion to the saints and Mary in the actions and pronouncements of the leaders of the church, and many of the obvious tensions between sound doctrine and pious practice remained unresolved. Nevertheless, official writings like the Acts of the Martyrs[145] stressed the conformity of the saints with Christ as an example of true discipleship for all Christians. By the same token the function of confessors, martyrs, and saintly ascetics who seemed to be "imitators of Christ" in an exceptional way was easily associated with Christ's sole intercession and mediatorship: such saints pray with Christ and can be prayed to.[146] Developments in the doctrine of the Holy Spirit during the trinitarian controversy of the fourth century helped Christians to perceive their martyrs and saints as instruments of God's Spirit, and the precision achieved with regard to the doctrine of the Word of God Incarnate during the christological struggles of subsequent centuries was a clear reminder that the saints must remain subordinate to, and at the service of, Christ the one Mediator.

(164) In the second century Justin and Irenaeus already suggested that, as Christ is the new Adam (cf. Rom 5:11-19; 1 Cor 15:45), so Mary may be seen as the new Eve.[147] This typology found a significant echo among patristic writers as well as in later Marian piety: "Death came through Eve, life through Mary."[148] As a consequence of the christological debates of the fifth century, the place of Mary in relation to Christ and other saints received further attention. By endorsing the Second Letter of Cyril of Alexandria against Nestorius and taking note of the attached anathemas, the Council of Ephesus in 431 accepted the doctrine of *theotokos*, i.e., the accuracy of the title "God-bearer" for the mother of Jesus, in order to insist that her son was the Eternal Word made flesh.[149] This decision marked the beginning of an enthusiastic wave of new Marian devotion which swept through all parts of the Empire and expressed itself

in many forms, including the dedication of churches in her honor.[150] Like the expressions of the cult of the saints, the expressions of popular devotion to the Virgin Mary had parallels in beliefs and practices of the surrounding culture connected with the veneration of female deities such as Aphrodite, Artemis, Isis, or the "Great Mother" of Asia Minor, but also in the concerns of ascetic movements which extolled virginity and abstinence. The conviction, not explicitly shared and sometimes rejected as unbiblical by writers of earlier centuries, that Mary not only conceived as a virgin (*virginitas ante partum*), but remained a virgin throughout her life (*post partum*), even in the act of giving birth (*in partu*), became now widely shared. It was understood both as affirming the totality of God's action in the incarnation of the Word and as enhancing Mary's role as a model for the church and the faithful, especially Christian virgins.[151] Both doctrines seemed to imply the unique holiness of Mary, although there was never unanimous agreement in the early church as to the implications of her divine motherhood for her own person. Comparison with the martyrs and apostles suggested to a few that she might have died a martyr herself, but the ancient writers were generally silent on this point, ignorant as they were of the time, the place, and the manner of her death.[152] Apocrypha from the Old Syriac, Coptic, and Ethiopic traditions speak of Mary's assumption into heaven at some point after her death.[153] Probably in the early part of the fourth century Mary was mentioned by name as an intercessor in the eucharistic liturgy of Syria where Marian praises in hymnody and panegyrics already flourished.[154] The practice spread from there to other areas, including Rome. Similarly, liturgical feasts of Mary began to be celebrated in the East. We know of a general feast in her honor in Cappadocia in the fourth century, the Feast of the Dormition in Jerusalem c. 430, and of others somewhat later, with the West slowly following suit.[155] Whether or not Mary had a place in private piety during the early centuries is not known; a form of the Marian prayer, *Sub tuum praesidium*, addressed to the *Theotokos*, has been dated to the third or fourth century on paleographical grounds.[156]

(165) The incarnational logic of the christological dogma is reflected in the formulation of the third article of the so-called Apostles' Creed, which comes from the early fifth century: the Holy Spirit is at work in the church, making it a *communio sanctorum* or community of saints (*sancti/sanctae*) through the sharing in the holy mysteries (*sancta*).[157] By their baptism all the Christian faithful have been made saints. Yet as they experience the reality of divine grace

in repentance and forgiveness, they also know themselves to be sinners. By contrast, in the case of the Virgin Mary the work of the Spirit in the incarnation of the Word of God was understood as having rendered the *Theotokos* all-holy (*panagia*).[158] For some fourth- and fifth-century Fathers such as Ambrose and Augustine, this meant that the God-Bearer, "full of grace," as the Latin Bible rendered Luke 1:28, could not be considered to be tainted by the same sinfulness as other human beings.[159]

(166) The polemics on original sin and on the nature of grace in which Augustine was involved have a bearing on the role of the saints in his thinking. Echoing Ambrose, Augustine exhorts the faithful that, while they must "worship God alone," they should also "honor the saints," specifically the martyrs.[160] In his sermons Augustine could be quite critical of devotional excesses and superstitions among his people, but he clearly encouraged the cult of the saints, including their invocation. In his eyes these saints are examples of the working of God's grace in sinful human beings, models to imitate as well as intercessors who pray to God for the faithful. An elaborate martyrs' cult, including the regular invocation of the saints, was a common feature of worship life in Africa at his time.[161] In this connection, pondering the old notion of a "cleansing fire" for the purgation of souls in the interim state after death (cf. 1 Cor 3:11-15), he suggested that belief in post-mortem purgatorial punishments was not impossible.[162] Chiefly in his later years, but already at the time of his conversion when he witnessed Ambrose promoting the cult of saints Gervaise and Protaise in Milan, Augustine admitted that the saints may, in and through Christ's sovereign power, intervene on earth through miracles.[163] Such posthumous miracles were told of Ambrose in a *Life* written at Augustine's request by Paulinus of Milan, who took as his model the famous *Life of Saint Martin of Tours* by Sulpicius Severus.[164] In all these saints, Augustine was convinced, Christ crowns his own gifts in a special way, granting the faithful a foretaste of the age to come and allowing them to see the power of the resurrection at work. Christ's millennial reign with the saints (Rev 20:4) has started already in the baptized here on earth and in the saints in heaven who are commemorated at the altars of the church.[165]

(167) Steeped in the full range of themes of Augustinian piety, Pope Gregory the Great (590–604) took special interest in the fate of the human soul after death. Book IV of his *Dialogues*, in which he answers the questions of Peter the Deacon about this topic, demonstrates that concerns of this kind were very much alive

among the faithful of his time. Gregory makes use of legends and hearsay tales of visions, apparitions, and extraordinary miracles in order to illustrate his teachings about the lively interaction between the saints above and the church on earth and about the interim state of the faithful departed. According to him, the souls of the saints (*sanctorum animae*) or of the righteous go directly to heaven after death. In heaven the saints enjoy different degrees of bliss according to their virtues. Conversely, in hell there is but one fire that burns with different degrees of intensity in proportion to the faults of each sinner.[166] It is necessary to believe also in a purgatorial fire after death whereby minor sins not remitted in this life are purged away. By intercessory prayer the faithful on earth may assist souls in the purgatorial state. Masses said by the living on behalf of the dead can be effective for this purpose. According to one of Gregory's stories, a suffering soul was released from punishment after thirty masses had been said for it on successive days.[167]

(168) At the end of the patristic period the basic soteriological affirmation of Christ's incarnation, death, and resurrection as the only channel of the divine grace bestowed upon the faithful in the Holy Spirit remained unanimous and unchallenged. At the same time, as examples of holy life multiplied through the growth of the monastic movement, the cult of saints and of Mary continued to expand without arousing a sense of danger for, or rivalry to, the unique mediatorship of Christ. But the ambiguity of the competing devotions remained. That Mary was proclaimed in Byzantine oratory as having been raised above all the angels[168] may been seen as a celebration of the divine grace exhibited in the *Theotokos;* in the understanding of others it may have served as a necessary critique of an excessive cult of other heavenly powers. But it may also be seen as having led to an exaltation of Mary which could eventually undermine faith in the unique mediatorship of Christ. All of these views could and did coexist. It was a constant challenge for church leaders, theologians, and the laity to keep all affirmations about the honor and veneration of the angels, the saints, and the Virgin Mary under the judgment of the christological affirmations established by the early church.

(169) The Christology of the early Middle Ages continued that of the Fathers and the great Councils. Yet ongoing debates on adoptionism and the hypostatic union of Christ's two natures as well as the Western addition of the *filioque* to the Creed of Nicaea-Constantinople were part of a religious climate in which new theological interpretations and new forms of piety would develop. Soteriology remained closely tied to Christology. Anselm's satisfaction

theory of the atonement provided strong support for the belief in the sole mediatorship of Christ.[169] At the same time a different kind of religious mentality took over as the moralizing tracts of monks and preachers exercised their influence on popular piety and spiritual aspirations. The decrees of the Synod of Orange (529), with their anti-Pelagian intentions, were no longer known among post-Carolingian theologians.[170] An inadequate revision of Pelagius's *Commentaries on the Pauline Epistles* circulated under the names of orthodox writers.[171] In the predestinarian controversy of the ninth century it became painfully clear that there was no firm agreement on the question of human freedom, cooperation with divine grace, and human capacity in relation to salvation.

(170) Compared with the East, however, the development and expansion of the cult of the saints, especially of the Virgin Mary, was relatively slow in the medieval West, being accompanied by the equally important deepening of a piety focused on the person of Christ, his cross, and his eucharistic presence. To be sure, Western devotion both to the saints and to Mary had strong roots in earlier centuries, partly under the impact of the exuberant rhetoric of the Eastern liturgical tradition, partly in response to tribal and local customs and emphases. There is ample evidence, for example, of a deeply felt veneration for Saint Peter among the Franks and the Anglo-Saxons, and the cult of Saint Martin of Tours in Gaul and in the Germanic territories reached its peak long before the eighth century.[172] The works of Gregory the Great and numerous monastic writers as well as the preaching of the Irish monks on the continent nourished a keen interest in the afterlife, in the benefits of penitential discipline, in purgatory, and in Western saints and their miracles. We find Mary's praise being sung here and there in Marian poetry and in sermons which echo the rich expressions of Eastern hymnody and oratory, and her perpetual virginity being extolled in line with its fervent defense by Western patristic writers, especially Jerome. There were also, however, echoes of a biblical critique of Mary, for example, in the interpretation of the marriage feast at Cana in Galilee (John 2:3-4).[173] It was in the eleventh century that mariological interest started to blossom in a fresh way, reaching new dimensions which perhaps are most clearly reflected in the works of the theologians of Chartres and Anselm of Canterbury.[174]

(171) The iconoclastic controversy of the eighth century in the East, culminating in the decrees of Nicaea II (787) and the restoration of icons (843), illustrates the different mentalities of the Christian East and West in regard to the saints and Mary.[175] In the East icons

of Christ, the *Theotokos*, and the saints had since the fourth century become a deliberate alternative to emperor-worship and popular as pilgrims' mementos.[176] Some images were believed to have been miraculously painted, providing a holy prototype for the iconography of Christ and the Virgin. Theologians carefully distinguished between *latria* or adoration (of God and Christ) and *dulia* or veneration (of Mary, the saints, and the icons). Nevertheless, they taught that images participate ontologically in the depicted subject, for they generally embraced a symbolic view of the world informed by a platonic understanding of reality. In the *Libri Carolini*, however, Charlemagne's theologians argued—following Gregory the Great—that holy images had their lawful use in the Christian church as educational tools only.[177] They rejected the notion of participation as applied to the icons and (wrongly) accused the Council Fathers of confusing veneration and adoration and of idolizing the saints. Their intention was to keep the material and spiritual realms separate and to follow the literal meaning of Scripture. Veneration, they claimed, was appropriate only for the cross, the elements of the Eucharist, and the relics of the saints—because the bones of holy persons will share materially in the resurrection. Several concerns seem to converge in this theology. The obvious fear of idolatry reflected an interest in preserving the theocentricity of Christian worship. A christological and soteriological motive was operative in the conviction that veneration of the saints and their relics was justified by the saints' presence in heaven, and in view of the future resurrection of the body. There was also a philosophical motive in that it was the immortal soul that was understood to be saved from eternal death, the body becoming associated with salvation in the future resurrection.[178]

(172) It has been suggested that the Frankish theologians exhibited a polemical attitude against any independent value given to the saints and their images which is not unlike that of the Protestant Reformers; the argumentation of Agobard of Lyons and Claudius of Turin is especially impressive in this regard.[179] Yet this critical attitude did not prevail. The decrees of Nicaea II were received and endorsed by the popes.[180] Platonic and Neoplatonic thought, already present in the Augustinian tradition, was greatly favored in the work of John Scotus Erigena (c. 815–c. 880) and later by the school of Chartres. Through John the writings of Pseudo-Dionysius the Areopagite became known and were much appreciated. Moreover, the cult of relics which had been endorsed by the *Libri Carolini* was of great importance for the functioning of feudal society. Relics

were sold, traded, and stolen.[181] Pilgrimages to the shrines of particular saints contributed to local pride and wealth. Monastic piety, which gave prominence to saints as founders, patrons, and protectors, served as a model for popular devotion. It fostered among the laity a fervent concern for personal virtue and meritorious works which was open to Pelagian distortions and tended to underplay the christocentric motif of *imitatio Christi*. The eschatological orientation toward final salvation provided a framework for moral efforts in which the saints had an important place as helpers and intercessors along the way. The prayer routine of the monasteries included the public celebration of the memory of the saints: the sanctoral cycle mushroomed. The elaborate liturgies popularized by Cluny gave the saints a prominent place, and there was a private flowering of Marian hymnody from the eleventh century on.[182] Lay piety, which largely followed monastic ideals, was instructed by preachers who urged the people on to do pious works. In all this the religious mentality of the people was nourished by ancestral customs, interest in local cults, concern for one's fate in the afterlife, and the conception of saints as ideals and heroes.

(173) During the following centuries Mary emerged among the saints as the object of special veneration.[183] Both the laity and the monasteries contributed to this development. The laity was sensitive to the chivalresque ideal of the lady honored by her knight and to the image of the queen of heaven in the splendor of her feudal court. Clearly, popular pressure pushed toward more extensive Marian devotions. From the twelfth century on, many churches were dedicated to the Virgin; shrines and pilgrimages in her honor multiplied; miracle stories were told; new feasts honoring Mary were celebrated and requested.[184] The monasteries cultivated the image of Mary as an ideal of purity, virginity, and holiness. Her role in the history of salvation was lifted up for contemplation. Christologically she was seen as the Mother of God, soteriologically as the most obedient actor in the process of salvation. Praises of Mary in hymns and antiphons were introduced into the liturgical hours;[185] votive masses were dedicated to her. New Marian titles appeared in poetry and art, often inspired by biblical images and types.[186] New prayers such as the *Ave Maria*, the *Angelus*, and the *Salve Regina* gained great popularity. The Theophilus legend, which came from the East and told of a sinner's dramatic rescue from the devil through the Virgin's intervention, was eagerly peddled and had a significant influence on the invocation of Mary as intercessor.[187]

(174) Both the monastic and the Scholastic authors of the Middle Ages provide ample evidence of the increasing importance of Mary in the piety of the age. Anselm of Canterbury, Bernard of Clairvaux, Bonaventure, and Thomas Aquinas were highly devout and eloquent in their extolling of Mary's virtues. Hugh of St. Cher, a Dominican theologian, and his confrere Albert the Great distinguished the *dulia* or veneration of the saints from *hyperdulia*, a higher veneration appropriate to the Virgin. The idea of Mary as the image of the church spread. The Song of Songs, which had been interpreted as a dialogue between Christ and the church or the soul in the earlier tradition, received a mariological interpretation in biblical commentaries from the early twelfth century on.[188] As monastic and lay piety urged each other on, lay devotees used monastic Marian devotions such as the "Little Hours of the Blessed Virgin Mary," just as monks sublimated the cruder forms of popular piety into a more reflective spiritual mood. There was a spiral of excesses exemplified by such projects as the rewriting of the biblical psalms into a "Psalter of the Virgin," or the adaptation of the traditional *Te Deum* to the praise of Mary.[189] From Mary's womb "as from a kind of ocean of the divinity have flowed the streams and rivers of all graces."[190] Mary's praise at times outshone that of Christ.

(175) Theologically one can also discern the continuation of a moderate line, a kind of *via media*, in the medieval attitude toward the veneration of the saints and Mary. Theologians whose personal Marian piety was emphatic remained nevertheless traditional and cautious in their teaching. The traditional christological context for the consideration of Mary in the history of salvation made them shun independently developed Marian doctrines. The references to Mary in Anselm's *Cur Deus Homo* and his other theological treatises are clearly restricted to the christological context.[191] Bernard of Clairvaux pioneered a new affective approach to Marian piety in his sermons while at the same time objecting to the new feast of Mary's Conception.[192] Bonaventure saw the sum of all perfections in Mary and preached a famous group of sermons on her virtues. Nevertheless, he rejected the doctrine of the Immaculate Conception and made no mention of Mary's bodily Assumption in his *Commentary on the Sentences* even though he endorsed the concept personally.[193] Thomas Aquinas expressed his praise and admiration for Mary's eminent dignity, but he was cautious in his Mariology. He accepted the Assumption but opposed the Immaculate Conception and in his *Summa theologiae* spoke of Mary strictly according to the biblical outline of the life of Christ.[194]

(176) Thomas's famous discussion of the conception of Mary (*S.T.* 3.27) provides clear evidence that new aspects were entering the discussion of the problem of the human soul during the Scholastic age. As a purely spiritual creature, the soul was believed to be immortal by its very nature. Under the influence of Aristotle's metaphysics it was regarded as the "form" of its "matter," the body, form, and matter being interdependent.[195] Thus the separation of the soul from its body results in an abnormal situation. This interpretation served to underscore the urgency of the issue of the interim state, which now posed itself as the question of the fate of the separated soul between death and the resurrection of the body. Concern for the interim state was instrumental in spreading the liturgical commemoration of all the faithful departed on All Souls' Day (November 2), one day after All Saints (November 1).[196] The personal piety embodied in the liturgy of the dead and powerfully illustrated by the thirteenth-century sequence *Dies Irae* obviously appealed to the popular imagination.[197] For many Christians the threat of the Last Judgment was very real, even though the image of Christ as the stern judge of souls, whose deeds are weighed by the archangel Michael, was balanced by that of Christ's gift of grace and mercy as epitomized in the holiness of the Virgin Mary, "advocate of sinners." The old theme of Mary as the new Eve who had reversed *Eva* into *Ave* was featured in sermons and hymns. Yet theological speculation about the interim state remained sober. The theologians generally affirmed the survival of the immortal soul, its waiting for the resurrection of the body and the final judgment, the legitimacy of prayers for the dead that their sins may be forgiven, and the availability of assistance for the souls suffering punishment. The nature of the interim state became a point of contention between the Byzantine East and the Latin West for Eastern theologians did not find the term "purgatory" in their tradition and refused to speak of a material cleansing fire.[198] The Second Council of Lyons in 1274 endeavored to obtain a consensus between the Latin bishops and the envoys of Emperor Michael Palaeologos. The confession of faith accepted by the emperor dealt explicitly with the fate of the dead prior to the end of the world. It included the statement that the living can assist the dead "through supplications, the sacrifices of masses, prayers, almsgiving, and other acts of piety."[199]

(177) The question, however, was not allowed to rest there. In several sermons preached in the years 1331–32, Pope John XXII proposed that until the Last Judgment the saints remaining "under

the altar" (Rev 6:9) enjoy the vision of Christ's humanity but not the vision of God.[200] Yet later he had to retract this opinion and described the lot of the saints with the biblical images of the kingdom of heaven, paradise, or being with Christ; the saints see God and the divine essence clearly face to face, at least insofar as the condition of a bodiless soul permits it.[201] John's successor, Benedict XII, tried to clarify the state of the saints before the final resurrection further in his constitution *Benedictus Deus* (1336): after the passion of Christ the souls of all the saints who had died earlier as well as of all the faithful departed—those in whom "nothing needed to be cleansed," and those who "have been cleansed after dying"—are in heaven with Christ. They see the divine essence "in an intuitive vision face to face," without the mediation of anything created.[202] The same issue was considered again by the Council of Florence in 1439, which endorsed the teachings of Lyons and of Benedict XII. The Council also stated that the saints see the Holy Trinity and that, in keeping with their respective merits, the bliss of one saint may surpass that of another. Without using the noun "purgatory," it taught that the soul after death is "cleansed in purgatorial pains" and endorsed the formula of Michael Palaeologos regarding assistance of the dead by the living.[203]

(178) On the eve of the Reformation an elaborate penitential system with contrition, confession, absolution, and satisfaction by pious works as the constitutive elements of the sacrament of penance was in place and functioning, designed to assure everyone of the opportunity to obtain forgiveness of postbaptismal sins. Yet the widespread presence of frightful threats to personal health and safety together with natural disasters and intense fear of death tended to increase concern for the state of the departed soul. Life itself was often seen as a penance in preparation for that state. In this situation the concept of the "treasury of merits" acquired prominence.[204] The church, it was believed, had at its disposal a wealth of merits from the saints and Mary as well as from Christ for the relief of temporal and purgatorial punishments. The widespread demand for indulgences in the fourteenth and fifteenth centuries was based on this understanding.[205] Spiritual writers tried to keep a balance between the concerns of the fearful conscience and the loving intimacy which the faithful are called to enjoy with Christ, the saints, and the Virgin Mary. John Duns Scotus and the theologians of the *via moderna* distinguished between God's omnipotence ("absolute power") and self-chosen immanence to his creatures ("regulated power"). This distinction allowed them to

emphasize that God's freedom is inscrutable and beyond all human norms and at the same time that God's mercy is fully and reliably accessible for the forgiveness of sins through Christ, the church, the sacraments, the saints, and the Virgin Mary.

(179) The history of the fourteenth and fifteenth centuries demonstrates that, despite considerable expansion in practice, there was hesitation and ambiguity in the church's official stance toward the veneration of saints. Local, diocesan, and national interests favored the proliferation of shrines, feasts, and pilgrimages. Yet official caution was often a retarding factor. New cults were less frequently accepted at random.[206] The earlier informal canonizations of saints by popular acclaim were replaced by formal and regular procedures.[207] The christological and soteriological principles inherited from the early church demanded attention, making it difficult to accommodate innovative developments in regard to the saints theologically. Attempts by preachers and theologians to push ahead and find a basis in Scripture or tradition for such views led at times to questionable readings of these authorities or mere arguments of "fittingness" and from there to a dubious "theology" of purgatory or indulgences. The invocation of saints could be justified in principle by age-old customs relating to the cult of martyrs and by appeal to the solidarity of the "communion of saints" in the Creed. But from the veneration of saints as the *Libri Carolini* envisioned it, medieval piety had progressed to their invocation as a focus of personal devotion. Moderate in the public liturgy of the church where the saints were chiefly asked to "pray for us" (as in the litanies of the saints and the confession of sins in the Mass), this invocation developed increasingly bizarre forms in extraliturgical piety, as when particular saints were claimed as patrons by families, guilds, and nations in competition with each other, or when the "fourteen auxiliary saints," popular in Southern Germany, were believed to have special areas of competence in answering prayer requests.[208]

(180) Similar ambiguities marked the official attitudes toward Marian piety in the Middle Ages. Bishops and popes often encouraged new steps in the devotion to Mary, yet they also experienced the need of having to curb excesses. Frequently local cults, new feasts, and enthusiastic titles for Mary were actively promoted despite initial hesitation. These titles included Mary as Queen of Heaven, crowned by the Father and her Son, and Mary as *auxiliatrix* or *mediatrix*.[209] A feast of Mary's conception had been celebrated in the West since the eleventh century in many places (earlier in the

East), and her sanctification in her mother's womb was generally acknowledged. At the Council of Basel in 1439 her conception was proclaimed to have been "immaculate"; the Council called this assertion "a pious doctrine in conformity with the church's worship, the Catholic faith, right reason, and sacred scripture."[210] Yet the session of the Council at which the proclamation took place was not recognized as ecumenical by pope or church, and the statement was therefore not received. In spite of vivid popular interest in reports of miracles and apparitions, bishops and popes demanded evidence to substantiate claims concerning such phenomena; they sometimes restricted local cults; they sought to verify claims of the Virgin's supernatural interventions. Above all, they did not formulate or proclaim Marian dogmas, despite the progress of theological support for the Immaculate Conception along the lines proposed by John Duns Scotus and considerable pressure from the secular powers at times.[211]

(181) Today both Protestant and Catholic historians would agree that late medieval developments in regard to the theological and popular concerns for the departed souls, the saints, and Mary were closely tied to the situation that resulted from the peculiar shape of a system in which the sacrament of penance, with the ensuing stress on satisfaction and the recourse to indulgences, had become a focus of popular attention and therefore of pastoral care. Doctrinally the christological framework of salvation was retained. Yet the weight of the assurance of salvation was shifting to human works and efforts for which the zeal of the faithful found a wide range of opportunities in practices and ideas connected with the cult of the saints and Mary. Undoubtedly these developments were perceived by many as abuses; there was theological resistance at many points, and calls for reform were commonplace. But the momentum seemed unstoppable. As a consequence, the christological foundation of soteriology and the biblical understanding of the justification of sinners were obscured.

III

From the Reformation to the Present

(182) In the post-Reformation period, to which we now turn, Lutheran and Catholic attitudes toward the saints and Mary disclose increasing divergences and a hardening of lines most apparent after the promulgation of the two Marian dogmas, the dogmas of the Immaculate Conception (1854) and of the Assumption (1950). Guided by the Council of Trent, Catholic piety and reflection continued to give a significant place to the saints and Mary, illustrated by many canonizations, additions of saints' feasts, and a renewal of devotion to Mary as one of the best ways to counter the influence of the Reformation. Lutherans viewed these developments with a mixture of suspicion and benign neglect before 1854, but then reacted with sharp polemics.

(183) Post-Tridentine Catholicism, anxious to offset the influence of the Reformation, emphasized specifically Catholic doctrines and forms of worship. Apologists and church leaders encouraged veneration of the saints and Mary, along with emphasis on the papacy and the Blessed Sacrament, as badges of Catholic identity. Peter Canisius,[212] Francis Suarez,[213] and Robert Bellarmine,[214] among others, responded to Protestant objections to the invocation of saints, the cult of relics, and the veneration of images. Canisius (1521–1597) composed a major treatise on Mary, *De Maria Virgine incomparabili*,[215] which ran through four editions in eight years. Polemical in tone, it defended traditional Catholic language about Mary and argued for the suitability of veneration of the Mother of God. The actual term "Mariology" seems to have been introduced in 1602 by Nicholas Nigido in his systematic work *Summa sacrae Mariologiae*.[216]

(184) In the sixteenth and seventeenth centuries, as dogmatic theology became increasingly abstract and as liturgy became more formalized, popular piety tended to become less theological and less liturgical. In the baroque period the Mass often took the form of a splendid celebration with a minimum of congregational participation. At the same time the devotion of the people found expressions in extraliturgical forms such as novenas, often in honor of the saints, pilgrimages, and visits to the Blessed Sacrament. The rosary received its definitive form in the sixteenth century, and in 1573 Pius V instituted the Feast of the Holy Rosary. In 1563 Johannes Leunis, S.J., established the first Sodality of Our Lady,[217] an increasingly popular lay movement that by 1576 had thirty thousand members and enjoyed rapid growth.[218] Canonizations of new saints took place in increasing numbers, including many founders and members of the religious orders.[219]

(185) Church officials were aware of the need to keep enthusiasm within bounds. Sixtus V in 1588 and Urban VIII in 1642 enacted new regulations for beatification and canonization. Subsequently Prosper Lambertini, as an official of the Congregation of Rites, wrote a voluminous treatise *De servorum Dei beatificatione et beatorum canonizatione* (1734–1736), in which he laid down norms for the recognition of miracles and sanctity.[220] In 1748, as Pope Benedict XIV, Lambertini defended the historian Ludovico Muratori's work, *De ingeniorum moderatione in religionis negotio* (1714), which had criticized certain exaggerations in piety toward the saints and Mary. The Bollandists, founded by Jean Bolland, S.J. (1596–1665), introduced critical principles of historiography into the study of the lives of the saints.[221]

(186) Theologians of the French school, following Cardinal Pierre de Bérulle (1575–1629), while promoting religious sentiment, sought to focus devotion primarily on the person of the Incarnate Word. Within this framework Marian piety flourished.[222] A typical representative of the French school, Jean Eudes (1601–1680), in his *Le Coeur admirable de la très sainte Mère de Dieu*, exalted the immense dignity of the heart of Mary, beating near the heart of Jesus in her womb.[223] Louis Grignion de Montfort (1673–1716), also of the French school, composed a *Traité de le vraie dévotion*,[224] in which he argued that, since grace comes to us from Christ through Mary, we should return to Christ through her. By cultivating devotion to Mary, the individual receives the influence of the Holy Spirit, who overshadowed Mary at Nazareth so that Christ is formed in the soul. On its first publication in 1842 this book gave rise to the

practice of renewing one's baptismal vows by making an act of personal consecration to Mary. The most popular of all books on Mary, appearing in close to a thousand editions since 1750, was *Le glorie di Maria* by Alphonsus Liguori, an Italian Redemptorist, (1699–1787).[225] More devotional than theological, this work teaches that all grace passes through the hands of Mary, to whom Christ has surrendered all the riches of his mercy.

(187) The Romanticism of the early nineteenth century brought with it a new wave of enthusiasm for medieval practices and a distaste for the rationalism of the Enlightenment. Marian piety was intensified by a whole series of apparitions, beginning with the visions of Catherine Laboure at Paris in 1830. The apparitions to Bernardette Soubirous at Lourdes in 1858 and the miracles worked at that site were taken by many Catholics as signs of approval of the dogma of 1854, since the Lady there was reported to have said, "I am the Immaculate Conception." Marian devotion was further stimulated by the apparitions at Fatima in 1917. New lay associations were founded, attracting millions of members, for example, the *Militia Immaculatae* founded by the Polish priest Maximilian Kolbe in 1917 and the Legion of Mary founded by the Irish layman Frank Duff in 1921.

(188) Devotion to the saints and to Mary spread in the English-speaking world with the help of two distinguished converts to Roman Catholicism, Frederick William Faber (1814–1863) and John Henry Newman (1801–1890). Faber attempted to popularize devotions in a radical Italian baroque style,[226] whereas Newman preferred a more sober English style. In his response to Pusey's *Eirenicon*,[227] Newman in 1865 was able to take as agreed points, accepted by his Anglican opponent, that the invocation of saints is, as the Council of Trent had put it, "good and useful" and that favors are obtained through their intercession. In this same response Newman presented a clearly christocentric view of the *theotokos*, reemphasizing the image of Mary as the new Eve, first propounded by Justin, Irenaeus, and Tertullian. He insisted that Mary "is nothing more than Advocate, not a source of mercy."[228]

(189) Seeking to integrate Mariology into the total system of Catholic dogmatics, Matthias Joseph Scheeben (1835–88) in his final masterwork, *Handbuch der katholischen Dogmatik*, situated the theology of Mary between the treatises on Christ and on the church. He singled out as the fundamental principle of Mariology the divine motherhood, understanding by this term not simply Mary's physical maternity but also her association with her son's redemptive

work.[229] Subsequent treatises on Mariology gave close attention to the question of the fundamental principle of Mariology, which was variously identified as the divine motherhood, spiritual motherhood, close association with Jesus, and the mission to represent humanity or the church.[230] Marian privileges such as the Immaculate Conception, the Assumption, and Heavenly Queenship were studied in great detail. A number of Marian theologians sought to pave the way for dogmatic definitions of new Marian titles, such as Coredemptrix and Mediatrix of all graces.[231] By the mid-twentieth century periodicals entirely devoted to Marian research were being published in several languages. In addition, regional, national, and international Marian congresses published volumes of their proceedings. The theological literature on Mary in this period is so vast that to date only a superficial survey has been attempted (e.g., at least 5,758 titles in 1952–57).[232]

(190) From Pius IX (1846–78) to Pius XII (1939–58) papal teaching and preaching carried forward theological reflection on Mary and devotion to her. Ranging in style from formal encyclicals to informal allocutions to pilgrimage groups, these papal pronouncements were enormously influential in furthering Catholic interest in Mary. Calling attention to the literary genre of these pronouncements, René Laurentin has cautioned:

> The most widely misunderstood consideration is this: the Marian documents issued by the papal magisterium in the last century had, for the most part, a devotional objective, notably the rosary. Although they include important doctrinal considerations destined to guide the piety of the faithful, they are not, for all that, dogmatic constitutions. They seek less to define a body of doctrine than to bring forward considerations for the nurture and guidance of fervor. For this reason they belong more to the homiletical genre. Moreover, their language is by choice oratorical, full of images, sometimes more generous than rigorous. They intend to stir up and excite emotions, not to promote opinions or solve academic disputes. It would be bad method to try to set up these suggestive expressions as dogmatic theses.[233]

In spite of that *caveat*, there can be no doubt that over a century of public papal encouragement of Marian piety left its mark on Catholic attitudes.

(191) The culmination of these Marian trends in popular, theological, and papal activity was the official definition of two Marian dogmas. The doctrine of the Immaculate Conception had been

discussed for centuries. Opposed by theologians of the caliber of Bernard of Clairvaux and Thomas Aquinas,[234] it nevertheless slowly gained ground, especially after Duns Scotus responded to the objection that it makes Christ's redemption unnecessary in the case of Mary. For Scotus, Mary in her Immaculate Conception was redeemed because Christ's merits preserved her from original sin, which she would have otherwise contracted.[235] In 1854, having consulted the episcopate and been given a response that was ninety percent affirmative, Pius IX issued the decree *Ineffabilis Deus*. After giving a history of this doctrine and showing the close link between it and Mary's dignity as Mother of God, the decree states:

> The doctrine that maintains that the most Blessed Virgin Mary in the first instant of her conception, by a unique grace and privilege of the omnipotent God and in consideration of the merits of Jesus Christ, the Savior of the human race, was preserved from all stain of original sin, is a doctrine revealed by God and therefore must be firmly and constantly held by all the faithful.[236]

With acceptance of the definition in the Catholic world, studies on the subject multiplied. The apparitions at Lourdes seemed to affirm the dogma and linked it with a deep well of piety. Churches, cities, schools, and countries (including the United States of America) were dedicated to Mary under the title of the Immaculate Conception.

(192) Almost a century later Pius XII consulted the episcopate regarding the doctrine of the Assumption and received a similarly positive response. Leaving open the disputed question of whether or not Mary actually died, he declared as divinely revealed dogma that:

> The Immaculate Mother of God, Mary ever Virgin, when the course of her earthly life was finished, was assumed body and soul to the glory of heaven.[237]

This dogma, too, was, with some exceptions, well received by Roman Catholics.

(193) Lutherans paid little attention to these Catholic developments since Trent. Seventeenth-century Lutheran Orthodoxy in its dogmatic formulations either defended the position of the Lutheran Confessions or ignored the saints and Mary. For example, John Gerhard, an influential theologian, spoke of Mary's virginity in the chapter on original sin and viewed deceased saints as examples for

strengthening character, thus disclosing the communion between the church militant and the church triumphant.[238] Conrad Dannhauer, a popular preacher and theologian (1603–66), expressed fears that Jesuit Marian spirituality would "end up in Mariosophy."[239] When Lutherans in Germany and Scandinavia began to stress individual piety in addition to and over against doctrinal purity, the saints and Mary played no significant role. The rationalistic tendencies of the Enlightenment only increased Lutheran disinterest in a veneration of the saints and Mary. Typical is the attitude of Johann Salomo Semler, a leading theologian (1725–91), who emphatically rejected any veneration of Mary and regarded it as part of Catholic superstition.[240]

(194) Under the influence of the Romantic movement, Mary became a popular symbol of the eternal mother, expressed by the poet Friedrich von Hardenberg, known as "Novalis" (1772–1801): "Mother, who thee once has seen, wholly lost hath never been."[241] The nineteenth-century revival of Lutheran Confessionalism, with its emphasis on the sixteenth-century Confessions, on liturgy, and on sacraments, also awakened interest in deceased saints as models of faith. Thus Wilhelm Löhe (1808–72), a leader of this movement, advocated a vigorous catechesis which was to depict deceased saints as models of faith, with Luther as the central figure.[242] Regarding Mary, influential theologians like Friedrich Schleiermacher summed up the sentiments of many Lutherans when in 1806 he declared in his reflections on Christmas that "every mother can be called Mary."[243] Some, like Paul de Lagarde, a German intellectual and a critic of a "Jewish" Paulinism (1872–91), even advocated the transformation of the Madonna cult into a symbolic expression of "German religion."[244]

(195) The dogma of the Immaculate Conception of Mary (1854) drew bitter criticism from Lutherans. The Lutheran king of Prussia, Frederick William IV, set out to organize an international protest which, however, failed because of disagreements among the parties involved. Popular Lutheran theological handbooks and massive tomes condemned the dogma as a betrayal of everything found "in Scripture, the Fathers, and reason."[245] Even those few Lutherans who had favored some rapprochement with Rome could not accept the dogma. The only Lutheran "mariologist" at the time who faintly praised the dogma, Pastor W. O. Dietlein, could not accept its infallibility.[246] The prevailing Lutheran attitude was repudiation of the dogma.

(196) Lutherans, however, were involved in many ecumenical trends. In the latter half of the nineteenth century a liturgical movement advocated a veneration of the saints and Mary based on the Lutheran Confessions. The head of the German deaconess house Kaiserwerth, Theodor Fliedner, continued the concerns of Wilhelm Löhe by compiling a massive work (1849–59) on martyrs and other witnesses of the "evangelical church." Friedrich Heiler (1892–1967), a Marburg professor and a convert from Roman Catholicism,[247] promoted a "high church" mentality by calling for Marian devotions, but without any sympathy for the Marian dogmas of 1854 and 1950. The "St. Michael's Brotherhood" (which grew out of the "Berneuchener Circle") was founded in Marburg in 1931 to promote liturgical reforms that included some Marian devotion and a Lutheran calendar of saints. The Brotherhood, though small in number, had considerable influence through prominent liturgiologists and journals.[248] Between World Wars I and II some individual theologians, such as Hans Asmussen (1898–1968), created renewed theological interest in Mary.[249]

(197) The 1950 papal definition of Mary's Assumption revived anti-Catholic polemics among Lutherans. Shortly before the promulgation of the dogma, the Heidelberg Evangelical Theological Faculty transmitted an "opinion" (*Gutachten*) to Rome, leveling severe criticisms against Catholic Mariology. The "opinion" noted that there is no scriptural or early patristic evidence in favor of the dogma and its promulgation would have the effect of a "painful estrangement" in ecumenical relations.[250] After the promulgation of the dogma, prominent Protestant leaders and bishops of the international ecumenical movement deplored this latest development in Catholicism. Walter Künneth, a Lutheran theologian, even charged that the new dogma created a "*status confessionis*" for Lutherans: it threatens the gospel itself.[251] The "Evangelical League" (*Evangelischer Bund*), which had been formed in 1866 to combat Catholic renewal in Germany, engaged in polemics on a popular level. Many Lutherans spoke of the paganization of the gospel through the elevation of Mary by this dogma; and the international journal of the *Una Sancta* movement, *Ökumenische Einheit*, identified the doctrine of Mary's assumption as a Gnostic legend.[252] Even Hans Asmussen, who had tried to revive Marian devotions in Lutheranism, deplored the promulgation of the dogma as an undesirable form of "Marianism."[253]

(198) Despite such polemics against the two Marian dogmas, an ecumenical appreciation of Mary and the saints existed among some

Lutheran groups which were linked to the liturgical and confessional renewals of the nineteenth century. After 1945 there were numerous experiments in communal living, stressing the veneration of the saints and Mary. Among these experiments are the "Sisters of Mary" (*Marienschwesterschaft*) in Darmstadt led by Klara Schlink, the sister of Professor Edmund Schlink. Many Lutherans were also influenced by the ecumenical community of Taizé, whose Marian devotions became widely known through Max Thurian's promotion of Mary as daughter of Zion and image of the church.[254] The veneration of the saints received particular attention through Max Lackmann, a German theologian, who argued in 1958 that deceased "saints" (*Heilige*) relate to "the holy" (*das Heilige*) in the Eucharist.[255] But on the whole all these groups and individuals promote a veneration rather than an invocation of the saints and Mary and as such reflect the limitations set by the Lutheran Confessions.

(199) The Lutheran liturgical tradition, especially in eucharistic prefaces, acknowledges a doxological link between living and deceased Christians.[256] Funeral liturgies include prayers for the dead commending them to God's care.[257] There are Lutheran calendars of saints in which one finds a great variety of names associated with "commemorations," e.g., Albert Schweitzer (September 4) and Dag Hammarskjöld (September 18).[258]

(200) In some Catholic circles the definition of the Assumption raised hopes that new Marian privileges, such as her role as Coredemptrix or as Mediatrix of all graces, would soon be defined. But tendencies in this direction were countered by the biblical, patristic, liturgical, and catechetical renewals, all of which, in combination with the ecumenical movement, favored restraint with regard to the saints and Mary. Focusing in fresh ways on the centrality of Christ, these movements prepared for the shift of emphasis that was to come at Vatican Council II (1962–65).

(201) Vatican II witnessed a certain clash of mentalities. The conservative minority (as it came to be labeled) pressed for continued Marian development in the directions pursued by Pius IX and Pius XII. Thus the Preparatory Theological Commission drew up a schema *De beata virgine Maria matre Dei et matre hominum* and presented it in 1962, strongly defending the title "*gratiarum Mediatrix*" and explaining that her universal mediation "in Christ" was totally dependent on the unique mediation ascribed by Holy Scripture to Christ himself (I Tim 2:6). As the Council focused attention primarily on the mystery of the church, the schema was revised and

put forward under the title, "On the Blessed Virgin Mary, Mother of the Church." In the fall of 1963 a debate took place on the question whether the schema on Mary should stand as an independent document or be incorporated into the *Dogmatic Constitution on the Church.* By a close vote on October 29 the latter alternative prevailed.[259]

(202) Vatican II attempted to deal with Christ, the saints, and Mary with sensitivity to Protestant concerns. Thus this teaching is contained chiefly in its Dogmatic Constitution on the Church (*Lumen Gentium*).[260] The very structure of this constitution provides a hermeneutical key to the relationship it asserts among Christ, the saints, and Mary. The first chapter on "The Mystery of the Church" opens with the definition: "Christ is the light of all nations" (§1). In the radiance of his light the church itself is brightened and, by proclaiming the gospel to every creature, helps to shed on all people the light of Christ. This, then, is the relationship: Christ the sole Redeemer, and the church as the assembly of all those who believe in him and witness to him to the world.

(203) The reality of the church is not exhausted in those who are still alive, for the bonds which unite believers to Christ are strong enough to perdure even through death. Therefore in chapter seven the *Constitution* turns its attention to the dead who are with Christ, those "friends and fellow heirs of Jesus Christ" (§50) with whom the living form one communion. This it does in tandem with consideration of the eschatological nature of the pilgrim church. It is within this context of those believers who are definitively with Christ (whom Catholics generally refer to as "saints") that chapter 8 considers the role of the Blessed Virgin Mary, Mother of God and preeminent member of the church (§53).

(204) In an age of individualism the *Constitution* thought it important to clarify both the fact and the foundation of the *koinonia* of all disciples. This lies in the truth that

> in various ways and degrees we all partake in the same love for God and neighbor, and all sing the same hymn of glory to our God. For all who belong to Christ, having his Spirit, form one church and cleave together in him (§49).

This is not a new belief. Historically, the church from its beginning centuries has always believed that the apostles and martyrs, as well as Mary and other holy people, are closely united with those living in Christ and "has always venerated them" in special ways (§50).

The church, the Council continues, has believed that they are inseparably united with Christ; in this relationship they contribute to the upbuilding of the church on earth through their holiness and their prayer, offered in and with him. The benefits which come to the living by remembering the saints are many. Our faith is inspired by theirs, our way is made more sure by their example, and the communion of the whole church is strengthened. Indeed,

> in the lives of those who shared in our humanity and yet were transformed into especially successful images of Christ (2 Cor. 3:18), God vividly manifests to human beings his presence and his face. He speaks to us in them, and gives us a sign of his kingdom, to which we are powerfully drawn, surrounded as we are by so many witnesses (Heb. 12:1) (§50).

The proper response of living disciples is to love these friends of Christ, to thank God for them, to praise God in their company (particularly during the eucharistic liturgy), to imitate them when appropriate, and (with reference to the Council of Trent) to invoke their intercession, which means to ask for their prayers. In the vision of the *Constitution* each one of these actions terminates through Christ in God, who is wonderful in his saints (cf. 2 Thess 1:10).

(205) Concerned that veneration of the saints has not always hewn to the proper christocentric/theocentric pattern, the *Constitution* calls for prevention and correction of "any abuses, excesses, or defects which may have crept in here and there" (§51). The faithful should be taught that authentic veneration of the saints consists not so much in external acts, but rather in the intensity of love; communion with those in heaven, provided that it is understood in "the more adequate light of faith," serves only to enrich the worship given to God through Christ in the Spirit.

(206) The eighth chapter of the *Constitution* does not aim at presenting a complete doctrine about Mary. Within the context of teaching concerning the church, it aims at describing both the role of Mary in the mystery of Christ and the church, and the proper cultivation of her memory (§§52, 54). The tone is set by the assertion that Mary at the Annunciation "received the Word of God in her heart and in her body, and gave life to the world" (§53). Thus Mary is identified as the one who in a singular way "heard and kept the Word of God" (§58; cf. Luke 11:27-28). If certain trends of the Marian era had tended to imagine Mary in a kind of privileged and splendid isolation, the Council makes clear that she is to be connected firmly

and in differing ways to Christ and to the church. As a preeminent and singular member of the church, she is related both to Christ and to us. Indeed, while her great dignity stems from her role as Mother of the Son of God, she is at the same time a daughter of Adam and, as such, one with all human beings in the need for salvation (§53).

(207) By means of a running commentary on scriptural and patristic texts, the *Constitution* tells the story of Mary's life in relation to the saving events of the life of Jesus Christ. What is emphasized throughout is the faith through which she responded to the call of God in different situations. With reference to the Annunciation, for example, the interpretation is made that,

> Embracing God's saving will with a full heart and impeded by no sin, she devoted herself totally as a handmaid of the Lord to the person and work of her Son. In subordination to him and along with him, by the grace of almighty God she served the mystery of redemption (§56).

In summation, her life is described as a "pilgrimage of faith" (§58) which led her all the way to the cross and to the subsequent waiting in the midst of the community of disciples for the outpouring of the Spirit. The reality of Mary's life, then, is intertwined with the great events of the coming of salvation in Jesus Christ.

(208) Recovering the patristic theme of Mary as a model of the church in faith, charity, and perfect union with Christ (Ambrose), the Council reflects on how Mary shines forth to the whole community as an exemplar of integral faith, firm hope, and sincere charity. It further develops this idea of Mary as *typos* of the church with reference to maternity and virginity. By accepting God's word in faith, the church too becomes a mother, bringing forth new children of God through preaching and baptism; the church is also a virgin in full-hearted fidelity to Christ (§§65, 66). As the *Constitution on the Sacred Liturgy* was to phrase the same idea, in Mary the church

> holds up and admires the most excellent fruit of the redemption, and joyfully contemplates, as in a faultless model, that which she herself wholly desires and hopes to be (§103).

(209) Within this framework the question of Mary's mediation is dealt with (§§60–62). This crucial section begins with the confession that there is but one Mediator between God and human beings, the human being Jesus Christ, who gave himself as a ransom for

all (1 Tim 2:5-6). In this context Mary is described as praying for wayfarers who are beset with difficulties. For this reason she is called upon in prayer in the church (not by the church, as some had wished to say) under many titles, including Mediatrix.[261] This, however, is to be understood in such a way that it neither adds to nor detracts from the dignity and efficacy of Christ the one Mediator. Mary's agency arises

> not from some inner necessity but from the divine pleasure. It flows forth from the superabundance of the merits of Christ, rests on his mediation, depends entirely on it, and draws all power from it (§60).

As a participation in Christ's mediation, Mary's "mediation," then, shows the power of Christ.

(210) The *Constitution* gives attention to the special reverence with which believers should venerate Mary. Differing from the adoration due to God alone, this veneration has taken diverse forms in various times and places and is to be encouraged. But the Council "earnestly exhorts" preachers and theologians to avoid excesses both of exaggeration and minimalism, and urges ecumenical sensitivity. The document ends by noting that, in glory with Christ, Mary is an image of the church as it will be in the age to come; as such, she is a sign of hope and solace for the pilgrim people of God.

(211) The theology of Mary developed and taught by Vatican II is integrated with major themes of Christian faith. Rooted in Scripture and the patristic tradition, it attempts to be christological, ecclesiological, ecumenical, and eschatological in perspective, presenting Mary in connection with the events of salvation history and the ongoing presence of Christ in the church. Mary in the midst of the community of saints in heaven; the saints as sharing the *koinonia* of all the people of God; and the whole church itself reflecting the light of Christ as the moon does that of the sun—such is the relationship set up by Vatican II among the one Mediator, the saints, and Mary.

(212) During and after Vatican II the liturgical year was modified so as to give greater emphasis to the sequence of feasts pertaining to Christ and the mystery of salvation. As a result, the feast days of the saints were reduced in emphasis and numbers.[262] On the other hand, the multitude of beatifications and canonizations has increased especially under Pope John Paul II.[263] The processes of beatification and canonization were simplified by Pope Paul VI in 1969 and again by John Paul II in 1983.[264] About thirty new causes

come to the Congregation for the Causes of Saints each year. About a thousand causes are at present under study.[265]

(213) A decade after the Council Paul VI wrote an apostolic exhortation on *Devotion to the Blessed Virgin Mary (Marialis Cultus)*.[266] After reviewing the Marian feasts and texts of the renewed liturgy of the Roman rite and meditating on Mary as a model of the church at worship, the pope concentrates on directives for the renewal of Marian devotion in the contemporary world. Conscious that some forms of piety show the "ravages of time" (§24) and need renewal, he calls for creative effort to revise pious expressions in keeping with recent theological and conciliar developments. To that end, theological principles and practical guidelines are pointed out as criteria for proper Marian devotion (§§25–37).

(214) The first and most detailed criterion is theological: Pious practices directed toward the Virgin Mary should clearly express a trinitarian and especially a christological focus; they should take note of the Holy Spirit and of the newer emphasis on the intrinsic ecclesiological content of Marian devotion. Next, such devotions should have a biblical imprint, being imbued with the great themes of the Christian message. They should, in addition, harmonize with liturgical prayer, be in some way derived from it, and lead back to it. Equally important, they should be ecumenical in tone, careful to avoid any exaggeration which could mislead other Christians about the true doctrine of the Catholic Church. Finally, they should be anthropologically sensitive, taking note of contemporary culture and life-style, especially the emergence of women into the public arena. It is in connection with the last-mentioned criterion that the pope, wishing to offset the alienation that increasingly arises when the domesticity of Mary of Nazareth is offered as an example to women today, observes that

> the Virgin Mary has always been proposed to the faithful by the church as an example to be imitated not precisely in the type of life she led. . . . She is held up as an example rather for the way in which, in her own particular life, she fully and responsibly accepted God's Will (Lk. 1:38), because she heard the Word of God and acted upon it, and because charity and a spirit of service were the driving force of her actions. She is worthy of imitation because she was the first and most perfect of Christ's disciples (§35).

(215) Throughout this document, in conformity with the Council, there are repeated calls for correcting abuses—vain credulity,

ephemeral sentimentality, errors and deviations, legends and falsity, self-seeking, one-sidedness—all of which separate Marian devotion from its proper doctrinal content. Only by removing these errors can the ultimate purpose of such devotion show itself, namely, to glorify God and lead Christians to commit themselves absolutely to the divine will. As examples of pious practices which are governed by the five principles, the pope describes the Angelus and the Rosary. These are practices that should be fostered, and new ones should be created.

(216) The conciliar stress on the relation of Mary to Christ and to the church is carried out here with attention to practical matters. Mary is venerated because of her singular dignity as Mother of the Son of God. At the same time she is "truly our sister, who as a poor and humble woman fully shared our lot" (§56). Her prayer, her example, and the divine grace which is victorious in her encourage us to follow Christ, who alone is the way, the truth, and the life (John 14:4-11). Thus did Paul VI envision the renewal of a proper postconciliar devotion to Mary.

(217) A few months before Paul VI published *Marialis Cultus*, the United States Catholic bishops had issued a pastoral letter, *Behold Your Mother: Woman of Faith*, in which many of the same emphases are found.[267] The central idea is that of Mary as model and exemplar of the church, and in that context the Immaculate Conception and the Assumption are explained as typifying the election and eventual glorification of the church. Dealing at some length with the biblical roots, this letter portrays Mary as a perfect disciple who heard and courageously followed the word of God, thus making herself "the model of all real feminine freedom." With a view to restraining excesses of enthusiasm, the bishops warn that the private revelations given even to canonized saints are never to be accepted as matters of Christian faith. The place of Mary in any sound ecumenism is adroitly treated.

(218) The same concentration on the twofold bond which unites Mary to Christ and to the church both structures and permeates John Paul II's encyclical *Mother of the Redeemer (Redemptoris Mater)*[268] written to herald the opening of a Marian year (1987–88). Most particularly he concentrates on Mary's life story as a pilgrimage of faith. Her pilgrimage, which made her blessed, is of significance not just for herself but for the whole people of God. While devotional in tone, this letter does not propose any new devotions. Rather, it limns the meaning of Mary's faith in the mystery of Christ and of the church in order to encourage all in the church to live

the life of faith more intensely. Vatican II and subsequent Catholic teaching[269] have thus sought to present the interrelationship of Christ the one Mediator, the saints, and Mary in more biblical and christological perspectives.

(219) In retrospect: Several difficulties have become manifest in our discussion of the one Mediator, the saints, and Mary. The doctrines in question are experienced through traditional forms and customs of piety that long usage has made venerable. But practices of devotion may be inspired by a variety of motivations (psychological, ethnic, national, etc.), which call for caution in the use of the axiom, *lex orandi lex credendi*. While such forms of piety are subject to judgment based on doctrine, the people who have found spiritual consolation in them should also be treated with pastoral prudence.

In addition, theological reflection cannot place all these doctrines and devotions on the same level. Some of them are close to the center of the gospel because they are directly implied in the incarnation (e.g., that Jesus Christ is the one Mediator, that Mary is the *Theotokos*). Others are more distant from this center (e.g., that Mary always remained a virgin, that saints may be venerated), while some are matters of speculation (e.g., how the saints in heaven pray, how they hear prayers addressed to them).

It remains our hope that the present report will contribute to a clarification of the matters we have examined and will help our churches to remove the remaining obstacles on the way to ecumenical reconciliation.

Catholic Reflections

(1) The sessions together have made clear to us as Catholics that our intellectual and dogmatic differences over "Christ the One Mediator, the Saints, and Mary" are rooted in part in deeply felt patterns of life and spirituality. After almost five centuries of living separately, Lutherans and Catholics have come to embody different ways of living out the gospel.

(2) One basic theological and liturgical conviction which has carried the Catholic tradition holds that Jesus Christ alone is never merely alone. He is always found in the company of a whole range of his friends, both living and dead. It is a basic Catholic experience that when recognized and appealed to within a rightly ordered faith, these friends of Jesus Christ strengthen one's own sense of communion with Christ. It's all in the family, we might say; we are part of a people. Saints show us how the grace of God may work in a life; they give us bright patterns of holiness; they pray for us. Keeping company with the saints in the Spirit of Christ encourages our faith. It is simply part of what it means to be Catholic, bonded with millions of other people not only throughout space in countries around the world, but also throughout time. Those who have gone before us in faith are still living members of the body of Christ and in some unimaginable way we are all connected. Within a rightly ordered faith, both liturgical and private honoring of all the saints, of one saint, or of St. Mary serves to keep our feet on the gospel path.

(3) Within a rightly ordered faith. There is the rub. For in the course of our history and even today some devotional practices operate within a disordered faith. This means that by the way they are structured they invite a person to transfer ultimate trust away from Jesus Christ and toward Mary or the saints. In time, the friends of Christ come to substitute for the saving Redeemer in the life of an individual or community. Such practices of piety are expressions of fruitless and passing emotion, vain credulity or exaggeration, to use the words of Vatican II;[1] they deserve critique.

(4) Popes and councils have frequently acted to restrain popular excesses, but at certain times, as in the late Middle Ages, have acted less vigorously than they should. Yet there are limits to what church authorities can do without destroying proper freedom or undermining the faith of believers. In this connection some authors appeal to texts such as Matt 13:29 (on not uprooting the wheat with the weeds).[2] In a secular age perhaps an immature sense of the transcendent is preferable to no faith at all. Yet it is far from the ideal.

(5) Pope John Paul II, aware of these dangers, has called for "the evangelization of popular piety." Pastors, he has said, must see to it that devotion to the saints, expressed in patronal feasts, pilgrimages, processions, and other forms of piety, "should not sink to the level of a mere search for protection for material goods or for bodily health. Rather, the saints should be presented to the faithful as models of life and of imitation of Christ, as the sure way that leads to him."[3]

(6) The purification of popular devotions is well addressed by the apostolic exhortation *Marialis Cultus* which Paul VI issued ten years after the council to guide the renewal of Marian devotion in the postconciliar church.[4] While its subject is the special saint Mary, the principles and guidelines which it proposes are just as applicable to devotion to any or all of the saints, and it is in that comprehensive light that we consider this pastoral teaching.

(7) The theological principles that serve as criteria for the proper honoring of the saints and Mary are trinitarian, christological, pneumatological, and ecclesial truths. These criteria stem from basic creedal faith. There is only one God, who is Father, Son, and Holy Spirit. There is only one merciful Savior, one Mediator between God and human beings, himself human, Jesus Christ. All the gifts of grace given to human beings show forth the working of the Spirit. In the church all the members are bonded together and concerned with each other's welfare; in a special way Mary typifies

what the church is called to be and ultimately hopes to be. Each of these theological principles should be at home, at least implicitly, in any proper devotional practice. Any such practice, therefore, which would overshadow the triune God, impugn the mercy and effective mediatorship of Jesus Christ, neglect the sanctifying power of the Holy Spirit, or isolate a particular church member or saint from the whole body is to be judged "out of order."

(8) In addition to these global theological principles, there are four practical guidelines which should norm devotion to the saints and Mary. These are drawn from the biblical, liturgical, ecumenical, and anthropological areas coming anew into consciousness since the Council. Devotional practices should be imbued with the Scriptures, not just a text or symbol here or there, but the great biblical themes of salvation history. Since the liturgy is the golden norm of Christian piety, these devotions should harmonize with its spirit, its themes, its seasons. In this ecumenical age care should be taken lest a wrong impression be given to members of other Christian churches, even unintentionally, especially with regard to Christ's unique role in salvation. Finally, devotional practices should accord with the cultural mores of the people engaging in them, for the church is not bound to the specific anthropological ideas of any period. In this regard, for example, given the emergence of women into all fields of public life, Mary need not be presented in a way that contemporary people might find timidly submissive or repellently pious, but rather as one who fully and responsibly heard the word of God and acted upon it. Thus she, and the other saints, can be held up as examples for believers today. These guidelines should function in the judgment of the adequacy of traditional devotional practices or the formation of new ones. Any such practice, therefore, which ignores biblical themes, does not accord with the dynamism of liturgical prayer, gives ecumenical offense especially with regard to the perceived role of Christ, or is out of tune with cultural advances is to be judged "out of order."

(9) With the experience of this dialogue clearly before us, we strongly recommend that our bishops, priests, pastoral leaders, preachers, teachers, and catechists disseminate these theological principles and practical guidelines and use them to judge the adequacy or inadequacy—even the danger—of preaching and devotional practices now in use. For example, the rather common idea that Mary or one of the other saints has a particular power over God or Christ and, if prayed to correctly, can obtain a benefit for the petitioner from an otherwise unwilling Almighty—this

"friends in high places" model of devotion—needs to be shifted toward a proper understanding of God's providential care and our solidarity in community. In this and other instances the integrity of the faith would be well served by good pastoral application of these norms. Taken together, they insure that honoring the memory of Mary, as well as other saints, remains coherent with the vital structure of Christian belief.

(10) One phenomenon of popular religion deserves special mention in these reflections, namely, apparitions or appearances of Mary or, less often, some other saint. These are puzzling phenomena to explain in ecumenical dialogue; even to many Catholics their status is not clear.

(11) The first key to their interpretation is the theological distinction between public and private revelation. What is named public revelation transpired in and through the person of Jesus Christ and the early generations of disciples who wrote the Christian Scriptures. It is this view which undergirds the axiom that revelation closed with the death of the last apostle. Subsequent to that death, the church hands on in a living tradition all that it has received, interpreting it anew in every age but not adding to the essential message. Private revelation, on the other hand, is insight granted to an individual person in the course of time. Private revelation when received by the church can be seen as a gift for the church, but it does not demand belief or allegiance as does public revelation.

(12) Different methods are used to investigate the claims of an individual to have received a private communication from heaven; all have in common that they are under episcopal direction. A very small percentage of apparitions or other such communications have ever been granted official approval by the church. When approval is given, what it signifies is simply this: the message and practices associated with the happening are in accord with the gospel. This message can be trusted, and participating in these practices will not lead a person astray. Prayer, penance, service to others—these are gospel values and characterize the message of those apparitions that have received official approval. But church approval does not oblige any church member to direct devotion toward the apparition or even to interest oneself in its story, for such matters belong to the sphere of private revelation and are not binding on the whole church.

(13) In a pastoral letter on Mary, the United States Catholic Bishops consider authenticated appearances such as at Lourdes or Fatima to be "providential happenings [that] serve as reminders to

us of the basic Christian themes: prayer, penance, and the necessity of the sacraments." In the context of this affirmation these happenings are then put into proper perspective:

> Even when a private revelation has spread to the entire world, as in the case of Our Lady of Lourdes, and has been recognized in the liturgical calendar, the Church does not make mandatory the acceptance either of the original story or of particular forms of piety springing from it. With the Vatican Council we remind true lovers of Our Lady of the danger of superficial sentiment and vain credulity. Our faith does not seek new gospels, but leads us to know the excellence of the Mother of God and moves us to a filial love toward our Mother and to the imitation of her virtues.[5]

What is important is the gospel of Jesus Christ, not a new invention. In the case of Mary genuine honor is expressed by love which shows itself in following her example. These cautions are necessary in the light of the tendency toward substitutions.

(14) There is no definitive church teaching about what actually happens during an appearance, and theologians interpret the phenomenon in various ways. Such an occurrence is a manifestation of the charismatic element in the church, a freely given moment in which the Spirit of God inspires the memory and imagination of a person to receive a message from God (Rahner). Or again, it may be interpreted as a hermeneutic of the nearness of God to people who feel themselves to be outside the normal official channels of access to divine power, such as the poor, the young, the nonordained, the uneducated, or rural women (Schillebeeckx). In particular circumstances, such a happening may be interpreted as a sign of God's compassionate solidarity with defeated people, unleashing a new power of hope and human dignity (Elizondo on Guadalupe).[6]

(15) In any event, these phenomena are in the domain of private, not public revelation, and as with other devotional matters the individual is free to participate or not, as the Spirit moves. Prudence would dictate that in the case of current happenings on which the church has not yet given a final judgment, great care and caution be exercised.

(16) In addition to the falsity of exaggeration on the one hand, Vatican II also exhorted that we equally avoid the excess of narrow-mindedness on the other. In our country and in the countries of the North Atlantic generally, a number of traditional practices of

veneration have diminished in importance in the postconciliar church. Thus, in addition to vigilance against abuses, there is need for creativity in doing for this age what our forebears in the faith did for theirs, namely, to renew inherited practices of devotion and shape new ones suitable to the temper of the times. Biblical prayer vigils, reflective reading of Scripture, preaching, litanies, the rosary, pilgrimages, and personal meditation have all been adapted in ways that cohere with the theological principles and practical guidelines of *Marialis Cultus*. These could well be encouraged, for within a rightly ordered faith they serve to enhance the life of the church.

(17) As our dialogue sessions have made clear and as the preceding considerations reflect, the most neuralgic difficulty over the issue of the "One Mediator, the Saints, and Mary" lies especially in the area of piety. Our different mentalities have interpreted "Christ alone" in different thought patterns, and this has had practical consequences in shaping pious practices. We have come to realize why certain Catholic practices appear so problematic to Lutherans. In embracing the criterion of justification by faith alone, Lutherans have developed a yardstick with which to measure deviations from adherence to the singular role of Jesus Christ in salvation. Both historically and theologically Lutheran sensitivity in this area is acute. We have come to appreciate the profound christocentric belief and piety which undergirds this stance.

(18) Furthermore, it has been encouraging to discover that we do share some common ground for honoring the saints and Mary. Scripture and patristic tradition are appreciated by both communions. In addition, Martin Luther's hymns and meditations, for example, his "Commentary on the Magnificat," and the Lutheran Confessions in part are also compatible with Catholic sensibility. Apology 21, in addition to criticizing the practice of invoking the saints, also gives a positive direction to honoring the saints: We may thank God for them, take courage from their faith, and follow their example where appropriate, elements that foreshadow *Lumen Gentium*, chapter 7. In trying to deal with the unfinished business of the sixteenth century, we have recognized that in spite of our real differences we are not as far apart as it seemed at first glance. From a common basis of belief Catholics challenge Lutherans to give clearer expression in ecclesial practice to the *koinonia* of saints which includes the living and the dead in Christ. At the same time Lutherans challenge Catholics to give clearer expression to the sole mediatorship of Christ in the devotional practices involving the

saints and Mary in which we engage. It is this challenge which we call to the attention of our church.

(19) The steps proposed in our common statement (Part I, Section III) may call for some elucidation. They are based on the supposition that the Catholic Church aspires to full communion (or fellowship, as it may also be called) with all Christians, including Lutherans. One obstacle to full communion is the suspicion sometimes voiced by Lutherans and others that the invocation of saints and the honor paid to Mary in the Catholic Church are idolatrous and injurious to the honor that belongs to God alone (cf. SA 2-3:26; *BC* 297). We believe that in light of the teaching of Vatican II, reinforced by many statements of Paul VI and John Paul II, it may now be possible for Lutherans to declare that such accusations are today unwarranted. We are gratified that the Lutherans of this dialogue join us in recommending that their church authorities make an acknowledgment to this effect.

(20) The second step envisages that Catholic church authorities agree that in an ecclesial communion Lutheran churches and their members might be left free not to profess belief in the Marian dogmas of 1854 and 1950 and not to invoke saints in their prayer. To prevent misunderstanding, three points should be kept in mind. First, we are in no sense maintaining these disagreements are unimportant. Within the closer fellowship we envisage these issues would continue to be seriously discussed. *Full* ecclesial communion would involve agreement with regard to all truths that either church holds to be binding in faith or inseparable from the gospel. Second, these divergences from Catholic belief and practice certainly do not preclude *all* communion, for it is Catholic teaching that a measure of communion already exists between the Catholic and Lutheran churches.[7] Third, if there is sufficient convergence—involving, presumably, mutual recognition of ordained ministries—it may be possible to have reciprocal eucharistic sharing between Catholics and Lutherans.[8]

(21) In the midst of the difficulties of this age, the Catholic tradition of the saints and Mary is a great resource for developing habits of the heart which cherish community, especially needed in contemporary Western culture which so emphasizes the individual. Our consciousness of participation in the life given in Christ expands as we acknowledge the graced lives of the great cloud of witnesses from times past, thank God for them, and receive benefit in their company on the road of discipleship. In the words of praise to God in the Preface for Holy Men and Women:

You are glorified in your saints,
for their glory is the crowning of your gifts.
In their lives on earth
you give us an example.
In our communion with them
you give us their friendship.
In their prayer for the Church
you give us strength and protection.
This great company of witnesses spurs us on to victory, to share their prize of everlasting glory through Jesus Christ our Lord.
With angels and archangels
and the whole company of saints
we sing our unending hymn of praise:
Holy, holy, holy. . . .[9]

Lutheran Reflections

(1) What does this Common Statement mean for actual life in Lutheran churches? Very much indeed. In summary fashion, it is possible to see we have much in common with Roman Catholics on the subject of the sole mediatorship of Christ, the saints, and Mary.

(a) *The sole mediatorship of Christ*: Together with the Roman Catholics we confess Christ as the one Mediator (1 Tim 2:5-6a) who "determines not only the content of the gospel and its communication but also all Christian life, including our own and that of Mary and the saints who are now in heaven" (CS § 103.2).

(b) *The saints*: We have become more aware of the doxological dimension of the church, i.e., the unity of the church militant on earth with the church triumphant in heaven. We affirm, along with Roman Catholics, the importance of honoring the saints as examples of Christian life and faith. (Cf. *CA* 21:1; *BS* 83b; *BC* 46; Ap 21:4-7; *BS* 317-18; *BC* 229-30.)

(c) *Mary*: We have become more aware of the place of Mary in the New Testament (CS §§ 143–55); of Luther's high view of Mary, notably his Christmas meditations on Mary and his exposition of the Magnificat where he extols the virgin who, faced with the incomprehensible role of bearing the Son of God, lived by faith alone (CS §§ 18–19); and of Mary in the Lutheran Confessions, in which statements are made that Mary is the "Mother of God" (*mater*

Dei; cf. *theotokos,* "God-bearer"), the "most blessed Virgin" (*laudatissima virgo*), and "perpetual Virgin" (*semper virgo*) (CS §§17, 38).[1]

Faced with a secularized world in which the spiritual is neglected or distorted, we rejoice that we are able to spell out another aspect of our common Lutheran and Roman Catholic witness to Christ and the doxological dimension of his church.

(2) What problems remain ecumenically? Lutherans and Roman Catholics encounter each other more and more and with heightened awareness at funerals, inter-Christian weddings, inter-Christian families, and the like. None can help sensing differences in style and practice. Differences may even be perceived as abuses. Here, too, ecumenical progress is evident.

(3) Spirituality does not have to be homogenized, Lutherans have learned in this dialogue. In some cases differences in piety and worship are merely differences in taste. Styles vary with the times as well as among groups. Present-day Roman Catholic spirituality, itself not unified, is the product of a long and complex development Lutherans know little about. We have learned that Roman Catholics made a serious distinction between worship (*latria,* for God) and veneration (*dulia,* for saints; *hyperdulia,* for Mary) and that they have a long tradition of fighting against abuses in worship and piety. (Cf. CS §§6, 82, 171, 174, 185, 204, 209, 214, as well as the Catholic Reflections.) We have also learned in this dialogue how incorrect it is for Lutherans to disdain Roman Catholic piety regarding the saints and Mary and simply condemn it as idolatry. (Cf. CS §§101, 104.1; SA 2:3:26; *BS* 425; *BC* 297.)

(4) It is just as incorrect, on the other hand, to disdain Lutheran worship and piety because it is said to lack elements found in another style of spirituality. Lutherans have a rich tradition of spirituality, of Bible reading, hymns, public worship, prayer meetings, family devotions, biblical and missionary heros, and reading devotional literature. With all of its complexities, the interaction between Orthodoxy and Pietism in the seventeenth and eighteenth centuries produced a deep spirituality largely unaffected by Rationalism.[2] This spirituality continued in the nineteenth century. In recent times Lutherans have profited from Roman Catholic liturgical renewal beginning in the last part of the nineteenth century and continuing up to the present as an increasingly ecumenical process. (Cf. CS §§195, 197–98.)

(5) But what of abuses? Abuses exist, of course. How are they to be discerned? Once again we can point to significant convergence between Lutherans and Roman Catholics. In our previous series

of dialogue we were able to affirm together that "our entire hope of justification and salvation rests on Christ Jesus and on the gospel . . ." so that "we do not place our ultimate trust in anything other than God's promise and saving work in Christ " (L/RC 7:4, 157). Our "fuller material convergence" on justification by faith (L/RC 7:155, cf. 152) has as "its counterpart" *solus Christus*: "He alone is to be ultimately trusted as the one mediator" (L/RC 7:160, cf. 117).

(6) Our dialogue was able to affirm "a significant though lesser convergence" on the "use" of this doctrine "as a criterion of authenticity for the church's proclamation and practice" (L/RC 7:152, cf. 121). It is a "lesser convergence" in that Lutherans hold to justification by faith alone in Christ alone as "the" criterion, "the" *articulus stantis et cadentis ecclesiae* (cf. L/RC 7:88-93, 117, 121, 154); Roman Catholics, in contrast, hold that our "ultimate trust" (L/RC 7:4, 157) is, to be sure, in Christ alone for salvation, but that the "alone" in the Lutheran "by faith alone" does not allow for "the traditional Catholic position that the grace-wrought transformation of sinners is a necessary preparation for that salvation" (L/RC 7:157); then justification is only "an" *articulus stantis et cadentis ecclesiae* (L/RC 7:155; cf. CS §62), along with the sole mediatorship of Christ, among "[o]ther critical norms" (CS §97) for judging doctrine and practice. Recognizing that we as Lutherans also face abuses in both worship and piety, we welcome the convergence we have discovered in these critical norms as criteria for judging all doctrine and practice.

(7) We do, however, disagree over whether there is one criterion or there are many criteria. The topic of the "saints and Mary" is a means of testing the extent and nature of our agreement as well as a possible model for dealing with other outstanding topics between Lutherans and Roman Catholics. (L/RC 7:116, 119, 153-54; CS §§3–4).

(8) Why this Lutheran insistence on the sole criterion, justification by faith alone in the sole Mediator? Because only such faith can be the assured faith (*certitudo*) that the sinner requires. *Certitudo* is not a psychological category, i.e., a kind of feeling. What produces such *certitudo* is solely faith in Christ, in contrast to *securitas*, i.e., a false faith based on any person or thing other than faith alone in the sole Mediator. By this Lutherans discern what is or is not abuse or error. The question of *securitas* is not for Lutherans basically a matter of spirituality. It is intrinsic to the working of the gospel. Here "gospel" is not a vague, general concept, but salvation solely

by faith in Christ (SA 2:1:5; *BS* 145; *BC* 292). Where this gospel is not proclaimed and the sacraments are not celebrated according to this gospel, Lutherans ask whether abuse or error have crept in (cf. CA 7; *BS* 61; *BC* 32). As we examine such a topic as the "saints and Mary," it is crucial that Lutherans see how this criterion functions.

(9) 1. *Proper understanding of the saints and Mary*. Because Lutherans emphasize doctrine, we all too readily make proper understanding the criterion for doctrine and practice. Proper understanding of the "saints and Mary" is important and has its place. Things need to be put in context, and we need to be challenged by different spiritualities and conceptualities. This does not mean, however, that to understand all is to accept all. The fundamental question is: Does spirituality involving the saints and Mary in any way undermine assured faith?

> It becomes necessary to make a careful distinction between faith as trust in the divine promises and those aspects of the faith of the Church which are responses to the divine promise through confession, action, teaching, and doctrinal formulations. These responses are necessary: the gospel (the promise of God) does indeed have a specifiable "knowledge" content. But the authority of this content, Lutherans believe, is established by its power to convict of sin and convince of grace through the work of the Holy Spirit and is not enhanced by saying that the teaching office or doctrinal formulations are themselves infallible. (L/RC 6:III, §10, p. 63)

(10) 2. *Extension of Biblical Passages on the Saints.*

a) Because the church militant and church triumphant are one (and here Lutherans do not disagree; see above [1][1b]). Roman Catholics go on to hold that invoking departed saints is a legitimate extension of asking living saints to intercede (Rom 15:30-32; 2 Cor 1:11; Eph 4:19; Col 4:3) and of the prayer of the righteous (Jas 5:16) (CS §§51, 80).

b) Roman Catholics appeal to tradition, including the extension of certain biblical passages in the tradition as well as other tradition established by the magisterium (CS §§67, 68, 78) as the basis for holding that the departed are aware of prayers addressed to them. On this point the biblical evidence is mixed (CS §§133-42), and some Roman Catholic theologians have asked whether departed saints are aware of what we who remain on earth are concretely asking and doing.[3]

c) Roman Catholics hold "that those who die in close union with Christ are taken up into eternal life and become outstanding members of the communion of saints" (CS §80). Those dying in an imperfect union with Christ are in purgatory and lack the beatific vision. (Purgatory is a topic involving biblical extension and magisterial tradition.) Those dying "in close union" have "a charity heightened by personal experience and awareness of the serious plight of wayfarers" (CS §67; cf. "so effective," §81) and, in the case of Mary, "exceptional power" in her intercession because of her divine motherhood (CS §84). Thus it is said to be "supremely fitting" (*summopere decet*) to invoke the saints (LG 50). The Marian dogmas of the Immaculate Conception (1854) and the Assumption (1950) are also based on biblical extension and magisterial tradition (CS §§84, 86, 88).

(11) To rehearse this material is to make evident that the use of Scripture remains controversial between Lutherans and Roman Catholics.

a) As Lutherans, we grant that the angels and "perhaps" the saints pray for us (Zech 1:12; Ap 21:10; *BS* 318; *BC* 230), yet even this needs to be kept within the perspective of the assured faith found only by faith in the sole Mediator. Prayer for the dead has not been frequent in Lutheran piety; funeral liturgies may include prayers that commend the deceased to God.[4] But there is no biblical promise that our intercessions can affect the situation of those already dead. Even if infrequent, such intercessions must be only by faith in Christ. Further, Lutherans should examine intercession by "living saints" to see if this is thought to be efficacious because it is intensive, because many intercessors are involved, or more "spiritual" Christians take part, rather than only because of faith in Christ.

b) Because the biblical evidence for the sort of awareness departed saints have is mixed and thus the Lutheran Confessions do not find "any decisive ground for affirming that the departed are aware of prayers addressed to them" (CS §79), Lutherans ask how one can be confident that prayers are heard.

c) The New Testament speaks of all believers, e.g., in Corinth, as "saints" or "holy ones" in Christ. All saints, living or departed, are equal because all are justified only by faith in Christ. While recognizing that "reward" language is found in the New Testament, Lutherans hold that these are rewards in a very different sense (cf. L/RC 7: pp. 94-110). Whatever the case may be, "rewarded" saints are not therefore more accessible or benevolent. Moreover, although Lutherans are very familiar with making both living and departed saints into spiritual examples of the faith, we are also very familiar with possible abuses. In Luther's exposition of the Magnificat he exalts Mary because she faces her situation by faith alone. An attempt to use Mary or another Christian to extol any other "virtue" than faith raises the question of undermining living only by faith in Christ.[5]

(12) When dealing with the issue of biblical extension, however, it is important to keep a wide focus. What is ultimately at stake is not a wooden approach to Scripture or endless delay while settling exegetical disputes. For Lutherans hold that "the scriptural witness to the gospel remains the ultimate norm" (L/RC 6:III, §11, p. 63), and this gospel is the gospel of God's unconditional mercy in Jesus Christ to which the biblical writings are the primary witness (L/RC 6:III, §7, p. 62).

(13) 3. *Invoking the saints and Mary.* Lutherans have been assured that the *Confutation,* although interpreted correctly by Melanchthon in the *Apology* as requiring invocation of the saints, was written in and for its own time and is not to be considered part of the official teaching of the Roman Catholic Church (CS §22). Thus what was a major problem for the Lutheran Confessors has been eliminated. And our present dialogue partners assure us that "in any closer future fellowship members would be free to refrain" from invoking the saints (CS §97), just as this freedom is presently enjoyed personally by Roman Catholics today (CS §94). What remains unclear is what would be required of Lutheran participation that is not just personal in official rites, such as baptism and ordination, where the saints are invoked.

(14) More importantly, whatever invocation might be as an ideal in and of itself, the Confessors held that it lacks a divine promise, produces insufficient spiritual certainty, and leads to abuses in devotional life, even though saints are to be honored (CS §83). Further, if "there is no expectation of return," the saints "will quickly be forgotten," (SA 2:3:28; *BS* 425; *BC* 297), and this actually happened.

(15) These are all, however, negatives. The positive, as the present dialogue has put it, is the freedom to proclaim the sole mediatorship of Christ clearly (CS §98). Then everything else will fall into place, including discerning abuses and errors, because everything will be only by faith in Christ.

(16) Once again, it is important to keep a wide focus. What the Lutheran Confessions meant and mean will be disputed, perhaps endlessly. Lutherans look to their Confessions for guidance concerning the invocation of the saints and Mary, yet we are aware of the fact that doctrinal formulations for Lutherans are, on the one hand, confessions and doxologies rather than promulgations of infallible dogma; and, on the other, they function as guides for the proper proclamation of the gospel, the administration of the sacraments, and the right praise of God rather than as statements which are themselves objects of faith (L/RC 6:III, §11, p. 63).

(17) 4. *Intent, experience, and the saints and Mary*. The criterion for judging doctrine and practice is not the intent of the believer, for example, that the believer intends the good or "feels good" concerning the saints and Mary. That would mean that assured faith depends on the individual and is individualistic. We do not judge the heart; we cannot even judge our own hearts (cf. 1 John 3:20). The same is true for experience, intuition, conscience, speaking in tongues, and private revelations. These all have their proper place, but they are not final criteria for right doctrine and practice. The criterion remains whatever is discerned solely by faith in Christ.

(18) A correlate is the problem of "communion" whenever the comfort of human solidarity is confused with the comfort we have *sub contrario* because we live in brokenness, finally dying, and the cross is our hope and comfort (*sola cruce*). In Christ we may be abased and we may abound. What is decisive is not our experience in all its brokenness and exaltedness, but whether our *communio* is solely by faith in Christ or is by another gospel.

(19) Therefore in any future fellowship with the Roman Catholic Church the freedom Lutherans would have clearly to proclaim the sole mediatorship of Jesus Christ would mean that at all levels of the church Lutherans would always be free to discern whether invoking of the saints and Mary is carried out in such a way that it produces assured faith (*certitudo*) because it is the proclamation (*usus*) of justification by faith alone in the sole Mediator, Jesus Christ. This methodology would be applicable to similar issues that still divide our churches, for example, indulgences and any proposal that the Marian dogmas be "accepted in some form" (cf. CS §101 and CS §17, n. 20).[6]

(20) We are alert to the fact that the question of Scripture and tradition lies behind much of what still separates Lutherans and Roman Catholics concerning the saints and Mary. We already signaled the importance of this question in our first round of dialogue

(L/RC 1: p. 32). It was fundamental for our dialogue on Teaching Authority and Infallibility in the Church (L/RC 6). In the present round of dialogue on the saints and Mary we have again discovered the need to investigate biblical extension and magisterial tradition (Lutheran Reflections, §§10–12; CS §100).

(21) Lutherans take the appeal to church history seriously, as is shown by our appeal to a lack of early testimony to invocation of the saints (Ap 21; *BS* 81–82; *BC* 46–47), even though there is now further evidence on the matter, as has been noted above (CS §80; cf. §88, on the Marian dogmas). We know that reception is integral to the life of the church (cf. L/RC 6:III, §14, p. 65: "interpreted by the community of faith"), and we are alert to the fact of development, particularly the development of the biblical canon. Our Confessional writings appeal to the teachings of the Fathers of the church: "This teaching is grounded clearly on the Holy Scriptures and is not contrary or opposed to those of the church catholic or even the church of Rome, insofar as its teachings are reflected in the writings of the Fathers."[7] Thus, even while holding firmly to the fact that "the scriptural witness to the gospel remains the ultimate norm" (L/RC 6:III, §11, p. 63), we also believe that "the unfailing guidance of the Holy Spirit" (L/RC 6:III, §14, p. 65) leads the church. We therefore rejoice in what we as Lutherans have been able to say together with Roman Catholics and look to the Lord of the church to bring us to unity as well as to guide us into all truth.

BACKGROUND PAPERS

JOSEPH A. FITZMYER, S. J.

1

Biblical Data on the Veneration, Intercession, and Invocation of Holy People

For our discussion on Mary and the saints there already exists the book, *Mary in the New Testament*,[1] prepared under the sponsorship of this dialogue. This enables me to concentrate on the other part of our main topic, the saints. The biblical data that bear on the veneration, intercession, or invocation of holy people are derived from various writings of the Old Testament and New Testament. I shall present the data in what seems a logical order under six headings: (1) the holy ones; (2) the remembrance and honoring of holy people of the past; (3) the honoring of persecuted holy people; (4) the communion of saints; (5) the prayer of holy people addressed to God on behalf of others; and (6) the invocation of saints as intercessors before God.

1. The Holy Ones

What was a holy person or a saint in the minds of biblical writers? One would have to cull a number of terms or phrases, for there are various ways in which a person's close association with God has been expressed: the "righteous" or "just" (*ṣaddîq*; LXX, *dikaios*), the "blessed" (*bārûk*; LXX, *eulogēmenos*), one "filled with the (holy) Spirit," or one "who has found favor with God." Such terms are used of Noah (Gen 6:8-9), Solomon (1 Kgs 2:45), Elijah (Jas 5:16c-18), the Baptist (Luke 1:15), Elizabeth (Luke 1:41), and Zechariah (Luke 1:67). But the term "holy one" (*qādôš*; LXX, *hagios*) feeds most directly into the traditional title of "holy" persons or "saints."

Holiness is a quality attributed to God's people as chosen by him. It is not to be understood as some intrinsic quality like sanctimonious piety or even as the transparent radiance of God's own image. It is rather the mark of Israel as a group or of individuals in Israel dedicated to Yahweh and to his awesome service. It comes from the idea that God dwells in the midst of his people; for this reason they are holy, an *ʿam qādôš*, an idea occurring often in Deuteronomy (e.g., 7:6; 26:19; 28:9). It is explicitly formulated in the Holiness Code (Leviticus 17–26). Succinctly put, "You shall be holy, for I, Yahweh, your God, am holy" (19:2). We cannot engage here in a metaphysical analysis of "the holy" or a thorough survey of the use of *qādôš/hagios* in the two Testaments.[2] Yet the discussion of the biblical roots of "holy people" has to reckon with the basic idea of the relation of Israel to Yahweh, his deliverance of it from Egyptian bondage (Lev 19:36), his separation of it alone for a covenant with himself (Lev 18:1-5; 20:26), and the dedication of it to himself as the God of a "holy name" (Lev 22:32; cf. Deut 26:19; Ezek 39:7).

Not merely Israel as a whole was so characterized. Individuals within the people were so regarded because of their special dedication to Yahweh or to the awesome service of him in his temple (so Elisha [2 Kgs 4:9]; Levites [2 Chr 35:3]; the Nazir [Num 6:5]).

In the New Testament holiness is further applied to Christian disciples in earthly life, who now become God's people in a new, extended sense. First Peter 1:15-16 explicitly quotes Lev 19:2, applying it to them. Paul uses *hagioi* as a designation for Christians to whom he writes (Rom 1:7; 1 Cor 1:2; 2 Cor 1:1); he sees it as a mark of their calling, a destiny also envisaged by John 17:17, 19. The term also expresses the relation between Christians and him who is "the Holy One," the "Holy One of God" (Acts 3:14; 4:27, 30).

The above passages refer to holy human beings in earthly existence, but *qĕdôšîm/hagioi* is also used of heavenly beings, angels. "Yahweh, your God, will come, and all the holy ones with him" (Zech 14:5). Or "to which of the holy ones will you turn?" (Job 5:1, where Hebrew *qĕdôšîm* becomes *angelōn hagiōn*, "holy angels" in the LXX).[3] The same usage occurs also in the New Testament, where "holy angels" not only appears (Mark 8:38; Luke 9:26), but "holy ones" means "angels." Paul speaks of "the coming [parousia] of our Lord Jesus with all his holy ones" (1 Thess 3:13).[4] The ambiguity here is seen when one compares it with 2 Thess 1:7, 10, where in the former verse "the revelation of the Lord Jesus from heaven with his angels of power" (*met' angelōn dynameōs autou*) is mentioned; in the latter, his coming on that day is "to be glorified in his holy ones and marvelled at by all who believe." Are the *tois hagiois autou* (1:10) the same as the *angelōn* (1:7) or as *tois pisteusasin*, with which they are in parallelism in 1:10? Is Paul referring to "angels" who will accompany the Christ of the Parousia or to Christians who have "fallen asleep"(1 Thess 4:14), "whom God through Jesus will bring with him"?

This double sense of *hagioi* eventually led to the use of the term for deceased Christian disciples. "Many bodies of the saints who had fallen asleep were raised" (Matt 27:52). The interpretation of this verse is difficult, but one notes at least that *hagioi* is predicated not of angels or heavenly beings, but of deceased believers.[5] I have used "saints" in translating this verse because it suggests the beginning of the specific use of *hagioi*. Whereas most of the Old Testament passages and many of the New Testament passages already cited fit under the generic sense of "holy ones," human or angelic, the specific Christian sense of "saints" emerges in time: members of God's people who have "fallen asleep" are remembered publicly in local or widespread celebration. They are regarded as having achieved their destiny (cf. Rev 18:20, 24).

Even if one admits the use of seven apocalyptic stage props in 1 Thess 4:14-18,[6] one must note its major affirmation about Christian destiny: "to be always with the Lord" (4:17). The imprisoned Paul later faced the prospect of his own death and debated with himself which was preferable: to live in fruitful labor or to die and "be with Christ" (Phil 1:21-24).[7]

The New Testament affirmation of Christian destiny also has to be understood against the biblical teaching about the resurrection of the dead, which emerged clearly in the last pre-Christian centuries of Palestinian Judaism (e.g., Dan 12:2) and of immortality, which surfaced in Judaism under the influence of Greek philosophical thinking (Wis 3:4; 4:1; 8:13) and which begins to pervade New Testament writings (e.g., 1 Cor 15:53-54; Mark 12:27).[8] These ideas color that of "eternal life," already found with various nuances in the Old Testament.

2. The Remembrance and Honoring of Holy People of the Past

Associated with the emergence in postexilic Judaism of resurrection and immortality were the remembrance and honoring of deceased holy forebears. Though Qoheleth could comment, "There is no remembrance of bygone human beings, nor will there be of those yet to come among those who come after them" (1:11),[9] Jews in time began to recall their holy forebears and to honor them. In the Book of Sirach one finds the eulogy of Israel's ancestors (44:1–50:24). This Old Testament passage provides a Jewish background for a similar New Testament passage to be discussed.[10] Sirach sings the praise of *ʾanšê ḥesed*, "men of piety" (44:1; cf. Isa 57:1), "our forebears, each in his own time," for the Most High has apportioned them great glory and "their righteous deeds have not been forgotten" (44:10); "their name lives on to all generations" (44:14); "the assembly recounts their wisdom, and the congregation proclaims their praise" (44:15). The passage illustrates the theme of Sirach 24, that true wisdom resides in Israel; the reader is to learn to see God's work in history and in the men of old. There follows the recital of the deeds of Enoch (44:16; cf. 49:14), Noah (44:17-18), Abraham (44:19-21), Isaac (44:22), Jacob (44:23), Moses (45:1-5), Aaron (45:6-22), Phinehas, son of Eleazar (45:23-26), Joshua, son of Nun (46:1-7a), Caleb (46:7b-10), the Judges (46:11-12), Samuel (46:13-20), Nathan (47:1), David (47:2-11), Solomon (47:12-25), Elijah (48:1-12a), Elisha (48:12b-16), Hezekiah (48:17-22b), Isaiah (48:22c-25), Josiah (49:1-7), Ezekiel (49:8-9), the Twelve Prophets (49:10), Zerubbabel (49:11), Jeshua, son of Jozadak (49:12), Nehemiah (49:13), Joseph, the patriarch (49:15), Shem, Seth, and Adam (49:16), and the high priest Simon II (50:1-21). It ends praising "the God of all" (50:22-24).

A few details in this recital should be noted. God is said (44:22) to have renewed the promise of old for Isaac "because of Abraham, his father." He makes Moses "equal in glory to the holy ones" (45:2 [LXX]). Of the Judges it is said, "May their bones return to life from their resting-place, and may the name of those honored live again in their children" (46:12). And of Samuel, "Even after his death he was consulted and made known to the king his ways; he lifted up his voice in prophecy from the grave to end the people's wickedness" (46:20), an allusion to Saul consulting the witch of Endor (1 Sam 28:3-25). Concerning Elisha it is said, "In his life he performed wonders and after his death marvelous deeds" (48:14). Finally, Sirach prays about the Twelve Prophets, "May their bones return to life from their resting-place" (49:10). Holiness is predicated only of Aaron (45:6), but God himself is praised as "the Holy One, the Most High" (47:8).[11] One also detects a belief that many of the deceased forebears are somehow still alive and can influence later generations.

Sirach's eulogy forms the backdrop for a similar remembrance and praise of forebears in the New Testament. The author of the Epistle to the Hebrews, having defined faith as "the reality of things hoped for, the proof of things that one cannot see" (11:1),[12] proceeds to praise Old Testament figures famous for such faith:[13] Abel (11:4), Enoch (11:5-6), Noah (11:7), Abraham (11:8-10, 12, 17-19), Sarah (11:11), Isaac (11:20), Jacob (11:21), Joseph (11:22), Moses (11:23-28), the people of the Exodus (11:29-30), Rahab of Jericho (11:31). Further extolled are Gideon, Barak, Samson, Jephthah, David, Samuel, the prophets, women—all persons of faith (11:32-39). "All these, though well attested by their faith, did not receive what was promised, since God had foreseen something better for us, that apart from us they should not be made perfect" (11:39-40). They become, however, "a cloud of witnesses" surrounding us (12:1). The author sees solidarity existing between his readers and such bygone people of faith. "Remember your leaders, those who addressed to you the word of God; contemplate the outcome of their lives and imitate their faith" (13:7; cf. 6:12).

Another mode of honoring "saints" of old is recalled in the Synoptic Gospels: Jesus mentions the practice of Jews who built "tombs of the prophets" and adorned "monuments of the righteous" (Matt 23:29). These phrases come from the woes addressed to the Scribes and Pharisees, whom Jesus quotes as saying, "'Had we lived in our fathers' days, we would not have shared with them in shedding the prophets' blood.' Thus you bear witness against yourselves that you are the children of those who murdered the prophets" (23:30-31). Jesus' remark was not directed against the building of tombs and monuments as such, but against those who, while honoring dead prophets and righteous persons of old, were ignoring the living one(s) among them.

J. Jeremias gathered much information about such graves and monuments of holy persons not only in Palestine, but in Syria, Egypt, Arabia, Mesopotamia, and neighboring lands, and not only of prophets, but of martyrs, priests, patriarchs, kings, and famous women.[14] The subtitle of his book relates all the information gathered to the *Volksreligion* of Jesus' time. His sources are mainly *Jubilees, Testaments of the Twelve Patriarchs*, 4 Maccabees, and Josephus, which would be pertinent; but some of his other materials (Jerusalem Talmud, *Prophetarum vitae fabulosae*, Samaritan and early Christian sources) are less pertinent as examples of *Volksreligion* in

Jesus' time. Enough of his evidence, archaeological and literary, however, does bear on the period in question and sheds light on the practice among Jews of honoring the memory of people of old regarded as servants of the God of Israel.[15] Burial sites of such people were known, whether or not elaborate monuments were built to their memory in all cases; their graves were visited and held in respect. Though the adornment of graves was regarded by H. Vincent and F.-M. Abel as "la renaissance du culte des tombeaux ancestrales,"[16] Jeremias rather ascribes such adornment to Herod the Great and calls it "ein Novum."[17] Such monuments were often cenotaphs (with pyramid caps in imitation of Egyptian styles), often inscribed (as in 4 Macc 17:9-10). Jeremias quotes A. Schlatter: the Jews of this period were convinced that "not only the bones of the prophet, but the prophet himself was in the tomb."[18] He cites Matt 2:18 as evidence for this opinion (reference to Rachel's tomb near Bethlehem). The presence of the holy person was considered manifest when miracles were wrought at the tomb (Sir 48:14 about Elisha). For Jeremias the most important conviction of Palestinian Jews about such holy people was the view of them as intercessors. To be noted is the lack of evidence that religious authorities in Palestinian Judaism saw any conflict of such *Volksreligion* with the monotheism of Israel.

3. The Honoring of Persecuted Holy People

The cases of the Scribe Eleazar and of the Seven Brothers and their Mother move the discussion of the honoring of holy people into another dimension. Certain features in the stories about these persons provide a background for the persecuted dead in the Book of Revelation and also fed historically into the cult of early Christian martyrs. For these persons were honored not only because of their faith, but because they chose to die rather than desert the faith of their fathers.

The story about the aged Scribe Eleazar surfaces in 2 Macc 6:18-31. Being forced to eat pork, Eleazar welcomed "death with honor rather than life with pollution" (6:19). Despite the exhortations of old friends, he would not even pretend to eat the pork. So he died on the rack, leaving "to the young a noble example of how to die a good death . . . for revered and holy laws" (6:28).

Then follows the story of the Seven Brothers and their Mother (7:1-42), who, though threatened with torture, refused to eat the unlawful pork. Tortured in diverse ways, the seven resisted Antiochus IV Epiphanes. The second brother to be killed addressed the king, "Cursed wretch that you are, you release us from the present life; but the King of the Universe shall raise us up to an everlasting renewal of life since we have died for his laws" (7:9). The fourth brother replied similarly, adding, "For you there shall be no resurrection to life" (7:14). The last brother exclaimed, "Our brothers, having endured a brief suffering, have drunk of everflowing life under God's covenant; but you, at God's judgment, will receive just punishment for your arrogance" (7:36). Finally, the mother comes to her ordeal, depicted as one "filled with a noble spirit." She "fired her woman's reasoning with the courage of a man" (7:21) and exhorted her sons to resist as they had. "Last of all died the mother, after her sons" (7:41).[19]

These stories are further embellished in 4 Macc 5:4–6:30 (Eleazar) and 8:3–17:10 (Seven Brothers). Recasting them in a philosophical discussion that stresses reason dominating the passions, the author records how fitting it was to inscribe a memorial over their resting place for future generations:

HERE LIE AN AGED PRIEST
AND A WOMAN FULL OF YEARS AND HER SEVEN SONS.
THROUGH THE VIOLENCE OF A TYRANT
DESIROUS OF DESTROYING THE HEBREW NATION,
THEY VINDICATED THE RIGHTS OF OUR PEOPLE,
LOOKING UNTO GOD AND ENDURING TORMENTS
EVEN UNTO DEATH.[20]

Neither death for one's faith nor the honoring of those who have so died is peculiarly Christian. Eleazar and the Seven Brothers reveal the Jewish antecedence.[21]

In the New Testament Stephen (Acts 7:58-60) begins the list of Christian martyrs; he is eventually called "the Protomartyr."[22] Acts also tells of a persecution of the Jerusalem church following the death of Stephen (8:1) and of the death of James, son of Zebedee, at the order of Herod Agrippa (12:2).

The Book of Revelation uses apocalyptic stage props to honor such Christians. They "have come forth from the great tribulation, having washed their robes and made them white in the blood of the Lamb" (8:14). Numberless, from every nation, tribe, people, and tongue, and clothed in white, they stand before the enthroned Lamb, holding palm branches. Such persecuted Christians—or perhaps other confreres, depending on how one relates the 144,000 of 14:1 to those of chapter 8—are considered to be "saints" who have endured: "those who keep God's commandments and the faith of Jesus" (14:12). "Blessed are the dead who died in the Lord . . . that they may rest from their struggles, for their deeds follow them" (14:13).

In such descriptions of persons called "saints" one cannot be apodictic about the symbolism used. But since apocalyptic literature generally emerged from a persecution context, we see in the Book of Revelation an honoring of Christians who, having died in persecution, are depicted with apocalyptic trappings enjoying that destiny of which other New Testament writers speak of as "being with the Lord." The apocalyptic genre has made of them "followers of the Lamb" (14:4). Thus this Christian author has not only adopted a Jewish literary genre, but in his own way continues the Jewish practice of honoring "saints" who have died for their faith.[23]

4. The Communion of Saints

Under the rubric of "communion of saints" we are not to think merely of the mass of deceased Christians such as the 144,000 followers of the Lamb (Rev 14:4) in their corporate, spotless existence before the heavenly throne, but much more concretely of the solidarity that Jews or Christians still in earthly life have with those who have passed on and are regarded as enjoying their eternal destiny. The Book of Revelation implies such a corporate relation or connection in its description of the souls of those put to death for the word of God, who are under the altar and are told to wait a little longer "until the number of their fellow servants and their brethren be filled up" (6:9-11). Here the solidarity is sensed by those who have already passed on (cf. 1 Cor 15:23, where mention is made of Christ the first fruits and of those who at his coming belong to Christ).

Without recourse to apocalyptic trappings, that sense of communion or solidarity is depicted in the Epistle to the Hebrews, when it refers to nineteen persons of faith, along with unnamed persecuted ones (11:35-38), as "a cloud of witnesses" that surrounds us still in earthly life, as we are exhorted to lay aside every encumbrance and run with perseverance the race set before us, "looking to Jesus the leader and the one who perfects all faith" (12:1-2).[24] Here famous persons of faith of bygone times are presented not merely as witnesses of what real faith is, but also as a compact throng of believers, whose company living Christians are already called to share.

A similar association of Christians on earth with the "saints" seems to be envisaged in Eph 2:19-21: "You are, therefore, no longer strangers and aliens, but fellow citizens (*sympolitai*) of the saints and members of God's household, built upon the foundation of the apostles and prophets with Christ Jesus himself as the capstone, in whom the whole structure is fitted together and grows into a holy temple in the Lord." Here much depends on the sense of *tôn hagiôn* (2:19). Does it designate merely Jewish and Gentile members of the Christian church on earth, or holy Christians who have passed on? The former sense is certainly possible; but given the reference to Christ Jesus as the capstone and the title of him as Lord (hence resurrected), it may suggest the second sense. Thus the passage would support the idea of a "communion of saints," a solidarity of earthly Christians with those already "with the Lord."

To such passages one would have to relate the Pauline teaching of the church as the body of Christ and the solidarity that that image implies (see 1 Cor 12:12-30, esp. vv. 14-26;[25] [note the development of his teaching in Col 1:18-20; Eph 4:15-16]). Per se, the image describes the church in its earthly existence; yet the development in Eph 1:20-23, referring to the risen Christ seated at God's right hand "in the heavenly places" with "all things under his feet" and made "head over all things for the church, which is his body," suggests that the "glorious inheritance of the saints" (1:18) is a New Testament way of speaking of what later came to be called *ecclesia triumphans*.

One also has to relate to the "communion of saints" the teaching about Christ's heavenly intercession with the Father on behalf of Christian believers: "Christ Jesus, who has died, rather has been raised, and who sits at God's right hand, also intercedes for us" (Rom 8:34). "He is also able for all time to save those who approach God through him, being always alive to intercede for them" (Heb 7:25). Hence, though *sanctorum communio* is not explicitly a New Testament expression, it is not without an implicit basis in such teaching.

5. The Prayer of Holy People Addressed to God on Behalf of Others

Though the biblical basis of *sanctorum communio* may not be wide, another aspect of it needs consideration, namely, examples in both the Old Testament and the New Testament of holy persons who pray to God on behalf of others. J. Jeremias, in speaking of Palestinian *Volksreligion* in the time of Jesus, distinguished—in dependence on a Göttingen dissertation by N. Johansson in 1940—between *Fürbitte* and *Fürsprache* (or *Interzession*).[26] He cited Gen 18:16-33 as an example of the latter: Abraham's intercession before God on behalf of Sodom and Gomorrah. It succeeds in eliciting a divine promise that the evil cities would not be destroyed if only ten, not fifty, righteous persons were found in them. Involved here is Israel's sense of solidarity; normally this is expressed in terms of the contamination of the whole by the wickedness of a few. But in the Abraham story it works in reverse, and Abraham makes a point of it in his intercession.

Another example is perhaps of less pertinence, that of Moses, who during Israel's battle with the Amalekites stood upon a hill and held up "the rod of God," supported by Aaron and Hur: "Whenever Moses held up his hands, Israel prevailed" (Exod 17:11). More pertinent, however, would be Moses' prayer for Israel after it had worshiped Aaron's golden calf (Exod 32:11-14). He is depicted supplicating God, with a memento of Abraham, Isaac, and Jacob and of the promises made to them. Here during the desert wanderings God favors his people at the intercession of his own chosen servant (cf. Exod 32:31-32).

Other examples of such intercession might be the Servant of Yahweh, the one "who bore the sin of many and who made intercession for transgressors" (Isa 53:12). Or again Job, who prays for his friends; "the Lord accepted Job's prayer" and turned his wrath from them (42:9). There is also intercession for a king (Ps 20:10) or even for the land in which Jews are exiled (Jer 29:7). Jews are depicted praying for pagan authorities (Ezra 6:10, "Pray for the life of the king, and his sons") or for Spartans (1 Macc 2:11; cf. Bar 1:10; 1 Macc 7:33). Moreover, Josephus records that sacrifices were offered daily for Caesar and the Roman people (*Jewish Wars* 2.10.4 §197; *Ag. Apion* 2.6 §77).

In the New Testament Stephen prays for those who stone him (Acts 7:60) and the converted, baptized Simon Magus requests of Peter and John that they pray to the Lord for him that nothing of what they had warned him about would happen to him (Acts 8:24). The last is, indeed, a fear-prompted request, but it depicts one member of the Christian community continuing to act in the conviction that God listens to prayers of such servants for others.

In writing to the Philippians, Paul thanks God "in every remembrance of you" (every time I remember you), "always in every entreaty of mine on your behalf" (1:3-4). His prayer is at once thanksgiving and supplication addressed to God. He is convinced that the Philippians' supplication on his behalf, joined with "the support of the holy Spirit" (1:19), will bring about his deliverance from prison (recall his requests for prayers on his behalf [e.g., 2 Cor 1:11; Rom 15:30]).

Similarly, the author of the Letter to the Ephesians exhorts them to "pray at all times in the Spirit, with every [mode of] prayer and supplication, keeping alert for this purpose with all perseverance, and with supplication for all the saints and also for me, that utterance may be given me in the opening of my mouth to proclaim boldly the mystery of the gospel" (6:18-19).

In James 5 church elders are summoned to pray for the sick; it is "a prayer of faith" (5:15). Christians are to "pray for one another that" they "may be healed" (5:16b); "the effective prayer of a righteous person is very powerful" (5:16c). Here *dikaios* is associated with intercession, and Elijah (5:17-18) is presented as such a person.[27]

The most important passage for our purposes is 1 Tim 2:1-6:

> [1]First of all, then, I urge that supplications, prayers, intercessions, and thanksgivings be made for all human beings, [2]for kings and all those in high positions, that we may lead a tranquil and quiet life in all godliness and dignity. [3]Such prayer is good and acceptable in the sight of God our Savior, [4]who wants all human beings to be saved and to come to the knowledge of the truth: [5]that God is one; that one too is the mediator between God and human beings, the man Christ Jesus, [6]who gave himself as a ransom for all—a testimony provided at the proper time.

Three things are to be noted here: (1) Verse 3 reads: "touto kalon kai apodekton enōpion tou sōtēros hēmōn theou." What is the antecedent of *touto*? The Revised Standard Version, the New International Version, and many commentators translate verse 3 merely as "This is good," preserving the ambiguity of the Greek, so that *touto* may refer to the supplications, prayers, etc., or to the leading of a tranquil and quiet life.[28] But the New English Bible and the New American Bible, which I have followed, refer *touto* to the main topic of the exhortation and not merely to that of the subordinate clause. If *touto* were to refer to the leading of a tranquil life, even "in all godliness and dignity" as something "good and acceptable to God our Savior," it would stress a banality. Why would the author insist "first of all" on supplications, prayers, and intercessions for human beings?

(2) If the antecedent of *touto* is the supplications and prayers, then they are seen as a means by which human beings may "come to the knowledge of the truth" about salvation coming from the one God, through his unique Mediator, Christ Jesus. It thus excludes the idea of Moses as a salvific mediator (Deut 5:27; Exod 19:3-6; cf. Gal 3:19) or even angels (Deut 33:2 [LXX]; Acts 7:53; cf. Josephus, *Ant.* 15.5.3 §136). Hence the unique mediatorship of Christ would not rule out supplications of holy Christians for one another. The collocation of the two ideas in one passage must be noted. God's concern for the salvation of all is proposed as the motivation for the prayers.[29]

(3) The author exhorts living Christians so to pray for other human beings; he does not envisage such Christians as part of the *sanctorum communio*. But one may ask whether his exhortation, with its close collocation of supplication and Christ's sole mediatorship, rules out a later theological extension of it, as at least part of the Christian tradition has understood it.

The New Testament ideas of both intercession and the sole mediatorship of Christ also have to be considered in the light of Col 1:24-26:

> [24]Now I am rejoicing in sufferings on your behalf, and in my flesh I am filling up what is lacking in the afflictions of Christ on behalf of his body, which is the church, [25]of which I have become a minister according to the divine commission given me regarding you, to make the word of God fully known, [26]that secret kept hidden for ages and generations, but which has now been made manifest to his saints.

The author admits his divine commission to complete the preaching of the Christian gospel to human beings who will make up Christ's body, the church. He is aware that "the sufferings" (*pathēmata*) endured "in the flesh" in his efforts to spread that "word of God" somehow contribute to the benefit of "the church" or God's "saints." Indeed, he sees them "filling up what is lacking in the afflictions of Christ" ("antanaplērō ta hysterēmata tōn thlipseōn tou Christou").[30]

The meaning of this clause is quite disputed.[31] But no matter which interpretation is preferred, the author's "sufferings" on behalf of the church or God's "saints" do not contradict the reconciliation wrought by Christ "in his body of flesh" and only "by his death," a reconciliation of which the author ("Paul") regards himself a "minister" (1:22-23).

6. The Invocation of Saints As Intercessors before God

Is there any biblical evidence that supports the idea of Christians not only honoring deceased "saints" (in the specific sense), but even invoking their intercession before God?

We may begin with a passage in an intertestamental writing: "There I saw another vision, the dwelling of the righteous and the resting-places of the holy. There my eyes saw their dwelling with the angels and their resting-places with the holy ones, and they were petitioning and supplicating and praying on behalf of the sons of men" (*1 Enoch* 39:4-5).[32] One could also cite the evidence that J. Jeremias has amassed about the Palestinian Jewish conviction about intercession made by the deceased before God and that H. Delehaye has gathered from the ancient world about departed persons being asked to intercede with God, including Greek and Latin Christian inscriptions from Rome.[33]

As for the Augsburg Confession 21, "it cannot be proved from the Scriptures that we are to invoke the saints or seek help from them." First Timothy 2:5, joined with Rom 8:34 and 1 John 2:1, is cited. Augsburg Confession 21 is correct when its affirmation is understood of explicit statements. But what we have presented above is an attempt to show what the biblical basis for it might be, such as it is. Whether 1 Tim 2:5 excludes such invocation is debatable, as we have seen, even when one asks about the invocation of "saints" in the specific sense.

JOHN REUMANN

2

How Do We Interpret 1 Timothy 2:1-5 (and Related Passages)?

This question was addressed to the dialogue in September 1985 by the Catholic caucus. The issue of "extension in meaning" beyond the literal, New Testament sense was also raised with regard to this and other New Testament passages such as Col 1:24; Rev 6:10 and 20:4. In Joseph Fitzmyer's paper, "Biblical Data on the Veneration, Intercession, and Invocation of Holy People," 1 Tim 2:1-6 and Col 1:24-26 are discussed. The two passages in Revelation will be treated briefly below as additional illustrative material on basic questions. Though the 1 Timothy passage is the focal point of the question, Col 1:24b has probably had more of a neuralgic history in Lutheran–Roman Catholic polemics. Accordingly we shall treat the Colossians verse first.

Colossians 1:24b

> Now I rejoice in (my) sufferings on your behalf, and I fill up what is lacking of the afflictions of Christ in my flesh on behalf of his body, which is the church. (Greek: Nyn chairō en tois pathēmasin hyper hymōn, kai antanaplērō ta hysterēmata tōn thlipseōn tou Christou en tēi sarki mou hyper tou sōmatos autou, ho estin hē ekklēsia.)[1]

Space does not permit attention here to the long history of exegesis of verse 24b.[2]

Today Lutherans and Catholics together can readily agree that, however certain details of 1:24 are interpreted, there is no disparagement in the passage of "the unique mediation of Christ" or anything clearly "in contradiction of the reconciliation wrought by Christ 'in his body of flesh' and only 'by his death,' a reconciliation of which the author (identified as Paul) regards himself a 'minister' (1:22-23)."[3] This emphasis on Jesus' sole, salvific death has been emphasized again and again by most exegetes throughout the centuries. It is consistent with the Pauline view of the cross in 1 Cor 1:13; 15:3; 1:18-25; 2:2; Rom 6:9-10; and Col 1:22.

As to the multitudinous attempts at explanation of 1:24, two lines of interpretation command greatest assent currently, namely what Fitzmyer terms in his listing: (d) "the apocalyptic 'woes of the Messiah,' " citing evidence of apocalyptic ideas in the context in Colossians 1, though he sets this view aside for lack of early evidence about messianic woes; and (e) "an expression of the sufferings that the author vicariously endures for the 'saints' or the 'church,' which unites them or it with Christ, as the author supplies in his preaching and suffering whatever may still be lacking in their/its share of the sufferings that all are called on to share for the sake of completing the preaching of the word of God." This is termed "the best interpretation." However, with so difficult and disputed a passage, one can scarcely ever be satisfied that "the" answer has been attained. Compare the lament of Photius in the ninth century, after giving what he regarded as the more probable view, that if someone found a better answer, well and good.[4]

Fitzmyer's preference (e) is in many ways close to that of Jacob Kremer,[5] but does not include sufferings of the historical Jesus, nor does it seemingly stress the author and the saints acting in Christ's stead. Fitzmyer's interpretation puts even greater emphasis on preaching the word of God as the context for the verse.

Explanation (d), the apocalyptic solution concerning a "quota of woes" before the final Day of the Messiah, is favored by such exegetes as Moule, Lohse, O'Brien, and Dunn.[6] In the history of exegesis this view dropped from sight by the second century, something not surprising with Jewish apocalyptic in a Gentile church. I would prefer this view but recognize the difficulties.[7]

The possible evidence for a Hebrew phrase "the travail of the Messiah," has been conveniently summarized by Fitzmyer.[8] Objections are that (a) the sort of woes listed there do not affect the Messiah (objective genitive) but occur in the world prior to Messiah's coming at the Day of the Lord; (b) none of the proposed intertestamental passages mentions a messiah except 2 Baruch; and (c) the rabbinic sources, which do mention *māšiaḥ*, are late. To these points it may be replied, with regard to (c), that, where only late materials exist from Jewish sources, it is admittedly a question of methodological rigor as to how far back one can conjecture an oral tradition extended.

As to (b), the intertestamental writings, 2 (Syrian) Baruch does mention "the Anointed One" (70:10) at whose coming there will be all sorts of tribulations and twelvefold calamities; its recent translator, A. F. J. Klijn, dates it early in the second century A.D. or at the earliest about A.D. 100.[9] We do have in Mark 13:8 parallel Matt 24:8, in connection with those who come and say, "I am the Messiah," the phrase "beginning of birthpangs" to describe a variety of apocalyptic events.[10] Does all this suffice for a phrase in a document so late as Colossians (if deutero-Pauline, perhaps shortly after A.D. 70)? Especially if it describes afflictions of Christ's people, not of Christ himself (point a), pertaining to the period between the time when "the mystery" (an Old Testament apocalyptic term, not Greek) has been revealed (1:26) and the time when Christ appears in the future (3:4)?

If this notion of a quota of end-time woes ("messianic" in that it applies to the period before Christ comes again) is not accepted, then we must see a paradoxical Pauline statement about joy amid sufferings in the context of missionary proclamation. As an "I-statement," reflecting Paul's role as minister, a suffering apostle-missionary, carrying out God's gospel-plan (*oikonomia*), the verse mentions his role uniquely (*Paulus in der Heilsgeschichte*); while it does not exclude significant and similar roles for others, the passage does not mention them either. What Paul does and experiences is not only for the sake of "you" in Colossae (v. 24a) but also "for the sake of Christ's body," the whole church in its missionary advance (cf. E. Schweizer, who speaks of the "missionary body of Christ"; that sense could justify the position that others share with Paul in similar missionary service[11]).

There is probably no particular force to the first prefix in the double compound verb *ant (i)-ana-plēroō*; it means "fill up" but with no emphasis on being "in the place of [the historical] Jesus." If *ta hysterēmata* is not a series of "messianic woes" in apocalyptic thought and one wishes something more than a general sense of "whatever may still be lacking in a share of sufferings," then we must conceive of a mass or quota of missionary afflictions that the suffering apostle endures with joy, for the sake of his Lord and the advancement of the word of God.[12]

In interpreting the passage one must also keep in mind that the Christ hymn of 1:15-20, as it stands, has departed from the view of the body of Christ in 1 Corinthians 12 and elsewhere (where the risen Christ permeates every member of the community and identifies himself with that body in all its parts, but is not identified exclusively with the head) in favor of a view where Christ as head is prior to and over the body of Christ, the church (1:18). Thus Paul's afflictions are for the church and for the word, but the Head and Lord, who is at God's right hand (3:2), can be declared to be "among you, as the hope of glory," precisely as the One proclaimed in the community (1:27-28), source of wisdom (2:3) and, though hidden, the pole star for the church's life (3:1-4).

1 Timothy 2:1-5

This passage lacks the complex interpretative history of Col 1:24 (or at least someone like Kremer to chronicle it).[13] The Fitzmyer essay focuses on two issues: (a) the antecedent of *touto* in verse 3—is it merely "that we may lead a tranquil and quiet life in all godliness and dignity" or does "this" refer to the whole of verses 1-2 and the sweeping enjoinder to pray? So, according to the New American Bible, "Prayer of this kind is good." (b) When this exhortation is connected with "the unique mediatorship of Christ" (v. 5), does "subsequent theological extension" of the theme legitimately include supplication beyond this life? Our emphases will be on *touto* (v. 3); Christ's mediatorship and supplications; and the question of theological extension.

At the outset Lutherans and Catholics together can affirm "the unique mediatorship of Christ," in the proper sense of "unique," i.e., with regard to " 'salvation,' achieved in Christ's giving of himself as 'a ransom for all.' In him alone is this salvation found"; Christ's mediation "thus excludes the idea of Moses as a salvific mediator . . . or even the angels."[14]

We need not here explore in detail the Greek term for "mediator," *mesitēs*.[15] A secular Greek word for umpire, intermediary, or negotiator, used of deities (like Mithra) or human figures like the king, priests, the *theios anthrōpos*, or founder of a religion, it is absent from the Old Testament with reference to God. Yahweh, however, had the angel of the Lord, the spirit of Yahweh, and wisdom to serve mediatorial functions for him, and, among human figures in the Old Testament, Moses and the Servant of the Lord in 2 Isaiah carried out tasks of mediation between God and people. In the New Testament, only in Paul and in Hebrews does *mesitēs* occur—

in Gal 3:19-20, negatively, of Moses; in 1 Tim 2:5; and in Heb 8:6; 9:15; and 12:24 for Jesus as Mediator of a better covenant. One goes further only by a general "biblical-theology" approach.[16] That *mesitēs* was used in the patristic writings above all for Christ as Mediator "between God and man" is shown by this classification and the references provided in Lampe's *Patristic Dictionary*,[17] but the term could also be used in one sense or another of an angel or of Mary occasionally, the saints, clergy, or John the Baptist, by the church fathers.

One may note also the term *engyos* (perhaps from *engys* = near at hand; therefore "under good security"; guarantee), as in Heb 7:22, "Jesus the surety of a better covenant." Oepke suggests the latter term "stresses the guaranteeing of salvation, the former [*mesitēs*] its accomplishment," i.e., by "mediatorial death."[18]

Exegetically, we find in 1 Timothy 2 a chapter that deals with public prayer in the Christian community: verses 1-7, prayer generally; verse 8, by men; verses 9-15, women and prayer. There are passing references to Paul's role as kerygmatic apostle-teacher (v. 7) and to women (wives?) *not* teaching (v. 12). I am extremely dubious about the claim of Holtz[19] that, because chapter 3 is about "offices" in church law, chapter 2 is of a piece with it, a liturgical-sacramental order, following an anathema (1:20). The attempt seems forced when he seeks to take *eucharistiai* in verse 1 as celebrations of the Eucharist; *enteuxeis* as including under *intercessio* the absolution, reconciliation, and kiss of peace; *proseuchas* as the offering prayer, *euchē pros phorou*; and *deēseis* as petitions in the liturgy, so that we have an order for worship here. More likely, chapter 2 reflects catechesis about prayer.

Paul's paraenesis urges that "first of all" you pray, pray, pray, and pray. It is doubtful that we can with any absolute precision distinguish among the four nouns.[20] The phrase *prōton pantōn* never is picked up with a "secondly," unless it is in verse 2b (see below) or in verse 8 and then verse 9 ("first, then, likewise"). Pauline letters are, however, perfectly capable of using "first" without ever following up with additional adverbs (cf. Rom 1:8; 2 Tim 5:4). The phrase here may mean nothing more than "above all" or "especially."[21]

That the prayers are to be "for all human beings" and specifically "for kings and all who are in high positions" reflects both a universal concern and a traditional interest for (foreign) governmental authorities and structures that goes back at least as far as Jer 29:7. There the prophet's letter to the exiles, in a diaspora situation, tells them to pray for the city (of Babylon!), "for in its welfare you will find your welfare."[22] The tone of Jer 29:7 is enough to explain in 1 Tim 2:2b the *hina*-clause that follows: prayers for the authorities have the further purpose that we, in the religious community, may then live at peace and in prosperity. There is a possibility, however, that a period should be placed after "all who are in high positions." Then the *hina*-clause could be taken as imperatival, i.e., first pray (vv. 1-2a), then "Let us live a quiet and peaceable life, godly and respectable in every way."

Before commenting on *touto* in verse 3, we may observe that, on the usual reading, the author is giving two reasons as to why the church should pray for the secular authorities: (1) so that we may live at peace, and (2) because such is God's will (v. 3).[23] If 2b is taken as a second imperative ("let us live a quiet, pious life . . ."), after "I exhort you to pray . . . ," then it is more likely that *touto* refers only to verse 2b and not to the exhortation to pray (cf. Rom 13:11). If it is banal to say that living a pious life is "good and acceptable to God our Savior," it is scarcely profound to say that to pray is God-pleasing and acceptable. The meaning may in any case be less clear to us than to the first hearers and readers of the document because we do not know against what, if any, opposing view in the situation the admonition is addressed.

Next note that, while we usually take verse 4, that God "wants all human beings to be saved [*sōthēnai*]" in the Christian sense of salvation, the verb could simply mean that all be "preserved" or "kept from harm"[24] (cf. 4:10, the "faithful saying" about God "who is savior [*sōtēr*, preserver?] of all human beings, especially of the faithful"; further, cf. Matt 14:30; John 11:12; 12:27 for this "weaker" sense of the verb). Such an interpretation would contrast, with wordplay, "God *our* savior" and the divine will to preserve "all." Such a reading may also allow a better sequence in verse 4, that, in a world where there is peace and security and people are kept by God from harm, they may then "come to knowledge of the truth," i.e., conversion to the faith (cf. 2 Tim 2:25; 3:7; Titus 1:1). On the usual reading, we have a case of *hysteron proteron*, saved first, then knowledge of the truth.[25]

The "truth" of which verse 4 speaks is specifically embodied in the creed or catechetical-liturgical formula of verses 5 and 6:

God is one [the passage is a *heis theos* formulation];
the mediator between God and human beings is one,
    the human being Christ Jesus,

who gave himself a ransom for all,
God's testimony at the appointed times.

Reference to Paul's appointed office as teacher for the Gentiles of this truth and faith rounds out the section (v. 8).

The word *touto* in Greek usually refers back to something preceding, though it may refer to something that follows.[26] If it points forward, *touto* would be picked up by the formula in verses 5-6.

A case can be made, as sketched above, for taking "this" in verse 3 as a reference back to the clause in 2b: the pious life is good and acceptable to God (though not on the grounds of Holtz's exegesis, since he gives no reasons for his judgment here). But it is far more common to refer *touto* to the prayer-emphasis of verses 1-2 or better to both the prayers and the living of the pious life.[27]

But in this paraenesis it must be remembered that the admonition is not for Christians to pray for one another but "for all human beings" and further for what were then pagan rulers. Moreover, there is nothing said about praying for their conversion. Rather the petition (if the *hina*-clause is taken in the usual way) is that they may so govern that "we may live a tranquil and quiet life." If one asks how such human beings, kings, and authorities might come to faith in God and Christ the Mediator, the only answer the passage suggests is through the proclamation of the word—through the *kēryx*, apostle, and teacher of the Gentiles (v. 7), Paul.

While the next verses speak of how men should pray (in public) and women should adorn and conduct themselves (in life generally and in the church assembly), it may also be said that these verses weave in details about what will contribute its witness to "the truth": no anger or quarreling; modest life-style; good deeds, on the part of those who profess religion (*theosebeia*; here only in the New Testament, but compare 3:16 and elsewhere for *eusebeia* and its doctrinal content; it is not just pious conduct).

To answer now our questions, of course the "unique mediatorship of Christ does not rule out the supplications of holy [-unholy] Christians for one another" (though this passage does not deal with prayers for other Christians). The will of God for "the salvation of human beings" is wider than prayers for our co-religionists, and if our exegesis is at all correct, the passage enjoins praying for "the world" and its rulers and our mutual preservation, even in Babylon. As Luther wrote, "Each of us should form the habit from his youth up to pray daily for all his needs, whenever he is aware of anything that affects him or other people around him, such as preachers, magistrates, neighbors, servants; and, as we have said, he should always remind God of his commandment and promise."[28]

The passage clearly exhorts "living Christians . . . so to pray for other human beings."[29] But there is nothing here about Christians in the next life praying, or about praying for the dead or for those in the next life. I see no such theological extensions demanded in this passage, nor can such extensions readily be based on 1 Timothy 2.

Revelation 6:10 and 20:4

Both verses refer to "the souls of those who had been slain for the word of God and for the witness they had borne" (6:9; 20:4, more specifically, "the souls of those who had been beheaded for their testimony to Jesus and for the word of God and who had not worshiped the beast or its image or had not received its mark on their foreheads or their hands"). In the first passage, as the fifth seal is opened, the narrator says, "I saw under the altar" these souls, who then cry out (v. 10), "O Sovereign Lord, holy and true, how long before thou wilt judge and avenge our blood on those who dwell upon the earth?" They are given each a white robe and "told to rest a little longer until the number of their brethren should be complete" (RSV). In chapter 20 these souls come to life and reign with Christ for a thousand years while the devil is bound.

Fitzmyer's paper does not deal with these verses. The *Book of Concord* does not cite them, and they have not come up in our work with the *Confutatio*. They seemingly were added to the list to see how we would deal with an apocalyptic passage where the martyred saints cry out to God in prayer and then reign in the millennial kingdom at the first resurrection.

The Revelation 20 passage perhaps causes the most exegetical problems, but these are not ones that divide Lutherans and Catholics. When Augsburg Confession Article 17 rejects as "Jewish opinions" the notion that "before the resurrection of the dead, saints and godly men will possess a worldly kingdom and annihilate all the godless," that can be read as a disavowal of views current in 1530[30] or even of the Book of Revelation itself in its millennialist speculation. But the article was aimed at the Enthusiasts or *Schwärmer* and the Jews, not Catholics. We shall therefore concentrate on 6:9-10 as more pertinent to our topics.

The opening of the fifth seal in 6:9 follows upon symbolic depiction of war, slaying, famine, death, and pestilence on earth in the breaking open of the first four seals. It will be followed by a great earthquake and all sorts of apocalyptic signs in the heavens. In verses 9-10 we catch a glimpse of the souls of the slain crying out to God. Presumably their bodies rest in their graves until the day of resurrection, but their souls wait in a kind of interim state (*Zwischenzustand*)[31] before they reign with Christ. "The altar" under which they repose has not been mentioned previously in Revelation but must be located in heaven (cf. 8:3-4; 9:13; 14:18; 16:7); perhaps one is meant like the temple altar of burnt-offering and/or that of incense. The imagery of the souls there is termed Jewish by most commentators.[32]

The outcry of these martyrs, "with great voice," is a prayer asking first "How long?" and then calling for vengeance and judgment in their favor. J. M. Ford [33] tries to blunt the vengeance theme by taking *ekdikeis* as "deliver" (as if it were the Hebrew *nqm*), but given what happens later in Revelation to the oppressors it is hard to read in such a sense here. R. H. Charles[34] would distinguish this passage from Jewish apocalypses in that the martyrs cry out only once (aorist tense verb) and are immediately answered. But they are not immediately answered with what they prayed for but only by a further wait (until ch. 20?). Presumably there is a "quota" of martyr-witnesses to be filled before God will finally act, who meanwhile clothes them with white and addresses them (*passivum divinum*, v. 11).

The passage deals only with the small group of martyrs from the Christian communities of the Apocalypse. They pray just once and then must, though God does respond to them, continue to wait and trust the word and the witness for which they have been slain. It would take considerable theological extension, severalfold, to apply this to saints in general, making intercessions for a variety of needs and concerns, for others, outside the devices of apocalyptic, in terms of a doctrine about the hereafter or general resurrection.

ROBERT B. ENO, S.S.

3

Mary and Her Role in Patristic Theology

During the patristic period, discussion about Mary revolved around the central issue of her relation to Jesus and his role in the plan of salvation.[1] Jesus' birth from Mary pointed to his true humanity while the virginal conception was seen as indicative of a more than human reality in Jesus' life and work. Mary herself came more into prominence when, by extension, related questions were asked: Was it necessary or just fitting that Mary's virginity never be lost in her lifetime? If she was "ever-virgin," then who were the "brothers and sisters of the Lord"? Given that Mary was the "mother of the Lord," what was to be thought of her as a believer and follower of Jesus? What was to be made of certain incidents in the Gospels which at first sight seemed to show Mary in a less favorable light? In a word, beyond the issue of perpetual virginity, there was also the question of Mary's holiness.

A. Early Patristic Views

Theologically, a breakthrough of sorts was reached at an early stage in considering Mary's place within salvation history. Justin, initially, and then in a more developed fashion, Irenaeus, spoke of the parallelism of Eve and Mary as negative and positive elements in the story of the human race. They built on the imagery of the old and the new Adam already found in Paul. Many have seen this as the origin of Marian theology. In a way of course it was, yet this particular line of reasoning in fact soon came to a dead end and the insight became a commonplace in the Fathers (e.g., Jerome "Mors per Evam; vita per Mariam").[2]

In the development of Christology an important milestone was reached with the definition of Mary as the *Theotokos* by the Council of Ephesus in 431. The term had certainly been used in the fourth century—perhaps even in the third. The roots of the modern Roman Catholic dogmatic developments can be found at least remotely in the pre-Ephesine phase. Speculations about Mary's sanctity combined with Augustine's emphasis on original sin will still need a very long period of development. Questions about Mary's destiny at death and beyond do begin in this time, but the more decisive steps came during the penumbral period between late antiquity and the early Middle Ages.

Before proceeding to the usual starting point, the Apostolic Fathers, there is one document of particular interest among the New Testament apocrypha, one which apparently had a considerable influence. This is the Book of James, later called the Protevangelium.[3] According to recent studies this was written in Egypt or Syria between 175 and 200. Its principal purpose seems to have been to counteract Jewish attacks against Jesus and Mary, attacks such as those repeated in the *True Doctrine* of Celsus written c. 180. There is present as well that general characteristic of the apocyphal gospels, i.e., a response to the popular desire that *lacunae* in the canonical gospels be filled in.

This book fills us in on the early life of Mary. Anna and Joachim are named as her parents. There is a certain parallelism suggested between Joachim and Elcanah; Anna and Hannah; Mary and Samuel. Mary was presented in the temple, where the priests saw a divine calling for her. She was raised in the temple until puberty, when she was espoused to Joseph, an elderly widower. At the birth of Jesus a midwife was present who testified to the miraculous birth. Clement of Alexandria later referred explicitly to this.[4] Another woman, Salome, who doubted that Mary was still a virgin, was punished with a withered hand. Much later Jerome ridiculed the *deliramenta* of the apocrypha, but the Book of James was influential nonetheless.[5]

Going on to the Apostolic Fathers, one is immediately reminded of the continuing preoccupation of Ignatius of Antioch (d. c. 116) with docetism. As a part of that concern, he stressed the birth of Jesus from a woman. "He is in truth of the family of David, according to the flesh, God's Son by the will and power of God, truly born of a virgin."[6]

The greatest of the Apologists was Justin, who died a martyr at Rome c. 165. One of his works, the *Dialogue with Trypho the Jew*, was concerned to a great extent with differing views about the interpretation of the Jewish Scriptures. The meaning of Isa 7:14 provided an ongoing focus for Jewish-Christian polemic. But Justin's work contains as well the seeds of several important later developments. The Eve/Mary parallelism is one of these: "For Eve who was a virgin undefiled, having conceived the word of the serpent, brought forth disobedience and death. But the virgin Mary . . . received faith and joy."[7]

The insight of Justin was developed by Irenaeus of Lyon (flourished c. 175). In refuting the various Gnostic teachings, he elaborated his theology of recapitulation. In saving the human race, Jesus, the new Adam, retraced the steps of the old Adam in the undoing of the race. Not surprisingly, other parallels were sought and the one mentioned by Justin, Eve and Mary, was seized upon. "In accordance with this design, Mary the virgin is found obedient. . . . But Eve was disobedient, for she did not obey when as yet she was a virgin. Eve . . . having become disobedient was made the cause of death, both for herself and the entire human race; so also did Mary . . . by yielding obedience become the cause of salvation both for herself and the whole human race. . . . The knot of Eve's disobedience was loosed by the obedience of Mary. For what the virgin Eve had bound fast through unbelief, this did the virgin Mary set free through faith."[8] "And if the former did disobey God, yet the latter was persuaded to be obedient to God, in order that the virgin Mary might become the advocate of the virgin Eve. And thus as the human race fell into bondage to death by means of a virgin, so it is rescued by a virgin."[9] Much later, theologians of a less biblical and more Scholastic turn would speculate whether such texts could be cited to show Mary's essential participation in the redemptive process. Is she a conscious and free participant or more like a passive prop in this drama?

Despite his high estimate of Mary's role, Irenaeus also exhibited traces of what would become a common thread running through Eastern exegesis. Commenting on Gospel incidents involving Mary, he could be critical of her. So, in the wedding at Cana, she is blamed for excessive haste, seeking to push her son into performing a miracle before his hour had come.[10]

Origen

Proceeding first along the trajectory of the Eastern tradition, we turn to Origen of Alexandria (d. c. 253). He wrote against Celsus and in so doing defended Mary as well as Jesus against calumnies about the latter's origins.[11] Since he preached on the Gospel of Luke, he had many opportunities to comment on relevant questions. In the sixth homily he called the *"kecharitōmenē"* a unique form of address, made to Mary alone. She was made venerable by the divine childbearing, and through her all women were blessed.[12] According to the historian Socrates, Origen used the term *Theotokos*, but this cannot be verified from the extant texts.[13]

While there is no question that Origen upheld the virginal conception, there is a dispute beyond that point. Although he believed that Mary had no further children, he did not clearly accept a physical *virginitas in partu*. "As for those who claim that she was united in marriage after giving birth, they have no way of proving that, for the children attributed to Joseph were not born of Mary and no text of Scripture recalls this."[14] Origen also brings John's Calvary scene to bear as evidence that Jesus was Mary's only child. "According to those who think wholesomely about her, Mary had no son but Jesus."[15]

Yet he also speaks of Mary's need for purification after the birth of Jesus: ". . . [concerning the purification] of Mary who had given birth, no question will be asked and we would say with a certain boldness: Mary, who belonged to the human race, needed purification after childbirth."[16] A little later, more directly, he said: "For the mother of the Lord, her womb was opened at the very moment of childbirth, since, before the birth of Christ, no man had approached the womb consecrated and worthy of the greatest respect."[17] Among those who have tried to reconcile apparent contradictions in Origen, the more common opinion is that, for him, the physical loss of virginity at childbirth did not disqualify Mary for the title of "ever-virgin." He looked, in other words, primarily at sexual intercourse as that which deprived a woman morally as well as physically of her virginity. In his commentary on Matthew, Origen repeated the story, mentioned in the Gospel (Matt 23:35), of how Zechariah came to meet his death. Mary, after childbirth, came to pray in the temple, in the section reserved for virgins (! ?). When the authorities tried to stop her, Zechariah explained that she, in spite of recently giving birth, was still a virgin. He was killed for his trouble.[18]

The role of Mary as model for Christian virgins would become increasingly important in the future. "Jesus was the first-fruits among men of the purity which consists in chastity and Mary among women. It would not be right to attribute to any woman other than Mary the first-fruits of virginity."[19]

Origen's exegetical views would also come to bear considerable weight with later commentators. One of the most influential of these opinions can be found in his remarks on the Calvary scene. The famous "sword" that will transfix Mary according to Luke (2:35) has been variously interpreted. For Origen this meant that on Calvary, in the hour of Jesus' suffering and death, Mary wavered in her faith; the "sword of infidelity" and uncertainty touched her. Origen took some of the sting away by adding that it was necessary that this happen so that she too would have some sin for which Jesus died.[20]

He speculated that Mary stayed as long as she did with her cousin Elizabeth because she doubted the angel's message and wanted to see for herself how it would come about.[21] Finally, he adds that even when Jesus was twelve years old and lost in the temple, the faith of Mary and Joseph was still quite imperfect. This passage is interesting because it indicates that Origen was aware of the discrepancy between Mary's disquiet here and her presumed awareness of Jesus' divine status as she should have learned it from the events recounted in the infancy narratives. His somewhat desperate solution was to explain that Mary and Joseph were upset because they feared that Jesus might have decided to return to heaven![22]

Tertullian

At the Latin-speaking end of the North African coast, there lived Origen's older contemporary, Tertullian (d. after 221). Because of his position as the first of the Latin theologians and his sparkling rhetoric, which contrasted with Origen's more plodding style, Tertullian's views may seem more significant than they really are. In fact, on many matters he was the exception. In the context of his comments on Mary, he was always concerned with refuting docetic christological views, especially those of Marcion. While he was a firm believer in the virginal conception, he stressed the reality of Jesus' humanity by expressing his belief that Mary was no longer a virgin after the birth of Jesus. Nor did he attribute to Mary any special sanctity.

It was a docetic commonplace to interpret the scene in Matt 12:48 as a denial by Jesus of his true humanity, a denial that he had any physical, human origins and family. But Jesus was really of the flesh of Mary, insisted Tertullian. He was "of" Mary, not just a heavenly being who had been "in" her womb for the sake of appearances. What would be the point of that? "If the Word was made flesh out of himself and not out of what the womb contributed, how did a womb which had wrought nothing, performed nothing, experienced nothing, decant its fountain into those breasts in which it comes only by the process of giving birth?"[23] Mary was a virgin "as regards her husband, not a virgin as regards child-bearing . . . and if as a virgin she conceived, in her child-bearing she became a wife. . . . For all other women, marriage opens it. Consequently hers was the more truly opened in that it was the more shut. Indeed, she is rather to be called not-virgin than virgin, having become a mother by a sort of leap, before she was a bride."[24]

Further, Mary as well as the "brothers" did not believe in Jesus' mission. Their arrival to see him while he was teaching showed that she "did not adhere to him." At this point their *incredulitas* was exposed. They did not go in to hear him "evidently not valuing what was being done inside." Mary thus becomes a figure of the synagogue. "Outside, in them, was Israel; whereas the new disciples, hearing and believing, and being inside, by cleaving to Christ depicted the church which, repudiating carnal kinship, he designated a preferable mother and a worthier family of brothers."[25] Similar ideas were expressed in the *Adversus Marcionem*. His reaction to his family outside was a disavowal, not a denial (i.e., that he had a physical family). He rather transferred the "titles of relationship" from them to others who were judged more closely related to him by faith. On another occasion, when Jesus replied to the woman who praised his mother that obedience to the word of God was worthier of praise, Tertullian commented that Mary was not present and that Jesus had in any event already rejected his mother and family.[26]

A summary of the pre-Nicene developments on Mary shows that the Protoevangelium remained unusual in that it showed some interest in and development on Mary for her own sake. Most of the patristic material as such is concerned primarily with the christological issues: that Jesus was a real human being, not just an appearance, nor just a heavenly being with a body composed out of some extraterrestrial matter.

While they were clear on the virginal conception, there was much less unanimity on other aspects of Mary's virginity. The Mary/Eve line of thought became a commonplace without much further development. However, most felt free to find fault with some of Mary's actions as reported in the Gospels. Positively, Origen showed the way when he asserted that it was appropriate to think of Mary as the starting point of dedicated Christian virginity for women.[27]

Between Nicaea and Ephesus: 325–431

The East

The "golden age of the Fathers," the fourth century, showed a basic continuity of ideas with the pre-Constantinian period. With the growth of the ascetic movement, there was more emphasis on Mary as the model for virgins. This is the aspect that stands out in Athanasius. His life of Antony, which played such an important role in making known the ideals of the desert monks, was paralleled by his letters to virgins, extant only in Coptic. These writings no doubt influenced Western authors, especially Ambrose, in their enthusiastic espousal of the ascetic ideal. Mary is portrayed as a nun; she had no desire to go forth from her seclusion at home, to be seen by men, to go about in public. She did not waste her time looking out the window but spent her time studying Scripture. She had devoted herself to those things from childhood (influence of "James"?). She could not even stand the sound of a male voice—hence her apprehension at the annunciation.

Athanasius also had a place for the Mary/Eve comparison/contrast. Eve is the mother of the dead, Mary of the living. Eve listened to Satan with dire results; Mary heeded Gabriel. "What a heavenly gift man has received through you. O true Virgin!"[28] In his letter of Epictetus, however, he does not seem to hold for physical *virginitas in partu*.[29] The first undisputed usage of *Theotokos* is found at the beginning of the Arian controversy in a letter by Athanasius' predecessor, Alexander.[30]

Perhaps it is surprising that someone so prominent in the development of trinitarian orthodoxy would have so little to say about Mary. The same is true of the Cappadocian Fathers, creative theologians though they were in other areas. In a letter Basil also speaks of Mary's shaken faith on Calvary, despite, he added, all the miracles, the annunciation, etc.[31] His friend, Gregory of Nazianzus, insisted that Mary must be accepted as *Theotokos*; Jesus is really her son. Thus a statement about Mary was urged as a criterion of orthodoxy, but once again the core of the issue here was christological—more specifically, anti-Apollinarian. Gregory wrote: ". . . [Christ was] conceived by the virgin, who first in body and soul was purified by the Holy Spirit for it was necessary both that child-bearing should be honored and that virginity should receive a higher honor."[32]

Basil's younger brother Gregory wrote more on Mary than the other two Cappadocians. He greatly extolled the virginal ideal, calling Christ the arch-virgin. He seems to hint at the idea that Mary made a vow of virginity, an idea made explicit later by Augustine. In the context of the annunciation scene, Mary asks Gabriel how the birth will come about since "her flesh is consecrated to God."[33] His sermon on the annunciation contains examples of the elaborate and high-blown rhetoric that will become characteristic of Byzantine Marian homilies after Ephesus.[34]

While we have spoken exclusively of theological views, the two Gregories also give us a glimpse of the growth of devotional aspects of Marian belief. In Nazianzen's *Oratio* 24 on the legend of Cyprian of Antioch and the virgin Justina, the latter, while being seduced by the wicked magus, first prayed for help to Jesus, the one who had protected Susanna and Thecla, and then to the Virgin Mary to assist a virgin in danger. More interestingly, in his life of Gregory the Wonderworker, Gregory of Nyssa described a vision of Mary and John, who appeared to the third-century apostle of Pontus in the first recorded Marian apparition.[35] To be sure, the two passages tell us more about the situation in the time of the writers than about realities of an earlier century. The legend of Cyprian of Antioch is historically worthless, and we have no way of verifying that Gregory Thaumaturgus ever had such a vision. Speaking of his mother in one of his poetic epigrams (§28), Gregory of Nazianzus wrote: "Nonna, . . . praying by this table, was taken up thence a pure victim, and now, one of the guardians of her sex, shares the glory of the pious women, Susanna, Mary and the two Annas."[36]

The origin and date of the prayer, *Sub tuum praesidium*, continue to be a matter of dispute. It is put forward as the earliest example of a popular prayer to Mary, from the fourth (?) century. "Mother of God, [hear] my supplications: do not allow us (to be) in adversity, but deliver us from danger. Thou alone. . . ." In the liturgy proper the mariological stratum of the sanctoral cycle is the most recent, not having been launched in earnest until after 431. Certain liturgical feasts existed before 431, such as the *Hypapante* (the Presentation of Jesus in the Temple), celebrated in Jerusalem since at least the middle of the fourth century. But it would be unwarranted to presume that liturgical feasts considered Marian in later history were primarily so at their origin.[37]

Whereas these well-known theologians tell us relatively little, it is the lesser-known and less able theologian, Epiphanius of Cyprus (d. 403), who added some interesting items to the growing tradition. In his compilation of heresies, the *Panarion,* he lists two dealing with Mary. The Antidicomarianites, who are anti-Marian, and, at the other extreme, the Collyridians, who treat Mary as a goddess, supply a perfect balance for his treatise.

The former try to besmirch Mary by denying her perpetual virginity. In this context Epiphanius elaborated upon the "data" of the Protevangelium. Joseph was an elderly widower of eighty with six children, four boys and two girls. He went into considerable detail about these children, especially James. Joseph died at a great age shortly after the return to Nazareth from the temple visit when Jesus was twelve.

As for the Collyridians, they are an example of the harm done in the church by women. Mary should be honored, but not to excess. The sacrifices offered to Mary by these women are the work of the devil. If women could have become priests, Mary would have been a priest. But she did not even baptize. If she could have, she, rather than John, would have baptized Jesus.

In speaking of the Antidicomarianites, Epiphanius broached another topic of interest. He was the first to pose questions about what happened to Mary in her later life. Because he wished to deprive the *virgines subintroductae* of ammunition, he maintained that Mary, after Calvary, did not remain with John. What happened? He maintained that we do not know, but he made several intriguing suggestions. He asked, for instance, whether the prophecy of the sword does not relate to a possible violent end for Mary. In equally elusive terms, he brought up the woman of Revelation 12. He ended by asserting that we do not know if Mary died and was buried but that he did not want to ascribe anything fleshly to her because of the "greatness of the vessel."[38] This question would be developed later in the *Transitus Mariae* and Dormition literature.

The final pre-Ephesine Greek Father to be considered here is John Chrysostom (d. 407), priest of Antioch and bishop of Constantinople. He had no problem with Mary's perpetual virginity, but he realized that the virginal conception was something many had difficulty accepting, and, he said, questions are many and frequent about it. He went into great detail in his homilies on the events surrounding the Annunciation and the Nativity. Some questions are familiar by now: Why do the Gospel genealogies of Jesus trace Joseph's lineage? Or new questions: Why is Mary told the news before the conception rather than after, as in Joseph's case? Answer: Otherwise Mary might have killed herself, if simply presented with a *fait accompli*. Why was Joseph reminded of the prophecy of Isaiah and Mary not? Answer: Because as an unlearned woman, it would have meant nothing to her. Origen had been of the opposite opinion, that Mary knew the Scriptures well and meditated on them.[39]

John, like many of his Eastern predecessors, had critical comments to make about Mary, but he also tried to temper them. "The virgin is made in no common degree glorious and distinguished."[40] Jesus loved and respected his mother. Any negative comments and reprimands show how much he loved her and was concerned with her spiritual well-being and salvation. It is interesting to see that whereas in the West the tradition of negative comments about Mary died after Tertullian, the Eastern writers and preachers continued to repeat the criticisms, but such statements did not seem to retard the simultaneous growth of devotion to Mary. Chrysostom tried to combine the critical and the devotional trends.

In his homilies on the Gospel of John, the Cana incident is once again a focus of attention. In urging Jesus to act, Mary wanted to help her friends in need but also to call attention to herself: "She, because she had borne him, claimed, according to the custom of other mothers, to direct him in all things, when she ought to have revered and worshiped him." Jesus rebuked her for her own good. "For if he cared for others and used every means to implant in them a becoming opinion of himself, much more would he do so in the case of his mother." He held her in high honor. "For the answer (given) was not the answer of someone rejecting his mother, but of one who would show that the fact that she bore him would have availed her nothing, had she not been very good and faithful." Jesus finally performed the miracle at Cana so as not to seem to shame and contradict his mother.[41]

In the incident of the family waiting to see Jesus during his public ministry, Mary was guilty of excessive vanity. What she needed to discuss was of little importance, but Mary wanted to show people that she had power over her son. Once again, Jesus' reply was not a repudiation but a reprimand to help her improve spiritually. "There is but one nobility: to do the will of God."[42] Nothing more is made by Chrysostom of the Calvary scene than the moralizing lesson that we are to take care of our parents.[43]

Before passing to the Latins, a word may be mentioned about Saint Ephrem (c. 306–c. 373) and the Syriac tradition. While that tradition is less well-known to us, it probably should be viewed as closer to the Greek tradition than has usually been recognized. Its outstanding representative, Ephrem, wrote poetry so that the content of his theology is still more difficult to interpret. His work in this regard is not without further problems, e.g., he sometimes confused the Virgin Mary with Mary Magdalene in his comments. Like his Greek neighbors, he could find fault with her. He speaks of her excessive haste at Cana.[44] But normally Ephrem is noted for his great praise of Mary. "You alone and your mother are more lovely than all others; there is no stain in you and no sin in your mother." "Even after the birth, he was still with you; he shone forth from you. His bright glory was spread through your beauty; the anointing of his body flowed over you. You fashioned a garment for him; but he spread his splendor over all your senses."[45]

The West

The three great Western Fathers of the fourth century all had something to contribute. Ambrose and Jerome in particular were greatly influenced by Eastern developments, especially the idea of Mary as the model for Christian virgins. At this time in the West there emerged protests against certain tendencies in church life and piety—against an excessive emphasis on virginity at the expense of marriage, against other forms of exaggerated asceticism, against the growing cult of relics, against pilgrimages, etc. Because the writings of the protesters such as Jovinian, Helvidius, and Vigilantius were destroyed, we know them and their ideas only through their adversaries. How and why did such complaints arise? We do not know. Jerome was not one to leave any argument unused against an opponent or, following the style of the time, to leave his character unstained.

Jerome. Jerome's interest lay almost entirely in the area of Mary's virginity, and one may ask whether her appearance in his works was not largely simply a function of his polemic in favor of asceticism. Not surprisingly, as the foremost Scripture scholar of Christian antiquity, Jerome engaged in a polemic with the Jews over the interpretation of Isa 7:14. A significant part of his propagandizing in favor of virginity consisted in denigrating marriage, e.g., as in *Adv. Jovinianum* 1.16.

Within the context of this polemic, Jerome authored what has been called the first treatise on Mariology, the *Adversus Helvidium* (383). Compared to the blast against Jovinian, this is a fairly brief work. Here he discusses most of the same issues others treated earlier. Whereas Helvidius claimed that Mary had had other children, Jerome strongly reasserted her perpetual virginity. One original feature is that he denied that the "brothers" of the Lord were children of Joseph by an earlier marriage. It is fitting that Joseph also be virginal. Thus the "brothers" must be more distant relatives.

Ambrose. Ambrose's interests were somewhat broader than Jerome's. We must ask how original some of his ideas were, however. His sudden propulsion into the episcopate of an important city made his previous lack of theological and biblical study painfully felt. He was thrown back upon such time for personal study as he could find. His views on Mary showed the influence of Origen and Athanasius. His descriptions of Mary in effect make her not just a model for nuns but a nun herself. "Modesty, the companion of purity, makes chastity safer. When in her chamber alone, she is greeted by the angel, she is silent and is disturbed at his entry. The virgin's face is troubled at the strange appearance of a man's form."[46] Before going to visit her cousin Elizabeth, Mary had always lived in the strictest seclusion.[47]

Some of Ambrose's statements illustrate his strong Marian devotion. Speaking of her marriage to Joseph in the context of having previously extolled virginity, he said: "The Lord would rather have some doubt cast on his own origins than on the purity of his mother. He knew how delicate was a virgin's honor, how fragile her reputation for purity, and he did not wish to build up faith in his own origins at the price of an insult to his mother."[48] He supported Mary's *virginitas in partu* and invoked Ezek 44:2 as a proof text. "And when he was born of Mary's womb, he yet preserved the enclosure of her modesty and the inviolate seal of her virginity." "Holy Mary is the gate of which it is written: 'The Lord will pass through it and it will shut.' "[49] The Calvary scene as recounted in John's Gospel is once again cited as proof that there were no other children. Joseph is gone. Indeed, the separation is termed a *divortium*.[50]

Following Origen, Ambrose believed that Mary's superiority to Zechariah was shown in the reaction of the two to the angelic revelations. What Mary was asked to accept was far more difficult to believe than the angel's message to the priest. She is truly blessed and greater than the priest. "It is not surprising that the Lord, wishing to redeem the world, began his work through Mary; the one through whom the salvation of all was being prepared would herself be the first to gather from her son the fruit of salvation." Addressing the devil, he said: "You were vanquished by Mary, who gave the conqueror birth."[51] "Mary was alone when she spoke with an angel. She was alone when the Holy Spirit came to her. . . . She was alone and she worked the salvation of the world and conceived the redemption of all."[52] He also utilized the Mary/Eve parallelism: "per mulierem stultitia, per virginem sapientia."[53] Finally, at Calvary he noted that, whereas the apostles fled, Mary remained by the cross. Looking at Jesus' wounds, she saw not her son's death but the salvation of the world. "Perhaps she thought her own death could add something to the grace accomplished for all. But Jesus did not need help to accomplish universal salvation."[54]

Augustine. The views of the third great Latin Father of this period would be vastly influential in setting forth both teachings and problems for the future of Western theology. As with all the Fathers, in dealing with Augustine the context of theological controversy must be attended to carefully. Thus there is considerable stress on the virginal conception of Jesus in the context of original sin. Since Jesus did not have a human father and was not conceived in the usual way, he was without original sin. He was not conceived in the heat of human lust (*libido, concupiscentia*). The overshadowing of the Spirit cooled the heat of such lust.[55]

"Although the body of Christ was taken from the flesh of a woman who had been conceived from the flesh of a sinful race, nevertheless, since it was not conceived in her womb in the manner in which she had been conceived, it was not sinful flesh but the likeness of sinful flesh. For he did not thereby contract the guilt that brings death. . . . But he received a body immune to the contagion of sin."[56] Christ has only the *similitudo carnis peccati.* "His flesh came from a virgin and was not conceived in lust, that he might be in the likeness of sinful flesh, but not in sinful flesh."[57] These thoughts recur many times. In his controversy with Julian of Eclanum, the latter asked whether, if, as Augustine taught, original sin was an integral part of the human condition, Jesus could really be human without it.[58] The "likeness" reference, of course, is to Rom 8:3, but Julian's question could also pose a problem for Augustine's Christology.

Within the context of Jesus' conception, Augustine stresses Mary's "yes" to God. Jesus' nature was "proper to one born of a virgin, one whom a mother's faith and not her lust had conceived." "Angelus nuntiat, Virgo audit, credit et concipit. Fides in mente,

Christus in ventre." "A virgin conceived without the embrace of a husband, not by the concupiscence of the flesh, but by the chaste submission of the mind." The subject lent itself to the impressive compression of Augustinian rhetoric—e.g., "conceptio filii; fides matris"; "credendo, non concumbendo, sancta est fecundata virginitas."[59]

Augustine clearly believed in Mary's perpetual virginity, although the *post partum* aspects claimed only a modest amount of attention. He noted that Ambrose had sufficiently refuted Jovinian, who impugned Mary's perpetual virginity. Mary had no other children; the "brothers and sisters" were Mary's relatives. "Did Mary give birth again? Certainly not. The dignity of virgins begins with her." As Mary conceived and gave birth as a virgin, so she died a virgin.[60]

The question of virginal conception and childbirth was also the object of skepticism and attacks. Concerning *virginitas in partu,* Augustine brought forward the example of the capabilities of Christ's risen body. It is another of God's miracles. The classic example of pagan doubts about the virginal conception is to be found in the exchange of letters between Augustine and Volusianus. Even here, Augustine could say ultimately only that God can do all things and that many of the things he actually does are beyond our comprehension, at least in this life. "This great miracle those people prefer to regard as fiction rather than fact."[61]

Concerning Mary's perpetual virginity, Augustine also saw her as the preeminent example for the dedicated virgins of the Christian community, although he is more restrained and less flamboyant than Ambrose and Jerome. Consecrated virginity is a state superior to marriage. "And so too Christ, who established his church as a virgin . . . in no wise deprived his mother of her virginity when he was born. . . . And you whom the church out of her unsullied virginity has begotten holy virgins, you who, disdaining earthly marriage, have chosen to be virgins also in the flesh, joyfully and solemnly celebrate this day the virgin birth. He who brought you what you should cherish, did not take what you do cherish from his mother. Heaven forbid that he who heals in you what you have inherited from Eve should injure what you have loved in Mary."[62]

Mary's famous vow of virginity should be mentioned in this connection. Augustine is well aware that such a vow was not in harmony with Jewish custom of the time, but he spoke of it in a particular context that made it useful as a hypothesis. In comparing the reactions of Zechariah and Mary to the angelic revelations of future births, Augustine sought a way of distinguishing them.

Zechariah's reaction to the announcement of the coming birth of John was one of disbelief and skepticism. Hence his punishment. Yet Mary too asked a question. But this was not prompted by lack of faith. On the contrary, Mary is the true model of faith. She did not doubt that what was predicted would come to pass, but because of her vow of virginity, she wondered "how" it would come to pass. "She did not doubt God's omnipotence."[63]

The Canadian Augustine scholar, Emilien Lamirande, has noted the general absence of "Marian devotion" in Augustine.[64] The fact is that the North African liturgical calendar of the time contained no Marian feasts. Much of Augustine's theologizing on Mary is to be found in his sermons for Christmas and the feast of the birth of John the Baptist. In his sermons the biblical saints are treated differently than the Christian martyrs. The martyrs are presented as models for living and as intercessors. This is not the case with Mary. There is no discussion of or exhortation to Marian intercession. Mary, as we have seen, is an example, albeit a specialized one, for Christian virgins. Mary was a holy virgin, but she was a human being.[65] Augustine ventured no speculations about her ultimate state.

One place where Augustine showed a special tenderness for Mary concerned the question of her sinlessness. Here we are not speaking of original sin. The debate over her immaculate conception comes later in theological history. In a famous passage from an early anti-Pelagian work, *De natura et gratia*, he states: "We must except the holy Virgin Mary, concerning whom I wish to raise no question when it touches the subject of sins, out of honor to the Lord; for from him we know what abundance of grace for overcoming sin in every particular was conferred on her who had the merit to conceive and bear him who undoubtedly had no sin."[66] As always, he stressed that only by God's grace do the saints accomplish what they do. To be sure, he does not assert here that Mary was without actual sin but simply that he does not wish to discuss it. Nevertheless, it must be noted that even this refusal to discuss it cost him in his argument with Pelagius. The teaching of Pelagius which he was contesting maintained that it was possible (with relative ease) for a human being to lead a sinless life.

Once Julian of Eclanum accused Augustine of being worse than Jovinian. The latter had denied Mary's perpetual virginity, but Augustine delivered her to the devil through his doctrine of original sin. Here would have been the perfect opportunity to claim that

Mary had somehow been exempted from original sin, but Augustine replied only that the condition of fallen nature was remedied by the grace of rebirth.[67] This is the solution for all human beings. Mary was not baptized, though no doubt was purified of original sin in some other way.

The Mary/Eve parallelism did not occupy a prominent place in Augustine's thought. But, like the others, he made use of it. "The devil holds him; Christ liberates him. Eve's deceiver holds him; Mary's son frees him; he holds him who approached the man through the woman; he frees him who was born of a woman that never approached a man; he holds him who injected into the woman the cause of lust; he liberates him who without any lust was conceived in the woman." "Our malady arose through the corrupted spirit of a woman; from the incorrupted flesh of a woman came salvation."[68]

The incarnation had to involve a woman to help women avoid despair because of their role in the fall. "By this defeat, the devil would be tormented over the thought of both sexes, male and female, because he had taken delight in the defection of them both. The freeing of both sexes would not have been so severe a penalty for the devil unless we were also liberated by the agency of both sexes."[69] If the "honor" of the female sex had been tarnished or lost, Mary and her part in salvation history won it back. "The honor of the male sex comes from the body of Christ; the honor of the female sex is in the mother of Christ. The grace of Jesus Christ has won over the cunning of the serpent."[70]

Augustine's skill as a rhetorician is evident in his preaching. Much of what he says about Mary is to be found in his Christmas homilies. Here he loves to dwell on the paradoxes of the incarnation, e.g., *Sermo* 184.3. For apologetic reasons Augustine also discussed the role of Joseph. Sceptics asked why, if Mary was a virgin mother, the genealogies in the infancy narratives of Matthew and Luke traced Jesus' lineage to Joseph. Among other points, Augustine argued that Joseph, though not the biological father, was nevertheless a true father to Jesus and a true spouse to Mary.[71] "Joseph might be called the husband of Mary though she was his wife only in affection and in the intercourse of the mind, which is more intimate than that of the body. In this way it might be proper that the husband of the virgin mother of Christ should have a place in the list of Christ's ancestors." Similarly, their marriage was a real marriage; did it not possess the three *bona coniugalia: proles, fides, sacramentum*?[72]

The Gospel passages that earlier led to certain exegetical traditions critical of Mary brought no such result in Augustine's interpretation, writing, and preaching. The "sword" that was to pierce her was not the sword of doubt but of sorrow for the loss of her son.[73] In the case of the wedding at Cana, the exegesis was more strained. He explicitly repudiated the thought that Jesus was in any sense insulting or repulsing his mother. In an involved explanation he maintained that Jesus was about to perform a miracle that would demonstrate his divine nature. Since Mary was the mother of the human nature, this was not her business. Later, on Calvary, her maternal role would be clearly acknowledged when his human nature was close to death.[74] Augustine may be laying himself open here to a charge of crypto-Nestorianism.

The scenes of the family's disbelief in Jesus during his public ministry have sometimes caused difficulties. In a way they help prepare the way for one of the more well-received aspects of Augustine's Marian teaching. In the kingdom of God spiritual relationship is decisive, not physical relationship. Hence Jesus asked: "Who are my father and mother?" And to the cry, "Blessed is the womb that bore you . . .," Jesus replied, "Blessed rather is one who hears the word of God and keeps it." For Augustine, Mary was first and foremost in a close spiritual relationship to Jesus. "So even her maternal relationship would have done Mary no good unless she had borne Christ more happily in her heart than in her flesh."[75]

"Should the Virgin Mary not have done the will of the Father, she who by faith believed, by faith conceived, who was the chosen one from whom our salvation should be born among men, who was created by Christ before Christ was created in her? Indeed holy Mary obviously did the will of the Father; and therefore it is greater for Mary to have been Christ's disciple than to have been his mother. . . . The truth of Christ is in the mind of Mary, the flesh of Christ in her womb; greater is what she bears in her mind than what she bears in her womb." Given the role of Mary in the plan of salvation, she is part of the body of Christ. "Mary is a part of the church, a holy member, an excellent member, a supereminent member, yet but a member of the whole body." The whole is greater than the part. Therefore "the church is better than the Virgin Mary."[76] Overall, Augustine's Marian teaching is moderate and integrated into his total picture of salvation history.

After Ephesus

Many have spoken of the great explosion of Marian devotion after 431. This did not arise from nothing. Our survey might lead one to think that previously almost nothing had been happening. This was probably not the case. Indeed, some have even claimed to see signs that things were already threatening to get out of hand. Who, they ask, were the Collyridians? Figments of Epiphanius's fertile imagination, or real evidence that there was a danger of making Mary a goddess? The *Sub tuum praesidium* prayer does not ask for Mary's intercession but asks for her help and direct intervention. Was the concern of someone like Nestorius proof of his stupidity or was it based on a sincere concern for serious theological misunderstanding and/or popular aberrations? Definite answers cannot be given because of our lack of extensive knowledge about popular Marian beliefs and devotions.

The preaching of some of Nestorius's opponents such as Proclus (bishop of Constantinople 434-46) and Theodotus of Ancyra (d. before 446) is not reassuring. Rhetoric begins to run riot. Paragraphs with sentence after sentence beginning "O" or "Hail" are common in such preaching. "O womb in which the contract of the common freedom was written! O belly, in which the weapons against the devil were forged!"[77] Increasingly divergent Old Testament texts were applied to Mary. There arose in Constantinople a tradition of liturgical poetry, with Romanos Melodos its greatest representative (flourished c. 540) and its culmination, the "Akathistos" hymn.

In the early fifth century there began to appear as well the *Transitus* literature, which claimed to describe the death of Mary and the taking of her body to heaven by angels. Emperor Maurice at the end of the sixth century instituted the feast of Mary's Dormition on August 15. Noteworthy Assumption sermons are known c. 600 by Palestinian bishops such as Modestus of Jerusalem and Theoteknos of Livias. Popular piety looked more and more to Mary as protectress.[78] The West remained relatively slow and theologically sober during this period of growth of Marian piety and poetry in the East.

KILIAN McDONNELL, O.S.B.

4

The Marian Liturgical Tradition

A privileged entrance into the Catholic understanding of the role of Mary is her place in liturgical celebration. In liturgy one sees the history of Marian piety, its power, its detours.

Primary in examining the liturgical cult is the use of Scripture in Marian feasts. The spiritual sense and biblical typology within the liturgy have contributed considerably to the development of Marian reflection. Marian devotion provided the types that would allow theologians to interpret Old Testament texts as Marian hymns.[1] Here one could point to the use of Sirach 24:5-16, which reads in part: "From eternity, in the beginning, he created me, and for eternity I shall remain." This text is evocative of the origin of the Eternal Wisdom and was applied to the engendering of the word by God. In Marian liturgies it was applied to Mary.

The scandal of such usage is diminished if it is recalled that this and other sapiential texts were in use for a primitive form of the Common of Virgins years before the first feast of Mary. "This was to entail an initial accent on the virginity of Mary which would be normative for the subsequent development of Marian liturgy."[2] The stage was set for the accent on virginity by the celebration in Rome of the feasts of Saint Agnes and Saint Agatha years before there was a Marian feast in Rome. No attempt was made to compare Mary to the Uncreated Wisdom because originally this passage was used indistinctly of all virgins.

Another wisdom text used in Marian liturgies is Prov 8:22-35, which reads in part: "The Lord created me at the beginning of his work, the first of his acts of old. Ages ago I was set up, at the first, before the beginning of the earth." Again this passage has to do with the Eternal Wisdom. No indication can be found which would suggest that it was ever used for any other saint, virgin or otherwise, before being used for the first time after the age of Charlemagne in the Mass of the Nativity of Mary (September 8). The key to its theological meaning in the liturgical context is found in the opening words: "The Lord created me at the beginning of his work." Theologians reflected that Christ lived in the thought of God from eternity. No one could think of Christ's beginnings without thinking of his mother, who was predestined to her role in the same thought—and this, without any desire to confuse creator and creature. This daring parallelism between son (Eternal Wisdom) and mother was not to blur the "distance" between them nor the radical difference in honor and dignity. Rather, it was to show how, solely through free divine election and unmerited grace, a creature was chosen to be associated in the work of redemption. This does not place her beyond redemption, but means she was redeemed more radically and in a different manner.

Preliturgical and Early Liturgical Texts

Liturgical praxis does not arise out of a void. Before the emergence of a specific Marian liturgical cult in the fifth century there was a preliturgical devotion to Mary that goes back to the second century—to Justin, Irenaeus, Tertullian.[3] Inspired by the Adam-Jesus typology of Paul (Rom 5:12-21), the early patristic writers elaborated an Eve-Mary typology.[4]

The date of the evident beginnings of the liturgical cult of Mary *Theotokos* is with justice given as the fifth century. Some years before the Council of Ephesus (431) a feast was celebrated in Kathisma, between Jerusalem and Bethlehem.[5] Though *Theotokos* was a christological title, intended to say something about Christ, Ephesus gave rise to a flowering of Marian piety. Previous to the Council the term was used by the authors of the Alexandrine school and by others.[6] The title of *Theotokos*, however, antedates Ephesus by about two hundred years. Hugo Rahner has demonstrated that Hippolytus of Rome used the title around the year 220.[7] Hippolytus was not a person at the cutting edge of new theological developments. A conservative puritan, he resisted a series of popes on disciplinary and doctrinal issues, for he thought they were abandoning the ancient tradition.[8]

Various readings of the old Roman creed contain some form of the phrase "born of the Holy Spirit and the Virgin Mary."[9] Liturgical expression tends to be conservative, drawing less on new ideas and more on time-honored themes. This being so, second-century creeds could represent older traditions.

A Marian liturgical prayer of surprising antiquity is the *Sub tuum praesidium*: "To your protection we flee, holy Mother of God (*Theotokos*); do not despise our prayers in [our] needs, but deliver us from all dangers, glorious and blessed Virgin."[10] In the Roman rite the borrowing of this text from the Greek rite does not go beyond the sixth or seventh centuries; in the Coptic, Greek, and in the Ambrosian rite (Milan) it cannot be dated earlier than the fifth or sixth centuries.[11] But in 1938 M.C.H. Roberts published a Greek text, somewhat corrupted, but still recognizable as the *Sub tuum praesidium*. There is evidence from the paleographic characters of the papyrus that the text goes back to the third century or earlier.[12] Given H. Rahner's dating of the first usage of the *Theotokos* to the early third century, this dating of the *Sub tuum praesidium* does not seem unreasonable. If this is true, then the prayer is the most ancient one to the Mother of God. The presence of the *Theotokos* in the *Sub tuum praesidium* is evidence that the term was more than just a theological term, but a word that had an ecclesiastical liturgical usage—and this before it became a conciliar term.[13] The presence of *Theotokos* in liturgical texts would help explain the savagery with which Cyril of Alexandria defended it against Nestorius, who was not rejecting just a technical term dear to the theological schools, but a faith expression rooted in the liturgy.[14]

However significant for a contemporary evaluation of the force of Marian liturgical texts, the appearance of the *Theotokos* in the *Sub tuum praesidium* does not seem tied to a marked increase of Marian liturgical forms or even of Marian popular piety. Up until 431 and the proclamation of the *Theotokos* at Ephesus the emergence of liturgical expressions of Marian piety was gradual and measured. Not only the actual proclamation at Ephesus but the public scenes of excitement accompanying it were the point of departure for a rapid and extensive development of a Marian liturgical cult. The external evidence of this is in the feasts dedicated to her and the number of churches erected in her honor. This rapid flowering of Marian piety is not tied to a proclamation about her, but to a statement about Christ. Possibly this joining of son and mother, a relationship not always honored in subsequent history, was the signal for a christologically oriented liturgical cult of Mary. The christological triumph of Ephesus was enough to give impetus to a pronounced Marian cult.

THE LITURGICAL HISTORY OF MARIAN FEASTS

After Ephesus Pope Sixtus III (432–40) built a basilica in Mary's honor, which subsequently was called St. Mary Major. Like churches in the East, the West wanted to relate the Marian cult to Christmas. In the seventh century the *Natale sanctae Mariae* was celebrated on January 1.[15] This was a generic feast of Mary, and it was made up of elements of the liturgy of virgins. In fact, the liturgy of virgins became the chief source for texts of Marian feasts. But this generic feast of Mary disappeared rather quickly. The introduction of new feasts from the East (the origin of many feasts to appear on the Western calendar) made this feast appear redundant. In the second half of the seventh century the West introduced the feast of the Dormition.

Toward A.D. 600 the Emperor Maurice ordered August 15 to be the celebration of the Assumption of Mary. This feast had been celebrated in the East at Kathisma, a sanctuary south of Jerusalem. At this time it was simply the feast of the *Theotokos* on August 15.[16]

At Rome itself there was mention of Mary in the *Communicantes* of the Roman eucharistic canon: "In union with the whole church we honor Mary, the mother of Jesus Christ, our Lord and God." The insertion of this prayer in the canon of the Mass very likely took place before the pontificate of Pope Leo (440–61), but the mention of Mary as *Theotokos* probably belongs to the sixth century. This prayer goes beyond the simple mention of Mary's name, as is done for the other saints, and shows her special veneration.

From the time of the seventh century the festival of Ember Days, which is part of the temporal cycle, has had some Marian content through readings from Luke 1:26-38 (Annunciation) and Luke 1:39-47 (Visitation).

Not to mention Mary in conjunction with the celebration of Christmas would be something of a feat. Both the Leonine Sacramentary of the seventh century and the Gelasian of the mid-eighth century mention Mary with some frequency. But the editor of the Gregorian Sacramentary, which might have been Gregory himself, avoided all explicit mention of Mary in the Christmas Masses, with the exception of the previously mentioned *Communicantes* and two other prayers that were relegated to an appendix labeled simply "Other Prayers."[17] The reason for this heavy-handed exclusion might be the institution of Advent in the second half of the sixth century. Advent, then, would form an extensive prelude to Christmas, and in this prelude Mary had her due place. In the East the larger framework out of which Advent came was the Nestorian controversy. Advent, then, was to serve as a strong affirmation of the close union between the humanity and divinity in the person of Jesus.[18]

Toward the end of the seventh century Pope Sergius (687-701) ordered processions in honor of Mary in Rome. They were to take place on the feasts of Annunication, Dormition, Nativity, and Purification. These remained the Marian feasts in Rome until the fourteenth century.[19] The Annunciation was liturgically celebrated on the Wednesday of the Ember Days in December. By the beginning of the sixth century it had been also celebrated on March 25. Here is one of the beginnings of liturgical doubling.

The feast of the Purification was, according to the witness of the pilgrim Etheria, celebrated in Jerusalem already at the end of the fourth century. In its beginnings this feast had as its object the meeting of Jesus (emphasis on the humanity) with Simeon, and was called the Feast of the Meeting. Only later, and then in the West, was attention drawn to Mary in such a way that it could be considered a feast of Mary, at which time it took the name of the feast of the Purification. Only somewhat later was the practice of lighting candles taken over by the Roman church, a custom that was noted by Etheria in her account of the liturgies of Jerusalem in the fourth century.

The emergence of these more specifically Marian feasts made redundant the generic feast of Mary on January 1. The reform of the liturgy, which became effective January 1, 1970, restored the first day of the year as a feast of Mary, naming it The Solemnity of Mary, Mother of God. Therefore it is the specific feast of the *Theotokos*.

Liturgy after the Ninth Century

The feast of the Assumption soon became the most important of the Marian feasts, not an astonishing development when one remembers that all the liturgical feasts of the saints were celebrated on the day of their entry into glory.

Soon there was also a feast of the Conception of Mary, a development furthered by the biblical story of the birth of John the Baptist. The same story that tells of the sanctification of the Baptist while still in his mother's womb led to the reflection on the conception of Mary. In this, as in so many matters liturgical, the East preceded the West, but in reality the celebration of the Conception of Mary in the West was independent of the Eastern festival. The first evidence of the feast in the West is to be found in the missal of Leofric in the eleventh century. Some of the texts of the Mass were taken over from apocryphal writings, something that was soon corrected. From England the feast passed over to France where it met one of its most formidable opponents, Bernard of Clairvaux, who, in spite of his opposition to the feast, has to be numbered among the greatest of the medieval Marian theologians and devotees. Thomas Aquinas was also opposed because he did not see how Mary could be conceived immaculately and still be in need of redemption. Christ was the universal Redeemer, and Mary was not to be excepted.

Rome resisted the pressure to recognize the feast. The exile of the papacy in Avignon and the pressure that the populace of France exerted led to the adoption of the feast by the papacy and curia. The doctrine received decisive papal support through the constitution *Cum praecelsa* of Pope Sixtus IV, a Franciscan, in 1476. From this date the papacy has not ceased to give support and encouragement, which led eventually to the solemn definition by Pius IX on December 8, 1854. The office and mass composed at this time both reflect the controversies that accompanied the previous development. These texts were replaced in 1863 by those that were in use until the revision of the liturgy in 1970.

Minor Feasts of Mary

Since the calendar reform of 1913–14 and 1970 only a few of these feasts remain in the calendar of the universal church. They are given here because they helped to form the Catholic consciousness of Mary.

On February 11 the universal church had celebrated the feast of the Apparition of the Blessed Immaculate Virgin Mary. The reference is to the apparitions that took place in Lourdes in 1858. Commenting on this feast, Bernard Botte suggested that "the spirit of welcome which the church has toward some divine manifestations which she wishes to guarantee is here carried to the maximum."[20] There is only one other comparable feast, that of the Translation of the House of the Blessed Virgin (December 10). It commemorates the supposed translation by angels of the house of Mary from Nazareth to Loreto, Italy, with a stop in Greece. At the time of the reform of 1913 this feast was suppressed almost everywhere, but was restored in 1916 for the dioceses of Italy and for others who requested it. It would be difficult to suggest that the church engaged the fullness of her authority in assuring that the house of Mary was miraculously carried from Nazareth to Loreto by angels.

The feast of the Seven Sorrows of the Blessed Virgin is celebrated twice, on the Friday after Passion Sunday and on September 15. There is no allusion to the seven specific sorrows in the first feast, but they are all counted in the feast on September 15. The feast is an expression of the Marian piety that arose in monastic circles in the Middle Ages. Bernard of Clairvaux and the Cistercians contributed to its propagation. Further assistance took the form of the foundation in Flanders in the sixteenth century of the Confraternity of the Seven Dolors. The Servites, founded in the thirteenth century specifically for the promotion of the cult of the Virgin, had a devotion to the seven joys of Mary and eagerly joined to it the celebration of her seven sorrows. It was the Servites who obtained in 1668 a liturgical celebration on the third Sunday of September, which Pius X transferred to September 15. During the time in the eighteenth century when the church in France was undergoing severe trials, Pius VII extended the feast to the universal church.

The feast of the Holy Name of Mary (September 12) is tied to the feast of the Nativity of Mary (September 8) in much the same manner as the feast of the Circumcision is attached to that of the Holy Name of Jesus (formerly celebrated on the Sunday between the feast of Circumcision and Ephiphany, or January 2). Originally the feast was granted to a diocese of Spain in 1513. Only with difficulty did the feast hold its place in the calendar. Pius V suppressed it, and it was restored by Sixtus V only to be threatened again by the liturgical policies of Benedict XIV. The deliverance of Vienna in 1683 was sufficient reason for Innocent XI to extend it to the whole church.

Our Lady of Mercy (September 24) is tied to Spain and the invasion of the Moors, with the consequent enslavement of a number of Christians. For a long time this was the feast of the Order of

Mercy or the Mercedarians, a religious community specifically dedicated to the ransoming of slaves. A tradition has it that the Virgin herself asked for the feast. Only at the beginning of the seventeenth century was a new solemnity given to the feast, and in 1896 it was extended to the universal church.

Our Lady of the Rosary (October 7) had its origin as a feast of a confraternity. The coincidence of the celebration of this feast with the battle of Lepanto (October 7, 1571) caused Pius V to order the confraternities of Rome to hold a solemn procession on this feast day for the success of the war. After the victory at Lepanto the feast was given a new impetus. The feast gradually became widely popular until it was extended to the universal church by Clement XI.

At the Council of Ephesus Mary was declared the *Theotokos* (October 11, 431). In 1751 Benedict XIV granted the petition to the king of Portugal for a feast in honor the Maternity of Mary. Benedict XIV himself composed the texts for the office and Mass of the feast. On the fifteenth centenary of the declaration at Ephesus Pius XI extended to the whole church a feast that had existed since the eighteenth century. It was to be called the feast of the Maternity of Mary (October 11).

The Presentation of Our Lady (November 21) was founded on a legend recorded in the apocryphal Protoevangelium of James. There it is recorded that Mary was presented in the temple at the age of three, where she was to serve the Lord. Already in the seventh century there was a feast of the Presentation at Jerusalem. The feast was attached to the dedication of a new church in honor of Mary at Jerusalem. It had great popularity in the East, as seen in the writings of John Damascene, but it was unknown in the West until the time of the Crusades. Toward 1340 Philip, the ambassador of the pope to the king of Cyprus, experienced the celebration of the feast on the island and took it upon himself to seek its establishment in the West. In 1371 Gregory XI permitted its celebration in Avignon and then granted it to the Franciscans. In spite of the appeal of the feast Pius V suppressed it, only to have it reestablished by Sixtus V for the whole church. Benedict XIV wanted to suppress it again, but it survived and was not further threatened. Clement VIII gave it new texts. He was quite discreet and did not insist on the fact of the presentation, but simply recalled the words of John Damascene without accenting historicity.

Other Liturgical Forms

Saturday gradually became a day consecrated to the Virgin, but the historical reasons are not clear. Even from antiquity Saturday was a sacred day on which the people fasted. From the writings of Peter Damian and Bernold of Constance we know that the Mass *de Sancta Maria* was celebrated everywhere. The Office of Holy Mary was already in existence, and it was recited on Saturday especially in the monasteries. The practice became general very quickly. In the eleventh and twelfth centuries one religious family after another (Cluniacs, Carthusians, Cistercians, and later the Dominicans) joined this office to the great offices of the day. The diocesan clergy soon followed. The laity then followed the lead of the clergy. Up to the end of the Middle Ages the hours of the Blessed Virgin were the preferred devotion of the laity.

Only the briefest of indications will be given of the mention of Mary in other liturgical books. The church invokes her before candidates for baptism are immersed.[21] Mary's intercession is invoked in favor of mothers who come to express gratitude for the gift of motherhood after childbirth.[22] The church prays to Mary on behalf of those who are dying.[23] Also the church prays to Mary for those who have already died.[24] Lastly, the church invokes Mary's aid for those who mourn the dead.[25]

The Contemporary Calendar

An extensive reform of the calendar became effective January 1, 1970. In promulgating this reform, Pope Paul VI in his Apostolic Letter of February 14, 1969, said: "With the passage of centuries, the faithful have become accustomed to so many special religious devotions that the principal mysteries of redemption have lost their proper place."[26] While reasserting the role the feasts of Mary have in the liturgical year, Paul VI again based her place in the church's liturgical worship on the role she played in the mysteries of her son—as Vatican II put it—"being joined by an inseparable bond to the saving work of her Son."[27]

The Marian feasts of the reformed calendar are:

January 1 *Solemnity of Mary, Mother of God*	Solemnity
February 11 *Our Lady of Lourdes*	Optional Memorial
May 31 *Visitation*	Feast

Saturday after Pentecost *Immaculate Heart of Mary*	Optional Memorial
July 16 *Our Lady of Mount Carmel*	Optional Memorial
August 5 *Dedication of St. Mary Major*	Optional Memorial
August 15 *Assumption*	Solemnity
August 22 *Queenship of Mary*	Memorial
September 8 *Birth of Mary*	Feast
September 15 *Our Lady of Sorrows*	Memorial
October 7 *Our Lady of the Rosary*	Memorial
November 21 *Presentation of Mary*	Memorial
September 8 *Immaculate Conception*	Solemnity

In the new calendar, therefore, there are thirteen feasts of Mary, but four of these are optional memorials and four are memorials.

Speaking in the context of the 1970 calendar reform, Paul VI called attention to Advent as presenting a happy balance between levels of piety with regard to Christ and his mother. "This balance can be taken as a norm for preventing any tendency to separate devotion to the Blessed Virgin from its necessary point of reference—Christ."[28] This balance is exemplified in the feast of Christmas, on which the church "both adores the Savior and venerates his glorious mother."[29] The Annunciation (March 25) is now restored to its ancient title as the Annunciation of the Lord and is, as it was in antiquity, a joint feast of Christ and his mother, commemorating the day on which Mary, "by receiving into her womb the one Mediator, became the true Ark of the Covenant and the true Temple of God."[30] The feast of February 2 also has been given back its ancient name, the Presentation of the Lord, it too being conceived of as a joint commemoration of the son and the mother. The Presentation of the Blessed Virgin (November 2) has been retained. Though one would have hoped that the calendar reform would have been a suitable occasion for suppressing a feast that has an apocryphal basis, it was retained, said Paul VI, out of reverence for a tradition in the Eastern churches. One wonders whether credibility with regard to things Marian should not have been of greater weight, especially in regard to the problems Mariology presents to other Christians.

Paul VI noted that not all feasts of Mary are found in the General Roman Calendar. Local feasts have generally, according to the liturgical norms, been allowed to local churches, e.g., in England Our Lady of Ranson (September 24) is celebrated as a memorial, but not in the United States. The Pope called attention to the commemoration of Mary in the Eucharistic Prayers. Besides the *Communicantes* in the Roman Canon, now Eucharistic Prayer I, the third canon contains the words "May he make us an everlasting gift to you [Father] and enable us to share in the inheritance of your saints, with Mary, the Virgin Mother of God."[31]

THE ROOTS OF MARIAN LITURGIES

In composing the offices for the Marian liturgies, the church drew heavily on the liturgy of virgins. This means that the doctrinal emphasis in the Marian liturgies would be on the virginity of Mary. This would explain the presence of bridal themes in the Marian feasts, something that distinguishes them from the Byzantine liturgy where the accent is on Mary—not as the bride but on the bridal chamber, and consequently with the emphasis on the maternity of Mary.[32] The bridal accent has theological importance, more specifically for ecclesiology. If Mary is the prototype of the church, the church has a bridal relation with the Christ. It is important to have in ecclesiology images both of identity (Mystical Body) and of differentiation (bride, people of God). If only images of identification are used, ecclesiology can easily become triumphalistic. Such images need to be complemented with images of differentiation. The bride is not the groom; the church is not in every respect absolutely the body of Christ. Both Mary, the bride, and the church, the bride, are in need of redemption.

Another source for Marian liturgies, as we have seen, is the Christmas season, including Advent, which accords well with the supposition that the place to do Mariology is Christology. Mary's significance derives from her being chosen to be associated with the work of redemption by her son. Or as Pius IX said in the bull defining the Immaculate Conception, "One and the same decree fixed in advance the *primordia* of Mary and decided the Incarnation of the divine Wisdom."[33] Therefore incarnational texts are properly chosen for Marian liturgies.

Besides the New Testament the liturgies of Mary draw on the Psalms, the Canticle of Canticles, and the Wisdom literature.

POPE PAUL VI AND *MARIALIS CULTUS*

In *Marialis Cultus* Paul VI touched on the theological context of the liturgical cult of Mary. The norms of correct veneration of Mary are to be found in the liturgy.[34] The liturgy makes it evident that there are trinitarian, christological, and ecclesial aspects to such veneration.[35] In particular, devotion should give particular prominence to the christological dimension. The liturgy when taken as a guideline prevents "any tendency . . . to separate devotion to the Blessed Virgin from its necessary point of reference—Christ."[36] One of the specific purposes of *Marialis Cultus* was "to purify Mariology and Marian piety of everything which would appear as more or less independent or destined only to the glorification of Mary."[37] What needs to be corrected is an autonomous Mariology. Devotion to Mary is seen as "an approach to Christ, the source and center of ecclesiastical communion, in which all who openly confess that he is God and Lord and Savior and sole mediator (1 Tim 2:5) are called to be one with one another."[38] Thus *Marialis Cultus* takes up the insistence on Christ, the one Mediator (1 Tim. 2:5), which the "Constitution on the Church" returned to seven times.[39]

In insisting that alongside liturgical worship "other forms of piety" should be promoted,[40] Pope Paul also recognized that some of these forms of piety have been "subjected to the ravages of time" and are in need of renewal.[41] The way to attain a reform and renewal of popular piety within this broad framework is to recognize "that every form of worship should have a biblical imprint,"[42] and that piety "should be imbued with the great themes of the Christian message."[43] Further, popular devotions should be in harmony with the sacred liturgy. According to Vatican II "They should somehow derive their inspiration from it, and because of its preeminence they should orient the Christian people towards it."[44]

Two attitudes toward popular piety stand in opposition to these biblical and liturgical norms. There are those who *a priori* scorn devotions of piety, even those that are in harmony with biblical and scriptural norms, and these persons create a vacuum which they make no effort to fill. "They forget that the Council has said that devotions of piety should harmonize with the liturgy, not be suppressed."[45] Then there are those who "mix practices of piety and liturgical acts in hybrid celebrations. . . . [These forget] that exercises of piety should be harmonized with the liturgy, not merged with it."[46] What Pope Paul VI says of Marian devotion could also be said of the veneration of saints, namely, "every care should be taken to avoid any exaggeration which could mislead other Christian brethren about the true doctrine of the Catholic Church."[47] Also to be commended is the avoidance of "the exaggerated search for novelties or extraordinary phenomena."[48]

From Cult to Creed

Lex orandi lex credendi cannot mean that there is a kind of automatic transfer from cult to creed, so that what is prayed is immediately and without reservation translated as obligation in matters of faith. The principle is broader. What the church does, especially during liturgical prayer, is a *locus theologicus*.[49] That the praxis of the church has such a theological force has been recognized as least since Origen.[50] The liturgy, then, is operative in the way the church norms doctrine; it is an element in the process of theological discernment. As a normed norm (*norma normata*) it is subordinate to the norming norm (*norma normans*) of Sacred Scripture. In its normative function liturgy does not stand by itself. Rather, it is part of a whole theological culture (Scripture, preaching, private prayer, evangelization, ordinary and extraordinary teaching, and the experience of the world), in a word, the totality of the church's experience.[51] Within this theological culture liturgy is a conservative element, reaching into the experienced past for its riches rather than pushing the boundaries of the future and anticipating new theological developments. Nonetheless, it belongs to history and is marked by its passage through theological styles and devotional preferences of a given historical moment. If an historical period is marked by a too elaborate theological specificity, by a theological superstructure that is too heavy for even undoubted firm foundations, this then will all be reflected in the liturgies which come out of that historical moment. Neither the church nor the liturgy is captive to a given age. What she celebrates at one moment in history she may barely allow at a later moment or not at all. Liturgy, too, is part of that sifting process that one calls theological discernment.

The liturgy has shown itself open to new initiatives by God. There is a primary and founding initiative, recorded in the word of God, and that is the Father's sending of the Son and the Spirit. But the people who are the recipients of that initiative are a people on the march, and God continues to take initiatives, touch their history, and make evident the divine presence. To these quite secondary or tertiary manifestations (e.g., Lourdes) the liturgy has shown itself open. Though the authority of the church is behind the celebration of these manifestations, that authority is not engaged in a definitive way. A person who sincerely did not believe in the authenticity of Lourdes would not be considered less a Christian. Interventions of this order are not a matter of faith. Of the various "interventions" that find some place in the liturgy, either universally or locally, one could mention the Battle of Lepanto (Our Lady of the Rosary, October 7), the apparitions at Lourdes (Apparition of the Immaculate Blessed Virgin Mary, February 11), and the apparition and giving of the scapular to Saint Simon Stock (Our Lady of Mount Carmel, July 16); the one that has had the most universal impact on the church is Lourdes—and this because of the experience of vast numbers of believers.

The various feasts of Mary celebrated in the liturgical year are not all of equal theological weight, in a way analogous to the theological weight of the Epistle to the Romans as compared to that of James. The Solemnity of Mary, Mother of God (January 1) is specifically a feast of the *Theotokos* and is of greater theological importance than the Presentation of Mary (November 21), which is based on an apocryphal document.

The theological climate and the style of popular piety of a given historical moment affect how a Marian insight is liturgically appropriated by each age. What was appropriate to one social and cultural context will not be appropriate to another. If a liturgy comes out of an age in which popular piety has already suffered what Paul VI called "the ravages of time," this will be reflected in the liturgies. If the Marian theology is overdeveloped and too highly nuanced, this might be reflected in a liturgical proliferation which a later age will recognize as excessive. The catalog of about 940 universal and local feasts of Mary compiled by Holweck at the end of the nineteenth century is an expression of this.[52]

What was admitted in an earlier age might not be acceptable in a later one. Fifty popes have honored the House of Loreto, which according to legend had been transported by angels from Palestine via Greece. The admission of the feast of the Presentation of Mary, which is based on apocryphal material, presents a problem.

With these general remarks in mind, something more specific can be said about the application of *les orandi lex credendi* to Marian doctrine. The liturgical cult of Mary reaffirms the central Marian truths: she is the Virgin Mother, chosen under grace and not by merit, to be associated in the work of redemption by her son. She is wholly and preeminently on the side of the redeemed. More radically than any other she is redeemed. She is honored because she heard the word of God and kept it. Because of the role that she played in the economy of salvation, she is rightly venerated publicly and privately. This recognition, which has often been affirmed in a structural way by councils and popes, has had a base in popular piety.

At a secondary level the liturgy teaches that God by his own sovereign initiative encompassed the whole of Mary's life, from beginning to end, surrounds her existence with a unique fidelity which comes from him, and this because of the part she played in the salvation Jesus was to win for all. She was the one who received and realized the fullness of redemption. Because of her *fiat* she is celebrated as the perfect receiver.[53] "The consent she gave in faith and obedience belongs not only to her private life, but to the public history of salvation."[54] In a singular way she belongs to the doxological tradition of the church, in which are celebrated in praise the *mirabilia Dei*. Among the marvelous things celebrated is the nature of redemption, touching not only spiritual reality but materiality and corporality. Here God triumphs wholly in the entirety of the person, and this is cause for public praise.

K A R L F R I E D F R O E H L I C H

5

The *Libri Carolini* and the Lessons of the Iconoclastic Controversy

The *Libri Carolini*, a document of about two hundred printed pages, belongs in the context of the so-called iconoclastic controversy of the eighth and ninth centuries. Much has been written on this episode from the viewpoint of art history. Of course, the question of the impact on artistic practice of the theories of art that are found in the polemics of both sides remains valid and important. For our purposes, however, we must emphasize that the controversy was only marginally about Christian art or its abolition. Art in a Christian context existed much earlier, its production in East and West was not halted during the controversy, and there is little incontrovertible evidence of systematic destruction even during the reign of the iconoclastic rulers. A much more substantial fact was the persecution of iconodules, which produced its own martyrs for later generations to commemorate.[1]

History of the Document

For the background of the *Libri Carolini* four interacting parties are of importance: (1) The iconodules, the friends of image worship, primarily represented by the bishops, clerics, and monks assembled at the Second Nicene Council in 787. Today we are able to see that before the Council their main theologian was John of Damascus, whose location at Saint Sabas in Muslim territory prevented his wider influence at that time; during the second phase after 787 the important theologians were Theodore of Studion and Patriarch Nikephoros of Constantinople. (2) The iconoclasts, theologically represented by the 338 bishops of the Synod of Hiereia in 754, but more importantly identified with the Byzantine emperors and court circles between Leo III (717–41) and Michael III (842–67). (3) The Roman bishops and the curia; Pope Gregory II (715–31) already protested against imperial iconoclasm and Gregory III (731–41) had it solemnly condemned at a Roman synod in 731. It is clear that Rome simply followed its own moderately iconophile tradition. Thus Pope Hadrian I (772–95) was eager to accept the invitation to attend the synod of restoration in 786/87. His two legates were honored participants at Nicaea and signed the Council's *Horos* which restored the veneration of images. (4) Charlemagne and the Frankish court theologians. Deeply interested in theology himself, Charlemagne had the help and advice of a group of able theologians from his Frankish realm and abroad, among them Alcuin of York, Paul the Deacon, Angilbert of St. Riquier, Theodulf of Orléans, and others. The author(s) of the *Libri Carolini* must be sought among them; procedures at Charlemagne's court suggest a somewhat collective approach to drafting.[2] Their attitude is often simplistically classified as iconoclastic. In reality their intended middle course comes closer to an adiaphoristic stance, as we shall see. Deep into the ninth century the Frankish theologians remained convinced that the truth was on their side. But the gradual shift toward a factual endorsement of the Nicene (or better: the Roman) position was inevitable, given their deep respect for Rome and its decisions in doctrinal matters.

The first iconoclastic actions taken by Emperor Leo III (717–41) must be seen in the context of a comprehensive reform program after partial victories over the Arabs. If the earlier Arab conquests had an influence, it probably lay in the religious perception of the Arab advances as another expression of God's wrath over the empire and in the suggestion that penitential action against the sins of society was called for, especially the root sin, idolatry.[3] The program had much support from clergy and people. At the height of the movement Leo's son Constantine V (741–75) convened the famous-infamous Synod of Hiereia in 754, which considered itself as the Seventh Ecumenical Council. Its iconoclastic *Horos* was the main target of the polemics at Nicaea II in 787. The text is preserved in the acts of that latter Council because, in a dramatic gesture, it was read aloud sentence by sentence together with its refutation at the sixth session and thus became part of the official record. It was only under Emperor Leo IV (775–80) that the official iconoclastic zeal abated so that his widow Irene, reigning for her young son Constantine VI, could signal her intention to restore the veneration of images. After an abortive attempt to convene a council at Constantinople in 786, the synod gathered at Nicaea the year after and acted on the sovereign's desire. The full *Acta* of this Council are available. They contain a wealth of material: transcripts of the discussion as well as supporting documentation of all kinds. For the study of the controversy as a whole the *Acta Nicaena* remain the most important single source.[4] Nicaea was not the end. At a period of renewed military threats, this time at the hands of the Bulgarians, and in reaction to the triumphalist reform zeal of iconodule monks, Emperor Leo V the Armenian returned to an iconoclastic policy. His synod of 815 reaffirmed the *Horos* of 754 but found as little support for its demand to abolish the images as the emperor himself. Theodora, widow of Emperor Theophilos, is credited with achieving the final restoration of the icons. In 843 she installed a monastic leader as patriarch and held a synod whose action is solemnly recounted in the *Synodicon* still being read in Orthodox churches at the "Feast of Orthodoxy," which is celebrated on the first Sunday in Lent each year.[5]

The Western involvement in the controversy reached its zenith when Pope Hadrian I sent two legates to Nicaea in 786/87. They carried a detailed memorandum (Hadrian's *Synodica*) on the issues. It was read at the second session of the Council, though not in its entirety and with "improvements" in the Greek translation, and was greatly hailed by the advocates of the iconodule cause.[6] It is likely that, upon their return, the legates brought a copy of the Greek acts of the Council back to Rome. The sequence of the following events is not entirely clear. Its most recent reconstruction runs as follows:[7] (1) A rather inept Latin translation of the Acts or portions thereof was made in Rome and reached the Frankish court by unknown channels; (2) Frankish theologians analyzed the text, believing that they had an original document from Constantinople, and began working on a refutation under Charlemagne's direction; a preliminary draft of eight-five capitula (*Capitulare adversus synodum*) sharply critical of the substance and translation of the *Acta Nicaena* was carried to Rome by Angilbert of St. Riquier for information and comment; (3) Hadrian answered with a detailed memorandum which took up all the incriminated points *seriatim*, explaining the traditional Roman position and that of the Council. This document, the so-called *Hadrianum*, is the first in this series to have been preserved. It broadened the patristic basis by adding carefully chosen references to the Western patristic tradition;[8] (4) The Frankish theologians, chastened by the unexpected rebuff, continued their work; the finished draft is what we call the *Libri Carolini*. The preface indicates that Charlemagne originally authorized the text to go out under his own name as a piece of anti-Byzantine polemic aimed at a broad readership. The history of the text, however, shows that publication was halted and the working copy with marginal notes was filed in the royal archives. It is preserved (as ms. lat 7207) at the Vatican Library, lacking the preface and Book IV. Only two other manuscript witnesses are extant: a complete copy made for Hincmar of Rheims c. 860 (now Paris Arsenal 663) and a single leaf from a copy written at Corbie in the ninth century (Paris nat. lat. 12125, fol. 157). The text was first published from the Paris copy by the Gallican publicist Jean du Tillet in Paris in 1549. John Calvin used it for his anti-iconic polemic in his *Institutes* I.xi.14f. The edition was immediately placed on the index. Catholic historians such as Bellarmin and Baronius suspected a forgery fabricated by Karlstadt. The Migne edition[9] gives the text of the Paris manuscript as published by Melchior Goldast in 1608. Both the Vatican and the Arsenal manuscripts form the basis of the critical text established by Hubert Bastgen for the *Monumenta Germaniae Historica* in 1924. Ann Freeman is preparing a new critical edition with an English translation and notes.[10]

Intent and Impact

If we want to appreciate the content of the *Libri Carolini*, we should not let ourselves be distracted by its tone and its apparent lack of order. The tone is aggressive, scornful, but also naively self-confident about the quality of its theology and learning. Harnack saw here "the expression of the discovery of self-worth and power in the Frankish church which bursts forth with youthful brashness." The critique takes up single terms or statements and does not follow the order of the Nicene Acts. The only stated principle of order is the division into four books which is explained by reference to the mystical qualities of the number four (IV: Praef.). This might be an argument for the thesis that the authors had only excerpts from the Latin *Acta Nicaena* without visible order and simply followed along with what they read.[11] Most important, however, is the question of the document's intent. Political goals are certainly involved.

The *Libri Carolini* asserts the Frankish independence and the equality of their king to the Byzantine rulers. Already the Preface makes this clear: The emperor is called "rex eorum Constantinus" and Charlemagne claims the care of the church in his realm ("in his partibus nostris"). This, the authors explain, means responsibility for correct doctrine, including the Frankish *filioque,* which they assiduously defend in III: 3f.; an important chapter (I:6) links Frankish orthodoxy to the authority of the Roman church, which must always be consulted because it has its primacy directly from the Lord via Peter; Frankish rulers have conformed church life in their realm to Roman teaching down to the *ordo psallendi.*

This all stands in stark contrast to the East, where irregularities abound. The Patriarch Tarasius holds an illegitimate appointment (III:2); the empress, a woman, presumes to teach in the church against the injunction of the Apostle (III:13); and the style of letters from the East betrays arrogance, pride, and vainglory (I:1-4). The picture of the East is that of a boiling volcano where one never knows what horrible novelty will be spewed up next. There is, for instance, the attempt to add a seventh universal council to the sacred number of six, a clear indication of the Eastern church seeking novelty in doctrine. In the eyes of the Frankish theologians the history of the two councils of 754 and 787 illustrates the danger inherent in the volatile turns of Eastern church politics: an extremism that equals instability and lack of balance. First, the Byzantines mercilessly condemn and destroy the images, then they turn around and demand not only that images be allowed but adored (III:11-12). The Western theologians shudder at the sight of "fathers anathematizing their children, and children their fathers" (Praef., p. 6.7-9). This point comes up time and again: How can a council condemn its own parent generation, violating the elemental law of piety, the commandment to honor father and mother? (I:9; II:23; II:31; IV:6).

Against this epitome of immoderation and frivolity stands the principle of the Frankish church: We choose the *via regia*, the middle road, *mediocritas*. In terms of the image controversy: "We neither break nor adore" (Praef., p. 6.3). This formula betrays the provenance of the Frankish stance. It was the sum of Pope Gregory I's famous letter to the iconoclastic bishop Serenus of Marseille,[12] to which an entire chapter of the *Libri Carolini* is devoted (II:23). The lavish praise of Gregory as the champion of *mediocritas* is an indication of his normative influence on the theology of the Frankish church. The authors are proud of him; clearly and precisely, without *involuti sermones*, he has formulated "what is to be observed in our realm." With respect to images, this ideal was a mild form of an Augustinian-Gregorian spiritualism which could at the same time accommodate what was important for Frankish popular piety, e.g., the cult of saints and their relics:[13]

> Having images for the decoration of churches and the remembrance of past events, adoring God alone, and expressing due veneration to his saints, we neither break [icons] with the one [group], nor do we adore them with the other. (Praef., p. 6.1-3)

How does this middle position look when we ask about the substance of the argument? The *Libri Carolini* do spell out the rationale for their rejection of the underlying theories of images on both sides. It seems that the Eastern iconoclasts insisted on an almost magical identity of image and essence; on the analogy of the image of the emperor, a religious icon is *homoousios* with its prototype. This is the reason why icons have no room in Christianity. A picture of Christ, Mary, and a saint painted in colors and set up for worship violates the first and second commandments and "is" an idol. The *Libri Carolini* reject the identity thesis time and again. What, they ask, is the content of a picture? Is its meaning in it by nature or by some magical act of consecration? Certainly not. A picture receives its meaning by being named. This naming may be an act of the artist who identifies his work in an inscription (I:2). How else can one know a pious painting from an idolatrous one—a picture of Mary from one depicting Venus (IV:21)? The naming may also be an act of the beholder: The similitude by which the skillful artist connects the portrait to its one source, the person depicted, may suggest the correct identification. Image "is" different from idol, but it may turn into one if the beholder makes it into a holy object and uses it for worship. It is interesting to note that the *Libri Carolini* direct this argument not against the iconoclasts but against the Fathers of Nicaea II; they are the ones who assert of pictures what they are not. They say that icons are holy and thus make them into idols.

The Frankish theologians likewise reject the theory behind the iconodule position expressed in the quote from Saint Basil: "The honor paid to the image passes on to the prototype" (III:16 title). Why is such mediation needed? Saints in heaven do not ask for such honors to be paid to them on earth. Christ did not say, "What you have done to images," but "What you have done to one of the least of my brethren you have done to me" (III:16). If there is an "image" of Christ in the world, it is the living human being, not a material picture. On balance, however, the censure of the iconoclasts throughout the *Libri Carolini* is much less vigorous than that of the iconodules. The former were certainly not as wicked as the Jews (I:27), and, while they were in error, at least they acted out of zeal for the Lord (I:28). The iconodules, on the other hand, are strongly suspected of actual idolatry (III:17—a misreading of a statement in the *Acta Nicaena* which said the opposite; cf. III:15); when they condemn iconoclasm, they wrongly lump together the Frankish position with that heresy. There is a great difference between "cruel destroyers" of images and "prudent avoiders" of their worship (II:1; cf. II:12; III:2).

The *Libri Carolini* spent an enormous effort on the refutation of biblical arguments in the *Acta Nicaena*. It seems that the authors felt especially well equipped and competent in this area. Their criticism is fully argued out and often relentless in its logic. Its tenor is a basic point of Augustinian hermeneutics: Scripture always aims at a spiritual meaning; it does not allow anyone to twist its sense into a material one (I:5). Instead of affirming this uplifting spiritual meaning, the iconodules "debase the mysteries" (II:4). This is evident when they use the brazen serpent (I:18), the metaphor of the "face of God" (I:23), and many other passages in support of their demand to worship material images. None of the passages adduced is applicable to this demand. They either do not speak of material images but of mysterious "types" of the new dispensation—such is the case with Jacob's pillar (I:10); Joseph's multicolored coat (I:12); the tablets of the law (I:19); Joshua's monument of twelve stones (I:21); God's footstool (II:5); or, where there is a command to make some material artifice, there is no mention of adoration—this is true of the two cherubim on the ark of the covenant (I:15); the artistic objects made by Bezaleel (I:16; cf. Exod 31:2-6); the fringes of hyacinth on the priestly garments (I:17; cf. Num 15:38). If Scripture occasionally speaks of "adoring" (*adorare*) something other than God, it refers to "saluting" human beings of higher rank or merit (I:9; I:10; I:22) or at most of "honoring" God's image and likeness in the human being. In this sense even the angels in heaven "worship" Christ's human nature (II:24). The apostles never allowed any worship of themselves beyond this understanding (II:25).

Other sections of the *Libri Carolini* refute the patristic evidence adduced by the *Acta Nicaena*. Again, the tenor of the criticism is that these texts either do not speak of painted pictures or, if they do, do not enjoin their worship. An instructive case is the Silvester legend (II:13), according to which Emperor Constantine asked the pope to bring him pictures of Peter and Paul; from the portraits he recognized the appearance of Peter and Paul in his dream and was ready for baptism. The *Libri Carolini* seem unaware of the Roman origin of the example; it was quoted in Hadrian's *Synodica*. They point out that Silvester brought the images for the emperor to see, not to worship. Even if he had encouraged their veneration (which he did not), he would have done it as a pedagogical measure, providing "milk" for infant faith, not the solid food of the believer. They add the caution that the story, while being read by Catholics, has no authority, according to the Gelasian decree. The last remark is typical. The *Libri Carolini* are highly suspicious of the Council's patristic quotations. They criticize distorted versions (II:20, Cyril of Alexandria), doubt the authenticity of iconophile passages (II:19, Ps. Chrysostom), and reject particular instances as apocryphal, e.g., the Abgar legend, for which the Gelasian decree is quoted again (IV:6). At two points they reject an iconophile text because the author "is unknown in our realm." Surprisingly, the two authors are Simeon the Stylite (IV:5) and Gregory of Nyssa (II:17). Discussing the latter, they spell out their preference: "We are content with the Scriptures, our Latin Fathers, and those of the Greek Fathers who are Catholics and have been translated by Catholics."

Finally, the criticism of the *Libri Carolini* is directed against the use at Nicaea of miracle stories connected with icons as well as dreams and visions. All this evidence is viewed with utmost suspicion. Much of it, the authors judge, is dubious, ridiculous, superstitious, or outright blasphemous (III:24-28; IV:11-12). Even if miracles do occur and are wrought by icons, this proves only that God uses material things to manifest his miraculous power.

What is the positive affirmation behind the elaborate polemic? What are the basic convictions from which the Carolingian theologians argued? We will discuss briefly their understanding of Scripture, of the nature of images, of sacred objects including relics, and of the saints. We noted the preeminence given to the biblical witness in the *Libri*. It seems that we are dealing here with the center of the authors' theology. Viewing the iconoclastic controversy from this biblical vantage point, they are asking two questions. First: If the issue concerns religious images, what do we find about it in the Bible? With the Jewish and the oldest Christian tradition their answer points unhesitatingly to the first and second commandments of the Decalogue, the interpretation of the second given by the first: "According to God's clear words, we are not allowed to worship elements, angels, nor any powers in heaven and on earth" (III:15). Pictures may have beauty but they have no sanctity (IV:27); they may be admired but "God alone is to be worshiped" (II:21). This sentence is used repeatedly to describe the essence of the *via regia*: "We do not want to stray right or left, but we worship God alone" (II:31; cf. Praef., p. 6.2). The second question is: What do we not find in the Bible about it? Again the answer is unambiguous: We find no warrant for the command to worship images in any form. Biblical warnings against images are far more numerous than commands to make them, let alone any implication of worshiping them. Even if the *Libri Carolini* had distinguished between "veneratio" and "adoratio" (we saw that they could distinguish "adoratio Dei" from "adoratio salutationis gratia"), images would not fall under either category. For them, reading the cult of images into the Bible must be compared to the devil's exegesis; even the devil interprets Scripture (Matt 4:6); but, as Jerome warns: "the devil interprets Scripture badly" (I:5). Turning one's zeal for image worship into the hermeneutical key for searching the Scriptures means placing images above Scripture. This, however, is exactly what must never be done.

Images cannot compare with Scripture. An entire chapter at the center of the outline, the longest one in the entire *Libri*, is devoted to demonstrating the inappropriateness of the comparison and the superiority of Scripture over images (II:30). Here our authors wax truly eloquent. Moses, Joshua, David, the prophets, even Jesus using his finger (John 8:6) did not paint but wrote. The Apostle penned not pictures but epistles, and the author of the Apocalypse was commanded to write, not to paint. If one is careful to read the Bible "in virtute sensuum, non in promulgatione verborum" (II:30; p. 97.30-35), it is the inexhaustible treasure store that answers any question asked in faith. Even simple observation demonstrates the limitation of pictures; they cannot depict the commandments of the law or the teachings of the prophets (III:23). Moses is greater than any painter (II:26). Pictures are dependent on the explanatory word to identify their content, not the other way around (IV:16). In fact, the only true "holy images" are biblical word images. Even in the case of the cherubim on the ark of the covenant (I:15) the word of the command to make them has priority over the artifice itself. If the *Acta Nicaena* cite Ps 49:9 ("as we have heard, so we see") to support their theory of a complementary role of visual images and word, they miss the logic of promise and fulfillment that these terms reflect here (I:30). If they quote Song of Songs 2:14 ("Show me thy face and let me hear thy voice") for the same purpose, they misread a type of the church for a bodily complement of hearing plus seeing (II:10). Listening and obeying are more important than seeing. It is the images in the words of Scripture that lead a person truly to the heights of spiritual meaning.

Here we come upon the issue of biblical hermeneutics. Our authors are certainly familiar with the distinction between various levels of meaning, specifically between a "simple" and a higher reading that scans the text for "aenigmata sive allegorica involucra" (II:7). The terminology of allegorical and tropological interpretation occurs occasionally along with other terms. The virtues of the saints that one must imitate may be found in Scripture *historialiter* as in the Decalogue, *mystice* as in the Old Testament allegories and types of Christ, and *tantum spiritualiter* as in the Song of Songs (II:10). The central methodological approach clearly is typology. Time and again the real sense of a passage quoted in the *Acta Nicaena* is explained typologically. In this procedure the *Libri* retain an emphasis from the Western church. Old-fashioned typology, the main form of second-century Christian allegorization, always remained popular in the Latin West, whereas Origen's allegorical hermeneutics only gained ground slowly. Nevertheless, recognizing prefigurations of the New Testament in the Old Testament or of the church's life in the New Testament is called "spiritual" or "mystical" exegesis in the *Libri Carolini*, and the method itself is understood as an anagogical tool, thus reflecting an emphasis in Augustinian hermeneutics. Against the iconodule reading of texts, this approach assumes that by definition the fulfillment of a type is a greater and more spiritual antitype, not a lower, more material one (I:19). True seeing is the seeing "spiritali intuitu" or "spiritalibus oculis" (II:2). The central antitype of most Old Testament types, including those in the psalm verses quoted, is Christ. An example is Jacob's pillar of Gen 28:18, which our authors declare to be a prefiguration of Christ on the strength of a host of "stone" *testimonia* (I:10). Several readers of the *Libri* have stressed the Christocentricity of their piety.[14] The Christ of whom Scripture speaks is for its authors a powerful, triumphant leader and companion, *rex noster, imperator noster*. As such he demands obedient followers, imitators of his real person, those practicing his virtues (I:29). If Christ is the hidden meaning of most biblical types, his person is sufficiently mediated, and this mediation is the only appropriate one. Our authors seem to fear that further mediation through images would remove from the inner vision this Christ whose spiritual immediacy is felt to be very real. They seem to oppose even the painting, not only the adoration, of icons of Christ, whereas such hesitation does not apply to the saints.

Where does this understanding leave the phenomenon of the painted image as such? A true icon or image is always "incorporeal," as the authors stress in their discussion of Gen 1:27 (I:7). The nature of a painted or sculpted image is the opposite. Such a picture is "material" only—it is wood, canvas, paint. It cannot hear or smell; burning candles in front of it is useless (IV:3). There is no mystery in it as there is in the types and word-images of the Bible; meaning is imposed, bestowed (I:2). Nevertheless, pictures are useful for something. They have their value in two respects: as decoration, and as a reminder of things past. The recurring formula reads: "propter memoriam rerum gestarum et ornamentum" (Praef., p. 6.1-2; II:13; II:21, etc.). It echoes Pope Gregory I, but the ambiguous term *memoria* seems to place less emphasis on the educational function which was Gregory's primary interest than on the simple function of "refreshing the memory"; for our authors painted pictures are nothing but a record of the past (I:10). Whether there are pictures in a Christian church or not makes no difference for catholic faith (II:22). According to this "secularized" concept of painting, artists choose freely what they want to do. Our authors reckon with art in many media (I:2). They refer to paintings of allegorical, mythological, and symbolic subjects, which are taunted as pagan but nevertheless considered a proper exercise of the craft (III:23). To be a painter is a matter of natural talent (I:16); painting religious icons is not a special *pia ars* but a craft, comparable to the exercise of other crafts such as farming, smithing, metal working (III:22).

To state the conclusion: pictures are not "holy." But the holiness that is denied to the images is affirmed of other "material" things. Our authors reckon with the existence of *res consecratae* (III:24; p. 153.36-38) and *instrumenta religionis* (II:21; p. 80.7), helps and incentives for our faith. First and foremost there is Holy Writ, the physical gospel books and codices—*scriptura, non pictura* (II:30). But there is more. In the Bible itself such material objects are present: the ark of the covenant with its two cherubim (I:15; II:26); the temple and its furnishings (I:29); the sacred vessels and garments (II:29); Solomon's oxen and lions (II:9). While the *Libri Carolini* always stress their typological significance, they never deny or downgrade their material existence as holy objects. These objects are holy because God commanded them to be made or simply because they are mentioned in Scripture.

In the opinion of the *Libri Carolini* Scripture itself endorses the religious value and thus the holiness of three other "real things": the cross, the Eucharist, and the relics of the saints.The cross was one of the symbols that the iconoclasts continued to hold in high regard, retaining it as a symbolic gesture in exorcisms and blessings as well as in representations placed in their churches. The *Libri Carolini* do not endorse representations of the cross; the only reference is to the iconodules (I:19; p. 44.22f.), and thus the *Libri* do not present a direct parallel to the practice of Eastern iconoclasts. They exalt, however, the cross (meaning the actual cross on which Christ hung) as the *vexillum*, the banner of the victorious Lord through which the ancient foe was vanquished (III:23) and as the instrument of our salvation, quoting at length the Pauline passages about the mystery of the cross (II:28). The main point is that the cross can never be compared to images; it surpasses them far and wide in power, value, and honor. "Not through material pictures made by artisans but by the mystery of the cross the proud wisdom of this world has been cast down" (II:28). The authors allude to the material wood, *lignum crucis*, but this does not lead to an endorsement of its material representations; it may well reflect, however, respect for the relics of the "true cross" which were increasingly in evidence in the West at that time.

The authors of the *Libri Carolini* knew a quotation from the *Acta Nicaena* which compared the Eucharist, prepared from the fruits of the earth, to icons painted by human craftsmen but leading the beholder to the prototype. A long chapter refutes this parallel (II:27). The Eucharist has its beginning not on the material, human level. It is the direct work of the Holy Spirit. As the sacrament of the Lord's true body and blood, it is made (*conficiatur*) by the hands of the priest and the invocation of the divine name: in contrast, the icon is and remains a purely human fabrication. In other words: The holiness of the Eucharist is real, that of the icon is not. "Without perceiving the Eucharist no one is saved; without looking at images everyone is saved who has the right faith" (II:27; p. 89.4-6).[15]

Relics as "holy things" to be venerated are discussed at III:24. Again, the main point is the denial of a parallel to the veneration of images. The difference, as an earlier reference explains (I:16), lies in the fact that relics come directly from the body of the saint or, in the case of clothing, have been in physical contact with that body. Images lack this direct connection. The authors start by noting that relics of holy martyrs and confessors are "venerated" by the faithful out of love for them. The term is significant. In an earlier context it was stated that "benedicere, habere, salutare, osculari, venerare" are not the equivalent of "adorare" (I:9; p. 27.36-37). The reason for this "veneration" is first of all that the real dust and bones from the bodies of the saints, in contrast to their icons, will be part of the resurrection "of the body," sharing in the eternal reign of Christ. But there is also biblical warrant: The authors cite burial passages concerning Abraham, Jacob, and Joseph in order to demonstrate the importance of burial sites and of proper respect for the *ossa sanctorum*. The climax is the story of the prophet of Bethel (1 Kings 13) who, after burying the man of God killed by the lion but not devoured, would not have said: "Bury me next to the bones of that prophet" (13:31) had he not been aware that veneration was due to holy bones. Relics of saints are "real" holy things, their pictures are not. Once this logic is understood, the summary of the chapter strikes the reader as less eccentric:

> We neither reject relics with Vigilantius and his followers, nor do we adore images with Simon (Magus) and his cohorts, but we exhibit appropriate veneration (*obsequium*) to relics or saints' bodies and decorate our churches with images of the saints as we please or even with gold and silver, but the service of adoration or worship we reserve for God alone to whom alone it is due. (III:24; p. 155.15-19)

This quotation demonstrates once more that the *Libri Carolini* object to the cult of images but do not object to the cult of saints. The Praefatio had already placed this veneration next to the worship of the one true God: "We worship God alone and we render appropriate veneration to his saints" (p. 6.2). It is surprising that there is no discussion of any biblical warrant. It simply is taken for granted that "sanctis . . . veneratio exhibenda est" (II:21; p. 80.28). Saints are persons now living in the company of angels (I:20). Not only must they be imitated in their pure lives and their virtues (I:17), but they can be invoked, and they intercede for the health of the erring soul (I:18). Both the sacrifices of prayers by the faithful and the offerings of the merits of the saints are laid down before God (I:11). It seems clear that the cult of saints, including their invocation and the veneration of their relics, had such strong roots in the piety of the people as well as the theologians of the Frankish realm that it could not fall under the suspicion of novelty. Nevertheless, the principle guiding the Frankish critique of the "novel" cult of images retained its full force in this area as well. The *Libri Carolini* make a clear distinction: "venerantur sancti—adoratur Deus" (IV:23; p. 217.4).

ISSUES THE DOCUMENT DOES NOT COVER

An appreciation of the *Libri Carolini* in the context of our deliberations must lead to some initial reflection on the major items that seem to be missing in the Frankish dialogue with the decision of Nicaea II. We cannot expect that our authors dealt with all the important issues. They may have had incomplete and unreliable knowledge of the Council's documents and may have felt attacked themselves. But these external deficiencies are no final excuse. There are more fundamental lacunae that may indicate deeper difficulties of communication and some real differences of perspective. It was during the eighth and ninth centuries that East and West drifted apart, not in 1054.

(1) As has often been pointed out, missing in the *Libri Carolini* is a recognition of the terminological distinction between *latreia* and *proskynesis*, or more precisely: *proskynesis latreukikē* (reserved for God) and *schetikē* (appropriate for icons), by which the iconodules thought to avoid any danger of idolatry. The two, they held, must never be confused. One could ask: Why not? What is the difference, practically speaking? The answer cannot point to clear differences in the external forms of "worship"; there always is and has been a confusing variety of devotional practices in both directions; the answer must be content to point to attitudes. In this awkward situation the distinction reveals itself as a compromise. Image worship now "was" the piety of the Greek East but had to be protected from misunderstanding. The Latin translation did not make the distinction in its terminology. It used *adorare* everywhere, giving the authors of the *Libri Carolini* an easy pretext to lash out against the Nicene "idolatry." But was the uniform translation really so wrong? Augustine already wrestled with the problem. In *De Civitate Dei* 10.1 he discussed the proper word for the exclusive worship of God which, as he knew, was *latreia* in Greek. He concluded that the Latin had no real equivalent, no single word for this activity since the translation *servitium* was applicable to human beings also. The *Libri Carolini*, as we saw, knew of a possible differentiation between *venerare* and *adorare* and therefore of the compromise at which the Eastern distinction was aiming. They applied the term *venerare* to the saints, but not to the icons, not because of the

meaning of "worship" but because of their understanding of "true image."

(2) This brings up the second point. Missing is also any wrestling with the deeper philosophical foundation of the Greek theory of image. For the *Libri Carolini*, an image is "only" image—picture—matter without mystery. This seems to be an easy way out of a complex problem. Art, not just crafts, was part of every culture, certainly in the Greek world. This fact must raise the question of relationship between image and reality, *Urbild* and *Abbild*. In the Greek view the two are related by nature. God is surrounded by ideas that take on form in their images in a hierarchy of being. The iconoclasts shared this basis. On the analogy of the emperor's image in their culture they claimed a metaphysical *homoousia* between image and prototype; this consubstantiality excluded all icons from Christian worship as idolatrous. The iconodules denied the identity and tried to focus on the dynamics of the relationship: *Abbild* is not *Urbild*, but it participates in its being. This being itself is relational. The prototype contains in itself the image; it reaches its fullness only when the image becomes reality. Who, they ask, was the first maker of images? God created because creating was his nature. In the anagogical movement of our worship, we need the image as the proper way back to the prototype, our Creator. The *Libri Carolini* had no use for this way of putting it. But was avoiding the problem sufficient to deal with the problem?

(3) Missing is especially any discussion of the underlying christological issues of the controversy that were at the very heart of passions in the East. The *Libri Carolini* see some difference between icons of Christ and of the saints, as we noted; but the reasons for the special treatment of Christ are not fully thought through. The older polemic against the icon of Christ (Eusebius, Epiphanius) argued from a somewhat docetic position for the impossibility of painting the form of a Christ who was risen and glorified. The iconoclastic emperors argued a similar case—but after the christological struggles of the fifth century. Claiming orthodoxy for themselves, they started with the hypostatic union. But they saw the union as so firm that the human aspect of Christ cannot be isolated and painted. One may call this a somewhat "monophysitic" perspective. The iconoclasts, of course, would object. Indeed, the *Horos* of 754 tried to place the iconodules under the double jeopardy of christological heresy: those who want to depict the entire Christ become monophysites; those who want to depict just the human nature are on the way to Nestorianism. Nicaea II also started with

the hypostatic union. From the standpoint of its theology, it is this very model that cries for the icon. Christ is the image of the Father; humans are made in his image. In the hierarchy of being it is the very honor of the prototype to be capable of descending into the image. The incarnation of the Word, the deity becoming fully human, is only complete when we in our human flesh are enabled to grasp our salvation by beholding the image of his humanity in the lowly icon. Christ's humanness can, even must, become material icon because the hypostatic union includes rather than excludes it.

(4) In other words: what is missing is a serious consideration of the incarnation and its consequences. The cross is present in the *Libri Carolini*, but its interpretation stresses it as the sign of triumph. Where is the humiliation, the humanness of the cross? Where is the incarnation? And what "really" happened there? For the iconodules it was not only the humiliation of the deity into the flesh. They argued that after the incarnation, through Christ's taking upon himself our humanity, this lowly nature of ours, even the entire creation, is hallowed, redeemed. With the incarnation everything is changed and has become new—even history, logic, and the old meaning of Scripture. In a redeemed world, in the Christian era, the command of Exodus 20 not to make images has lost its old absolute validity. Even this material world can now be seen as "holy" and can provide the starting point for our journey home. Iconophobia reveals a lack of appreciation for the new world God has created in the coming of Jesus Christ in the flesh.

GEORGE TAVARD, A. A.

6

John Duns Scotus and the Immaculate Conception

There have been two main theological approaches to the question of the Immaculate Conception of the Mother of God. The older approach found in the patristic and medieval periods lasted until, and included, Thomas Aquinas. A new approach was attempted at the end of the thirteenth century. It was widely, though not totally, accepted at the end of the Middle Ages and in the Counter-Reformation. It prevailed in Roman Catholicism during the nineteenth century. The major difference between the two approaches hinged around the problem of Mary's conception. From the patristic tradition of both East and West the church had inherited a piety that considered the Mother of God all-holy and all-pure. Following Saint Augustine (*De Natura et gratia*, ch. 36), the theologians usually exempted the Virgin Mary from consideration when they studied original sin and its consequences. But such questions as whether the *Theotokos* was subject to original sin for any length of time after her conception, whether she was born in sin, or how she was made all-holy by the grace of God could not be postponed indefinitely, even when this was done out of reverence for the Mother of God. The occasion that brought such questions to the fore was liturgical.

The Feast of Mary's Conception

Since the middle of the sixth century there was in the East a Marian celebration on December 9. This feast honored an apocryphal story contained in the *Protevangelium of James*: an angel announced to

Mary's parents, who were sterile, the conception of their child. Nuances in understanding this feast made it a feast of Saint Ann when the stress was on the "active" role of Ann in the conception of her daughter, or a feast of the Virgin Mary when the stress was on the "passive" role of Mary. In the East this celebration was never associated with the suggestion that Mary could have been conceived without original sin.

It was the gradual spread of a similar feast in the West that brought up Mary's conception as a theological problem. The traditional Western feasts of Mary were the Annunciation, the Nativity, the Presentation, and the Assumption. Around 850, however, a feast of the *Conceptio sanctae Mariae Virginis* was introduced in Naples, under Oriental influence, since much of southern Italy practiced the Byzantine liturgy. Mention of this feast is made in Ireland during the ninth or tenth century (*Tallaght Martyrology*), though it is doubtful that it was actually celebrated in Ireland. In England, however, around 1030 the feast is celebrated on December 8 in the Benedictine abbeys of Old Minster and Newminster, both in Winchester. Whether the feast was borrowed from Naples or went back to the Greek archbishop of Canterbury, Theodore of Tarsis (669–90), is a matter of conjecture. In any case it spread through the eleventh century, chiefly under the influence of the abbeys. It inspired another legend: Helsin, abbot of Ramsay, would have been saved from shipwreck in exchange for the promise to promote the feast of Mary's Conception on December 8! And the legend in turn, when taken to be history, provided an argument in favor of the feast. The *Leofric Missal* (given by Leofric, bishop of Exeter from 1050 to 1075, to his cathedral) contains three liturgical prayers for the feast.

When the feast of Mary's Conception was adopted by the chapter of the cathedral of Lyon in France, Saint Bernard of Clairveaux (c. 1090–1153) protested. Liturgical feasts, Bernard taught, should celebrate the grace of God as it is given to a human person for sanctification. But like everyone else besides her son Jesus, Mary was conceived in original sin, even though she was soon purged from it and shielded from its consequence, the tendency to sin (*fomes peccati*). The objection was based on the universality of sin and of the need for redemption by Christ, as attested in the Epistle to the Romans: "It was through one man that sin entered the world, and through sin death, and thus death pervaded the whole human race, inasmuch as all have sinned" (Rom 5:12).

This criticism indicated the direction to follow if the feast of the Conception of Mary was to be maintained: one should look for a way to show that Mary was in fact not conceived in original sin. Seen in the Western problematic, the feast of Mary's Conception thus implicitly raised the question of the Immaculate Conception. But the challenge was not immediately picked up. In England Lanfranc of Canterbury and Alexander Neckam, abbot of Cirencester, opposed the feast. But the theologians who supported the feast were more numerous: Eadmer of Canterbury, Osberto de Clara, Nicolaus Magister, Peter Abelard, Pseudo-Peter Comestor, Anselm the Younger (a nephew of Saint Anselm), and the anonymous authors of three manuscripts that are preserved in Austria.[1] Yet they offered no theological argument to support the celebration. No one among them was bold enough to affirm that Mary was conceived without original sin. The claim would not be made before the last decades of the thirteenth century. For no one could see how the universal need for a Redeemer and the holiness of Mary's Conception were compatible. Yet medieval theologians were universally devoted to the Virgin Mary in their liturgical and, presumably, their personal piety. They generally taught that the Virgin was sanctified by divine grace in her mother's womb shortly after her conception. This was precisely the reason why the feast of Mary's Nativity was theologically justified and that of her Conception unacceptable. The basic position of Saint Bernard was supported by the great Dominicans, Albertus Magnus and Thomas Aquinas,[2] and by the first Franciscan theologians, including Bonaventure.

The Franciscan Tradition

The main argument in favor of the Immaculate Conception was eventually formulated in the Franciscan order. Saint Francis of Assisi (1181/82–1226) had a warm devotion to the Virgin, and he spoke of her in poetic or lyrical terms.[3] This type of piety remained among Franciscan theologians. On the one hand, Saint Bonaventure (1217/18–1274) asserts with Saint Bernard that Mary was conceived in sin. Yet he is willing to tolerate the celebration of her Conception on the basis of the Helsin legend. And his sermons abound in what he calls "metaphorical similitudes." While his Scholastic conclusions are reached through rigorous reasoning, his oratorical similes come from his pious imagination. Mary is then "the Empress of every creature," "the Queen of Heaven," "the Star of the Sea," the "third Paraclete."[4]

In the Franciscan friaries Bonaventure's rhetoric was added to the example of Francis. John Duns Scotus was heir to both.

THE OPINION OF HENRY OF GHENT (HENRICUS GANDAVENSIS, DIED 1293)

Between the theory of Mary's prenatal sanctification as defended by Thomas Aquinas and by Bonaventure and the theology of Mary's conception that was later proposed by John Duns Scotus, the theology of Henry of Ghent ought to be mentioned, be it only because Scotus's survey of the question gives it special prominence, both in *Opus Oxonense* and in *Reportatio Parisiensis*.[5] Henry discussed the question in his *Quodlibeta*.

"One doctor says that at the same instant she was in sin and in grace" (*Rep. Par.*). This is Scotus's summary of Henry's position. At first hearing it sounds very much like Martin Luther's *simul justus et peccator*. In reality Henry is far from Luther. He is not at this point analyzing Christian life in general. He is referring only to the first instant of Mary's existence. This instant bears what Henry calls "two signs." When (this example is taken from Aristotle) a bean is thrown against a millstone, the instant when it hits the stone is also that when it jumps back from the stone. In such an instant there are an arrival sign (*signum*) and a departure sign. Likewise, in Mary's conception the instant of being conceived in sin by her parents is concretely identical with that of receiving sanctifying grace from God. Yet these two events in one instant are as conceptually distinct as sign one is from sign two (or, as one might put it today, as [-] is from [+]). After this first instant of her conception, Mary is not in sin. She is only in grace. She received the sign of sin from her parents as these transmitted the cause of original sin to her body. But as God created her soul at the same moment, he also gave it the sign of grace.

SCOTUS'S CRITIQUE OF HENRY OF GHENT

John Duns Scotus rejects Henry's opinion on the basis of a philosophical principle that was universally accepted among the Scholastics: two contraries cannot coexist in one place.[6] The principle of the noncoincidence of contraries is a form of Aristotle's principle of noncontradiction or, said positively, of the principle of identity. Henry's explanation, Scotus objects, is not compatible with "the first principle" because it "posits true contraries together in one instant." The true contraries in question are sinfulness and sinlessness.

Scotus also objects that the initial formation of the body is necessarily a motion (*motus*). And since a motion or movement implies succession and duration, it takes time. The gift of grace, on the contrary, is not a motion, but a change (*mutatio*). As such, it is instantaneous. In Mary's conception, however, God's gift of sanctification is neither a pure motion nor a pure mutation. Rather, it partakes of both. This gift, actively given, is her sanctification. As passively received by her, it is her justification. This *justificatio-passio* has something of a mutation in that it is given as a "simple and indivisible form" that is necessarily instantaneous. Yet it has something of a motion in that it is not given "in an indivisible moment, but in time" (*Op. Ox.*). But if there is both instantaneity and duration in Mary's purification in the womb, then this purification cannot coincide with the first moment of her existence.

Scotus's Critique of the Common Opinion

Scotus continues with a critical exposé of what was the common opinion: the Virgin was conceived in original sin, but sanctified in the womb. The main argument in support of the common view is taken from the universality of redemption: an exception in favor of Mary would detract from the universality of redemption and thereby from the nobility of her son. Scotus, however, marshals up to four reasons against this argument:

First, the dialectic may be reversed.

> From the fact that the Son of God was the universal Redeemer it follows that he was a perfect Mediator, and therefore that he used the most perfect mode of redemption that he could use for the most excellent person who was under him. But the most perfect act [of mediation] preserves from all sin, since no one perfectly intervenes for another unless the offense is prevented when this is possible. . . . Therefore, if Christ is a perfect Mediator, he prevented all offense in his Mother.

Second, a perfect Mediator "should prevent all pain" and hence all guilt, "for guilt is the greatest pain."

Third, a perfect Mediator prevents all actual sin, as "all concede concerning the Virgin Mary"; but universal redemption deals more immediately with original sin than with actual sin; therefore it "more perfectly and more immediately prevents original sin than actual sin."

Fourth, mediation creates an obligation in its beneficiaries. The more perfect the redemption, the greater the obligation. But it is greater to preserve someone from committing sin than to purify from sin committed. "Therefore, if the Mother was to be supremely obligated to her Son, the Son had to prevent her from all original sin."

A second argument in favor of the common opinion is taken from the propagation of original sin through the process of generation, which is "the cause of original sin in the natural descendants of Adam." Mary, being such a "natural daughter," must have inherited the same sin. Yet this, for Scotus, proves nothing. For "the infection of sin is not a necessary cause of original sin." This is illustrated by the fact that the infection remains after baptism, when original sin has been erased. "Notwithstanding that the flesh thus inseminated can be a cause of original sin, it is not a necessary cause." In other words, exceptions to the common consequence of generation are possible.

THE SCOTIST ALTERNATIVE

After presenting these arguments pro and con, Scotus proposes an alternative, with the noncommittal formula, *Potest dici aliter*.

In the first place, "all the descendants of Adam have a sufficient cause of original sin if nature is left to itself." In the second, "this does not prevent the divine power from causing the contrary in Mary's soul." Thus one may think that Mary "has a sufficient cause of original sin," yet without its effects. What God can do in the second instant of her existence (as in some form of the common opinion), he can do just as well in the first. In so doing, God does more for Mary than for any other of those who are saved:

> Mary needed redemption more than anyone else, because the greater the redemption she needed, the greater the good that was bestowed on her after her redemption. But perfect innocence is a greater good than forgiven sin.

Accordingly, "a greater good was granted her by preserving her from original sin than if she had been purified later." That Christ had not yet died for sin when she was conceived is not a valid objection, since "Abraham was purified of original sin—that he had—by virtue of the foreseen merits of Christ," and "the gate was opened to many by virtue of the foreseen passion." The entire Old Testament implicitly testifies that anticipation of Christ's redemption has been a common occurrence.

One may further argue against Scotus's proposal that "in the first instant of her nature" Mary was "a natural daughter of Adam," namely, that she was deprived of original justice. Here, Duns Scotus replies that "the first instant of nature" is logically anterior to both justice and injustice. From her "not being just" in the first instant, it does not follow that Mary was unjust. The only thing one may affirm with certainty is: "In the first instant one understands what is, namely, that the soul is only soul."

Up to this point Scotus has based his arguments for an immaculate conception of Mary (though not called this by him) primarily on belief in God's sovereign power, and secondarily on the possibility that redemption may have taken a special form in Mary's case, the merits of the passion of Christ being anticipated by divine decree. The second perspective flows from the former. The focus of the argument has been on possibility, not on actuality or factuality. All that has been said is that a preventive exemption from original sin was possible. To argue further along the line of *potuit, decuit, fecit* is not Scotus's way.[7]

Yet the question of fact is faced squarely. Scotus asks, "Quid ergo tenendum in questione?" "I affirm nothing," he replies, "yet it could be that. . . ." In fact, three options are listed by him as acceptable: (1) the Virgin could have been in original sin for one instant and then immediately restored to grace (the common opinion); (2) she could have remained for some time in original sin, and then placed in grace before she was born; or (3) "it could have been that she was never in original sin." The first case is possible by virtue of the divine power, since it implies no contradiction. But if the first case is possible, so is the second. As to the third—"that it could have been that guilt was never in her"—it is "patent as proven by the previous reasons."

Did John Duns Scotus fully endorse as a fact the theoretical option that he proposed and defended? His formulas so far seem noncommittal. In a later passage of the *Opus Oxonense,* however, one finds the following remark:

> There is also [in heaven] the most blessed Mother of God, who was never an enemy [of God], either actually on account of actual

> sin, or originally on account of original sin. But she would have been, had she not been prevented.[8]

Strictly speaking, this is not an endorsement of what was later called "the Scotist opinion." For if Mary was exempted from original sin immediately after contracting it, she had no time actually to be made "an enemy of God" by Adam's sin.

Outcome

When it arose, the question of Mary's Conception was focused on whether it should be celebrated liturgically. Later, attention shifted to the moment when Mary was sanctified by the Holy Spirit. With the great Scholastics the debate bore on the principle of Mary's exemption or nonexemption from original sin. At the University of Oxford where John Duns Scotus lectured in 1300-1302, the question of Mary's Conception was somewhat different still. Among the masters whom Duns Scotus could have known directly, Thomas de Sutton, a Dominican, defended the opinion that the Virgin Mary remained for some time—more than one instant—in original sin before being sanctified in the womb. Robert de Cowton, a Franciscan, argued for the possibility of sanctification at the second instant of her existence. Both opposed Henry of Ghent as well as Scotus's proposal regarding the Virgin's anticipated redemption.

The difference between Bonaventure and Duns Scotus does not derive only from their diverse settings. Both Cowton and Scotus, while not forgetting Scripture or the tradition, were eager to assess the extent of the power of God (*potentia Dei*) in the matter under study. The central question had become: What can God do or not do? Once it had been ascertained that God can indeed redeem the Virgin from original sin so that she would not contract it, the next question will logically be: Why should God not have done it? This query opened the gate to the broad acceptance of John Duns Scotus's alternative. Mary's devotees appealed to the principle of Saint Anselm (1033/34–1109): "It was proper (*decens*) that the Virgin should enjoy a purity than which, under God, none greater can be conceived,"[9] whence the axiom of Francis Mayro, a Franciscan (d. 1325), that was to become a powerful tool in mariological speculation: *potuit, decuit, fecit*.[10]

The most notable criticism of Duns Scotus's proposal came from Gregory of Rimini, an Augustinian (d. 1358): if it was more perfect for God to redeem the Virgin Mary in advance, it would have been still more perfect so to redeem all of humankind.[11] Gregory concluded that since God did not do the latter, neither did he do the former. The Franciscans generally defended the "maculist" theology of Saint Thomas, but with no new arguments.

Yet most of the Nominalist theologians, following William of Ockham (1290/1300–1349/50), eventually endorsed the Scotist idea. Given their major interest in the two orders of God's *potentia absoluta* and *potentia ordinata*, it was not difficult for them to assert that what God could do for Mary he did. Pierre d'Ailly (1369–1420) and Jean Gerson (1369–1429) supported this position. Alphonsus V (1416–58), king of Aragon, made it the official policy of Christian Spain to promote the definition of the Immaculate Conception of Mary. In 1435, at the conciliarist Council of Basel, Jean Roceti, a canon of Le Puy, asked for such a definition. In the absence of the papal legates, who had left Basel in 1437 for reasons that were unconnected with Mariology, the continuing Council of Basel on September 17, 1438, at its thirty-sixth session, solemnly proclaimed the Immaculate Conception of the Virgin Mary. The definition spoke of Mary's sanctification, of her fullness of grace, of God's "prevenient and operative grace," of Mary's honor, and of her son's honor. But it did not mention redemption or the foreseen merits of Christ. The formula of the definition remained independent of the Scotist argument.[12]

The decision was accepted for a time as a formal definition of faith in the areas that recognized the ecumenicity of the Council of Basel. But the whole Catholic Church eventually aligned itself with the bishops of Rome, who admitted the ecumenicity of the first twenty-two sessions only. In his *Tractatus de veritate conceptionis* Juan de Turrecremata (Torquemata) (1388–1468), a great papalist ecclesiologist, Master of the Sacred Palace, and himself a Franciscan, called the definition of the Immaculate Conception the "firstborn of the synagogue of Satan"!

CARL J. PETER

7

The Communion of Saints in the Final Days of the Council of Trent

Is it at best a matter of historical curiosity to ask how Roman Catholic teaching about the communion of saints came to be formulated? And even more to investigate what that teaching amounts to as proposed by the Council of Trent? Perhaps it has greater importance than such questions imply. At least a number of recent ecumenical developments suggest this by focusing attention on indulgences, purgatory, and the cult of the saints.

In the summer of 1986 the general convention of the Lutheran Church in America addressed itself to the statement *Justification by Faith* that had been issued three years earlier by the Lutheran–Roman Catholic dialogue in the United States. The text adopted by the convention notes that the dialogue laid claim to having reached a "fundamental consensus on the gospel." Reacting to that claim, the convention said this consensus needs to be tested further; the doctrine of justification as a criterion of authenticity must be applied to issues that divided Lutherans and Roman Catholics during the Reformation: e.g., *indulgences*, papacy, and *purgatory*.[1]

During the same summer of 1986 the statement *Justification by Faith* was the object of a report made by another church body, this time the Inter-Church Relations Committee of the American Lutheran Church. In its report to the church's general convention, the committee reached a conclusion about that statement: "sufficient clarity concerning the gospel is not present to affirm that there is consensus in the gospel." Before this the committee had referred to "the proof of the pudding" and asked various questions clearly intended to serve as test cases. One of those questions was: "But what happens when justification by faith is applied to *purgatory*, the papacy, and *the cult of the saints*?"[2]

Later Pope John Paul II invited Roman Catholics to celebrate a Marian Year beginning on Pentecost 1987. Harding Meyer has reflected on the ecumenical implications of that celebration. In so doing he calls attention to the linking of Mary, the church, and Christ. For him this means that the issue of the church's cooperation and instrumentality in the salvation event has come center stage.[3] The saints and this time Mary especially—once again!

Thus retrieving the past may be part and parcel of ecumenical responsibilities in the present. And in this case that means not only trying to grasp the meaning of Tridentine teaching on the communion of saints but inevitably considering the state of the Council of Trent in 1560.

Historical Background

A new pope had been elected in December of 1559, the third to hold office in a little over five years. After an election resulting from a conclave that lasted almost four months, Cardinal Giovanni Angelo Medici of Milan became Pope Pius IV and had to face up to the problem of an unfinished Council of Trent.

Luther had called for a council on November 28, 1518. That of Trent met for the first time on December 13, 1545, during the pontificate of Paul III. Given the threat of typhus, this assembly later voted in its eighth session on March 11, 1547, to move to Bologna. The majority favored the transfer, but a strong minority opposed it. The emperor, Charles V, wanted the Council to remain in Trent, which in fact the minority never left. France approved the change—a point that will be important later. For his part Paul III allowed the Council at Bologna to discuss issues but not to publish any decrees. An impasse resulted and allowed imperial consideration of having the minority at Trent become the Council. Sensing the possibility of schism, Paul III reacted by decreeing the suspension of the discussions at Bologna in February of 1548. The Council was to defend the legality of the transfer before a tribunal in Rome. The minority at Trent was also given the opportunity to send a representative group to Rome but did not do so. The issue was not resolved when Paul III died on November 10, 1549.

The new pope, Julius III, had been Council President (Cardinal Del Monte) when the assembly voted to move to Bologna. After his election he nevertheless agreed to the return of the Council to Trent, where it reopened on May 1, 1551. Having recognized the transfer to Bologna, France did not participate in this second set of deliberations at Trent. When the tides of war turned against Charles V (he would be forced to flee from Innsbruck), the Council voted to adjourn indefinitely in its sixteenth session on April 28, 1552.

Less than eight years and all of two popes (though one held office for less than a month) later, Pius IV had an unfinished Council of Trent as a specter staring him in the face. His predecessor, Paul IV (1555–59), had resolved to reform the church without a Council. But his efforts had clearly failed. And in the meanwhile the Religious Peace of 1555 recognized the Augsburg Confession as legal in the empire. The great plan of Charles V had not worked out: to conquer the Lutherans on the battlefield and then require them to attend the Council. When he was winning, the majority of the Council had moved to Bologna; to expect the Lutherans to go there was out of the question. When the council was back in Trent, Charles was no longer in control of the situation militarily.

Should Pius IV try again? After all, none of the doctrinal decrees (including the one on justification) that the Council had adopted under Paul III and Julius III had as yet received papal approval. And the reform decrees had made little impact on the life of the church. Fear of conciliarism held Pius back, but events over which he had no direct control pressed him on to action.

Another Medici—unrelated, in France, and Catherine by name—was queen mother while her son Francis II was king at the age of fifteen. Though the administration of the realm had been delegated to the Catholic Guises, they were discredited after the Conspiracy of Amboise in March of 1560 and the vengeance dealt out to the conspirators. At this point Catherine assumed a new role. She summoned an Assembly of Notables at Fontainebleau. After convening in August of 1560, that Assembly resolved upon: (1) a convocation of the Estates General for December; and (b) in default of a general council an Assembly of Prelates for January of 1561.[4]

The reaction of the pope is described as follows by Hubert Jedin: "When the Imperial Diet of Nuremberg had, forty years before, announced a German National Council in Speyer, Emperor Charles V had forbidden this. Now, however, the pope himself had to act."[5] Pius summoned a general council to meet in Trent on April 6, 1561.

A New Council or the Old One Reconvened?

In 1556 Charles V had resigned the imperial throne in favor of his brother. The new emperor, Ferdinand, had cause to worry. First, Catholics had become weaker when the empire was divided with Philip II as King of Spain. Second, the Lutherans objected to Trent as a locus for the Council and rejected what had already been approved there in their absence after they declined the invitation to attend. As a result, Ferdinand was in favor of starting *ab ovo* with a new Council. For its part, France contested the legitimacy of all the sessions held at Trent under Julius III after the Bologna episode. Thus the emperor had France as an ally on this issue. But Philip II insisted that the assembly at Trent must be a continuation of the Council that had met there earlier. Indeed, he wanted the new gathering to give explicit approval to all the decrees that had been passed in earlier sessions. In this he was destined to win out, for that is exactly what the Council did in its final session.

Here was the problem. The major Catholic powers were in disagreement as to whether the Council should be a new one or a continuation of the one that had been suspended in 1552. Obviously what was at stake was more than a matter of juridical niceties.

In the bull of convocation Pius IV spoke of what he was doing as the act of indiction (*indicimus*) or determining that the Council was to meet within a certain period of time. This seemed to favor the wishes of the emperor. But the text also contained an ablative absolute (*sublata qualibet suspensione*) indicating that any prior suspension of the Council had ceased. This inclined toward the position of the "Catholic King." As might be expected and was in all likelihood foreseen, this pleased nobody fully but provided time for the process of persuasion and other events to take their course.

With this issue unresolved and after being delayed, the Council finally opened on January 18, 1562, when 109 cardinals and bishops, four abbots, and four generals of orders were in attendance. Whatever opinions have been since then, the numbers impressed Cardinal Seripando, who said that in comparison with this, the opening session of 1545 was like that of a diocesan synod.[6]

The emperor appointed three envoys, who arrived not long after the Council opened. What was most impressive about Spain was its representation by bishops who would prove to be perhaps the most important group in the assembly.[7] As one author has put it, the "orthodox and austere Spaniards would now present the Pope and his legates with their severest problems."[8] With their theological expertise and integrity, those Spaniards would prove to be a very great threat when they resisted the closing of the Council almost to the end. After all, they just might remain behind after the others left Trent, as another minority had done earlier![9]

As for France, Catherine was now acting as queen regent for her second son, who at the age of ten became King Charles IX after the death of his older brother in December of 1560. She was disillusioned as a result of the failure of the religious colloquies that had been sponsored first at Poissy and later in the chateau of Saint Germain. After their discussions at the latter, Catholics and Calvinists remained unreconciled on the subject of sacred images. Shortly thereafter, in February of 1562, Catherine ordered her bishops to go to Trent. On November 13 the cardinal of Lorraine (Charles Guise) arrived there with twelve bishops, three abbots, and eighteen theologians. Could it be that one Medici viewed the Council as his last resort? Is it plausible that after the failure of the colloquies at Poissy and Saint Germain another saw it as hers too? In any event, the latter colloquy was destined to have an impact later: the formulation of the Tridentine decree about saints and their images was influenced by the majority opinion among the Catholics (who had been divided among themselves) at Saint Germain a year earlier.[10]

A Taking of Bearings

So far this essay has dealt with the beginning of the end of the Council of Trent. Now it must center in on the end to which that beginning led. For the communion of saints figured in decrees that were approved by the Council literally at the last moment.

A mere listing of the topics on which the Council was able to reach agreement between the beginning of its third period, on January 18, 1562, and its twenty-fourth session, on November 11 a year later, gives no idea of how difficult an accomplishment this was. Nonetheless such a list may have at least the value of showing how and why the communion of saints came to be addressed at all—this in the twenty-fifth and final session, which was held on December 3 and 4 in 1563.

In that third period the Council followed a procedure that had been adopted during its first period as a compromise. To avoid having to resolve the divisive issue as to which deserved priority, it dealt simultaneously with matters of belief and with measures to promote reform in the life of the church. Between January 18, 1562, and November 11, 1563, it produced doctrinal decrees dealing with: (a) Communion under Both Species and the Communion of children;[11] (b) the Sacrifice of the Mass;[12] (c) the Sacrament of Orders;[13] and (d) the Sacrament of Matrimony.[14]

During that same time span, reform decrees were approved. The one that caused the most serious and bitter debate, leading to a stalemate and the near collapse of the Council, dealt among other things with the obligation of bishops to reside in their sees.[15] Also deserving special mention are those decrees referring to the pope: (a) a decision about the reception of communion under both species, and (b) canons dealing with clandestine marriages—the celebrated *Tametsi*, requiring the presence of a priest and at least two witnesses for the validity of a Catholic's marriage.

Counting its two earlier periods at Trent, the Council had by November 11, 1563, dealt with the following matters of belief by issuing doctrinal decrees on each: (a) the biblical canon and tradition; (b) original sin; (c) justification; (d) the sacraments in general as well as baptism and confirmation in particular; (e) the Eucharist; (f) penance and extreme unction; (g) communion under both species as well as the communion of children; (h) the sacrifice of the Mass; (i) holy orders; and (j) matrimony. Thus by the second week of November in 1563 nothing had been said directly and in their own right about purgatory, the saints, and indulgences. To some, as will be seen, the doctrinal agenda appeared incomplete for that reason. Filling that lacuna would be one of the Council's tasks before it closed for the final time less than a month later.

But to round out the picture, something more must be said. Between its twenty-fourth session on November 11 and its close on December 4, the Council approved decrees dealing with: (a) purgatory together with the invocation, veneration, and relics of the saints as well as with sacred images; (b) reform of the religious life (monasteries, priories, convents, etc.) as well as a general reform of the church; (c) indulgences; (d) feast days and fasting; (e) the Index of Forbidden Books, Catechism, Missal, and Breviary; (f) the preservation of the *status quo* with regard to certain rights hitherto enjoyed by heads of state; (g) the reception and observance of the Council's own decrees; (h) provision for a formal rereading and approval of all the decrees previously adopted by the Council (with this Philip II would be satisfied and the *Placet* of France would be given to those passed under Julius III); and (i) a request in the name of the Council that all its decrees be approved by the legates and by the pope. Our concern here is with the decrees listed under (a) and (c) above.

Nature, Origin, and Content of the Decrees Dealing with the Communion of Saints

What was the genre of the decrees that Trent approved with regard to purgatory, the saints, and indulgences? How were those decrees formulated? And what do they say? Each of these questions will be dealt with in turn.

The Decrees' Literary Form

It will be recalled that the Council usually formulated its teaching in dogmatic or reform decrees. In this regard what it approved on December 3 and 4 in 1563 with regard to purgatory, the saints, and indulgences involved a departure from its previous practice. What Jedin says of the first two decrees (those dealing with purgatory as well as the saints and sacred images) is very much to the point. They contain only a brief summary of Catholic teaching and for the rest are directed to practice, more precisely, to a concisely articulated program of reform. The same description could be extended to the decree on indulgences. All three are instances of a hitherto undeveloped genre for the expression of the Council's meaning and intention.[16] Of itself this was enough to lead to considerable hesitation, and the fact that they were—when presented to the assembly on December 2—going to have to be treated in the greatest of haste only added to this.[17]

Before proceeding, it may be of some interest to note that the three decrees were formulated in this genre because of two processes working themselves out simultaneously. Among influential Council members there was a conviction that silence with regard to purgatory, the saints, and indulgences would be a bad mistake.[18] At the same time the desire was widespread (especially among the French but by no means restricted to them) to bring the Council to a close and return home.[19] It is not surprising that a somewhat novel literary form resulted in such circumstances.

For his part, Philip II is reported to have regarded treating this subject matter in what he apparently took to be the genre of reform decrees as *grande inconveniente*. The "Catholic King" did not think that was the way to deal with "canones de fé."[20]

As to the "quality" of the results that were achieved through the literary genre that was chosen, it is not easy to determine how satisfied the Council was. Sometimes assemblies, like the persons who constitute them, give free and informed consent to a test that they regard as true and likely to be helpful but which does not represent what they know to be the best possible treatment of the subject matter involved.[21] That seems to have been the case with the Tridentine decrees on purgatory, the saints, and indulgences. At any rate a remark made in the next century by Pietro Sforza (later Cardinal) Pallavicino, S.J., is worth recalling in this context. By appointment of his superior general he was writing a history of the Council of Trent in answer to an earlier one, that of Paolo Sarpi.[22] Noting that the decrees on purgatory, the saints, and indulgences were approved by the Council, Pallavicino adds:

> . . . even though the one dealing with purgatory appeared to some to be superficial and scarcely worthy of the Council. To this a reply was given, which came to this. In every great edifice there is a part that is imperfect. [In this case] precautions taken to prevent the evils that would result from delay [the final departure of the French before the Council's close?] make it excusable and even laudable to overlook the omission of some slight refinement.[23]

Origin and Approval of the Decrees

To this day it is still difficult to answer many questions about what was involved in putting together the three decrees with which we are presently concerned. As early as 1935 Hubert Jedin called attention to the sketchy character of the minutes recording the way in which the decree on the saints and veneration of images came to be formulated and approved by the Council. He was not questioning the accuracy but rather lamenting the brevity of the account given by the Council's secretary, Angelus Massarelli.[24] Later Jedin was able to rely on his own research of forty years and in 1975 gave details from which one can reconstruct the sequence of approval of all three decrees.[25]

On December 3, the first day of the Council's final session, the two decrees that dealt respectively with purgatory and as well as with the saints and veneration of images were approved by the Council. There were no negative votes. One bishop said that because of the lack of time provided, he could not offer a judgment of his own and preferred to leave the matter to the judgment of the pope and Apostolic See. A second voted *Placet* with regard to the truth of the decrees but *Non Placet* with regard to the haste surrounding their approval. All others voted *Placet*. Two hundred seventeen were present and voting. As to the thirteen French bishops who had already left the Council, they were represented by procurators.[26]

The third and final decree that is of interest in this essay dealt with indulgences. The final session of the Council took place on two successive days; December 3–4, 1563. But after the work of December 3 was finished, there was need for a break and other action before proceeding to that of December 4. The reason was simple enough. There were materials on which it was proposed that action be taken in the session but which had not yet been discussed in a general congregation of the Council. This involved a number of decrees.

Therefore a general congregation had to be held on the morning of December 4. Jedin rightly points to the irony of history involved here. Only that morning did a general congregation approve a decree dealing with the Roman Catholic Church's teaching and practice with regard to indulgences—a matter that in 1517 was the occasion of controversy leading to the division in Western Christianity.[27] In that general congregation the decrees in question were approved. Only with regard to the one dealing with indulgences was there any objection. As a result of interventions, a passage that would have excluded the Crusade collection on the occasion of preaching general or jubilee indulgences had been removed from the draft of the decree on indulgences; behind this lay an objection that had come from Spanish bishops.[28] After the general congregation and in the final session on December 4, it was just the opposite. The decree on indulgences was approved but with some conditioned affirmative votes seeking the restoration of the very thing that had been deleted that morning.[29] It was not the Council but a pope—Pius V—later in the century who would prohibit monetary offerings in connection with the gaining of indulgences.

It is true that the decrees on purgatory, the saints, and indulgences were approved by the Council on December 4. But as late as November 27 it was by no means determined that there would be any decrees at all on these subjects. What happened in the meanwhile were meetings, negotiations, and committee work.[30] But of what kind?

On the morning of November 28 Cardinal Guise went to the residence of the Cardinal President, Morone. Some French bishops had already left Trent because of religious troubles at home. Guise said that because of family obligations and political concerns, he had to be on his way by December 9. First, though, he wanted the Council to deal with purgatory and the veneration of images.

Morone knew full well that it would pose a great problem if France were not present when the Council did finally close. Given that the pope himself wanted closure on December 9, Morone was quick to act. He called a meeting of Council notables in his home that evening. The principals were represented. Guise repeated his desire and intentions. The Archbishop of Granada agreed to the scheduling of a session on December 9, but only on condition that there would be another within fifteen days to deal with matters in a less hectic fashion. With this the other Spaniards who were present (along with some of the Italians) agreed. The emperor's representatives said they thought it was important to treat indulgences but that if this could not be accomplished before Guise had to leave, they would approve the closure of the Council on December 9 without it. The others present went along with this.[31]

As a result, things started to happen. Three committees had been put to work earlier in November to deal with the remaining doctrinal issues. During the preceding summer, theologians had been appointed to study the three themes. But now a new deputation was set up to formulate decrees—this *de facto* under the leadership of Guise and even in his residence. Greater urgency was felt when during the night of November 30 word reached Trent that Pius IV was seriously ill and might die. On December 2 Morone reminded the members of the Council that if the pope died before they had concluded, all their work would be endangered and the likelihood of national councils was real.[32] The closing session was moved up to December 3-4 and was not put back again when later word reached Trent to the effect that the pope was out of danger.

The committee working with Guise produced the drafts of the decrees. In their work the members relied on the discussions of purgatory that had taken place at Bologna after the ill-fated transfer. For the text on the veneration of images they made use of a *sententia* (with modifications) that had been proposed by Catholics in connection with the colloquy at Saint Germain in 1562.[33] The discussions of indulgences that had taken place at Bologna did not prove to be of much assistance.[34]

It was in this way that decrees on purgatory, the saints, and indulgences came to the Council of Trent and were approved on December 3-4, 1563. The Spaniards voted for those decrees and dropped their opposition to the Council's closing. The lone holdout was Count Luna, the representative of Spain, who did not formally protest the closure because he had no explicit instructions from his sovereign to object.

Content of the Decrees

Three decrees from the Council of Trent concern us in this essay. They have to do with the communion of saints. Each will be considered in turn.

(1) Purgatory. The doctrine contained in the Tridentine decree on purgatory is to be found in an introductory subordinate clause that reads:

> Since the Catholic Church, instructed by the Holy Spirit, has taught—from the Sacred Scripture and the ancient patristic tradition—in sacred councils and most recently in this ecumenical synod that purgatory exists and that the souls detained there are helped by the suffrages of the faithful and most especially by the pleasing and acceptable (*acceptabili*) sacrifice of the altar. . . .[35]

The long periodic sentence then continues: "this sacred synod commands bishops to. . . ."[36] The teaching thus enunciated will be considered first and only then the mandate for reform.

It may be helpful to point out some things that are missing in this degree regarding purgatory. First, it is not in any way proposed that purgatory is a place. The adverb *ibi* (there) can refer to a state as well as to a place. What is most likely at work in this context is the memory that Eastern Christians had long objected to designating purgatory as a place. Second, there is reserve with regard to what purgatory amounts to; unless one takes the name itself as indicating more than a reference to a condition of need, this is clearly the case. One looks in vain for any mention of fire or duration. Third, no effort is made to deal with the "how" or the mode of efficacy (e.g., an exchange of merits) that is attributed to the prayers of the faithful and especially the Sacrifice of the Mass. Finally, the grounds of the conviction, thus succinctly expressed, are not specified any further than by reference to Scripture and the patristic tradition. As far as the teaching of the Council of Trent is concerned, it is an open question which scriptural texts and instances of patristic witness are more relevant in this regard.

Clearly the intention was: (a) to express the conviction of faith in an unmistakable but careful fashion; and (b) to draw on this conviction of faith to see what consequences should follow for the life of Roman Catholic Christians. Those consequences were then spelled out one after the other. It is, namely, sound doctrine about purgatory (that handed down by the Fathers and councils) that bishops are to promote vigorously. As for difficult questions on this matter as well as those that have little to do with edification and are for the most part not conducive to growth in piety among the faithful, they are to be kept out of ordinary preaching. Furthermore, ideas that are uncertain or may even be downright false are not to be circulated. That which has more to do with idle curiosity or even superstition and smacks of filthy lucre is to be prohibited as a scandal and offense to the faithful. Suffrages for the dead and obligations that have been assumed in this regard are to be carried out with piety and devotion according to the law of the church—this not perfunctorily but with care and concern for the wishes of the donors.[37]

Doctrinally this intentionally short formula manifestly rests on a conviction of faith that: (a) disciples may die neither so justified in Christ as to need no further forgiveness prior to eternal salvation in heaven nor so resistant to justification in Christ as to be unable to receive his forgiveness; and (b) the grace of the crucified and risen Christ empowers disciples yet living to pray hopefully and effectively for deceased disciples in such need. Hubert Jedin acknowledged this when he observed that this decree together with those on indulgences and the veneration of the saints form "a development of the article of faith" regarding "the communion of saints."[38]

(2) On the Invocation, Veneration, and Relics of the Saints as Well as on Sacred Images.[39] This decree, longer than the one on purgatory, figured very prominently in the discussions of the Lutheran–Catholic dialogue in the United States during the February meeting in 1986. At that time the author of this essay presented a summary of the decree's content to the members of the dialogue. The text was discussed, appropriately modified, and substantially incorporated into the common statement, *The One Mediator, the Saints, and Mary*, as §§32–37.

It will not be repeated here. But one point made in the original presentation and relevant to the dispute about invocation in the sixteenth century may be of ecumenical interest today.

In its decree Trent concerned itself with the position denying that saints are to be invoked. It connected that denial with four claims; namely, that the saints in heaven do not pray for human beings; that invoking them to pray for us as individuals is idolatry; that such invocation is at odds with God's word and with honoring the one Mediator, Jesus Christ; and that it is ignorant to beseech with voice and heart those who reign in heaven. That denial or those contentions it rejected as impious (*impie sentire*). It was silent about abstention from such invocation on other grounds.

For its part, the Second Vatican Council described as "supremely fitting" our invocation of the saints and in so doing referred to this Tridentine decree.[40] It made, however, no judgment about a position denying that saints should be invoked. At the same time it regarded their invocation as appropriate because every genuine testimony of love shown the saints in heaven of its nature reaches beyond them to Christ, the crown of the saints.

Both Trent in its decree and Vatican II in *Lumen Gentium* were concerned with the vital relation between Christ's disciples who are now in heaven and those who are still on earth. That concern came from shared faith in the communion of saints.

(3) Indulgences. As early as 1518 Luther and Cajetan had argued about the role of the saints and their merits in the church's bestowal of indulgences.[41] This did not resolve the dispute nor did the subsequent decree of Pope Leo X, which directed itself to the subject.[42] As was noted earlier, the discussion of indulgences by conciliar theologians at Bologna revealed too many unresolved issues for Trent in 1563 to derive much help from that source. Later Paolo Sarpi would give a whole list of such issues which had been cataloged by Morone, the Bishop of Modena, and which had allegedly led the latter to propose that Trent deal with indulgences without coming down on one side or the other in those disputes.[43]

With this in mind, one is in a better position to understand what the Council said and left unsaid in its decree. It taught that the power of conferring indulgences was both granted by Christ to the church and used by the church from the earliest days. That practice, approved by councils and salutary for the Christian people, is to be retained. On these grounds those who maintain that indulgences are useless or who deny the church the power to grant them are anathematized or excommunicated. At the same time moderation, as in the days of old, ought to characterize the church's use of indulgences; laxity enervates discipline. In this regard abuses have led to blasphemy on the part of heretics. For the most part it has been the profit motive that has led to those abuses; this avarice must be completely eliminated. But there are as well abuses resulting from superstition, ignorance, irreverence, and other sources. Because situations vary according to locale, each bishop is to make a list of abuses found in his diocese and report his findings at the first meeting of the synod for the province to which the diocese belongs. When the opinions of the other bishops at that synod have been heard, the abuses are to be brought to the attention of the pope. He in turn is to decide in prudence and with his authority—as the good of the universal church requires—what is to be done so as to insure that indulgences are dispensed to all the faithful with godliness, holiness, and without corruption.[44]

The Council read past practice and teaching regarding indulgences with a hermeneutic occasioned by pragmatic concerns, but combining trust in the church with suspicion mandating reform. That there were many theological issues which remained both unmentioned and unresolved resulted from a conscious and deliberate choice.

And Then What? Some Later Developments

Texts have a future as well as a present and past; sometimes that future involves efforts to interpret those texts. Both are true of the Tridentine decrees with which this essay has been concerned.

On an issue, for example, where Trent was reticent about purgatory, a contemporary scholar has spoken. In a very important book Jacques Le Goff maintains that: (a) at some point the souls in purgatory came to be thought of as having the power to transfer their merits to the living; and (b) this reversibility of merits eventually won a place in doctrine.[45] That the souls in purgatory can help the faithful on earth did become a conviction operative in the piety of many Catholics. But that it became a point of doctrine is simply not true. Nothing of the kind appears in the Tridentine decree. And when asked to deal in the seventh chapter of *Lumen Gentium* with aid sought by the living from those in purgatory, the Doctrinal Commission of the Second Vatican Council decided not to act on the request. The reason they gave was desire to avoid giving the impression of resolving an issue freely disputed among theologians.[46]

As to the Tridentine decree on the saints and their images, the Second Vatican Council put it into a broader historical context and thereby interpreted it. In *Lumen Gentium* the Council sought precedents as it expressed its faith regarding the vital union which because of Jesus Christ exists between his living and deceased disciples. In so doing it proposed again the decrees of the Second Council of Nicaea, Florence, and Trent[47] and thus once more the communion of saints.

Finally, a project discussed by the Second Vatican Council was left for Pope Paul VI to finish. He did this in his apostolic constitution *Indulgentiarum Doctrina*. There he commended the traditional practice of the church as he dealt with indulgences. But he added to this significantly when he wrote: "Nevertheless the church allows each member to make use of this kind of means of purification and sanctification in the holy and just liberty of God's children."[48]

In the same document he described the treasury (*thesaurus*) on which the church relies in granting indulgences. He interpreted that treasury as being "Christ himself" but as including in God's eyes the value of the prayers and good works of Mary and the saints who followed in Christ's footsteps by his grace.[49] Responses are thus offered to questions left unanswered in Trent's decree.

In this ecumenical age it is up to the sons and daughters of the Reformation to decide whether these developments, which presuppose but are not reducible to the three Tridentine decrees dealt within this essay, help, hurt, or leave matters unchanged. In this process a background essay on the communion of saints in the teaching of the Council of Trent may be of some assistance.

E R I C W. G R I T S C H

8

The Views of Luther and Lutheranism on the Veneration of Mary

Martin Luther

Luther's view of Mary evolved in the context of his work as a biblical theologian who encountered the intense late medieval cult of the saints and Mary. Throughout his career as a priest-professor-reformer, Luther preached, taught, and argued about the veneration of Mary with a verbosity that ranged from childlike piety to sophisticated polemics.[1] His views are intimately linked to his christocentric theology and its consequences for liturgy and piety.

Early Years to 1521

The young Luther was nurtured in a spiritual environment that stressed the cult of Mary either in personal piety or in liturgical celebration. Thus it is not surprising that the twenty-year-old law student cried out, "Mary, help!" when, on his way from Erfurt to Mansfeld in 1503, he fell and cut an artery in his leg with his dagger.[2] Two years later, when frightened by a storm, he again cried out, "Help, St. Anna! I will become a monk!"[3] Luther confessed that Saint Anna was his idol;[4] she was the patron saint of miners, and Luther's father mined copper in Eisleben.

In Saxony, where Duke George had ordered the veneration of Saint Anna, Mary's mother, the cult of Saint Anna had become quite popular. Elector Frederick "the Wise" claimed to possess Saint Anna's thumb as a part of his extensive collection of relics. In Erfurt, where Luther encountered the cult of Mary and Saint Anna, there was a group known as "servants of Mary" (*Marienknechte*) as well as a fraternity dedicated to Anna.

Marian devotions were intense at the monastery of the Augustinian monks in Erfurt. Some of the theologians there whom Luther revered, such as John of Paltz, based the assertion that Mary was Christ's co-redemptrix on the doctrine of Mary's Immaculate Conception.[5] John Gerson (1363–1429) had already argued that Mary's body was immaculate even before her soul was infused.[6] Luther was quite aware of these Marian reflections, but he placed Mary in a christocentric context in his early sermons and biblical commentaries, especially in his commentary on Psalms: she is the "blissful Mother" who is humble in the faith and shows the faithful what great things God can do.[7] He also warned against a too zealous veneration of Mary at the expense of Christ.[8]

Luther intensified his criticism of the cult of Mary during the controversy over indulgences. Thesis 75 of the Ninety-five Theses was directed against John Tetzel's claim that papal indulgences could absolve a man even if he had done what seemed impossible, namely, rape the Mother of God.[9] To Luther's surprise, his Catholic opponents defended Tetzel and argued that an indulgence could indeed forgive such a sin as the sexual violation of Mary.[10] Luther consequently set out to protect her title of "Mother of God" (literally "Bearer of God") from any notion that Christ needs her as co-redemptrix to save humankind.[11]

The Magnificat (Luke 1:46-55) of 1521

This is the centerpiece of Luther's Marian views.[12] He completed the exposition during his exile at the Wartburg and dedicated it to young Duke John Frederick of Saxony, who, unlike his uncle Frederick "the Wise," openly supported Luther's cause. To Luther the theme of the canticle was quite clear: Mary is the embodiment of God's unmerited grace, and in her are contrasted true humility and the arrogance of worldly power.

a. Mary is the prototype of how God is to be "magnified." He is not to be "magnified" or praised for his distant, unchangeable majesty, but for his unconditional, graceful, and ever-loving pursuit of his creatures. Thus Mary magnifies God for what he does rather than magnifying herself for what was done to her. "She finds herself the Mother of God, exalted above all mortals, and still remains so simple and so calm that she does not think of any poor serving maid as beneath her."[13] This is truly "humility" (*humilitas*), "lowliness" (*Niedrigkeit*), indeed "nothingness" (*Nichtigkeit*).

b. "Being regarded by God" is the truly blessed state of Mary. She is the embodiment of God's grace, by which others can see what kind of God the Father of Jesus Christ is. This is Luther's interpretation of verse 48b, "All generations will call me blessed." She does not say, Luther contends, that people will call her blessed because of her virtue, her virginity, or her humility. Rather, she is blessed by the fact that God regarded her. "Not *she* is praised thereby, but God's grace toward her."[14]

c. Mary is a model for theologians who need to properly distinguish between human and divine works. "She divides all the world into two parts and assigns to each side three works and three classes of men, so that either side has its exact counterpart to the other."[15] Like Jeremiah (9:23, 24), Mary sees wisdom, might, and riches on one side and kindness, justice, and righteousness on the other. The former reflect human works, the latter the works of God. God uses his works to put down the works of men, who are always tempted to deify themselves. God's works are "mercy" (v. 50), "breaking spiritual pride" (v. 51), "putting down the mighty" (v. 52), "exalting the lowly" (v. 53), "filling the hungry with good things," and "sending the rich away empty" (v. 53).

d. Mary is the "Mother of God" who experienced his unmerited grace. Her personal experience of this grace is an example for all humankind that the mighty God cares for the lowly just as he cares for the exalted. That is God's work in history. Mary has no special qualifications for becoming the "Mother of God." The church, therefore, should not praise her for being worthy to bear the son of God. She was chosen because she was a woman, just as the wood was chosen to bear Jesus on the cross.[16] Thus she incites the faithful to trust in God's grace when they call on her. "She does nothing, God does all. We ought to call upon her, that for her sake God may grant and do what we request. Thus also all other saints are to be invoked (*anzurufen*), so that the work may be every way God's alone.[17]

From 1521 to Luther's Death in 1546

Luther's views on Mary after 1521 are not substantially different from those he presented in the Magnificat. He tolerated the "Hail Mary" in "A Personal Prayer Book" of 1522, which was to be an evangelical alternative to existing prayer books advocating the wrongful veneration of Mary as co-redemptrix. Luther urged people to understand this well-known addition to the Lord's Prayer "as a meditation in which we recite what God has given her" and as an admonition "that everyone may know and respect her as one blessed by God."[18] That is why the "Hail Mary," like the Lord's Prayer, is concerned "purely with giving praise and honor"; it is "neither a prayer nor an invocation" to Mary as the one who prays for us.[19] Instead, Mary should be regarded as being without sin, that is, as being "full of grace" (*voll Gnaden*) in the sense of being "graced" (*begnadet*);[20] all she did was done by God in her, that is, "God is with her"; "she is blessed above all other women" because she became fertile through the Holy Spirit, and through Christ's birth, not through her participation in it, humankind is redeemed from death and damnation. To bless her with rosaries and a constant mouthing of "Hail Mary" takes the honor away from Christ, who alone mediates salvation.[21]

In 1527 Luther dealt with the Immaculate Conception of Mary, advocating a middle position favored by a majority of theologians. Following Augustine, Luther told his congregation that Mary had been conceived in sin but had been purified by the infusion of her soul after conception. Her purification was complete due to a special intervention of the Holy Spirit, who preserved her from the taint of original sin in anticipation of the birth of Christ.

> Thus the Virgin Mary remains in the middle between Christ and humankind. For in the very moment when he was conceived and lived, he was full of grace. All other human beings are without grace, both in the first and second conception. But the Virgin Mary, though without grace in the first conception, was full of grace in the second. That is quite proper. For she was a medium between all generations: she was born from a father and mother, but gave birth without a father and mother, partly spiritually and partly bodily, because Christ was conceived of her flesh as well as of the Holy Spirit. But Christ himself is a father of many children, without a carnal father and mother. Just as the Virgin Mary remains in the middle between physical and spiritual birth, finishing the physical and beginning the spiritual, so she rightly remains in the middle concerning conception. Whereas other human beings are conceived in sin, in soul as well as in body, and Christ was conceived without sin in soul as well as in body, the Virgin Mary was conceived in body without grace but in soul full of grace.[22]

These and other statements concerning the Immaculate Conception of Mary are always made in the context of a christocentric theology which focused on the birth of Christ rather than that of Mary. She became immaculate as the mother of Christ. As Luther put it in 1540: "In his conception all of Mary's flesh and blood was purified so that nothing sinful remained. Thus Isaiah is correct in saying, 'There was no deceit in his mouth' [53:9]. Each seed was corrupt, except that of Mary."[23]

In the same vein, Luther also affirmed the traditional doctrine of Mary's perpetual virginity. She was a virgin before the birth of Christ (*ante partum*) and remained one at the birth (*in partu*) and after the birth (*post partum*).[24] She did not become a wife "in the usual sense."[25] When Scripture speaks of "brothers" of Jesus (John 2:12), what is meant is "cousins" because the Jews call cousins brothers. Luther, however, contended that none of this is important. "It neither adds nor detracts from faith. It is immaterial whether these men were Christ's cousins or his brothers begotten by Joseph."[26] Throughout Luther's career he nevertheless defended Mary's perpetual virginity, siding with Jerome, who had defended this opinion against Helvidius, a Roman layman (c. A.D. 385).[27] Luther saw Mary's perpetual virginity prophesied in the Old Testament (Isa 7:14: "a virgin shall conceive and bear a son, and shall call his name Immanuel."), and he promised one hundred gold pieces to anyone who could prove that the Hebrew *alma* meant "young woman" rather than "virgin."[28]

Luther's theological view of Mary also informed his liturgical reforms. He retained the use of the Magnificat in the Vespers, with the *tonus peregrinus* (pilgrim tone) as the most frequently used congregational setting. The Wittenberg Order of 1533 also stated that the German Magnificat is to be sung before a particular feast and after the sermon.[29] During and after the Reformation Lutheran composers created elaborate choir settings for this canticle.[30]

Although Luther incorporated his views on Mary into his hymns, only one of his hymns is dedicated to her: "To Me She's Dear, the Worthy Maid" (*Sie ist mir lieb die werte Magd*).[31] The hymn, perhaps composed in 1534, is based on Rev 12:1-6 (the woman and the dragon) and is subtitled, "A Hymn About the Christian Church, Based on the Twelfth Chapter of Revelation." Medieval exegetical tradition related "woman" to "church," and Luther may have followed this tradition. Other hymns mention Mary, but usually only in connection with the lordship of Christ. Luther's favorite and autobiographical hymn, "Dear Christians, One and All, Rejoice"

(*Nun freut euch liebe Christen gemein*; 1523), is typical: Mary is mentioned, but not praised, in the sixth stanza. "The Son he heard obediently/ And by a maiden mother/ Pure, tender—down He came to me/ For He would be my brother."[32]

Other hymns praise Mary's unique role in the incarnation: "Whom all the world could not enwrap/ Lieth He in Mary's lap" (*Den aller Welt Kreis nie beschloss/ der liegt in Marien Schoss*);[33] "Many a virtue from her shone/ God was there as on His throne" (*Leucht herfür manch Tugend schon/ Gott da war in seinem Thron*);[34] "From heaven high the godlike grace/ In the chaste mother found a place;/ A secret pledge a maiden bore—/Which nature never knew before" (*Die göttlich Gnad vom Himmel gross/ sich in die keusche Mutter goss/ ein Meidlein trug ein heimlich Pfand/ das der Natur war unbekannt*).[35] Thus Luther always mentioned Mary in the context of the christocentric theology that permeates the more than thirty hymns he composed for congregational singing.[36]

Luther was equally consistent in his view of artistic representations of Mary. There is evidence that he kept a painting of Mary with the baby Jesus in her arms in his study at the Black Cloister, though the painter is not known.[37] He opposed the iconoclasts, especially the radicals (*Bilderstürmer*) in his own camp, but he also opposed abuses in art. Some pictures, for example, exposed Mary's breasts, which, according to legend, had nurtured Bernard of Clairvaux. That goes too far, Luther declared. "I do not like Mary's breasts or milk, for she did not redeem or save me," he commented in 1537.[38]

Luther's christocentric theology also determined his view concerning the significance of the Marian festivals in the church year: Mary and her Magnificat should lead worshipers to give thanks, hear the gospel, and meditate on her as a model of faith. These norms guided him as to which festivals to keep.[39] He rejected the festivals of Mary's Immaculate Conception, December 8, and her Assumption, August 15. It is not quite clear which festivals he did favor, but in the sixteenth century most Lutheran territories celebrated the festivals of Purification (February 2), of Annunciation (March 25), and of Visitation (July 2).[40] Luther considered these festivals to be festivals of Christ also. Mary can be celebrated as the "Mother of God" precisely because Jesus is the son of God. But it is the son who gives her the honor she deserves. To Luther this was the unanimous testimony of the apostles and of the postapostolic creeds.

To conclude: to Luther Mary was the prime example of the faithful—a *typus ecclesiae* embodying unmerited grace. Mary is a paradigm for the indefectibility of the church.[41] But Mary is not the "mother of mercy" (*mater misericordiae*), interceding with God and Christ for humankind.[42] Luther defended Mary's perpetual virginity and regarded her Immaculate Conception as "a pious and pleasing thought" that should not, however, be imposed on the faithful.[43] In a similar vein Luther affirmed Mary's assumption into heaven but did not consider it to be of benefit to others or accomplished in any special way.[44] According to Luther Mary should be honored in festivals that focus on Christ, which is why he eventually rejected the celebrations of her Immaculate Conception (December 8), her birth (September 8), and her Assumption (August 15). He did honor her in the festivals of the Annunciation (March 25), the Visitation (July 2), and Purification (February 2), since these are connected with the birth of Christ.[45] "We dare not put our faith in the mother but only in the fact that the child was born."[46]

Lutheranism

The Lutheran Confessions of 1580

Philipp Melanchthon, the author of the Augsburg Confession of 1530, supported Luther's christocentric stance, grounded in the scriptural statement that Christ is the only Mediator between God and human beings (1 Tim 2:5).[47] He had encountered liturgical practices, particularly in formulas of absolution, that were based on the view that the invocation of Mary and the saints is a divinely instituted order.[48] He conceded that Mary prays for the church, but insisted that Christ's merit alone saves one from sin, and any transfer of saints' merits to sinners must be rejected and indeed considered pagan in origin.[49]

In the Smalcald Articles of 1537 Luther reaffirmed Mary's perpetual virginity, calling her "ever virgin" (*semper virgo*).[50] The Formula of Concord of 1577 repeated Mary's ancient ecumenical title "God-bearer" (*Theotokos*) and praised her as "the most blessed virgin" (*laudtissima virgo*).[51] The normative, Confessional Lutheran view of Mary, however, is linked to the perspective that saints in general are memorable examples for the faithful, who are called to serve their earthly neighbors in need.[52] The Lutheran Confessions exhibit frustration and anger over existing abuses in Marian devotions, which ranged from confusing Christ's merits with hers to granting her magical powers.[53] "Even though she is worthy of the highest honors, she does not wish to be put on the same level as Christ, but rather to have her example considered and followed."[54] Mary, therefore, is considered to be the foremost example of what it means to be a saint.

The Periods of Orthodoxy and Pietism (1580–1800)

Lutheran territories, largely created and protected by peace treaties (Augsburg [1555] and Westphalia [1648]), discouraged the veneration of Mary. Marian festivals were not celebrated, and, in reaction to a Catholic "counter-reformation," were regarded as an infiltration of the old undesirable religion. True, the mid-seventeenth century, with its bitter interconfessional polemics, saw the founding of a Lutheran order of sisters at Mount St. Mary in Helmstedt, Germany.[55] But Lutheran orthodoxy was generally guided by the judgment of Martin Chemnitz (1522–86), a well-known theologian, that neither Scripture nor tradition justified the invocation of Mary and the saints.[56] Johann Salomo Semler (1725–91) and other theologians with rationalistic leanings rejected any notion of Marian devotion, calling it Catholic superstition.[57]

The Lutheran pietistic movement, begun in Germany by Philip Jacob Spener (1635–1705) and propagated in Norway by Hans Nielsen Hauge (1771–1824), stressed individual piety, mission, and, to some extent, unity between the church militant and the church triumphant. But there was no interest in a veneration of Mary. Novalis (Friedrich von Hardenberg, 1772–1801), a German poet who had been a pietist in his youth but preferred a secularized romanticism, praised Mary as the symbol of eternal motherhood but made no reference to her place in the Christian tradition.[58]

From the Nineteenth Century to the Present

The 300th anniversary of Luther's Ninety-five Theses in 1817 precipitated a Lutheran revival that focused on the Lutheran Confessions and liturgy.[59] The revival was an attempt to overcome a bland territorial Lutheranism characterized by "unionism"—e.g., with Calvinism—and "rationalism," e.g., the Enlightenment. Typical were the efforts of August F. C. Vilmar (1800–68), a theologian, to reinstitute a true Lutheran territorial church in Hesse, with considerable success. The most influential Lutheran voice was Wilhelm Löhe (1808–72), pastor in Neuendettelsau, Bavaria, who stressed Marian reflections and piety in his work for a renewed Lutheran spirituality. He published a liturgical calendar that retained three Marian feasts (Annunciation, Visitation, and Purification) and included appropriate lessons and collects. Citing Luther, Löhe affirmed Mary's perpetual virginity, and he revived Lutheran interest in deceased saints as examples for the saints on earth.

This Confessional and liturgical revival received a second strong impetus in 1917, after the 400th anniversary of Luther's Ninety-five Theses. German pastors founded the "High Church Movement" (*Hochkirchliche Bewegung*) in 1918, which focused on liturgical renewal and on ecumenism. One of the strongest advocates of the movement was Friedrich Heiler (1892–1967), a professor of the history and philosophy of religion at Marburg University and a convert from Roman Catholicism. Heiler called for Marian devotion in Lutheran churches, although he had no sympathy for Marian dogma. He advocated making room for the commemoration of Mary in the eucharistic prayer in a Lutheran "German Mass": "Remembering our Dear Lady, the praiseworthy God-bearer and ever virgin servant Mary, together with all the saints, we dedicate ourselves to each other and to God for our entire life."[60] In the breviary published in 1932, vespers include a similar commemoration of Mary and the Magnificat. The liturgical calendar lists seven Marian feasts (Conception, Purification, Annunciation, Mother of Sorrows, Visitation, Dormition, Birth of the Virgin).

In 1931 a Lutheran "Brotherhood of Saint Michael"(*Evangelische Michaelsbrudershaft*) was established in Marburg, consisting of men who vowed mutual spiritual support and committed themselves to spiritual "retreats" that both clergy and laymen could attend. The commemoration of Mary as the foremost of all the saints is a part of the brotherhood's commitment to nurture "a connection with the world above." Some of the brotherhood's liturgical proposals, particularly celebrating the three biblical Marian feasts, have become part of the official Lutheran liturgy in Germany (since 1956).

Hans Asmussen (1898–1968), a prominent member of the "Confessing Church" (*Bekennende Kirche*) and the president of the Berlin Seminary (*Kirchliche Hochschule*) from 1935–41, paid particular attention to the veneration of Mary. He, Max Lackmann, and some others founded the ecumenical group called "the Gathering" (*Die Sammlung*) in 1954 (until 1963), which was dedicated to a "catholic" Lutheranism. Asmussen even argued, with little success, for a Lutheran Mariology: "As long as the veneration which we direct to the Lord Jesus Christ remains without the echo of the blessing granted by God to the Mother of Jesus Christ, we may have to live with the suspicion of not being serious in our attention to the one Mediator, Jesus Christ."[61] Klara Schlink, the sister of Edmund Schlink, a famous Lutheran theologian, founded a "Sisterhood of Mary" (*Marienschwesternschaft*) in Darmstadt. Known as "Mother Basilea," Sister Klara published several meditations on Mary.[62]

There is also the case of Richard Baumann, a Württemberg pastor and a student of Heiler, who favored papal authority in the Lutheran churches. He was suspended from the ministry in 1953 and converted to Roman Catholicism in 1982. His publications on Mary, filled with rhetoric referring to her as "the future," "the rescuer," and to "her hour," were not popular.[63] Another unpopular Lutheran Mariologist is Ulrich Wickert, professor at the Berlin Seminary, who has advocated a "mariocentric" view of salvation history: Mary stands at the confluence of God's saving activity; her assumption into heaven demonstrates the "integrative" moment in history which must be seen and understood from its goal (*telos*).[64]

The German Lutheran Marian devotion represents a parallel to the French community of Taizé, whose roots are Reformed rather than Lutheran. Influenced by, and contributing to the revival of Marian devotion, is Max Thurian—a Reformed theologian who converted to Roman Catholicism—who viewed Mary as the daughter of Zion and as the image of the church.[65]

Reaction to the Marian Dogmas

The dogmas of the Immaculate Conception of Mary (1854) and of her Assumption (1950) unleashed grave ecumenical concerns and some sharp polemics in Lutheranism.

The Immaculate Conception. Some critical Lutheran voices could be heard even before the dogma was promulgated. Ernst Wilhelm Hengstenberg, the editor of the *Evangelische Kirchenzeitung*, a popular conservative Prussian church paper, declared the dogma unscriptural[66] and expressed his gratitude to God that Lutherans had been mercifully snatched away from the bonds of Roman Catholicism.On December 8, 1854, the day the dogma was promulgated, Frederick William IV of Prussia set out to organize an international protest, to be led by continental Lutherans and to include the Church of England and other Protestant representatives. He failed because the parties could not come to an agreement.[67]

Popular Lutheran reactions were summarized in 1862 by Karl August von Hase, a theologian in Jena, in a *Handbook of Protestant*

Polemics Against the Roman Catholic Church.[68] Von Hase suggested that the reason Catholics had simply accepted the dogma was because they were indifferent to its theological details; ordinary Catholic folk would consider it just another recognition of Mary as the Virgin Mother of Jesus, and educated Catholics neither know nor think much about original sin and so Jesus' privilege of being conceived and born without sin is not at all incredible. According to von Hase the principal function of the dogma was to secure papal infallibility, although Pius IX had naïve and juvenile ideas concerning Mary when he issued the decree.

A massive attack against the 1854 dogma was launched by Eduard Preuss, an "orthodox" Lutheran theologian, in a 1865 tome entitled *The Roman Dogma of the Immaculate Conception, Presented on the Basis of the Sources and Refuted on the Basis of the Word of God.*[69] The book is written with pathos and is dedicated to "Jesus Christ, my Lord and my God." "God's wars have been and must be waged," Preuss stated in the Preface, "as long as the world endures. We, too, are obliged to draw our sword against the Roman error which is as alive today as is rationalism."[70] Preuss then offered a lengthy chapter on the dogma's history from the time of Mary to that of Pope Pius IX, testing his findings in light of "Scripture, the Fathers, and reason" and concluded that the dogma was "unapostolic" and indeed contrary to the principles of tradition as formulated by Vincent of Lerins. Although there was some Lutheran resistance to Preuss's fundamentalistic use of Reformation insights, his condemnation of Catholicism was widely shared. Konrad Martin, the Catholic bishop of Paderborn, was drawn into a literary debate with Preuss, but no change of mind on either side resulted.[71]

An exceptional reaction came in 1863 from W. O. Dietlein, a German Lutheran pastor, in a little book entitled *Ave Maria.*[72] He wanted to offer an alternative to the Protestant stance of "a continual flight from the Mother, anxious not to grant her even a word of the greeting, the Ave, which the eternal Father transmitted to her through the mouth of an angel."[73] But Dietlein had only faint praise for the dogma. He recognized in it a careful clarification (*Läuterung*) of theological opinions, but "the infallible decree is nothing less than an exaggerated opinion (*überspannte Meinung*) which goes beyond an appropriate veneration of Mary."[74]

After World War I some Lutheran theologians assessed the dogma in terms of its effect on the principles of *sola fides* and *solus Christus.* Walther von Loewenich's assessment is typical: the theological content of the dogma can be tolerated by Lutherans because

Mary's sinlessness "is derived from a special privilege of grace granted to her by God in respect to the merits of Christ." But Mariology is developing toward a doctrine of Mary as Mediatrix and Co-redemptrix, and that raises the question whether her merits are truly subordinated to the merits of Christ.[75] He repeated his views, though in a less pointed fashion, in his treatment of Mary in the American *Encyclopedia of the Lutheran Church*.[76]

Jaroslav Pelikan and Arthur Carl Piepkorn may well represent the reaction of contemporary ecumenically committed Lutherans toward this dogma. Pelikan viewed the dogma as the completion of "the chain of reasoning begun by the surmise that the sinlessness of Jesus . . . depends upon His being free of the taint that comes from having two parents. Now Mary may conceive immaculately because she herself has been conceived immaculately."[77] If, however, the veneration of Mary as the "mother of God" should lead to the view of her as "co-redemptress of Christ," as the Marian cult tends to assume, according to Pelikan, an old ecumenical temptation threatens the center of the Christian faith. "The dogma of the Catholic church has always run the danger of glorifying Christ so much that it cut Him off from the humanity He was to save. Now the dogma of the Roman Catholic Church is running a similar danger in its Mariology."[78]

Piepkorn believed that there is a significant convergence on the matter of Mary's Immaculate Conception between classical Lutheranism (as represented by such seventeenth-century theologians as Martin Chemnitz and John Gerhard) and Catholicism.[79] But any dialogue about it and other mariological assertions "would require Roman Catholic partners who realize that an appeal to the authority of the Roman Catholic Church or of the bishop of Rome to define doctrine would carry little weight, and that in consequence the dialogue would have to be on the basis that both partners could accept the Sacred Scriptures as the primitive Church understood them."[80]

The Assumption. Lutheran reactions to this dogma range from solemn protests by church authorities representing national churches to theological repudiation by groups of theologians and individual scholars.[81]

Even before the promulgation of the dogma on November 1, 1950, an official "Opinion" (*Gutachten*) had appeared in print (in July) in the name of the Heidelberg Evangelical Theological Faculty. It was drafted by Edmund Schlink with the assistance of Günther

Bornkamm, a New Testament scholar, Hans Freiherr von Campenhausen, a church historian, and Peter Brunner and Wilfried Joest, systematic theologians.[82] Bishop Stählin transmitted it to Rome, but it seems to have arrived too late to influence Pope Pius XII. The "Opinion" spelled out "serious misgivings" (*schwere Bedenken*) about the dogmatization of the Assumption of Mary: it had no biblical evidence, it obscured the incarnation of Christ, and it caused painful ecumenical estrangement. In short, Rome was promulgating "the dogmatization of a myth lacking historical foundation."[83]

Church leaders and prominent members of the ecumenical movement launched solemn protests shortly after the promulgation of the new dogma. German bishops issued a pastoral letter,[84] and similar protests were made by the Swedish Conference of Lutheran Bishops, the Austrian Lutheran Bishop, and the organizers of the *Landeskirchentag* of the Lutheran-Reformed Church in Northwestern Germany.[85] The sharpest criticism came from Walter Künneth, a theologian in Erlangen, who contended that the dogma of the Assumption of Mary created a *status confessionis*, i.e., it was opposed to the gospel, which must be defended against such enmity.[86]

The "Evangelical League" (*Evangelischer Bund*), which had been formed in 1886 to combat Catholic renewal in Germany, carried out popular Lutheran polemics against the dogma. One member of the League concluded that both dogmas had made Mary "a goddess alongside the holy God."[87] The journal of the *Una Sancta* movement, "Ecumenical Unity" (*Ökumenische Einheit*), subscribed to by Lutherans and Catholics after World War I, linked the dogma of the Assumption to the Transitus legend, a version of the Gnostic legend about Saint John, which had been debated among Eastern theologians in the seventh century. The journal also offered comments from anonymous Catholics opposed to the dogma.[88]

The Lutheran group called "The Gathering" (*Die Sammlung*), headed by Hans Asmussen, published "Twelve Evangelical Theses of Catholic Truths" in 1957, warning of a new "Marianism" that tends to be pagan rather than Christian.[89] Even Max Lackmann, who had advocated closer Lutheran-Catholic relations, vented his disappointment over the dogma by declaring that such "doctrinal development exceeds the proper limits of a Christian and Catholic theology."[90]

Readers of *Die Religion in Geschichte und Gegenwart*, a theological encyclopedia, were presented with the judgment of J. Weerda, a Lutheran theologian in Erlangen, regarding the dogma: Scripture is silent about it, and "the tradition is heard late and without clarity"; the structure of the relationship between revelation and tradition has been changed because the church "creates salvific facts on its own, and of itself effects the event of salvation."[91]

Gerhard Ebeling's response to both dogmas may represent wide Lutheran reaction: these dogmas illustrate Catholic perceptions of salvation history in which Mary is the mythical personification of the church as the "Mediatrix of all grace" (*mediatrix omnium gratiarum*); "the mariological dogmas mean the dogmatization of the basic structure of Catholicism."[92]

ROBERT W. BERTRAM

9

Luther on the Unique Mediatorship of Christ

Not As Means of Grace

First we should warn against anachronizing Luther's sixteenth-century terminology. Christ was Mediator, of course, but not in the sense, say, of "mass media." Christ did not mediate in the manner that the "means of grace" (*media gratiae*), the word and the sacraments mediate. About these Luther could say, they are "a means and a way and, as it were, a pipe, through which the Holy Spirit flows and comes into our hearts."[1] Gospel and sacraments are the public means, thus the mass media upon which faith depends, much though our innate *Schwärmerei* (enthusiasm) tempts us to denigrate them in favor of an immediate, privileged subjectivism. As a remedy for such false *Innerlichkeit* (subjectivity) the biblical God "has always observed the custom of giving a visible sign, a person, place or spot, where he desired to be found without fail."[2]

In Luther's enumerations of such biblical *Gnadenzeichen* (signs of grace) or *Gnadenmittel* (means of grace) he is not in the habit of including Christ, whose mediatorship is of another sort and unique. Christ is not just a revelatory transmitter of grace from God to us-ward, much less the first in a series of such mediations. Rather, he is the only Mediator between God and humanity in "both" directions, also God-ward. At least it would not be typical of Luther to proceed in the manner of a Christian Neoplatonism, ancient or modern, with Christ as a primal emanation or as a "sacrament of the encounter with God," who in turn founds a church, which in turn institutes sacraments, and so on, until the divine has finally trickled down to our nether level. That much the "intermediary" Moses might do, though—in the absence of another quite different kind of mediator—with disastrous results.[3]

If what we today mean by mediation is the communicating of God's love as something already assumed as a given, waiting only to be made known, then Luther by contrast would probably not speak of Christ as Mediator in that sense, as God's "self-revelation." For that matter, Christ needs revealing quite as much as God does, both of them by the Spirit through the word. But first of all there must be a divine love worth revealing, one which so loves sinners out of their sin as to vindicate God's love as just. True, Luther does say that in Christ is the divine "majesty sweetened and mitigated to your ability to stand it."[4] And true, such Luther quotations have been invoked to support recent revelationist theologies, though usually only by omitting Luther's prefatory statements about this "human God," "no other God than this man Jesus Christ."[5] Notice, "*human* God," not Barth's "humane" God.

Yet if it is that "human God" that the gospel mediates to us, in the sense of transmits or reveals, then that in turn only begs a prior mediation of another, not a revelationist sort. What Luther, but perhaps also his papal opponents, still believed to be necessary is a Christ as Mediator in the sense of a medium of exchange, a fair exchange. Christ is the point of transference, the crossover at which God replaces sinful people with righteous ones, thus doing justice, of all things, precisely by doing mercy—not the one without the other. In this "human God" humans become pleasingly God's, even become junior gods, yet in a way that squares or reconciles God's compassion altogether with God's honesty. No one else but Christ provides that kind of mediation, not even his mother or his saints.

When mediating, however, means revealing or transmitting or communicating, then it might be said by Lutherans today as well as by Roman Catholics that Mary and other departed saints do indeed function for us as mediators of revelation or even in an overextended sense as "means of grace." They are, as the Apology said, "examples of [God's] mercy, revealing [*significaverit*] his will to save humanity." "When we see Peter forgiven after his denial, we are encouraged [*erigimur*] to believe that grace does indeed abound more than sin."[6] For that communicative, transmissive function a mediator does not need to be a "human God." Even the Holying Spirit, to whom all such communicating is credited, does not need to be that, God incarnate. But Christ does if he is to be the "one mediator between God and humanity" (1 Tim 2:5).

The Joyous Exchange

Probably the one passage not only in the Lutheran Confessions but in all of Luther's writings that most Lutherans would choose as their favorite image of Christ as "mediator of redemption" is the Small Catechism's explanation of the second article of the Apostles' Creed. There the catechumen says of Christ—"true God, . . . also true man, . . . my Lord"—that "he has redeemed me . . . in order that I may be his own." Notice, both assertions, that Christ is "my Lord" and that I am "his own," are complementary, inseparable realities in a single mutual relationship. Christ becomes ours, and we his—*der fröhliche Wechsel*. What is rightfully ours—"lost and condemned [creaturehood], . . . all sins, . . . death, . . . the power of the devil"—Christ has not only identified with but has taken on incarnately as his own identity—"with his holy and precious blood and with his innocent sufferings and death." Conversely, however, and thus exceeding a merely one-directional, imputational atonement, we in turn now "live under him in his kingdom and serve him." From our side, too, we gain as ours what is rightfully his: "everlasting righteousness, innocence, and blessedness." "Even as he is risen from the dead and lives and reigns to all eternity," so therefore do we.[7]

Our Sin Becomes Christ's

What follows is a sampling from Luther's "joyous exchange" Christology, restricted in the interest of brevity to only one side of the transaction, namely, to how God in Christ, the "kindly Mediator," so intervened historically as to "purchase and win" us as "his own" and, since "us" here means us sinners, how he assumed our sinnerhood. Even such a restricted sample requires that we turn to something more extended than Luther's Small Catechism (which on this subject amounts to only one sentence), piecing together some scattered references from Luther's lectures on Galatians in 1531.

We confront a problem in predication. By reason of what can Christ be both the sinless God-man and at the same time a sinner? And we encounter Luther's characteristic solution. What finally makes the predication meaningful and real is that it is soteriologically necessary. Unless Christ was our sinner, we ourselves must be; but since through him we are not sinners, it follows that he was a sinner and had to be. "Our sin must be Christ's own sin, or we shall perish eternally." "If he is innocent and does not carry our sins, then we carry them and shall die and be damned in them. 'But thanks be to God, who gives us the victory through our Lord Jesus Christ!' Amen."[8]

Just as Luther's affirming Christ's sinnerhood is necessitated by soteriological, not only christological considerations, so the opponents' denying Christ's sinnerhood is likewise inspired by their contrary soteriology. And there, for Luther, lies their "infamy and shame." The papists' real motive for clearing Christ of sin, Luther claims, is not to honor Christ but rather to promote "justification by works." "They want . . . to unwrap Christ and to unclothe him from our sins." However, "to make him innocent" is "to burden and overwhelm ourselves with our own sins, and to behold them not in Christ but in ourselves." And the reason the papists do this is that they prefer to have their sins removed and replaced, not in Christ but within their own selves—"by some opposing motivations, namely, by love" or by the sort of faith that is actualized in love. It is this wish of theirs to be valuable inherently and biographically that prompts them to protest that he "is not a criminal and a thief but righteous and holy," or that "it is highly absurd and insulting to call the Son of God a sinner and a curse." But, says Luther, "this is to abolish Christ and make him useless."[9]

Ironically, it was the Scholastics' (and the Scriptures') whole profound understanding of moral predication, that same grammar of legality which insures that our sins are ours and no one else's and least of all the Son of God's, which now furnishes Luther with the key for discovering the way that sin, our sin, belonged instead to the Son of God. True, our sins did not belong to him in the sense that he committed them. Still, it is that kind of culpability, a guilt by active commission, to which Luther appeals for a comparison to underscore how real a sinner Christ was. Our sins "are as much Christ's own *as if* he himself had committed them."[10] Our sins are Christ's not by means merely of some transcendent, superhistorical imposition in which God simply "regards" our sins as his or simply "imputes" our sins to him, but by means also of his own immanent, historical "bearing" of those sins. He did not commit them, of course. But that does not mean for Luther that there is only one other way by which our sins can then be his, namely, by divine imputation. No, Luther comes as close as he can to saying our sins are Christ's by reason of his committing them yet without actually saying that. And as we shall see, Luther adopts this procedure not only for rhetorical effect but for an important theological purpose.

Six Ways to Predicate Sin of Christ

How much our sins truly are "Christ's own" Luther elaborates in at least half a dozen ways, recalling strangely the very ways in which our sin ought ordinarily be "our" own. These half-dozen variations on how our sin is rightfully and culpably predicated of Christ (culminating in the reminder that his guilt was after all intentional) will occupy us in the next six sections of this essay. Then in the essay's concluding section we shall note how it was precisely this recourse to ordinary moral predication in his portrayal of Christ's sinnerhood that enables Luther finally to explode that type of predication in his discussion of Christ's surprise victory. In other words, it was just because Christ "was made under the law" that he could be the death of the law—the law and its whole tyrannizing mode of predication.

For in the end Christ's intentional self-incrimination, which rightfully rendered him guilty before the law, was the selfsame intention that in turn incriminated and annihilated the law—his intention, namely, of invincible divine mercy. Here in the selfsameness of Christ's loving will, willing to be a sinner in order to be a Redeemer, Luther finds the secret bond that unites the personal subject with its paradoxical predicate, the sinless God-man with the sins of all sinners. When that merciful determination of God becomes immanent in this Man in this law-bound world, it becomes a guilty will, but only temporarily—for an ulterior "delightful" purpose.

Under the Law

For example, first of all, our sins are so much Christ's own that we dare not say he bore merely our punishment. What he bore was our sin. If he did not, the law had no reason to punish him. Luther refuses to explain away Paul's statement that Christ was made a curse for us or that he was made sin for us, by so diluting "sin" and "curse" that they mean merely the "consequences" of sin. The critics who "want to deny that [Christ] is a sinner and a curse" prefer to say rather that he "underwent the *torments* of sin and death." But that is not all that Paul says, and "surely these words of Paul are not without purpose." Neither are the words of John the Baptist, about "the Lamb of God." And remember the way Isaiah speaks of Christ: "God has laid on him the iniquity of us all." Of course, for Christ to bear iniquities, Luther agrees, does include his bearing our punishment. "But *why* is Christ punished? Is it not because he has sin and bears sins?" What is it that causes the law, the whole retributive order of things, to retaliate with punishment at all? What else but the culprit's sin and accursedness? It is for that reason that the law says to Christ: "Let every sinner die! And therefore, Christ, if you want to reply that you are guilty and that you bear the punishment, you must bear the sin and the curse as well." For that reason Paul was correct in applying to Christ "this general law from Moses." To predicate sin and accursedness of Christ is lawful and rational: "Christ hung on a tree, therefore Christ is a curse of God"[11]—a lawfully accursed sinner, not merely the innocent bearer of sin's punishments.

Fraternized with Sinners

Second, our sins are so much Christ's own that, when he fraternized with sinners, he stood himself condemned for the company he kept. And rightly so. For, says Luther, "a magistrate regards someone as a criminal and punishes him if he catches him among thieves, even though the man has never committed anything evil." "Among thieves," indeed. Jesus was consorting with the enemies of God. He was a *socius peccatorum*. Of this Christ Luther complains, "the sophists deprive us when they segregate Christ from sins and from sinners and set him forth to us only as an example to be imitated."[12] They err in their too aloof definition of Christ, but also in their too sanguine definition of "the world," in which Christ dwelt. For what is required here is that "you have two definitions, of 'world' and of 'Christ.' " That is to say, we must remember that Christ delivered us "not only from this world but from this 'evil world,' " "from this evil age, which is an obedient servant and a willing follower of its god, the devil."[13]

What links sinner to sinner in this worldwide syndicate of evil is not merely that they all misbehave in the same way, or even that they all aid and abet one another. Rather, they are all under the tyrannical jurisdiction of a common demonic lord so that, whatever their efforts at good behavior, "the definition still stands: You are still in the present evil age." What makes it evil is that "whatever is in this age is subject to the evil of the devil, who rules the entire world."[14] The company of sinners is a kingdom, a realm, of evil. This realm, being under divine curse, is off-limits. Yet it is into this realm that Christ came. "He joined himself to the company of the accursed." "And being joined with us who were accursed, he became a curse for us." "Therefore when the law found him among thieves it condemned and executed him as a thief."[15]

"I Have Committed the World's Sin"

Third, our sins are so much Christ's own that, no matter who committed them originally, all of them have now been committed in effect by Jesus Christ personally. The sins he bore, as John says, are nothing less than "the sins of the world."[16] And "the sin of the world," as Luther understands the phrase, is not sin in general, an abstract universal. It is exhaustive of every actual sinner and sin in history: "not only my sins and yours, but the sins of the entire world, past, present, and future." Luther represents Christ as saying, "I have committed the sins that all men have committed,"[17] "the sin of Paul, the former blasphemer, . . . of Peter, who denied Christ, of David, . . . an adulterer and a murderer and who caused the Gentiles to blaspheme the name of the Lord."[18]

Still, even in the face of such specific enumerations, we in our false humility are wont to exempt Christ from our sins, at least from those sins of ours that seem to us more than Christ should be expected to bear and which, alas, we alone must bear.

> It is easy for you to say and believe that Christ, the Son of God, was given for the sins of Peter, Paul, and other saints, who seem to us to have been worthy of this grace. But it is very hard for you, who regard yourself as unworthy of this grace, to say and believe from your heart that Christ was given for *your* many great sins.

But false humility is what this is, and disdain for Christ. Luther shows small sympathy for the neo-pharisaic pseudo-publican who prays, "God be merciful to me a sinner," and yet who means no more by "sinner" than the doer of trivial sins, "an imitation and counterfeit sinner." "Christ was given, not for sham or counterfeit sins, nor yet for small sins, but for great and huge sins, not for one or two sins but for all sins." "And unless you are part of the company of those who say 'our sins,' . . . there is no salvation for you."[19]

Conversely, it is only because "the sin of the world" is no mere abstraction but an enumerative totality of every real sin and sinner that Luther can perform the inference he repeatedly does: Christ is "the one who took away the sins of the world; if the sin of the world is taken away, then it is taken away also from me."[20] Accordingly, Luther describes the Father sending his Son: "Be Peter the denier, Paul the persecutor, . . . David the adulterer, the sinner who ate the apple in Paradise, the thief on the cross; in short, be the person . . . who has committed the sins of all men."[21]

Sin Itself

Fourth, our sins are so much Christ's own that, by his acknowledging them as his, he himself—not only the sins he bore, but he who bore them—becomes a sin and a curse. This drastic conclusion is suggested by Paul's strong use of "curse" in its substantive rather than its adjectival sense. Christ is said to have been made a curse and not merely accursed, not just a sinner but sin itself. And is not this the way it is, Luther recalls, whenever "a sinner really comes to a knowledge of himself?" He can no longer distinguish nicely between his sin, on the one hand, and himself, on the other, as though the two were still separable. "That is, he seems to himself to be not only miserable but misery itself; not only a sinner and an accursed one, but sin and the curse itself." And not only is that what he *seems* to be. "A man who feels these things in earnest *really becomes (fit plane)* sin, death, and the curse itself."[22]

Luther is all but saying the same thing of Christ. Although Christ did not commit sin, he so acknowledged our sins as his own and himself accursed because of them that this very acknowledgment alienates God and makes Christ a sinner "not only adjectivally but substantively."[23]

> All our evils . . . overwhelmed him once, for a brief time, and flooded in over his head, as in Psalm 88:7 and 16 the prophet laments in Christ's name when he says: "Thy wrath lies heavy upon me and thou dost overwhelm me with all thy waves." And: "Thy wrath has swept over me, thy dread assaults destroy me."[24]

Luther can even say of Christ: "He was not acting in his own person now; now he is not the Son of God, born of the virgin, but he is a sinner."[25] For that is the way it is with the law. "All it does is to increase sin, accuse, frighten, threaten with death, and disclose God as a wrathful judge who damns sinners." And "where terror and a sense of sin, death, and the wrath of God are present, there is certainly no righteousness, nothing heavenly, and no God." In the case of Christ, the law raged even more fiercely than it does against us. "It accused him of blasphemy and sedition." It frightened him so horribly that he experienced a greater anguish than any man has ever experienced." Witness his "bloody sweat, the comfort of the angel, his solemn prayer in the garden, and finally . . . that cry of misery on the cross, 'My God, my God, why hast thou forsaken me?' "[26] "A man who feels these things in earnest really becomes sin, death, and the curse itself."[27]

In His Body

Fifth, our sins are so much Christ's own that he bore them not only psychologically but also, as we do, bodily—"in his body." That prepositional phrase, sometimes quoted directly from 1 Pet 2:24, occurs so often and so habitually in Luther's christological discussions that its very frequency demonstrates how somatically Luther conceived of sin, whether ours or Christ's. There is for Christ no bearing of our sins without his doing so "in his body." Why?

The function that Luther most usually ascribes to Christ's bearing our sins "in his body" is that by his bodily dying he put those sins in his body to "death." "He bore and sustained them in his own body,"[28] where, by his death and apparent defeat, they were exterminated. Christ "conquers and destroys these monsters—sin, death, and the curse—without weapon or battle, in his own body and in himself, as Paul enjoys saying (Col 2:15): 'He disarmed the principalities and powers triumphing over them in him.' "[29] "All these things happen . . . through Christ the crucified, on whose shoulders lie all the evils of the human race— . . . all of which die in him, because by his death he kills them."[30]

Something else remains to be said. Christ bears our sins in his body not only because they are thereby destroyed but also because they are ours. There is no question in Luther's mind that Christ could have vanquished the tyrants without submitting to the cross, by an outright exercise of his divine sovereignty. But such an alternative completely overlooks how intimately his victory was to be ours and how it was therefore to be achieved "in our sinful person."[31] Luther has Christ saying,

> I could have overcome the law by my supreme authority, without any injury to me; . . . but for the sake of you, who were under the law, I assumed your flesh; . . . I went down into the same imprisonment . . . under which you were serving as captives.[32]

That is why "all men, even the apostles or prophets or patriarchs, would have remained under the curse (1) if Christ had not put himself in opposition to sin, death, the curse . . . , and (2) *if he had not overcome them in his own body*."[33] For Christ does not bear our sin as ours unless he assumes "our sinful person," and our sinful person is inseparable from our bodies.[34] "The old man . . . is born of flesh and blood."[35] John Osborne has captured a characteristic insight of Luther's in the line, spoken by Hans to his son: "You can't ever get away from your body because that's what you live in, and it's all you've got to die in."[36]

Spontaneously

Sixth, our sin is so much Christ's own that, since it is his by choice, it incriminates his motives, his innermost self. Because he attached himself to our sins "willingly" (*sponte*), he has only himself to thank for the fact that he is liable for them. "Because he took upon himself our sins, not by compulsion but by his own free will, it was right for him to bear the punishment and the wrath of God."[37] The deliberate, intentional character of Christ's sinnerhood seems to illustrate most graphically for Luther how truly Christ bore our sin "in himself." And it may be that at this point Luther's meaning comes closest to being intelligible to an age like our own with its definitions of selfhood in terms of "responsibility" and "decision." "Modern man," Bultmann reminded us, "bears the sole responsibility for his own feeling, thinking and willing."[38] Similarly, in his lectures on Galatians Luther can agree with the moral philosophers that what characterizes a man's actions as really and personally his is the ethical quality of his motives, his rational will.[39] In an earlier quote we heard Luther speak of Christ as a *socius peccatorum* and heard him explain, "Thus a magistrate regards someone as a criminal and punishes him if he catches him among thieves, even though the man has never committed anything evil." But in the case of Christ this was no arbitrary guilt by association. Christ could not plead that, though he was indeed among sinners, he was there in innocent ignorance or against his will. For as Luther adds immediately, "Christ was not only *found* among sinners; but of his *own free will* . . . he *wanted* to be an associate of sinners." Accordingly, "the law came and said: 'Christ, if you want to reply that you are guilty and that you bear the punishment, you must bear the sin and the curse as well.' "[40]

A Most Joyous Duel

It was not for nothing that Luther invoked every biblical description of Christ's sinnerhood which would show that, according to the moral grammar of predication, Christ was rightfully and legally subject to the law's condemnation, that our sins "are as much Christ's own as if he himself had committed them."[41] For by granting the legal order its maximum due, it is now drawn into the fray, not at its worst—not as the emasculated legalism of the "Scholastics," not as some miscarriage of justice by the Sanhedrin—but at its best. As a consequence, it is the divine law in its own holy integrity—that is, as it justly condemns every sinner, no matter how pious, as the enemy of God—which now does what it has to do to this *peccator peccatorum* (sinner of sinners). And it is this same law at its holiest and best which, in the *mirabile duellum* that ensues, is eternally discredited. The other antagonists as well—sin, devil, curse, wrath, death—are present not as caricatures but at the height of their power.

It is only because the enemies involved are the real enemies—the ones, in other words, with whom people have to reckon for life and death before God—that the *mirabile duellum* becomes indeed a "very joyous duel," *iucundissimum duellum*.[42] Here we find Luther applying his own hermeneutical rule, exploiting the antithesis of the opponents in order not only to "reveal their infamy and shame"[43] but to celebrate in turn our "knowledge of Christ and most delightful comfort."[44] The whole legal mode of predication, so elaborately employed for what seemed a merely negative detailing of Christ's sinnerhood, now "by contrast serves to magnify the grace of God and the blessings of Christ."[45]

Out of Great Love

"The grace of God and the blessings of Christ"—that is the secret of the *iucundissimum duellum*. Or rather what is the secret is that this divine grace, "the blessing," is locked in mortal combat with the curse "in this one person." "Now let us see," asks Luther, "how two such extremely contrary things come together in one person."[46] The answer, as might be expected, is that when they do come together it is the divine powers—divine righteousness, life, and blessing—which of course prevail over the lesser contraries, sin and death and the curse.[47] But the secret, indeed the prerequisite, of the victory is that it all occurs "in his own body and in himself."[48]

Both sets of contraries are really his. If the sin had not been his, as truly as the righteousness was, the law could easily have avoided its blasphemy against him by cursing only the one and not the other. However, "he joined God and man in one person. And being joined in us who were accursed, he became a curse for us; and he concealed his blessing in our sin, death, and curse, which condemned and killed *him*."[49]

Christ's intentional self-incrimination, his personal decision to attach himself to the enemies of God—the reason he was cursed, and rightfully—was the selfsame decision of the selfsame person (the merciful decision of the divine person) which for the law to curse would incriminate the law as blasphemous. The wonder, therefore, is not just that the curse was conquered by the blessing. The prior wonder is: Why should the curse, the law, want to attack the blessing in the first place? Luther's answer is that because God's blessing and our sin were so intimately joined in this one person (as intimately as the "person" and his "work"[50]), therefore the curse, which had no choice but to condemn our sin, necessarily condemned the divine blessing as well. "This circumstance, 'in himself,' makes the duel more amazing and outstanding; for it shows that such great things were to be achieved in the one and only person of Christ."[51]

We began the essay by asking, as a problem in theological predication, by reason of what can such a contradictory predicate as sin, our sin at that, really and meaningfully belong to Christ, this "purest of persons, . . . God and man?"[52] Luther's answer must finally be, by reason of Christ's love. He "did this because of his great love; for Paul says [of Christ, in Gal 2:20]: 'who loved me.' "[53] In the last analysis the explanation of Christ's paradoxical sinnerhood is simply that "he is nothing but sheer, infinite mercy, which gives and is given"; "the kind of lover who gives himself for us and . . . who interposes himself as the Mediator between God and us miserable sinners."[54]

Yet to speak of Christ as the "Mediator between *God* and us miserable sinners" seems to suggest that while Christ may lovingly have predicated our sins of himself, "God" may not concur in such a predication. Accordingly, the final explanation, which really and meaningfully predicates our sin of Christ, is that same loving will which he who "is God by nature" shares with his Father. "The indescribable and inestimable mercy and love of God" who saw "that we were being held under a curse and that we could not be liberated, . . . heaped all the sins of all men upon him." The culpable decision by which Christ attached himself to the enemies of God is simultaneously the decision of this very God. "Of his own free will and by the *will of the Father* he wanted to be an associate of sinners."[55] In fact, it is "only by taking hold of Christ, who, by the will of the Father, has given himself into the death for our sins" that we are "drawn and carried directly to the Father."[56]

> The human heart is too limited to comprehend, much less to describe, the great depths and burning passion of divine love toward us. Indeed, the very greatness of divine mercy produces not only difficulty in believing but incredulity. Not only do I hear that God Almighty, the Creator of all, is good and merciful; but I hear that the Supreme Majesty cared so much for me . . . that he did not spare his own Son, . . . in order that he might hang in the midst of thieves and become sin and a curse for me, the sinner and accursed one, and in order that I might be made righteous, blessed, and a son and heir of God. Who can adequately proclaim this goodness of God? Not even all the angels.[57]

In his Apology to the Augsburg Confession Melanchthon accused the current cultus of promoting departed saints from "mediators of intercession" to "mediators of redemption," thus displacing Christ or, worse, reconceiving him as a dreaded judge "approachable" only through nearer mediators. Quite a different danger that neither Melanchthon nor Luther seems to have reckoned with, nor yet needed to, is the sort of reductionist Christology in which the saints are not so much promoted to christological responsibilities as Christ is demoted to theirs. In this alternative all Christ does is what the saints admittedly do, too: transmit, communicate, reveal us-ward—in that sense "mediate"—a preassured divine grace that would have obtained anyway, with or without Christ, except that we might not have known about it.

On such a view, from the outset there never was any real alternative to divine mercy being like divine judgment or wrath, which only in Christ—that is, in God as a human being—is historically overcome for all other humans. Against such a tepid christological background the danger of the saints competing with Christ is probably a nonproblem because by contrast with more classical Christologies this revelationist Christ has little to do that is all that unique and might not just as well be shared or delegated among his members. The question that does remain—and the old controversy over the cultus of the saints may help to reinstate that question—is this: What is it about Christ's mediatorship that is unique to deity, incarnate deity? That question faces today's Lutherans as well as Roman Catholics.

FREDERICK M. JELLY, O.P.

10

The Roman Catholic Dogma of Mary's Immaculate Conception

The essential dogmatic content of the mystery of Mary's Immaculate Conception is contained in the following decree of the apostolic constitution or papal bull, *Ineffabilis Deus,* issued by Pope Pius IX on December 8, 1854:

> We declare, pronounce, and define that the doctrine which holds that the most Blessed Virgin Mary, in the first instant of her conception, by a singular grace and privilege, granted by Almighty God, in view of the merits of Jesus Christ, the Savior of the human race, was preserved free from all stain of original sin, is a doctrine revealed by God and therefore to be believed firmly and constantly by all the faithful.[1]

This particular passage of the papal bull teaches as a solemnly defined dogma of Catholic faith (because it is a "doctrine revealed by God") two basic truths about Mary: that she was preserved free from original sin at the very first instant of her existence as a human person in her mother's womb, and that this unique grace and privilege was bestowed upon her by God "in view of the merits of Jesus Christ."

The principal purpose of this essay is to propose historical and theological explanations of the ways in which this precise doctrine appears to have developed in the tradition. Because the papal magisterium had a particularly important role to play in the development of this dogma, the first part of this essay traces and reflects briefly upon its influence on the events that led to the definition in 1854. The second section considers the other significant factors in the dogmatic development of the Immaculate Conception which address more directly the difficulties of its doctrinal content as well as the sense in which it is a dogma revealed by God. The final portion of this essay reflects upon the contemporary significance of this dogma, particularly in the context of Vatican II's "order or 'hierarchy' of truths"—with its special relationship to the ecumenical issues involved.[2]

A Historical Overview of the Papal Magisterium Leading to 1854

To assess more accurately the role of Pius IX in the exercise of his extraordinary or solemn teaching authority in 1854, just sixteen years before papal infallibility would be defined by Vatican Council I in 1870, it seems wise to glance at the part played by his predecessors in the process.[3] The magisterial activity of the popes in this regard took place along three distinct but closely connected lines: the feast of the Conception, the differences about its proper title, and the frequently acrimonious disputes about the doctrine that was its object. It is important to bear this in mind as the basis for distinguishing between disciplinary and doctrinal decrees.

The Feast

This very influential factor in the dogmatic development of the Immaculate Conception is discussed more directly in the next section of this essay. Actually it inspired the terminological and doctrinal questions and provided the ecclesial setting in which these difficulties were gradually resolved. The feast of Mary's Conception, as it was traditionally called right up to 1854, originated in the East toward the end of the seventh century, but Pope Sixtus IV (1471–84) was the first bishop of Rome to recognize and confirm it officially, as well as to celebrate it personally, publicly, and solemnly in the curia itself. Although he significantly enriched the feast liturgically, he did not go so far as to prescribe its celebration for the universal church, for this took place only in 1693.

Saint Pius V, a Dominican pope, took the next major step when he was implementing the liturgical reform mandated by the Council of Trent. In his papal bull, *Quod a nobis postulat*, issued July 5, 1568, he preserved the feast of the Conception for December 8, reducing its solemnity but extending its celebration to give greater unity to the liturgy in the church. After gradual elevation in rank and the further spread of its observance, the feast was extended to the universal church by Pope Innocent XII on May 15, 1693. Then on December 6, 1708, Clement XI made it a feast of obligation for the whole church. The feast, however, was not raised to the highest rank, i.e., a "solemnity" according to current liturgical usage, until Leo XIII did so December 5, 1879, after the dogmatic definition.

Title of the Feast

The doctrinal significance of the name for the feast was the basis for the initial debate between "sanctification" and "conception." The latter was the only title known to the Greeks and was used during its twelfth-century celebration in the West. The former title derived from the "maculists," who doubtless based their claim upon the teaching of Saints Bonaventure and Thomas Aquinas that the feast really celebrates her sanctification in the womb of her mother. In all the acts of the papal magisterium, "conception" was the only name used for the feast. Even a Dominican pope, Saint Pius V, who would have been expected to use "sanctification" in accord with the custom of his Order, chose the title "conception" as more general and of greater antiquity in the tradition. He allowed those who had used "sanctification" for two hundred years or more to retain it. This exception was excluded by Gregory XV on May 24, 1622, a decision to help unify the church, which had been divided by the diverse usages. The "maculists," however, interpreted "conception" to mean that Mary was freed from original sin in the second instant of her conception.

The conflict over using "immaculate" was very complicated, and it is beyond the scope of this brief essay to examine the matter in any detail. Both sides in the controversy, the "maculists" and the "immaculists," used every means available to win over the authority of the Holy See to their opinion. The use of "immaculate conception" to designate the opinion of the "immaculists" became more acceptable in the Roman Catholic Church generally, but the popes avoided it and used *Conceptio Immaculatae Virginis* instead since the doctrine involved was not yet definitive. With respect to its usage in the title of the liturgical feast, a turning point did emerge when Pius VII on May 17, 1806, granted permission to the Franciscans to add "Immaculata" to ". . . et te in Conceptione . . ." of the Preface for the Mass on December 8. Gregory XVI in 1838 granted the same privilege to any orders or dioceses that might petition it, and by the end of his pontificate about three hundred had done so.

When even the Dominicans appealed for the privilege in 1843, doubtless on account of a definite invitation from the Holy See, and the difficulties of some of them that their oath of allegiance to follow the teaching of Saint Thomas Aquinas prevented them from pronouncing such a formula as "Immaculate Conception" were resolved, the last bastion of Roman Catholic resistance to the dogma disappeared.

The Doctrine

Prior to Sixtus IV (1471–84) there is no papal document favoring the Immaculate Conception. But it is remarkable that even though the popes leaned toward the side of the "maculists" to emphasize the universality of original sin, following the tendency in the twelfth to fourteenth centuries, they did not use their magisterial authority to confirm the theological opinion that Mary had been infected by original sin.

The first of a series of papal documents to have the mystery of Mary's Immaculate Conception as their direct object were two disciplinary decrees with a doctrinal orientation favorable to it. These are the two papal bulls issued by Sixtus IV, a Franciscan pope. Both are called *Grave nimis* and were issued successively in 1482 and 1483. He pronounced an excommunication reserved personally to the Holy See against any who taught that the church's feast celebrates merely the spiritual conception or sanctification of Mary or who called heretics those who believe in the Immaculate Conception. Likewise, he condemned those who called heretical the belief that Mary had not been preserved from original sin. The second papal bull extended the decision of the first to the entire church and also clearly indicated their disciplinary character, leaving open the question of the precise doctrinal object of the feast.

These disciplinary decrees did not achieve the purpose of promoting greater peace between the "maculists" and "immaculists." The disputes continued, often in an atmosphere of acrimony, despite the fact that succeeding popes reinforced and strengthened their prohibitions against either side accusing the other of heresy. A significant step in the direction of the definition in 1854 took place when Alexander VII issued the papal bull, *Sollicitudo*, December 8, 1661, in which he actually took up the doctrinal implications found in Sixtus IV and extended them in terms that Pius IX would use in 1854:

> By a special grace and privilege of God, and in view of the merits of Jesus Christ . . . Redeemer of the human race, (Mary's) soul

> was preserved from the stain of original sin, in the first instant of its creation and infusion into her body.[4]

Although he declares that this teaching represents the Church of Rome, where the faithful hold to it, he is careful to make clear that he is not defining the Immaculate Conception as a dogma of faith.

The definition of the doctrine by the Council of Basel, published September 17, 1438, is considered invalid because it was made when the Council was in schism from the Holy See. But it did reflect the pious beliefs and practices of the time and even contributed to their spread because many places throughout Christendom considered Basel to have been a legitimate ecumenical council in the church.[5] During Lateran Council V (1512–17) Leo X considered a definition, but the opposition of Cardinal Cajetan, who was appointed to examine the question, put an end to it. At the Council of Trent in 1546 in the context of the decrees on original sin, a lively discussion arose about the issue, and the following compromise was reached:

> This holy Council declares that it does not intend to include in this decree on original sin, the Blessed and Immaculate Virgin Mary, Mother of God; but that the constitutions of Pope Sixtus IV . . . are to be observed under the penalties contained in those constitutions, which [the present Council] renews.[6]

In retrospect one might say that this compromise actually favored the progress of the Immaculate Conception toward 1854, but in the minds of those who formulated it, notably the "maculists," it was neutral.

During the seventeenth century the popes had to resist the pressures from both secular and religious sources for a definition. The debate reached its peak in that century, while the eighteenth century was relatively calm. At the outset of the nineteenth century, petitions for a definition resumed with renewed vigor from bishops and religious orders, but not from princes and states, which had become quite secularized by then. The three immediate predecessors of Pius IX, even though unable to see their way clear to define the dogma, did pave the way for 1854 by introducing immaculist formulas into Christian prayer and liturgy.

On October 28, 1847, *Pio Nono* congratulated Father J. Perrone, a Jesuit, for his book, *De Immaculata Beatae Virginis Conceptione*, the purpose of which is clearly indicated by its subtitle: *An dogmatico decreto definiri possit?* Then on June 1, 1848, Pius IX proposed the question of definition to twenty theologians, seventeen of whom favored it. On December 6 of the same year a preliminary congregation was established to inquire whether it should be defined and how. Responding affirmatively to the first question, they recommended that the second be answered by consulting the bishops of the universal church. Therefore the pope issued the encyclical *Ubi Primum* on February 2, 1849. Of 603 bishops consulted, 546 favored a definition of the Immaculate Conception; fifty-six or fifty-seven opposed it for a variety of reasons—four or five were against its definability, twenty-four were undecided about its timeliness, about ten wanted an "indirect" definition without condemning the contrary opinion as heretical, and a final category would make no judgment in the matter. The pope had these results published and proceeded to consult further. On September 20, 1850, three theologians were asked for their views; one of them opposed the definition. On July 28, 1851, he named three new consultants, and on August 4 three more, all of whom favored the definition of the Immaculate Conception as a dogma of faith.

Meanwhile Pius IX had entrusted Perrone with the task of drawing up the first plans for a papal bull, which were given to Pius IX on March 26, 1851. That November and December he held five audiences with Dom Guéranger, Abbot of Solesmes, whose *Mémoire sur la question de l'Immaculée Conception* had been published the previous year and was considered by the pope the best thing that he had seen on the subject. On February 6, 1852, Guéranger received from Pius IX Perrone's schema, which he revised and submitted to Passaglia, who annotated it. Together both put it into final form, and the schema was ready for the pope on March 24, 1852. There were eight schemata, and it took many meetings to discuss them before the final revision of the papal bull, *Ineffabilis Deus*, the details of which are beyond the scope of this essay. Suffice it to say for our purposes that the bull was not ready in its entirety on December 8, 1854, when Pius IX read only the decree or official definition of the dogma (cited at the beginning of this essay), which was taken substantially from the bull of Alexander VII, *Solicitudo*, to which previous reference has also been made. The entire bull was probably completed in early January 1855 because the first copies were in the mail soon after January 14.

The body of *Ineffabilis Deus* explains the meaning of and the reasons for the definition, which are not exactly its adequate causes nor are they the direct object of the charism of papal infallibility. It is important to note the inherent distinction between the magisterial act of a pope and the methodology of an historian. The former is directly concerned with the extent of the development of a doctrine and not with the process or progress itself. A pope is concerned with the realities that are the objects of faith, which it is his special ministry to define for the sake of unity in the church. The historian is occupied with the literal meaning of statements in their temporal context. For instance, the feast of Mary's Conception was celebrated for centuries by the faithful with only vague notions about its proper meaning, but their faith did reach the total reality of the mystery in its liturgical setting. The work of the magisterial act, under the special guidance of the Holy Spirit, is to define the extent of a dogmatic development that exceeds the explicit awareness that their sources were able to have. The two distinct formal objects are by no means contradictory and ideally ought to be complementary, as is true for the service of a scientific theology to the magisterium of the church as a whole. The papal bull *Munificentissimus Deus*, in which Pius XII defined the dogma of Mary's glorious Assumption in 1950, shows a greater awareness historically and theologically than was possible for Pius IX's bull a century before.

Bearing in mind the special character of the magisterium, there is a rather remarkable continuity in the series of papal decisions in the dogmatic development of Mary's Immaculate Conception. One can perceive a pattern of prudent watchfulness, a succession of interventions to preserve peace amid conflicting opinions, and finally an authoritative decision that was sometimes preceded by judicious measures intended to meet the obstacles. In the process the liturgical feast seems to have been the most influential factor both by raising the pertinent questions regarding its doctrinal object and also by setting the context in which solutions would eventually be worked out. Thus the popes whose disciplinary decrees were instrumental in spreading the feast indirectly helped pave the way for the solution of doctrinal difficulties.

A wisdom transcending the merely human appears to have been operative in the basic consistency of the papal magisterium over the centuries—the work of no single pope. Once a man became pope his private opinions did not prevail, and he did not allow himself to be pressured into an untimely decision regarding the development of the dogma. The fact that Franciscans (immaculists) and Dominicans (maculists) alternately occupied the papal chair did not disrupt this basic continuity. The question has been raised, however, whether or not the real reason why *Pio Nono* deemed 1854 opportune to define the dogma is that his mind was set upon the definition of papal infallibility at Vatican I and so he would be able to refer to 1854 as a precedent. Who can discern the motives hidden in any human heart save God! Whatever may have been the case, the fact remains that the development of the dogma already discussed in this essay makes most credible the decision of Pius IX that it was opportune to define it in 1854 for many other reasons than as a "test case" for papal infallibility.[7] The next section of this essay should shed further light upon the question of its timeliness.

Analysis of the Factors in the Doctrinal Development of the Dogma[8]

Vatican II has clearly put into proper perspective the role of the church's magisterium in the development of doctrine, particularly in its relationship to Scripture and tradition. In the tradition that comes from the apostles, there is a "growth in insight into the realities and words that are being passed on."[9] The task of interpreting authentically the Word of God, of which Scripture and tradition make up a "single sacred deposit" has been "entrusted" to the magisterium, which "is not superior to the Word of God, but is its servant" and can propose for belief as being revealed by God only what is "drawn from this single deposit of faith."[10] The magisterium is not the total bearer of tradition, of what is passed on from the apostles, but the proximate norm of determining just what is authentic and so somehow divinely revealed in the transmission and development of that deposit of faith. The transmitters of tradition are actually all who are graced with apostolic faith in the church of Christ, some of whom are obviously called to have a greater hand in it than others, but embracing all in the "sensus fidelium."[11] The Council has left open to much further theological inquiry and dialogue many questions concerning the precise relationship between Scripture and tradition, e.g., whether or not the whole "Word of God" may be said in some sense to be contained in the Bible. The theological presupposition of this essay is that "implicitly" it is. Just how one explains the process of explication through a multiplicity of factors—not only directly doctrinal, but devotional, esthetic, evangelical, etc.—depends upon one's theological theory of the development of dogma within the tradition.

Possible Insinuations of the 1854 Dogma in Scripture and Tradition

Obviously there is no explicit biblical revelation of the dogma as it came to be defined in 1854. Is the consequence of this that we must search for it in "tradition alone" apart from any reference to the Scriptures? There seems to be no such thing as *sola traditio* any more than there is a *sola scriptura* without any serious relationship to a living community of faith, worship, and mission in the setting of which the inspired Scriptures manifest their real meaning. If we look to the traditional testimony of the Fathers, we find that their teachings about the apostolic faith are rooted in the Bible. If we turn to the magisterial statements of the church, we soon see that any defined dogmas are proposed with some foundation in the Scriptures. In accord with the theory of a contemporary systematic theologian, a Marian dogma such as the Immaculate Conception is not just virtually revealed or logically deduced by mere human reasoning from the revealed premises of that which is explicitly and formally revealed in the Scriptures, as though the conclusion of a theological syllogism. Actually the dogma of the Immaculate Conception is formally revealed, but implicitly, i.e., "suggested" or "insinuated" in what has been explicitly revealed.[12]

As we glance briefly at those biblical references that seem to have been most influential in the development of the dogma in 1854, let us keep in mind that the tradition in which they unfolded a fuller meaning is not one of purely intellectual reflection upon the archives of our faith in the Scriptures, but an atmosphere in which that faith grows both extensively and intensively through the experience of the triune redeeming God in worship and mission. The main biblical texts that have been invoked in support of the dogma are: Gen 3:15, "I will put enmity between you and the woman, and between your seed and her seed; he shall bruise your head, and you shall bruise his heel"; Luke 1:28, "And he [Gabriel] came to her and said, 'Hail, full of grace, the Lord is with you"; and Luke 1:42, "and she [Elizabeth] exclaimed with a loud cry, 'Blessed are you among women, and blessed is the fruit of your womb!' " These texts are referred to in the papal bull *Ineffabilis Deus*, and Vatican II makes reference to Luke 1:28 when teaching that Mary was "enriched from the first instant of her conception with the splendor of an entirely unique holiness."[13]

Does the "woman" of Gen 3:15 have any conscious connection in the intention of the fourth evangelist with his "woman" at Cana and at the foot of the cross? Is there any Marian symbolism revealed in the "woman clothed with the sun" of Revelation 12? Did Luke have in mind the "Daughter of Sion" motif in his portrait of Mary as the perfect disciple? Although it is not possible for us to answer such questions with certainty, it does seem reasonable to believe that such texts were influential factors in the development of Marian doctrine and devotion in the Catholic tradition and thus in some sense a biblical basis for the dogma of 1854. This approach appears to be at least implicit in Vatican II's interpretation:

> The earliest documents, as they are read in the Church and are understood in the light of a further and full revelation, bring the figure of a woman, Mother of the Redeemer, into a gradually clearer light. Considered in this light, she is already prophetically foreshadowed in the promise of victory over the serpent which was given to our first parents after their fall into sin (cf. Genesis 3:15).[14]

The key phrase for our purposes is "as they are read in the Church and are understood in the light of a further and full revelation." In light of the *lex orandi, lex credendi* axiom, this includes the "liturgical sense" of the Scriptures or the new insights that they can offer in the context of the church's official worship.[15] Being more sensitive to the historical critical methods of contemporary biblical scholarship, the fathers at Vatican II were more nuanced in their reference to Gen 3:15 than Pius IX and his collaborators could have been well over a century earlier. The above quotation carefully phrases it by saying that Mary "is already prophetically foreshadowed in the promise of victory over the serpent" and does not speak as though it were explicitly known to the writer.

The impact of the "woman" in Gen 3:15, of the woman who is clearly Mary in Luke/Acts and John's Gospel, and of the "woman" who might be the secondary Marian symbol in Revelation 12 upon the faith-understanding about Mary in the Catholic tradition has been considerable. She has come to be seen as the "exalted Daughter of Sion" and the "New Eve" who was perfectly associated with Christ in his complete conquest of sin and earth, which are symbolized by the "serpent." If she had been tainted by original sin, even for an instant, it would have marred the perfection of her son's redemptive work because his own mother would have come under the dominion of Satan.

As always, there is a number of theological ways to attempt an explanation of the process whereby biblical implications may develop into dogmatic explications in the tradition. The basic thrust of one such theory follows.[16] The same Holy Spirit who inspired the Scriptures is always active in the body of Christ, the church. That Spirit can also inspire the church to make explicit truths of revelation that were originally only implicit or divinely hinted at in the Bible. It is not as though we were reading something into the Scriptures (*eis-egesis*) but we read what was truly inspired, even though not in the actual intention of the inspired author. The Spirit, the eternal God who sees all simultaneously, put into the text or theme of the Bible a "prophetic expandibility" that has become clear and explicit in the course of the church's salvation history. According to this theory such a reading is a genuine exegesis of the text because the Spirit has inspired an "objective dynamism" that would eventually move toward an emergence into an explicit doctrine of our faith in light of the tradition. Thus we have been trying to show that tradition is not precisely a parallel source of revelation with Scripture but dynamically penetrates it for the sake of the complete word of God.[17]

Patristic Testimony

The earliest image of Mary after the New Testament revelation is the New Eve or Second Eve typology.[18] This antithetical parallelism between Eve and Mary, particularly as developed by Saint Irenaeus (d. after 193), portrays the mother as receiving an intimate share in the total victory of the son over sin and death, over satan the ancient "serpent."[19] Cardinal Newman (1801–90) believed that the Immaculate Conception (as well as the Assumption) is a doctrine that follows directly from the New Eve typology and is part of the tradition handed down from the apostles.[20]

In glancing briefly at the witness of the Fathers of the church, let us bear in mind the significant difference between the traditions of the East and West after Saint Augustine. His theologoumenon about the transmission of original sin through the marital act has not been accepted by the East to this day. At the same time the tradition of the East, especially as celebrated in the divine liturgy, has been most effusive in its praise of Mary as the "all-holy" one. In one of his Nisibene hymns Saint Ephraem of Syria (c. 306–73) sings the praises of the son and the mother as alone being "in all things fair" and of Mary as having "no stain."[21] There appears to have been a development among the Eastern fathers from the teaching that Mary was graced with a special holiness to her complete holiness. Saint Andrew of Crete (c. 660–740), Saint Germanus of Constantinople (c. 635–733), and Saint John Damascene (c. 675–753) are the great Marian theologians of eighth-century Byzantium, the end of the patristic era. In a sermon on the Presentation Saint Germanus calls Mary "most pure," "surrounded by untouched and immaculate virginity," "wholly without sin," "holier than the saints," and "more glorious than the cherubim."[22] Again, however, since the East did not conceive of original sin in the same categories as those used in the West, it cannot be said that such testimony explicitly exempts her from original sin—as the dogma of 1854 does. We might well note here that the ecumenical dialogue between the Roman Catholic and Orthodox churches should help resolve the problem.

Liturgical Witness

The feast of Mary's Nativity was celebrated in the East at least by the latter half of the sixth century. Because in the tradition only the birthdays of one considered sanctified at the time of his/her birth were recognized as liturgical feasts, it is certainly a testimony to the belief that Mary was sinless at birth. Now a feast celebrating Mary's conception did appear toward the end of the seventh century, which probably originated in the monasteries of Syria and spread throughout the Byzantine world. It reached England about 1050, but was suppressed for a time after the Norman conquest under William the Conqueror (1066–87). When the feast was revived about 1125, an argument arose in which for the first time there was a critical discussion about the doctrinal object of the feast. This debate gradually brought the doctrine of the Immaculate Conception to general attention. After its revival in England the feast spread into Normandy, France, Belgium, Spain, and Germany and helped provide the basis for the development of the dogma of 1854 that seems most significant, namely, the *sensus fidelium*, the belief and the devotion of the faithful.[23]

Medieval Doctrinal Debate

The earliest extant defense of the doctrine of the Immaculate Conception is found in a treatise, *On the Conception of the Blessed Mary*, by Eadmer (1060/64–1130), an English monk and intimate associate of Saint Anselm of Canterbury (1033–1109), to whom the work had been attributed for a long time. Although Eadmer was unable to settle the doctrinal difficulties regarding the Augustinian theologoumenon about original sin and the need for redemption by Christ on the part of every descendant of Adam, he contributed by encouraging the *sensus fidelium* through his promotion of the feast of Mary's Conception.

Saint Bernard of Clairvaux (1090–1153) opposed the celebration of this feast on the basis of Saint Augustine's great authority in the tradition of the West. Doubtless he had considerable influence upon the great Scholastics of the thirteenth century, notably Saints Albert the Great, Thomas Aquinas, and Bonaventure, who could not reconcile the Immaculate Conception with their theologies of Christ as the Savior of the whole world, including his own mother. In fact, their insistence upon this fundamental article of our Christian faith helped pave the way for the notion of "preservative redemption" as an essential component of the definition of the dogma in 1854.

Although historical research reveals that others made their contributions, particularly William of Ware (d. c. 1305), it is still generally agreed that the real breakthrough to the notion of preservative redemption was made by Scotus (1266–1308).[24] His position seems to rest essentially upon the perfection of Christ who as the most perfect Mediator was capable of exercising the most perfect act of mediation. But this would not have occurred unless he merited to preserve his mother from original sin. The Blessed Trinity, he argued, is not entirely appeased unless the offense of all sin is prevented in at least one of the redeemed. And unless it is contrary to the authority of the church or Scripture, it is most fitting to attribute to Mary the Immaculate Conception which actually makes her need for the redeeming act of Christ even greater since it was required by God to prevent her from contracting any sin.[25]

Such theological reasoning by Scotus ought not to be judged a direct principle in the development of the dogma in 1854, but it did remove a formidable obstacle to the doctrinal object of the feast of Mary's Conception. As we well know from the first section of this essay, it certainly did not put an end to all theological debate. But the Scotistic solution cleared the way to continue it with a focus upon the center of the mystery of the Immaculate Conception in a church where its liturgical celebration gradually grew. And this is the factor that seems to have been the most influential principle in its dogmatic development. Referring to Newman's essay "On Consulting the Faithful in Matters of Doctrine," J. Pelikan observes that the "mutual concordance of devotion and dogma in the mariology of Athanasius deserves consideration as another principle and method of the development of doctrine" and that "proper praying and proper teaching together make the Church orthodox."[26] The axiom that is usually stated, *lex orandi, lex credendi,* takes its origin from the lay monk Prosper of Aquitaine, who formulated it between 435 and 442: ". . . legem credendi lex statuat supplicandi."[27] It may be literally translated: "Let the rule of supplication establish the rule [norm] of belief." Whether or not the axiom may be interpreted in the tradition as meaning that the norm of liturgical worship has a priority over the norm of magisterial teaching of the faith is still open to debate, but the historical development of the dogma of 1854 might favor the opinion that liturgical devotion shapes official doctrine.

Reflections on the Theological and Spiritual Signifcance of the Dogma

The primary reason given in *Ineffabilis Deus* for the doctrine of Mary's Immaculate Conception is that she was chosen to be *Theotokos* by the triune God.[28] This harmonizes with the constant theological testimony in tradition that Mary was blessed by God with special and even unique graces and privileges so that she might be a "worthy" God-bearer. It also accords with Vatican II's "hierarchy of truths," to which reference has been made at the outset in this essay. Within this hierarchy, in which the primary or central truths are the Trinity, incarnation, and redemption, Mary's Immaculate Conception would indeed be considered secondary or peripheral.[29] The function of such revealed truths or dogmas is to shed light upon the central mysteries of our Christian faith and also to inspire us to live more fully in fidelity to them. Besides the trinitarian and christocentric characteristics of the Immaculate Conception, by reason of the dogma's inherent relationship to Mary's motherhood of God the Son or Word made flesh, it has soteriological and ecclesiotypical aspects as well, which help enlighten us about the central mystery of our redemption by Christ alone and inspire us to more devoted discipleship.

Karl Rahner clearly affirmed: "Mary is intelligible only in terms of Christ. . . . It may be said that a sense of Marian dogma is an indication of whether Christological dogma is being taken really seriously."[30] It is only in the context of accepting her as the *Theotokos,* essentially a christological dogma defined at Ephesus to overcome the Nestorian crisis, that one can truly believe in the other Christian dogmas concerning Mary. Of all the redeemed she alone was included with Christ in the Trinity's predestination of the redemptive incarnation. Only she was so intimately involved by divine decree in the saving mystery of the Word made flesh that her free consent at the Annunciation was deemed a necessary condition for the redemption of the whole world. The fact that Mary was "full of grace" or "highly favored" by God made the right use of her freedom possible, but it did not diminish the freedom of her total consent.

In Mary's preservative redemption we behold the fullest revelation of God's redeeming love in and through Jesus Christ. In her the graces of the Holy Spirit were totally uninhibited by the consequences of original sin. As the first fruits of her son's redemptive activity, she shared in his total victory over sin and so was a completely undivided person, able to give herself entirely to love of God and neighbor. In her everything is grace, *sola gratia*. There is no guilt to hinder her freedom to hear God's word and faithfully follow his holy will (cf. Luke 11:28). Because of our faith in the mystery of Mary's Immaculate Conception, we can be convinced that, thanks to the redemptive work of her son, even in our sinful world grace has an absolute priority over guilt.[31] Even we who are conceived and born in original sin come into a world where the power of the triune God's redeeming love, totally victorious in her who was predestined to be the *Theotokos*, makes the mystery of good predominate over that of evil. Even before our own baptism, our own being conceived immaculately and born again in Christ, we enter a history immersed in salvation. The grace of Christ that was completely victorious in Mary from the beginning inspires us to be confident in and cooperative with the gracious God who makes all things possible, even her Immaculate Conception and our birth into eternal life.

Are there any ecumenical implications in such reflections regarding the relationship between the Immaculate Conception and the central dogmas of our Christian faith?[32] John Macquarrie seems to think so in his reformulation of the dogma of 1854.[33] He begins by removing from the notion of sin its metaphor of "stain" and proposes the analogy of "alienation" or "estrangement" in its place. He then defines original sin as "that corporate alienation of the whole race from God that distorts human society."[34] Mary's freedom or preservation from original sin means more positively that she enjoys divine grace in the fullness of grace a redeemed person has and that in her the alienation is not found. Mary's Immaculate Conception means that the original righteousness intended by God for all humankind is restored. He carefully distinguishes between her "receptive righteousness" and the Redeemer's righteousness which "is a dynamic, creative, innovating righteousness . . . [that] brings an eschatological promise . . . [which brings us to] a doctrine of incarnation: the creative righteousness of God himself has in Christ come among men."[35] Surely Macquarrie's approach, and that of others in the context of Vatican II's "hierarchy of truths," summon us to further dialogue about the possibilities of reformulating the dogma of 1854.[36]

AVERY DULLES, S.J.

11

The Dogma of the Assumption

After the proclamation of the Immaculate Conception of the Blessed Virgin in 1854, the definition of the Assumption was only a matter of time. The same kind of Marian piety underlay both doctrines. Practically all the biblical texts and theological arguments supporting either of these doctrines may be converted into arguments for the other. Of the two doctrines, the Assumption had a longer tradition in its favor, a firmer liturgical grounding, a greater consensus of theologians, and a broader ecumenical appeal. While there were difficulties in the way of the Assumption, nearly all these difficulties would tell at least as strongly against the Immaculate Conception, which had already been defined as a dogma. Once the Immaculate Conception had been defined, it could be used as a source of additional arguments for the Assumption. The two dogmas together represent the most problematic examples of the Catholic magisterium claiming a revealed status for doctrines having a relatively tenuous basis in Scripture and early tradition.

Before the meeting of Vatican Council I (1869–70) the Roman Jesuit periodical *Civiltà Cattolica* predicted that the Council would be a short one and that it would proclaim by acclamation two new dogmas: the infallibility of the pope and the bodily Assumption of Mary.[1] The first of these two dogmas was in fact defined, but only after lengthy debates. At Vatican I some 195 bishops from various parts of the world signed petitions that the Assumption be defined, but because of the premature adjournment of the Council these petitions were not acted upon.[2]

The petitionary movement, after temporarily subsiding, flared into new activity between 1900 and 1914 and again after World War I. Pius X (1903–14) and Benedict XV (1914–22), conscious of the grave difficulties that stood in the way of a dogmatic definition, responded with reserve, but Pius XI (1922–39) encouraged the movement.

Pius XII in many ways earned for himself the title, "pope of Mary."[3] In his first allocution to the college of cardinals (March 12, 1939) he declared that he was placing his pontificate under the patronage of the Blessed Virgin. Later in the same year he ordered the collection and publication of all the petitions received between 1849 and 1940 for the definition of the Assumption. They were accordingly published in two bulky volumes (each exceeding a thousand pages).[4] On May 1, 1946, the pope directed a brief encyclical, *Deiparae Virginis Mariae*, to all the bishops of the world.[5] In it he referred to the two volumes of petitions, requested prayers that he might be guided to God's will in the matter, and put to each of the bishops two questions: "Do you, in your outstanding prudence and wisdom, judge that the bodily Assumption of the Blessed Virgin can be proposed and defined as a dogma of the faith? And do you, with your clergy and people, desire this?" As summarized by reliable authors,[6] more than 98 percent of the bishops answered by August 1950. Of the bishops who answered, 1,210 (more than 98 percent) were in favor of both the possibility and the opportuneness of the definition. Only twenty-two (less than 2 percent) expressed doubts. Sixteen doubted the opportuneness and only six (less than half a percent) doubted the revealed character of the Assumption.

On February 24, 1948, Cardinal Ernesto Ruffini of Palermo suggested the convening of an ecumenical council.[7] On March 4 Pius XII discussed the possibility with Cardinal Ottaviani. According to the original plans the council would, among other things, solemnly proclaim the dogma of the Assumption. But as disagreements arose about the agenda and as the world's bishops registered a lack of enthusiasm, plans for the council were abandoned in 1951. Much of the proposed agenda had meanwhile been accomplished through the encyclical letter *Humani generis* (August 12, 1950) and the proclamation of the dogma of the Assumption by the pope himself in the apostolic constitution, *Munificentissimus Deus* (November 1, 1950).

The dogma was not defined without careful preparatory work, to which the pope called attention in a semipublic consistory held on October 30, 1950, just before the proclamation. He appointed a special commission to study the testimonies of the church's magisterium, sacred Scripture, the ancient liturgy, and the teaching of the Fathers and theologians.[8]

During the 1940s there was an intense inner-Catholic debate occasioned by the likelihood of a dogmatic definition. The indispensable reference point for the issues is a 747-page work by Martin Jugie, A.A., entitled *La Mort et l'Assomption de la Sainte Vierge*, published at Vatican City and dedicated to Pius XII.[9] In the first two parts of this work Jugie traced the history of the material from Scripture through the ninth century and from the tenth century to the present. In the third and last part he gave his own reflections on the state of the question regarding both the death of Mary and her Assumption. Eleven points in this comprehensive study may be singled out for special mention.

(1) There are no direct testimonies in Scripture about the death or glorification of Mary, but several biblical texts such as Revelation, chapter 12, can be, and have been, interpreted as referring to these events.

(2) The patristic tradition of the first five centuries offers no clear and explicit affirmation of the Assumption as the term is understood today.

(3) The apocryphal legends of the *Transitus Mariae*, widespread in the sixth and seventh centuries, do not appear to be based on historical testimonies; they reflect beliefs current at the time of their composition.

(4) Some of the liturgical texts for the Feasts of the Dormition and the Assumption, both in the East and in the West, refer to a transfer of Mary's body to a celestial paradise.

(5) A number of Greek Fathers after the ninth century hold that Mary was exempt from bodily corruption.

(6) The few Western Fathers who even raise the question express ignorance of the fate of Mary's body (Isidore of Seville, the Venerable Bede). In the early Middle Ages some affirmed the Assumption on the basis of Pseudo-Augustine, but others professed ignorance on the basis of Pseudo-Jerome.

(7) Beginning with the thirteenth century the disciples of Pseudo-Augustine became more numerous. They include the major doctors of the church from Bonaventure and Aquinas through Bellarmine, Canisius, and Francis de Sales. Several of these expressed horror at the thought of the body of the Blessed Virgin being consumed by worms.

(8) In the nineteenth and early twentieth centuries pressure for a dogmatic definition of the Assumption was increased through a strong petitionary movement. While no doubt directed by the Holy Spirit, this movement was sometimes theologically naïve and imprecise, thus indicating that the doctrine still needed to be clarified theologically before solemn definition.

(9) Patristic sources show no unanimity about when or how Mary died. Jugie speculates that she may have simply departed from this world without dying.[10]

(10) Prescinding from the death of Mary, the Assumption may be judged to be formally revealed by reason of its evident connection with other revealed truths, such as the Immaculate Conception and the Divine Motherhood. The way appears to be clear for a solemn definition of the Assumption provided that this be detached from all reference to her bodily death.

(11) It would also be possible for the pope to proclaim as a "dogmatic fact" that Mary is in heaven, body and soul. This proclamation, while engaging the infallibility of the pope, would leave open the question whether the Assumption is part of the apostolic deposit of faith.

Subsequent scholars made abundant use of Jugie's work, but many found fault with it. Carlo Balić rejected the charge that the modern mariological movement was generally superficial and uncritical. He accused Jugie of departing from the sound method of traditional theology and of indulging an "uncatholic skepticism" based on Descartes's method of doubt. Maintaining that the death and resurrection of Mary would be obliquely contained in a definition of the Assumption, Balić especially challenged Jugie's doubts about whether Mary actually died.[11]

At the other end of the spectrum, Berthold Altaner, an eminent Catholic patrologist, while applauding Jugie's critical assessments of the evidence, contested his conclusion that in spite of its feeble support in Scripture and the Fathers the Assumption could fittingly be defined.[12] The typological and allegorical exegesis was of no scientific value and could not be used to establish the Assumption as an article of faith.[13] The arguments from the theological tradition proved only that the Assumption was admissible as a "pious opinion." Theological speculation could produce nothing better than arguments *ex convenientia*, which are never probative. While many of the faithful do believe in the Assumption, it is not clear how many believe that it belongs to the apostolic deposit of faith. In view of the present world situation of mounting atheism, and especially in view of the developing ecumenical relations with other Christian communities, the dogmatization of the Assumption would be inopportune.

More moderate than Altaner, but still opposed to a dogmatic proclamation, was the Belgian exegete Joseph Coppens.[14] Writing in 1947, he seconded Jugie's critiques of the petitionary movement. Against Balić he objected that one could not rely simply on the magisterium and on the lived sense of the faithful. A definition would require convincing evidence from Scripture and tradition that the Assumption was contained in the apostolic deposit of faith. It could not be deduced by aprioristic arguments, for God always remains free to do the unexpected. The scriptural arguments are inconclusive, giving only hints of Mary's Assumption. The patristic testimonies are contradictory, confused, and partly influenced by apocryphal legends. Systematic arguments from Mary's Immaculate Conception and from her close association with Christ's redemptive work can certify the Assumption as a theological conclusion but not as a revealed truth.

The total concept of the Assumption, according to Coppens, includes the death and resurrection of Mary as well as her full glorification. Even with the help of faith, however, we cannot achieve certitude about the death of Mary and the reanimation of her body. For this reason the integral concept of the Assumption should not be defined. In the present dechristianized world, moreover, the Assumption is too remote from the kernel of Christian faith for its definition to be opportune. It would offer grounds for unbelievers to reproach the church for yielding to the fabulatory tendencies of religious feeling.

Jugie's suggestion of an integral canonization of Mary (body and soul) appealed to Coppens. The object of such a canonization would be the full heavenly glory of Mary, without anything being said about her death and resuscitation. The grounds for the canonization would be Mary's unique sanctity and the experience of the church in worship throughout the centuries. Canonization would certify Mary's heavenly blessedness as a "dogmatic fact" but would obviate the need to affirm the doctrine as resting on historical testimonies going back to the apostles.

Theologians favoring the dogmatic definition took Coppens's proposals seriously but did not fully agree. Gérard Philips, a colleague of Coppens at Louvain, published an article in 1948 that does not mention Coppens but is evidently intended as a reply.[15]

An integral canonization of Mary, according to Philips, would not suffice because the infallibility of such canonizations is not universally admitted. Furthermore, the glorious exaltation of Mary should not be seen as a mere dogmatic fact but as bound up with God's revelation in Christ; it tells us something about Christ's divinizing work and the effect of that work upon the body. There are convincing theological reasons for holding that Mary, as Mother of God, was associated in a very intimate way with the salvific mission of her son. She was the object of a unique election that preserved her from all sin and consequently rendered her incapable of being held by the bonds of death. What scholarly analysis could establish as a theological conclusion might then be validated by the magisterium, with its charism of discernment, as a truth implicit in revelation.

Doctrines such as the Immaculate Conception and the Assumption, according to Philips, were the fruits of progressive doctrinal reflection. To appreciate the process it was important to realize that theological reasoning in such matters does not proceed by rectilinear or syllogistic logic but by a convergence of probabilities in the light of the church's living tradition. It would be a mistake to seek either a proof or a disproof of a mystery such as the Assumption by the methods of scientific history.

At Rome Joseph Filograssi, a Jesuit, published another carefully reasoned response to Coppens.[16] In answer to Coppens's critique of the petitionary movement he called attention to the value that Jugie himself had seen in the movement and to the pope's favorable reference to the two volumes of petitions in his 1946 encyclical. Since then, Filograssi argues, the consensus has become clearer than when Jugie wrote his book. As for the object of the petition, the pope had expressly asked whether the bishops and their faithful held that the Assumption could and should be defined as a matter of faith. Thus there need no longer be any suspicion that the petitions were attesting mere "pious opinions."

As for the content of the definition, most of the petitions make no mention of Mary's death or resurrection, which Coppens described as pertaining to the "integral" concept of the Assumption. The essential is simply that Mary has passed into the full life of heavenly glory—a fact not knowable by historical testimonies but only by revelation. While Filograssi is personally convinced that Mary did die, he does not think that this would need to be included in the doctrine as defined.

The fact of the Assumption, according to Filograssi, is certain by reason of the faith-consciousness of the contemporary church. Admittedly neither Scripture nor early tradition, studied by the methods of philological exegesis and academic history, can yield a cogent argument. But theology uses a dogmatic approach, reading the sources in the light of the church's developed faith. Once the Assumption has been accepted as a revealed truth—as it ought to be on the basis of the faith of the church today—it can be seen to be implicitly contained in other truths and especially in three other privileges of Mary: her divine maternity, her Immaculate Conception, and her virginal motherhood.

Finally, as regards opportuneness, a dogmatic proclamation would fulfill the desires of the whole Catholic world; it would enhance the glory of Mary and her son; it would strengthen the resurrection hope of the faithful; and it would lead to deeper reverence for the human body.

In one of several subsequent articles on the Assumption, Filograssi responded at length to Altaner.[17] He objected to Altaner's tendency to read the sources (Scripture and tradition) with the tools of philology and scientific history rather than in the light of the church's living faith. Filograssi, on the contrary, worked regressively, beginning with the present consensus of the bishops and the Catholic faithful and deducing that what the church today believes as a matter of faith must be contained in the sources. For him the only question was "how" the Assumption was contained in Scripture and apostolic tradition; the "whether" was not debatable. Taking his notion of tradition from Franzelin and Billot, Filograssi practically equated tradition with the doctrine of the magisterium, which perpetuated the apostolic preaching.

The bull of definition, *Munificentissimus Deus*, issued on November 1, 1950, scarcely requires any explanation, but some comments may be made about the organization, method, and selection of materials.[18] The introductory section has three divisions. First, the pope expresses his satisfaction at the growing devotion to Mary, which in recent years has led to greater clarity about the bodily Assumption of Mary. Then he remarks on the intrinsic links between the mysteries of the Immaculate Conception and the Assumption.[19] Finally, he rapidly surveys the petitionary movement from the time of the First Vatican Council and recalls the two questions he had put to the bishops in his encyclical of 1946.

The body of the apostolic constitution is structured according to the "regressive" method approved in the encyclical *Humani generis*.[20] This method gives pride of place to the living magisterium, which authoritatively proclaims the content of revelation, and to the existing consensus of the faithful, and then seeks to garner support in Scripture and tradition. The responses to his questionnaire, the pope states, make it indubitable that the Assumption is accepted as a revealed truth by a morally unanimous agreement of the bishops and faithful. Thus the Assumption is already a tenet of divine and Catholic faith. Since, moreover, the faith of the church extends only to contents of the apostolic deposit of faith, it follows that the doctrine of the Assumption is contained in the sources, namely, in Scripture and tradition, even though not so clearly that it could be found there with full assurance by purely exegetical and historical study.

In the next major segment Pius XII assembles "various testimonies, indications, and signs of this common belief of the Church," beginning from patristic times. Five groups of testimonies are successively treated: popular piety, liturgical texts, patristic teaching, Scholastic theology, and modern theology.

Commenting on popular piety, the pope observes that the faithful, enlightened by divine grace, became convinced that Mary's holy body had never been reduced to dust and ashes. Many churches, dioceses, regions, and religious institutes have been placed under the patronage of the *Assumpta*. Since the early sixteenth century the Rosary has included the Assumption among the glorious mysteries.

Under the heading of liturgy the pope deals with the ways in which the Dormition or Assumption has been celebrated in the Eastern and Western churches since about the seventh century. Numerous texts from the Byzantine liturgy allude specifically to the incorruption and glorification of Mary's holy body. In the West the sacramentary that Pope Adrian I (772–97) sent to Charlemagne contains the collect prayer *Veneranda*, asserting that the blessed Virgin "could not be held down by the bonds of death" ("nec tamen mortis nexibus deprimi potuit"). The Gallican sacramentary, slightly later, has an Introit that powerfully suggests the death and bodily resurrection of Mary. In the Roman liturgy the observance of the Assumption was prescribed by Saint Sergius I (687–701) as one of the four Marian feasts. Saint Leo IV (847–55) elevated it as a solemn feast, preceded by a vigil and followed by an octave.

The divine office and the martyrology would have afforded less powerful arguments than the Mass-texts to which the bull refers. The ninth-century martyrologies of Ado of Vienne and Usuard state that the sacred body of Mary is not found on earth, but that it is better to confess ignorance than to indulge in frivolous and apocryphal speculations. The breviary read in much of the West contained readings from Paschasius Radbertus to the effect that it is not known whether Mary's body returned to life. Only in the time of Saint Pius V (1570–72) and Gregory XIII (1584) were the breviary and martyrology, respectively, reformed so as to include unequivocal statements about the Assumption.[21]

In the next section, dealing with the Fathers of the church, the pope cites three Eastern writers, John Damascene (d. 749), Germanus of Constantinople (d. 733), and an unnamed author generally identified either as Modestus or as Pseudo-Modestus of Jerusalem (late seventh century). All of these witnesses are very clear, though somewhat influenced by the Apocrypha.

Pius XII does not speak of any Western Fathers, for none of them clearly attests the Assumption. He also passes over in silence the disputes that began during the Carolingian Renaissance, when the Eastern legends of the *Transitus Mariae* became popular in the West. It was at this time that Pseudo-Jerome (Paschasius Radbertus, d. 865) expressed ignorance concerning the fate of Mary's body. Nor does the pope mention Pseudo-Augustine, whose *Liber de Assumptione*, circulated as a work of Augustine himself, was to have great influence on the Scholastic theologians.[22] This author, whom some identify as Ratramnus (d. 868), argues to the bodily Assumption of Mary on the grounds of "reasons of suitability."

Passing on to the early Scholastic period, the bull mentions several biblical texts that were often injected into the speculative discussion about the Assumption. Four such texts are cited: Ps 131:8, Song of Songs 3:6, Luke 1:28, and Rev 12:1-6. While none of them in its literal meaning refers to the Assumption, these texts are capable of suggesting it to devout minds and of being used effectively in homiletic and devotional literature about the Mother of God.

Turning to individual witnesses, *Munificentissimus Deus* mentions from the early Scholastic period Blessed Amadeus of Lausanne (d. 1159) and Saint Anthony of Padua (d. 1231). A variety of other witnesses from this period, although cited in standard works,[23] are omitted by Pius XII. Saint Bernard, for instance, preached five sermons on the feast, but his vague expressions could be interpreted as referring to an exaltation of the soul alone. By contrast, Bernard's great rival, Peter Abelard, in one of his sermons gives a lengthy defense of Mary's corporeal Assumption. Several of the Victorine theologians (Richard and Walter) are quite explicit in favor of a bodily Assumption.

Passing on to the golden age of Scholasticism and the baroque period, the apostolic constitution cites a large number of major theologians and doctors of the church from the thirteenth century (Bonaventure, Albertus Magnus, Thomas Aquinas), the fifteenth century (Bernardine of Siena), the sixteenth century (Peter Canisius, Francisco Suarez), the seventeenth century (Robert Bellarmine, Francis de Sales), and the eighteenth century (Alphonsus de'Liguori), all of whom clearly taught the fact of Mary's bodily Assumption. This list could be amplified.[24] It is difficult to find any Catholic theologian of modern times overtly doubting or denying the doctrine.

Parenthetically it should be remarked that these authors, while accepting the Assumption, did not regard it as a dogma of the faith. Suarez, favoring the definability of the Assumption, held that prior to definition, it would be rash but not heretical to deny the doctrine.[25] Cardinal Prosper de Lambertinis (who later became Pope Benedict XIV, 1740–58) took the same position.[26] The approved Latin manuals of the nineteenth and early twentieth centuries generally held that the Assumption is a theologically certain doctrine, the denial of which would be temerarious but not heretical (see H. Hurter, A. Tanquerey, C. Pesch, G. von Noort, F. Diekamp, etc.). These authors were not of one mind as to whether the Assumption was revealed and thus definable as a matter of divine and Catholic faith.

Munificentissimus Deus goes on to state that all the arguments and considerations of the holy Fathers and theologians are based on sacred Scripture as their ultimate foundation. It offers a somewhat complex argument drawing on various texts from the Old and New Testaments. Genesis 3:15 predicts an enduring conflict between Eve and Satan and their respective progeny, suggesting the ultimate defeat of Satan. Paul speaks of redemption as a swallowing up of death in victory (1 Cor 15:54). Relying on the patristic identification of Mary as the new Eve, closely associated with the new Adam in his struggle and victory, the pope concludes that she must share in his triumph just as Eve shared in Adam's fall. If Mary's body had been given over to corruption, rather than being taken up into heavenly glory, Satan would have triumphed over her in some measure.

As an auxiliary argument, with an implicit reference to Exod 20:12, the bull suggests that Jesus would not have duly honored his mother had he not preserved her body from the corruption of the tomb. This would appear to be an argument *ex convenientia*, resting on a human estimation of what it would have been fitting for Jesus to do.

Pius XII then proposes reasons based on the *analogia fidei*, the harmony of the total economy of revelation. It presents the Assumption as the crowning privilege that follows upon, and is the appropriate complement to, four other privileges: (1) Mary as Mother of God is from all eternity joined with Jesus Christ in one and the same decree of predestination; (2) she is immaculate in her conception; (3) she is a perfect virgin in her divine motherhood; and (4) as the most noble associate of Jesus she obtained complete victory over sin and concupiscence. These harmonies, though not proffered as stringent proofs of the Assumption, render it antecedently probable, at least for Christians who accept the other Marian doctrines.

At the end of his survey of the testimonies the pope summarizes the state of the question. He recalls the unanimous teaching of the bishops, the consent of the faithful, the biblical foundations, the approved liturgies, and the harmony with other revealed truths, as well as the wisdom of the theologians who have scrutinized the evidence. In view of all these convergent testimonies and the petitions received from so many bishops and faithful, he judges that the moment for a solemn definition has now arrived.

Before actually formulating the new dogma, Pius XII considers the opportuneness of the definition. As positive grounds he adduces the importance of recourse to Mary as a remedy against the widespread evils of our time, the glory that the definition will give to God, the anticipated contribution of the definition to Marian piety, the inspiration afforded by Mary's union with God, and the added force that her Assumption can give to our understanding of the dignity and destiny of our own bodies. The Holy Year of 1950 provides an auspicious occasion for the definition.

The definition itself is briefly and cautiously phrased: It is "a divinely revealed dogma that the Immaculate Mother of God, the ever Virgin Mary, having completed the course of her earthly life, was assumed body and soul into heavenly glory." The affirmation proceeds, as it were, backward from the present situation of Mary in glory rather than forward from her earthly history, thus avoiding many of the problems raised by the lack of reliable historical testimonies, and by conflicting theological speculations, about the death and entombment of Mary.

The definition is followed, as is customary, by an anathema: "If anyone, which God forbid, should dare willfully to deny or to call into doubt that which We have defined, let him know that he has fallen away completely from the divine and Catholic faith." This warning is given on the principle that faith disposes a person to believe everything contained in divine revelation and taught as such by the church.[27] The concluding anathema applies only to those who willfully presume to doubt or deny ("si quis . . . voluntarie ausus fuerit"). Nothing is here said about those Catholics or non-Catholics who doubt or deny the Assumption because they are in good faith unconvinced that it has been divinely revealed.

The doctrine of the Assumption raises very trenchantly the problem of the development of dogma. It is an axiom in Catholic theology that the full contents of Christian faith were revealed by the end of the apostolic age. The Assumption, however, is not attested either in Scripture or in the early monuments of tradition. How, then, can it be reckoned as a revealed truth? In answer to this problem three basic positions may be distinguished.[28]

One school, represented by F. Marin-Sola's monumental study,[29] holds that the magisterium is capable of dogmatically defining truths that are homogeneous with, and logically deduced from, the original deposit of faith. The infallibility of the magisterium can guarantee the equivalence between the apostolic deposit and conclusions inferred from that deposit. Under certain conditions truths syllogistically deduced from the sources of revelation can be converted into dogmas.

Theologians of a second school deny that virtually revealed truths, even under the conditions specified by Marin-Sola, could attain the status of dogma. If the conclusion is a new truth, over and above what was contained in the deposit, it is not believed simply on the authority of the revealing God and thus cannot be proposed by the church as revealed. Every dogma, according to R. Schultes, the leading proponent of this second theory, must be formally, rather than only virtually, implicit in the deposit of apostolic revelation.[30]

If the apostolic deposit consists simply of the verbal statements contained in Scripture and apostolic tradition, as these two theories seem to presuppose, it is difficult to explain how dogmas such as the Assumption, which does not seem to be either virtually or formally implicit in the texts, could be defined. Thus theologians were under pressure to devise a more adequate theory of development. New Scripture studies and epistemologies were already indicating that revelation was not originally communicated or subsequently transmitted in merely propositional form. It was communicated and transmitted through persons and events contemplated by believers under the grace-given light of faith. From this it seemed to follow that the true bearers of dogmatic progress would be believers who perceived the significance of the realities of revelation with the help of a God-given instinct, known as the *sensus fidei*. Theology, with its rigorous inferential processes, could assist and monitor the process, but theologians themselves must be open to the leading of the Spirit. The magisterium, which is charged with the responsibility of judging the authenticity of the developments, has a charism for assessing whether they correspond to the objective meaning of the patrimony of faith.[31]

According to this third explanation, favored by many contemporary theologians—such as Karl Rahner, newly defined dogmas simply make explicit what was implicit in revelation from the beginning.[32] To this extent the third theory agrees with the other two, but it differs from them in maintaining that the movement from implicit to explicit is not accomplished only, or even preponderantly, by syllogistic logic. It appeals to the kind of informal reasoning analyzed by Newman under the rubric of the "illative sense." Although the first and second theories are quite helpful in explaining certain historical developments of dogma, the third would seem to give the most satisfactory account of dogmas such as the Assumption.

It goes without saying that *Munificentissimus Deus* is not a timeless document. Written in 1950, it bears the mark of the Marian movement, which was then cresting, and of the neo-Scholastic theology canonized in *Humani generis*. The definition was proclaimed in an atmosphere of great Marian enthusiasm and magisterial self-confidence. Since the definition theologians have had to reflect soberly on its contents and its grounds. To narrate the whole history of theological interpretation, for the forty-odd years since the definition, would exceed the limits of this essay. It may be sufficient to mention several major theologians.

Karl Rahner published an important article on the Assumption in 1951[33] and treated it again in his small book, *Mary the Mother of the Lord*.[34] He also made the Assumption the primary theme of his 479-page course on Mariology at the University of Innsbruck.[35] In the course he noted three types of significance in the new dogma: the mariological, the eschatological, and the anthropological.[36]

Mariologically considered, the Assumption is the consummation of Mary's career. This consummation is not an extrinsic addition but rather the inner *telos* toward which the entire existence of Mary from the beginning was already tending. If the fundamental mariological principle is that Mary is perfectly redeemed, the Assumption is the mystery that most fully exhibits what Mary was and is. Unless or until she was glorified in body and in soul, Mary could not be the completed sign of the redemptive power of grace.

Eschatologically considered, the Assumption is closely connected with the resurrection of Jesus. His body, which remains a piece of this world, was taken up and glorified at the moment of his resurrection, thus inaugurating the end of time. Jesus, however, did not rise for himself alone, but as the first fruits of the new creation. Following H. Zeller and others, Rahner maintains that the saints who arose and appeared in Jerusalem, according to Matt 27:52-53, entered with Jesus into the life of glory. If so, it is natural to suppose that Mary, as the most perfect fruit of the redemption, would also have been taken up into heavenly glory. In proclaiming this as a fact, the church is faithful to its vocation to attest to the realities of salvation. The church announces that in Mary the flesh is already saved.[37]

In its anthropological significance the Assumption reminds us that a human person is not just an accidental combination of body and soul, but a substantial unity of both, and that the whole human race is involved in a single history of salvation leading to the final consummation that has already begun in the flesh of Christ. In her total redemption Mary is not just an exception to be admired, but the very type of redeemed humanity. What she is, each of us hopes to become. Far from divinizing Mary (as some opponents of the dogma have alleged), the Assumption asserts of her only what is promised as the final destiny of all the redeemed.

From a rather early period in his career Rahner had difficulties with the Scholastic theory of the "separated soul," which seemed to him to reflect an unbiblical, Hellenistic anthropology. In his later writings he several times proposed the hypothesis that for all human beings the resurrection might occur immediately after death.[38] If this hypothesis is correct, the dogma of the Assumption "does not refer to something granted to Mary alone, but to what belongs generally to all who are saved, while appropriate to her in a special way in virtue of her function in salvation history."[39] In thus eliminating the hypothesis of an "intermediate state" between death and the general resurrection, Rahner thinks it possible to make the dogma of the Assumption more credible and convincing, especially to Protestant theologians.[40] The conviction that the dead already enjoy some kind of corporeal existence reduces the temptation to imagine the resurrection of the flesh in mythological ways.

Rahner's views on the "intermediate state" seemed to be rejected by a declaration of the Congregation for the Doctrine of the Faith in 1979. This declaration warned against theories "that would deprive the assumption of Mary of its unique meaning, namely the fact that the bodily assumption of Mary is an anticipation of the glorification that is the destiny of all the elect."[41]

Joseph Ratzinger, among others, has dissociated himself from the idea that for all human beings the resurrection takes place at the moment of death. While acknowledging that this theory removes much of the scandal attached to the dogma of the Assumption, he suspects that this theory does not do justice to the corporeal element in resurrection, for it attaches no importance to the body, which is ordinarily left behind at death.[42] It also does away with the clear interval between the death of Jesus and his resurrection "on the third day."[43]

In his little book, *Daughter Zion*, Ratzinger points out that the dogma of the Assumption takes its rise from doxology. It is a solemn form of hymnology, "an act of Marian veneration in the form of a dogmatic statement."[44] Hence we should not look for historical evidence, as in the case of the resurrection of Jesus. Yet the dogma is grounded in the affirmations of faith. It fulfills both the biblical prophecy, "Behold, henceforth all generations will call me blessed" (Luke 1:48), and the words of Elizabeth, "Blessed is she who believed" (Luke 1:45). These texts give a special applicability to Mary of the teaching of Ephesians that God raises up the baptized with Christ and makes them sit with him in heavenly places with Jesus (Eph 2:6).

Ratzinger sees a predominantly ecclesial significance in the dogma of the Assumption. The church, he states, is already saved in Mary. Because in Mary the New Israel has already ascended into heaven, its election is sure; it can no longer be rejected. In Mary as she has been assumed the church has not only the promise but a bodily realization of the promised salvation.[45]

Writing from an ecumenical point of view after Vatican II, John Macquarrie, an Anglican, observes that the linkage established by the Council between the church and Mary as its type, model, and preeminent member may be used to go back and interpret the dogma of 1950.[46] One reason for believing the Assumption, he maintains, is the impossibility of supposing that Mary—who conceived Christ, bore him, and gave him milk—could be separated from him at the end of her earthly life. Mary's solidarity with her son is such that his Ascension implies her Assumption, since it is Christ's desire that those whom the Father has given him should be with him where he is (John 17:22, 24). The feast of the Assumption, Macquarrie concludes, is thoroughly humanistic: it is not just a celebration of Mary (though it certainly is that) but a celebration of redeemed humanity. The dogma helps us to understand the church eschatologically. The church will reach its completeness only in the end, but it receives flashes of the final glory to encourage it on its way. The Assumption of Mary, then, is the beginning of a vaster and, indeed, a cosmic assumption. Speaking autobiographically, Macquarrie closes by saying: "From a vague half-belief, for the most part not understood, I have come to see the dogma of the Assumption as the expression in appropriate theological symbols of some of the most hopeful affirmations of the Christian faith."

CARL J. PETER

12

The Saints and Mary in the Eschatology of the Second Vatican Council

THE COUNCIL'S VIEW OF MARY

On October 24, 1963, a crucial exchange took place between two speakers addressing the fifty-fifth general congregation of the Second Vatican Council.[1] At issue was the way in which the Synod would formulate its teaching on Mary.

By way of background, this should be noted. A year earlier a draft-text had been distributed under the title *De Beata Maria Virgine Matre Dei et Hominum*.[2] Already at that time seven speakers had touched on the question of Mariology in addresses to the Council.[3] But it was widely recognized that many more reactions would be needed. These were sought and time was given (until the end of February in 1963) for the submission of opinions on the schema dealing with Mary. Eighty-five participants responded to this call for input.

The Council worked not as a committee of the whole but through commissions. It was of course the Doctrinal Commission (*Commissio de doctrina fidei et morum*) that had responsibility in this instance. But the members of that commission were unable to reach agreement. Some (actually a majority in a divided vote on October 9, 1963) wished to integrate the conciliar teaching on Mary into the schema on the church. The alternative would be to deal with Mariology in a separate document. More was involved than an appropriate division of subject matter. The schema before the Council had been given a new title: *De Beata Maria Virgine Matre Ecclesiae.* It was clear that something had to be done. A solution was found; each side would be provided an opportunity to make a case for its position.

The first to speak to the question on October 24, 1963, was Cardinal Rufini Santos of Manila.[4] He argued for a treatment of Mariology in its own right, that is, in a separate conciliar document. In the process he asked whether Mariology should be reduced to ecclesiology—whether the dimensions of the latter are broad enough to include all of Mariology. His answer to both was in the negative. Such a reduction ought to be avoided because Mariology is related to Christology and soteriology as well.[5] This would not be brought out if Mary were treated solely in the context of the church. What is more, he said he thought the most likely place for a treatment of Mary in the schema *De Ecclesia* would be after the presentation of the church as mystery in the divine plan. This would associate Mary's work too closely with that of the Trinity[6] and be every bit as misleading as making her another member of the church. A separate document was needed to avoid saying too little and too much.

Next to speak was the Archbishop of Vienna, Cardinal Koenig, who favored including Mariology in the Council's teaching on the church.[7] In an effort to make a case for this position he faced head-on an objection that he knew would be forthcoming. Some of his hearers would surely say he was asking the Council to embrace a Mariology that was "exclusively ecclesiotypical." By this they would mean a presentation of Mary as "one church member among others—a member passively receiving the benefits of the Redeemer."[8] In reply Koenig made it clear that he wished to see the role of neither Mary nor the church presented in any such fashion. The church is not, he said, a mere fruit of the redemption; it is as well an instrument of redemption in the hand of Christ—an instrument "actively cooperating in the process of salvation."[9] Let the church be described from this perspective! Then Mary can be presented as the one who "in the most sublime way and as a result of His grace cooperates with Christ in bringing about and expanding the work of salvation."[10]

A way out of the impasse had to be found. The next day, October 25, copies of the addresses delivered by Santos and Koenig were distributed. Members of the assembly were given time to reflect on the matter. On October 29 they were asked to determine whether the schema on Mary should be modified by being incorporated into the draft of the document dealing with the church.[11] Of those casting ballots 1,114 voted *Placet* (i.e., to treat of Mary in the teaching on the church) and 1,074 *Non Placet* (i.e., they wished to deal with Mariology in a separate document). Two violated the rules; they suggested amendments (*Placet juxta Modum*). There were as well three other invalid ballots (*Nulla*).[12] The margin of victory was narrow, less than 2 percent of those voting.

But the figures should not deceive one.[13] Underlying them is a shared faith about Christ as well as the nature and results of justification. To the question whether Mary is an agent with Christ or rather a passive beneficiary of redemption, Santos and Koenig replied: (a) her place is not with the Trinity but with the other recipients of her son's redemption; (b) not despite the fact but precisely because of the fact that she is always one redeemed *sola gratia*, she is, like the community which is the church, actively engaged in the work of the redemption; and (c) because of the unique grace she has received, her role is of surpassing importance in God's plan of salvation.

The close vote meant there would be future disputes about what should or should not be said regarding Mary (e.g., as Mediatrix) in the context of teaching about the church in relation to Christ. But paradoxically enough the agreement clearly present, despite differences in the opposing speeches of Santos and Koenig, would later come to expression in chapter 8 of *Lumen Gentium* and win almost unanimous conciliar approval. Thus to understand the Mariology of Vatican II one must have recourse to its ecclesiology and Christology: Mary is associated both with Christ the Redeemer and with the redeemed. To put it another way, it is at very least misleading to describe the conciliar Mariology as being exclusively either christotypical or ecclesiotypical.

What About Other Saints?

Before proceeding to a consideration of this Mariology, a number of questions suggest themselves. Is Mary the only one who is holy because of Christ? What, for example, of other holy people who lived after her day down through the centuries? If it is important to relate her justification and sanctification to the mystery of Christ and the church, what about theirs?

Saints other than Mary had not been forgotten by Pope John XXIII as he envisioned the work of the Second Vatican Council.

During the period when preparations were under way, he asked for a special study dealing with the cult of the saints: "in particular, its spirit, nature and limits, its indispensability within Catholic worship and its authentic forms."[14] Initially it was intended that there would be a special document dealing with these matters—just as in the case of Mariology. To this end and prior to the death of John XXIII, Cardinal Larraona, Prefect of the Congregation of Rites, together with a small commission which he chaired, produced a text.

After Pope Paul VI's election on June 30, 1963, he approved the project and sent the text to the Council's Doctrinal Commission. The work that had been done was then subjected to scrutiny by a subcommission of that body. Those charged with the task included Cardinals Santos and Koenig as well as the Archbishop of Toulouse, Gabriel Garrone. This group made important decisions about the treatment of the saints.

The Council's decision about the locus for teaching about Mary suggested that other saints as well should be presented in relation to both Christ and the church. The obvious place was "after" the treatment of the church in time and "before" that of Mary, who is with her son in heaven. Opting for this order, the subcommission decided to give the teaching about the saints the place it now occupies as a chapter in *Lumen Gentium*. To this end they added an introductory section to the text they had received and thereby called attention to the "eschatological" character of the pilgrim church as well as its relation to the church in heaven.[15] At the same time they excised the final section, which proposed new procedures for beatification and canonization. The result was a revised document dealing with the church; this was sent by mail to the Council members in the summer of 1964.

That fall the text dealing with the saints came to the floor and was discussed in general congregations of the Council in mid-September. Seventeen speakers addressed themselves to the draft; twenty-eight members of the assembly submitted their observations in writing.

The result was more work for the Council's Doctrinal Commission, namely, that of considering changes that had been suggested by the discussion. When this task was completed, a revised text dealing with the saints was presented to the Council by Cardinal Santos. He explained why some amendments had been accepted and why others had not. The four sections into which the text was divided were then voted on individually. This was on October 19,

1964; each of the four was approved by over 99 percent of those voting.[16] Then the text was voted on as a whole. This time amendments were allowed (*Placet juxta Modum*), but given the prior approval of each paragraph in such overwhelming numbers, the *modi* were not to change the substance of the text. The results: 1,921 voted *Placet*; twenty-nine voted *Non Placet*; 233 offered *modi*.[17] Of the 233 fifteen were accepted. Finally, the text dealing with the saints (chapter 7 of *Lumen Gentium*) was voted on in its entirety and approved by a majority of 2,127 out of 2,131.[18] This meant that first the saints and then Mary would be dealt with and eschatology would provide the link uniting both to the earlier treatment of God's pilgrim people. Attention must now be directed to that eschatology.

THE ESCHATOLOGICAL NATURE OF THE PILGRIM CHURCH AND ITS UNION WITH THE HEAVENLY CHURCH

Of the future to which God's people on earth look forward because of Jesus Christ, *Lumen Gentium* speaks in the four sections (48–51) of the seventh chapter. Each of these will be considered in turn.

The text of section 48 begins by speaking of Christ's church as looking to the future for its final perfection. The eschatology that is being expressed here is clearly one involving a completion of work that God has already begun.

That future is described as a renovation involving not merely the entire human race but the rest of the world as well. Everything is going to be reestablished in Christ; the eschaton is therefore not to be an event confined to the human psyche with no effect on the cosmos. The agents already involved in bringing this about are the glorified Christ and his life-giving Spirit. To put it another way, the future that has been promised is a restoration already begun in Christ and continuing through the Holy Spirit in the church. There it is that believers: (a) learn the meaning of their temporal existence, (b) hope for a future better than the present, (c) carry out tasks that are theirs to accomplish because God so wills, and (d) work out their salvation. Despite its imperfections, the church's holiness anticipates that renewal toward which the world is heading in this its final age. Until the end, when justice will finally triumph, the church will have sacraments and institutions that belong to this age rather than that which is to come. During the interim the church takes on a form that is destined to pass away; it dwells in the midst of creatures that cry out in labor pains and await the final revelation—which is birth into the divine family.

The final paragraphs of section 48 bring out further the similarities and the differences (as well as the nexus) between the church in the present and in its final consummation. This is accomplished by an accumulation of biblical images.

Because of Christ and the Spirit, who is a pledge (Eph 1:14), the church's members are already God's own children (1 John 3:1). Their life is now hidden; when Christ appears in glory, they will too (Col 3:4). Then they shall be like God, whom they shall see as he is (1 John 3:2). Their life at present is exile (2 Cor 5:6); the first fruits of the Spirit are already theirs; still they groan (Rom 8:23) and long to be with Christ (Phil 1:23). They are urged to live for him (2 Cor 5:15) while they seek always to please the Lord (2 Cor 5:9) and put on God's armor to resist temptation (Eph 6:11-13). They must stand guard always—on the Lord's advice. In this way—at the end of their earthly life, which is the only one they will have (Heb 9:27)—they will merit admission both to the marriage feast with Christ and to the number of the blessed (Matt 25:31-46). In this way too they will avoid ultimate failure. They will not, that is, like wicked and profitless servants (Matt 25:26), be ordered into eternal fire (Matt 25:41) and exterior darkness where there will be weeping and gnashing of teeth (Matt 22:13; 25:30). But before the church's members reign with Christ, each must appear before him to receive what his or her works have won (2 Cor 5:10). At the end will come a resurrection to life or judgment (John 5:29; Matt 25:46). Between the sufferings of the present and the glory of the future there is no comparison (Rom 8:18; 2 Tim 11-12). In faith the church of the present awaits its blessed hope, the coming of Jesus Christ, God and Savior (Titus 2:13). He will refashion the lowly bodies of believers and make them like his own in glory (Phil 3:21). He will come to be glorified in his saints—to be a source of wonder and admiration in all who have believed (2 Thess 1:10).[19]

The next section (49) of chapter 7 begins by referring to the promised future. When the Lord comes in majesty (Matt 25:31), death will be conquered and nothing will any longer be opposed to him (1 Cor 15:26-27). Of course not all this has yet happened! The Lord has at present: (a) some disciples who are exiles on earth, (b) some others who have died and are being purified, and (c) still others who are glorified and enjoy the vision of the triune God.[20] These are not three unrelated groups. They form a solidarity united by the same charity and in the same praise of God. They are all

Christ's and the Spirit is in all of them. They form one church and are united one to the other (Eph 4:16). Far from being broken, the union of Christ's disciples is strengthened by death—in an exchange of spiritual gifts. In fact, because the saints in heaven are present to the Lord (2 Cor 5:8) and more closely united with Christ (than they were before dying), they make a great and positive contribution to the holiness of the church and to the worship it offers God in time and space. Their solidarity with Christ's disciples on earth has its effect in the church's upbuilding (1 Cor 12:12-27). Through, with, and in Christ the saints in heaven do not cease to make intercession with the Father on behalf of the living. They are also role models in the accomplishments (merits) they achieved on earth through the one Mediator, Christ Jesus (1 Tim 2:5). While yet in the flesh, they filled up what was lacking in Christ's sufferings for the church (Col 1:24). By their care and concern they are of great assistance to brothers and sisters who need to be strengthened.

The mystical body of Jesus Christ has bonds linking members on both sides of the pale of death. Mindful of the biblical commendation found in 2 Macc 12:46, the church on earth offers prayers for the dead; this practice reveals an important relation that exists between Christ's disciples.[21]

But this relation of the living to the deceased is not the only one worth noting. The faithful on earth have devotion toward and seek to imitate the saints, whose closeness to Christ was shown in: (a) a testimony of faith and charity even at times to the shedding of blood, (b) conformity to his poverty and virginity, and (c) the practice of other Christian virtues as well as charisms given by God.

The church's members look to the saints for a good example in seeking the city which is to come (Heb 13:14; 11:10) and in finding a concrete path to holiness. More yet, a holy life is a sign of God's kingdom and exerts a powerful influence because of the faith that it involves. Finally, in an observation that deserves more attention than it has received, another benefit is said to come from remembering what the saints did and endured; their lives offer those on earth a confirmation of the truth of the gospel.

But cherishing the memory of the saints serves another purpose as well. That is the strengthening of the whole church in the Spirit through the practice of charity (Eph 4:1-6). On earth union among his disciples is conducive to closer union with the Lord himself. The same is the case when there is solidarity between disciples on this side of death and saints in heaven on the other. Christ is the crown of the saints; because of its nature love for them reaches out toward and ends in him. They are rightly asked for benefits that are needed and that only God can give (here the Council of Trent is cited on invocation, which is placed in the context of a charity that binds friends together across the pale of death).[22] The church venerates the memory of Mary and the saints in the liturgy of the Eucharist. It is in this worship of God that the saints in heaven as well as their brothers and sisters on earth are united *par excellence.*

The final section of chapter 7 shows the Second Vatican Council concerned about precedents in the past and proper instruction in the present. Attention is directed to the Second Council of Nicaea, the Council of Florence, and the Council of Trent. But what is significant is this; Vatican II has its own point to make. It does not say it wishes to repeat verbatim or even equivalently what II Nicaea taught about the veneration of images, Florence about the present state of the dead, and Trent about purgatory. To be sure, it does not deny or show any hesitation about the three. But that is not its direct concern. It rather wishes to associate itself with the faith of these three Synods regarding the solidarity of the church on earth with brothers and sisters in glory or in purgatory. That solidarity, effected by Jesus Christ and the Holy Spirit, is the theme of the whole chapter; Vatican II is confident it is not the first Council to teach of this. The resurrection of Jesus is of a power sufficient to hold together in unity his followers, whoever and wherever they may be.

But when the living and dead are thought to be in relation to one another, abuses may occur. These are to be prevented or corrected. So section 51 continues. Proper instruction must be provided, especially regarding devotion to the saints. The latter are honored not so much by the number and frequency of certain practices as by love of God and neighbor. Such solidarity between the living and dead strengthens rather than weakens the worship given to the Trinity. For in their mutual charity and in their joint praise of God, Christ's disciples on earth and the saints in heaven anticipate the liturgy that will be celebrated forever after the appearance of the Lord and the resurrection of the dead.

The Blessed Virgin Mary, Mother of God, in the Mystery of Christ and the Church

The final chapter of *Lumen Gentium* was the only one that was given subdivisions with headings to help distinguish and relate its various themes. The text begins with a Preface that traces the origin of the church back to God's "supreme goodness and wisdom." In that church, the mystery of salvation is revealed—it is there that the faithful are united with Christ and all the saints. It is there as well that they venerate the memory "above all of the glorious and perpetual Virgin Mary, Mother of our God and Lord Jesus Christ." Singled out for special mention at the outset are Mary's reception of the word in heart and body, her sublime redemption through her son's merits, her union with Christ, and her divine maternity. It is by reason of this grace of God that she surpasses all other creatures.[23] At the same time as an offering of Adam she stands in solidarity with all others in their need for salvation.[24] Her union with those others is in fact unique; by charity she cooperated so that in the church they might come to the birth of faith.[25] For this reason she is an utterly unique member of the church, whose model she is in faith and charity.

The Catholic Church looks to her as to a mother most dear.[26] For this reason the Council wishes to express its mind about her role in the mystery both of the Word Incarnate and of the Mystical Body. At the same time something will be said about the way in which others ought to relate to Mary.[27]

First to be treated is Mary's role in the economy of salvation.[28] The sources relied on are both the Old and the New Testaments as well as tradition (*veneranda traditio*). As the following passages are read in the church and understood in the light of further and full revelation, they already point to her: the promised victory of Adam and Eve after their sin (Gen 3:15); the virgin who is to conceive and bear Emmanuel (Isa 7:14; Mic 5:23; Matt 1:22-23).[29] Greeted as "full of grace" (Luke 1:28), Mary replies: "Behold the handmaid of the Lord; be it done to me according to thy word" (Luke 1:38). In this she was impeded by no sin; in fact, she was entirely holy and free from all stain of sin from the first instant of her conception.[30] She has been and is rightly spoken of as cooperating in salvation by her faith and obedience. Her union with Christ was manifested: at the visitation; at his birth, which sanctified and preserved her virginity intact; at the coming of shepherds and magi; at the presentation, loss, and finding in the temple; at Cana and the beginning of the miracles; in his declaring blessed those who hear and keep God's word (Mark 3:35; Luke 11:27-28) as she was faithfully doing (Luke 2:19, 51). During his life she advanced in a pilgrimage of faith and stood at the foot of his cross

(John 19:25) where he gave her as mother to his disciple (John 19:26-27). She was with the apostles at the outpouring of the Spirit (Acts 1:14); taken up body and soul into heavenly glory; exalted by the Lord as queen of all.[31]

Figuring thus in the work of salvation effected by Jesus and the Spirit, she is related to the church, which has but one Mediator, whose power is not threatened but rather manifested in her present role. Her association with Christ's work continues. Therefore she is invoked in the church by the titles of Advocate, Aid, Helper, Mediatrix.[32] None of these titles adds or detracts from the dignity or efficacy of Christ. No more than a sharing both by the baptized and by those in the priesthood adds or detracts with regard to the one priesthood of Christ! No more than the goodness of creatures supplements or diminishes the goodness of God! Christ's mediation does not exclude but rather gives rise to manifold cooperation. This subordinate role of Mary the church does not hesitate to profess.

The church too is mother: imitating Mary's charity, fulfilling the Father's will, accepting God's word in faith.[33] In Mary the church has reached the perfection that is without spot or wrinkle.[34]

The penultimate division of chapter 8 deals with devotion to Mary, whose words in the Magnificat are described as prophetic: "All generations shall call me blessed; because he who is mighty has done great things for me" (Luke 1:48). Devotion to her at one and the same time differs essentially from and contributes to worship of the triune God. All of this means fostering Marian devotion without exaggeration or narrow-mindedness. "True" devotion proceeds from true faith.[35]

Already glorified in body and soul in heaven, the Mother of Jesus is the image and beginning of the church that will be completed only in the age to come. But until the day of the Lord arrives she is for God's pilgrim people on earth a sign of sure hope and consolation.[36]

Thus the Council's teaching about Mary ends where all good Christian eschatology should both begin and end—with hope. And on that same note *Lumen Gentium* also reaches its conclusion.

JOHN FREDERICK JOHNSON

13

Mary and the Saints in Contemporary Lutheran Worship

The churches of evangelical catholicism at the time of the Reformation retained the biblically grounded Marian festivals: Presentation, February 2; Annunciation, March 25; Visitation, July 2. It is not surprising that these are still celebrated in a christological context by Lutheran Christians. Luther declared that it was exceedingly difficult for him to tear himself away from worship of the saints. He retained a deep reverence for the mother of our Lord and came to see that honor accorded Mary ultimately glorifies God for his revelation of grace in Christ. Due in large part to the influence of Rationalism, Marian commemorations were downgraded. In extreme instances they were abolished. Fortunately, evangelical catholicism has rediscovered the value of Marian celebrations. In addition to the three festivals named, contemporary Lutheran worship calls for the observance of a fourth: Saint Mary, Mother of our Lord, August 15.

The Reformers called assemblies of Christians "worship." They thereby intended to confess that God must be able to assent to all that happens when the community assembles. True worship depends neither on pious meditative concoctions nor on uncontrolled mystical experiences, but on what truly pleases God. And the Christian community knows that it is pleasing God when it is faithful to the fundamental conviction of the Reformation, to wit, the justification of the sinner before God by grace, for Christ's sake, through faith. This not only reflects a proper confessional concern for worship; in Lutheran understanding it is determinative for piety and practice.

This speaks an evangelical word to the ancient question of the relationship between worship and creed (*lex orandi et credendi*). Evangelical Lutheran Christians continue to hold that outward forms of worship never make one righteous before God. Since God is pleased only with rites instituted in accordance with the gospel and observed in faith in the forgiveness of sins found alone in Christ, the purpose of all ceremonies is to teach people what they need to know about Christ. Luther was anything but an iconoclast when it came to cultus. He was concerned that worship lead people (especially youth) into the Scriptures where one finds Jesus Christ, the object and foundation of true worship.

In 1965 Joerg Erb issued *Geduld und Glaube der Heiligen*. Festivals of Mary and a host of witnesses are to be remembered by evangelical Christians.[1] A sampling includes: Albert the Great, Ambrose, Augustine, Benedict, Birgitta, Bonaventure, Clement, Ephraim the Syrian, Francis, Gregory, Hedwig, Ignatius, Justin, Catherine of Siena, Lorenz, the Martyrs of Sicily, Monica, Origen, Patrick, Polycarp, Severin, Tauler, Thomas, Vincent, Wulfida. The author acknowledges the work of Bishop Wilhelm Stählin in developing the calendar, which was approved by the Lutheran Liturgical Conference in 1962. Purpose of the calendar is a proper remembrance of saints in accordance with Confessio Augustana, Article 21: "Saints should be kept in remembrance so that our faith may be strengthened."

The Lutheran Book of Worship

This nonexhaustive overview of the place of Mary and the saints in contemporary Lutheran worship does not deal with devotional practices of various Evangelical Sisterhoods and Communities. It restricts itself primarily to the *Lutheran Book of Worship* and *Lutheran Worship*.[2]

The *Lutheran Book of Worship* is used principally by congregations of the Evangelical Lutheran Church in America. It contains a split liturgical calendar.[3] The first part treats Sundays and Principal Festivals. The second part treats Lesser Festivals and Commemorations, which include apostles, All Saints, bishops, martyrs, missionaries, renewers of the church, priests, and pastors. Listings under June include: Justin; John XXIII; Boniface; Columba; Saint Barnabas; Basil of Caesarea; Gregory Nazianzus; Gregory of Nyssa; the Nativity of Saint John the Baptizer; Presentation of the Augsburg

Confession; Philipp Melanchthon; Irenaeus; Saints Peter and Paul; and Johan Wallin, Archbishop of Uppsala. Under July: Jan Hus; Benedict of Nursia; Archbishop Söderblom; Vladimir; Olga; Saint Mary Magdalene; Birgitta of Sweden; Saint James the Elder; J. S. Bach, Heinrich Schütz, and Handel; Mary, Martha, and Lazarus of Bethany; and Olaf, King of Norway.

In this section are commemorated the Presentation of our Lord (February 2), Annunciation of our Lord (March 25), Visitation (May 31), and Mary, Mother of our Lord (August 15). Collects and songs for Lesser Festivals are provided for the apostles, Saint Stephen, Holy Innocents, Name of Jesus, Holy Cross Day, Saint Michael and All Angels, Reformation Day, and All Saints' Day. Under Commemorations are listed prayers and psalms for saints, martyrs, missionaries, renewers of the church, pastors and bishops, and even theologians. Collects for Presentation and Annunciation contain no reference to Mary. The Collect for Visitation reads: "Almighty God, in choosing the Virgin Mary to be the mother of your Son, you made known your gracious regard for the poor and the lowly and the despised." The Collect for Mary, Mother of our Lord, reads: "Almighty God, you chose the Virgin Mary to be the mother of your only Son. Grant that we . . . may share with her in the glory of your eternal kingdom." The Collect for All Saints' Day reads: "Almighty God, whose people are knit together in one holy Church . . . grant us grace to follow your blessed saints in lives of faith and commitment." The Collect for Commemorations of Saints and Martyrs petitions God to encourage us by their example and faithfulness, which led them to the way of the cross and victory. A petition for saints thanks God for Abraham, Sarah, Moses, Aaron, Miriam and Joshua, Deborah and Gideon, Samuel and Hannah, Isaiah and all the prophets; Mary the mother of our Lord; Peter and Paul; Mary, Martha and Mary Magdalene; Stephen the first martyr, and all saints and martyrs of every time and in every land. "In your mercy, give us, as you gave them, the hope of salvation and the promise of eternal life."

Prayers included in the service for the Burial of the Dead ask for understanding "to believe and trust in the Communion of Saints, the forgiveness of sins, and the resurrection through life everlasting." Intercessions conclude: "God . . . you are the rest of the blessed dead. We rejoice in the company of your saints. We remember all who have lived in faith, all who have peacefully died, and especially those most dear to us who rest in you. . . . To your name, with the Church on earth and the Church in heaven, we ascribe all honor and glory, now and forever." At the place of burial the pastor prays: "Almighty God, by the death and burial of Jesus you have destroyed death and sanctified the graves of all your saints. Keep our brother/sister . . . in the company of all your saints. At the last raise him/her up to share with all your faithful people the endless joy and peace won through the glorious resurrection of Christ our Lord." The Litany of Evening Prayer calls upon the worshiper to give thanks to the Lord "for the faithful who have gone before us and are at rest."

Lutheran Worship

Lutheran Worship, used primarily by congregations of the Lutheran Church–Missouri Synod, divides the calendar according to Sundays and Major festivals, and Minor Festivals.[4] Minor Festivals commemorate apostles, martyrs, pastors, confessors, doctors of the church, All Saints, and presentation of the Augsburg Confession. Festivals associated with Mary are: Presentation of our Lord (February 2); Annunciation of our Lord (March 25); Visitation (May 31); and Saint Mary, Mother of our Lord (August 15). Commemoration of the faithful departed is observed November 2.

The Introit for Presentation, Annunciation, and Visitation is from Psalm 48. Collects for Presentation and Annunciation stress the incarnation of Jesus Christ, his cross, passion, and the glory of his resurrection. The Collect for Visitation reads: "Almighty God, as you dealt wonderfully with your servant, the blessed Virgin Mary, in choosing her to be the mother of your dearly beloved son. . . ." It stresses God's regard for the poor, lowly, and the despised and asks for the grace of humility and meekness to receive God's word with faith. The Introit for the Feast Day of Saint Mary, Mother of our Lord, is a portion of Psalm 34. The collect for the day reads: "Grant we humbly pray, O Lord, to your servants the gift of your heavenly blessing that, as the Son of the Virgin Mary has granted salvation, we may daily grow in your favor." The Collect for All Saints' Day refers to the communion and fellowship of the mystical body of Christ and petitions God "to follow your blessed saints in all virtuous and godly living that we may come to those unspeakable joys which you have prepared for those who love you."

The Collect for Commemoration of the Faithful Departed, which states: "Almighty God, in whose glorious presence live all who depart in the Lord and before whom all the souls of the faithful who are delivered of the burden of the flesh are in joy and felicity," thanks God for his lovingkindness to all who have finished their course in faith and rest from their labors. It implores the mercy of God that "we, together with all who have departed in saving faith, may have perfect consummation and bliss in both body and soul in your eternal and everlasting glory."

In the Holy Communion liturgy the Preface for All Saints declares that "the multitude of your saints did surround us with so great a cloud of witnesses." It also petitions that, rejoicing in their fellowship, "we may run with patience the race that is set before us and with them receive the crown of glory. . . . Therefore with angels and with archangels and with all the company of heaven, we laud and magnify your glorious name evermore praising you and saying. . . ."

Commemorations for the Saints and Mary

Both the *Lutheran Book of Worship* and *Lutheran Worship* contain hymns designated as appropriate for Lesser Festival and Saints' Days. The *Lutheran Book of Worship* lists particular hymns for Saints Andrew, Thomas, and Stephen; the Confession of Peter; Saints Peter and Paul, Apostles; Saints Mary Magdalene and Mary, Mother of our Lord; Saint Michael and All Angels. Of special note is the listing of "Ye Watchers and Ye Holy Ones" as a Marian hymn. After invoking seraphim, cherubim, archangels, and angelic choirs, it invokes Mary as higher than the cherubim and more glorious than the seraphim. As bearer of the eternal Word and the most gracious, she is petitioned to magnify the Lord (as she once did on earth). For some unknown reason *Lutheran Worship* places this hymn in the section dealing with the Church Triumphant and omits the invocation of Mary. *The Lutheran Hymnal*,[5] replaced by *Lutheran Worship*, contains the verse of invocation.

The hymn "By All Your Saints in Warfare" states that "now they shine in glory" reflected from the throne of God.[6] Verses speak specifically of saints and martyrs: Saints Andrew, Thomas, Stephen, John, Matthias, Mark, Philip and James, James the Elder, Bartholomew, Matthew, Luke, Simon and Jude; the Nativity of Saint John the Baptist; Holy Innocents and Martyrs; the Confession of Saint Peter; the Conversion of Saint Paul. (No verse serves as an invocation of the saints.) The hymn is in reality a doxology that reflects the hagiology of Confessio Augustana, Article 21. Other hymns appearing under Lesser Festivals commemorate Circumcision, Annunciation, Presentation, All Saints, John the Baptizer, and Holy Innocents. The Presentation hymn states:

In the arms of her who bore him
Virgin pure, behold him lie
While his aged saints adore him
Ere in perfect faith they die.[7]

In *The Lutheran Hymnal* a Collect for Advent reads: "Most merciful God, who hast given thine eternal Word to be made incarnate of the pure Virgin, grant unto thy people grace . . . so they may be ready for thy visitation." A Collect for Annunciation reads: "Almighty God, who didst will that agreeably to the angel's message thy Son become incarnate of the Virgin Mary, mercifully grant that our sinful conception may be cleansed by his immaculate conception." Collects for Visitation refer to the Virgin Mary as God's handmaiden and the object of God's gracious exaltation. The Gradual for Visitation carries the Versicle: "Blessed art thou, O Mary, among women, and blessed is the fruit of thy womb. Behold, there shall be a performance of those things which were told thee from the Lord." In *Lutheran Worship*, the Collects for Advent implore God to "stir up" the faithful, but all references to Mary are curiously (and, I think, unfortunately) missing.

There will probably never be a full-bodied evangelical Mariology simply because Mary has no truly independent standing for evangelical Christians. At the same time there will always be an evangelical concern for Mary because of her intimate link with Christology. As long as there is a doctrine regarding Christ, there will be a doctrine regarding Mary.

Contemporary Lutheran worship has a large place for the honor and commemoration of Mary and the saints. It especially has a healthy reverence for Mary and sees value in observing those traditional, truly catholic festivals of Mary which, because they are biblically grounded, are truly festivals of Christ.

ELIZABETH A. JOHNSON, C. S. J.

14

Mary as Mediatrix

Both theology and devotion regarding Mary as Mediatrix have had a variegated history. Originating in the East after Ephesus (431) and moving to the West by the eighth or ninth century, the idea of Mary's mediation received different nuances in succeeding centuries. Devotion seems to have been at its most enthusiastic pitch in the late medieval period. The most intense theological scrutiny occurred in the decades of the twentieth century before the Second Vatican Council (1962–65). At that Council proper expression of the theme was a matter of intense debate. There is, then, no simple story to tell.

The Late Patristic East

It is not clear who actually first used the title Mediatrix for Mary.[1] It is clear, however, that it originated in the East as an offshoot of reflection on the incarnation. In its original form the idea referred to her unique role in this saving event. Conceiving Christ first in her spirit through faith, she then conceived him in her body and, through her physical pregnancy and childbirth, delivered to the world its Savior. Thus she was understood to be the means by which God came to earth, the female mediator of Christ's saving presence in history. As a corollary of this insight into her maternity, Mary's present intercession in heaven was envisioned as a continuation of her gracious maternal role on earth. In a special way among the apostles and other saints she joined in the prayer of

Christ for those still struggling on earth, thus cooperating with the salvific plan of God by means of which saving grace was poured out on sinners.

Early references to Mary's historical and heavenly roles as Mediatrix of the divine presence were usually made (when they were noted—it was by no means universal) in the genre of praise:

> Hail, thou through whom the Creator became a babe . . .
> Hail, heavenly ladder by which God came down;
> Hail, bridge that carries the earth-born to heaven. . . .
>
> (Akathistos Hymn)

> You also by fulfilling the office of Mediatrix, and being made the ladder of God descending to us, that he should assume our weak nature and join and unite it to himself . . . you brought together what had been separated. . . .
>
> (John Damascene—*PG* 96:713)

> When you, God-bearer, were made the dwelling of the Holy Spirit, then did human beings become spiritual. No one is filled with the knowledge of God except through you, O most holy one; no one is saved except through you, O Mother of God; . . . no one secures a gift of mercy except through you, O worthy one who holds God.
>
> (Germanus of Constantinople—*PG* 98:349)

It is interesting to note that the first Western editor of this sermon of Germanus saw fit to add a footnote explaining that these claims should be understood in light of the fact that Mary gave birth to Christ.[2] In his preaching this patriarch of Constantinople (d. 733) was likely the first to make explicit two other points that would be influential in later ages, namely, that Mary's intercession is all-powerful, for God obeys her as a good son his mother; and that her intercession turns away the sentence of damnation justly passed on sinners, for as a mother her heart is inclined to be merciful. In no way, however, were these ideas very common among theologians.

In sum, during the late patristic period in the East, Mary's mediation of God's historical presence and saving grace was preached and sung about largely in relation to her maternal role in the incarnation of Jesus Christ.

The Medieval West

In addition to Mary's historical birthing of the Savior and her continued heavenly intercession, the medieval West connected her mediation more immediately with the individual's need for a safe approach to Christ.[3] Peter Damien sounded the theme: "Just as the son of God has deigned to descend to us through you, so we also must come to him through you."[4] This insight found expression in the influential image of Mary as the neck, a metaphor embroidered on the Pauline symbol of Christ, the head of his body, the church: "Our Lady is rightly understood to be the neck of the holy church, because she is the mediatrix between God and human beings."[5]

More than anyone else it was Bernard of Clairvaux (d. 1153) who expressed the idea of Mary's mediating role in a mellifluous rhetoric which gave his insights far-reaching influence. While only 4 percent of his works deal with the person of Mary, that material has been quoted innumerable times to affirm Mary's gracious ways in the ongoing story of salvation. In one key sermon Bernard compared Christ to the source of the floodwaters of divine grace, while Mary was likened to an aqueduct which receives this water from its source and conducts it to our dried-out hearts. It is God's wish that we venerate Mary with great tenderness, for God "wills us to have everything through Mary."[6] True, he went on, the Father has given us Jesus as our effective Mediator. But while he is our merciful brother made of our flesh, we might tremble to approach him, for he is also our majestic God. Mary, however, is simply and only human and can be our advocate with him. The son hears his mother, and the father hears his son: "This is the ladder of sinners, this is my greatest trust, this is the whole reason for my hope."

In another famous sermon on the woman crowned with twelve stars (Rev 12:1), Bernard stressed the need for a purely human Mediatrix due to weak souls' possible fear of Christ's divinity. While Christ learned by suffering the compassion that makes him merciful, he is nonetheless our judge. We need a link to the Mediator, and no one plays this role more effectively than Mary. Weak though we may be, she removes our fear for she is wholly sweet and gentle, full of mildness and mercy. How greatly we should give thanks to Christ, who in his mercy has provided us with such a Mediatrix.[7] Set within the medieval mind-set with its quest for salvation, this idea of Mary as "Mediatrix with the Mediator" gained widespread acceptance.

Mediatrix now evoked a threefold function of Mary in the history of salvation: she was the means of the Savior's historical incarnation, the channel through which divine grace continued to flow to sinners, and the one through whom sinners had access to the merciful Savior. Saving grace was the grace of Christ, won for sinners by his death on the cross; but the communication of that grace to individuals required certain means, among them prominently the intercession of Mary. As a mother her prayer could soften the heart of her son and obtain mercy for undeserving sinners. Toward the end of this period Bernardine of Siena (d. 1444) trenchantly summed up this understanding:

> Every grace which is communicated to this world has a threefold procession. For from God to Christ, from Christ to the Virgin, from the Virgin to us, it is dispensed in a most orderly fashion. . . . I do not hesitate to say that she has received a certain jurisdiction over all graces. . . . They are administered through her hands to whom she pleases, when she pleases, as she pleases, and as much as she pleases.[8]

Post-Reformation Catholicism

While the Council of Trent briefly addressed the issue of proper veneration of the saints, it did not give systematic treatment to any doctrine concerning Mary—including mediation. The following centuries, however, saw this theme grow in popularity in both devotional life and theological reflection.

Spiritual Writers

The two most popular books on Mary during these centuries give ample evidence of how the idea of mediation formed the basis of gently chivalrous devotion. In *True Devotion to the Blessed Virgin Mary* Louis Grignon de Montfort (d. 1716) echoed Bernard and Bernardine as he pellucidly affirmed:

> God the Son has communicated to His Mother all that He acquired by His life and His death, His infinite merits and His admirable virtues; and He has made her the treasurer of all that His Father gave Him for His inheritance. It is by her that He applies His merits to His members, and that He communicates His virtues and distributes His graces. She is His mysterious canal; she is His aqueduct, through which He makes His mercies flow gently and abundantly.

> God the Holy Ghost has communicated to Mary, His faithful spouse, His unspeakable gifts; and He has chosen Her to be the dispensatrix of all He possesses, in such sort that she distributes to whom she wills, as much as she wills, as she wills, when she wills, all His gifts and graces.[9]

Having established this theological framework, he described how one should renew one's baptismal vows by acts of consecration to Mary, entrusting all one's body, soul, and goods to her care. Seeing Mary in such a soul, the Holy Spirit will fly there as at the Annunciation and Christ will again be brought forth. The axiom that summed up this approach in the popular mind was "To Jesus though Mary," and while criticized by some theologians, it shaped a way of devotion followed by many in the church.

A second widely popular work, written as a counterblast to the rationalism of the Enlightenment, was *The Glories of Mary* by Alphonsus Liguori (d. 1787). Here the idea of Mary's universal mediation of graces, which some scholars such as L. Muratori had considered to be "pious exaggeration," was vigorously upheld:

> God who gave us Jesus Christ wills that all graces that have been, that are, and will be dispensed to men to the end of the world through the merits of Jesus Christ should be dispensed by the hands and through the intercession of Mary.[10]

This idea was developed within the dichotomous mercy-justice framework, so that prayer to Mary insured that the sinner would have a kind advocate with Christ, the justly irritated judge.

The ideas in these two works—Mary's mediation of Christ's grace to us, and her mediation of our well-being before Christ—were reiterated by innumerable spiritual writers and preachers. While not universally accepted, they formed the devotional life of a large number of people in the church during these centuries.

Popes

The writings of nineteenth- and twentieth-century popes contributed significantly to the theme of Mary's mediation. By all accounts the "Marian Era" opened with Pius IX (1846–78). In his speaking and writing he encouraged people in all difficulties, fears, and needs to pray to Mary, for she has a mother's heart and is solicitous about their salvation:

> The foundation of all Our confidence, as you know well, Venerable Brethren, is found in the Blessed Virgin Mary. For God

> has committed to Mary the treasury of all good things, in order that everyone may know that through her are obtained every hope, every grace, and all salvation. For this is his will, that we obtain everything through Mary.[11]

Standing at the right hand of Jesus Christ, she presents petitions in a most efficacious manner. What she asks she obtains. Her pleas can never be unheard.

In numerous encyclicals on the rosary the next pope, Leo XIII (1878–1903), expounded the theses that Mary is the channel of absolutely every grace, that her help and aid are constantly directed toward struggling people, that her intercession appeases and softens her divine son, and that therefore the church puts all hope and trust in her. In one instance, after reflecting that the Son of God did not become incarnate without Mary's free consent, this pope wrote in terms reminiscent of Bernard:

> Thus as no man goeth to the Father but by the Son, so no man goeth to Christ but by His Mother. How great are the goodness and mercy revealed in this design of God! What a correspondence with the frailty of man! We believe in the infinite goodness of the Most High, and we rejoice in it; we also believe in His justice and we fear it. . . . Thus do those whose actions have disturbed their consciences need an intercessor mighty in favor with God, merciful enough not to reject the cause of the desperate. . . . Mary is this glorious intermediary; she is the Mother of the Almighty; but—what is still sweeter—she is gentle, extreme in tenderness, of a limitless loving-kindness. As such God gave her to us.[12]

Perhaps the clearest and most often quoted passage penned by this pope on Mary's mediation notes that the rosary involves saying only one Our Father but ten Hail Marys; hence,

> Thus is confirmed that law of merciful mediation of which We have spoken, and which St. Bernardine of Siena thus expresses: "Every grace granted to man has three degrees in order; for by God it is communicated to Christ, from Christ it passes to the Virgin, and from the Virgin it descends to us." And if we, by the very form of the Rosary, linger longest upon the last and lowest of these steps . . . it is precisely that our failing and defective prayers may be strengthened with the necessary confidence.[13]

Such a presence of Mary in our prayer awakens the warmth of love, joy, and trust, and we are led to glorify God's goodness.

In similar fashion subsequent popes carried on this custom of stressing Mary's mediation. She is the "supreme Minister of the distribution of graces" (Pius X);[14] the "Virgin treasurer of all graces at the side of God" (Pius XI);[15] the one who gives us her son "and with Him all the help we need, for God 'wished us to have everything through Mary' " (Pius XII).[16] It was not as though papal teaching focused on the mediating role of Mary to the exclusion of other interests relative to faith and morals. Encyclicals on the church, liturgy, Scripture, peace, marriage, the rights of workers, etc., give evidence of a broad range of issues to which these popes gave their attention. But in tracing just this one thread, the above sampling is certainly representative of the teaching of these popes on Mary's role as Mediatrix. Their exhortations in this regard were highly influential.

Theologians

With few exceptions neo-Scholastic thinkers understood Mary's mediation to mean that by God's will she had a key and active role in the process by which the treasury of graces merited by Christ was communicated to individuals. Many scholars worked to clarify, justify, and promote this idea with ever more detailed refinements.[17] They explored its nexus with other Marian doctrines such as Mary's sinlessness, her spiritual maternity, and her subordinate role as Coredemptrix in the saving work of Christ. The universality of her mediating role was explained to include the gift of every grace (albeit there was a debate about sacramental grace) to every member of the human race. Her knowledge of what was needed by struggling people, her loving care that led her to seek to obtain it, and her effective power to do since Jesus loved her as his mother and was beholden to her requests were elements that received scrutiny. The nature of the causality involved, whether physical or moral, with God the principal cause in either case, and the precise manner in which her role was exercised were matters of dispute. No one, however, questioned the basic theme of her mediation. By one count, over three thousand theological works were produced on these subjects before 1950.[18]

A typical excerpt from one of the most prolific writers may give some sense of the tenor of this theological reflection:

> Mary deserves the title of universal mediatrix, subordinated to the Redeemer, if she is an intermediary between Him and men,

> presenting to Him their prayers and obtaining benefits from Him for them. But that is precisely Mary's role. For, though a creature, she reaches by her divine maternity to the frontiers of divinity, and she has received a fullness of grace which is intended to overflow on us. . . . Thus Jesus is the principal and perfect Mediator, in dependence on whose merits—and they are superabundant and sufficient of themselves—Mary exercises her subordinate mediation. But Mary's mediation has nevertheless been willed by God because of our weakness, and because God wished to honor her by allowing her the exercise of causality in the order of salvation and sanctification.[19]

Thus was the mediation of Mary studied and discussed with great attention by Catholic theologians in the period preceding the Second Vatican Council.

Activities

Early in the twentieth century a movement developed with the goal of promoting Mary's mediation to the status of a dogma of the church by means of an official papal definition. At the urging of Joseph Cardinal Mercier of Belgium and others a worldwide campaign was launched to elicit petitions to the Vatican in favor of a definition. These petitions, including some from national hierarchies, began to come in. In 1950 an international group of Catholic theologians convening in Rome passed a resolution that was sent to Pius XII:

> Since the principal, personal attributes of the Blessed Virgin Mary have already been defined, it is the wish of the faithful that it should also be dogmatically defined that the Blessed Virgin Mary was intimately associated with Christ the Savior in effecting human salvation, and accordingly, she is a true collaborator in the work of redemption, spiritual Mother of all men, intercessor and dispenser of graces, in a word, universal Mediatress of God and men.[20]

It was reported, however, that the pope felt that the doctrine of Mary's mediation was not yet theologically mature enough for such a definition, that the time was not yet "opportune."[21] Once Vatican II had been called, the preconciliar consultation of the world's Catholic episcopate showed that 382 bishops wanted the Council to make a strong affirmation, even a definition, of Mary's mediation. At the same time the Mariological Society of America petitioned the Preparatory Commission to put on the agenda of the Council a definition of Mary's co-redemption.[22]

This movement, which wished to give ever greater importance to the role of Mary as Mediatrix, was not the only preconciliar movement, however. Also brewing were renewals in biblical, patristic, and liturgical studies, catechetical methods, and the theological areas of ecclesiology and grace.[23] Each of these currents coupled with a new ecumenical openness flowed into Vatican II and affected that body's teaching on the mediation of Mary.

Second Vatican Council

There were several successive official drafts of the Council's document on Mary, due to competing insights. On the one hand, there were those who wished to honor Mary by stressing her unique prerogatives in glowing language. On the other hand, there were those who wished to take what they called a more "sober" approach, treating Mary in a way calculated to avoid biblical and ecumenical difficulties. And there were those who, once the controversy between the first two groups came into the open, tried to find a way of unity and compromise between them. In reality there was no division on the matter of basic doctrine. All agreed that Jesus Christ was the sole Mediator between God and human beings and that Mary, the mother of Jesus Christ and a preeminent member of the church, participated in the saving work of Christ. Disagreement came over the matter of the appropriate language, thought patterns, formulas, and titles with which to express the insights agreed upon. Both Karl Rahner and René Laurentin, who were present as *periti*, have analyzed the clash as due to differences in national cultural characteristics, with the Mediterranean temperament stressing Mary's prerogatives in exuberant and affective terms, while the Northern temperament took a more critical and rational approach.[24] In addition, Rahner noted a differing methodological approach, as those more enthusiastic for Marian privileges drew heavily on papal teaching as a source, while those who wished a more tempered approach engaged in the return to scriptural and patristic sources. In any event, the theme of Mary's mediation was the occasion for spirited clashes both on the Council floor and in the Theological Commission charged with overseeing the draft's revisions.

The original text prepared before the Council met reflected the mariological approach taken by nineteenth- and twentieth-century theologians and popes as described above. The document called for a formal proclamation of Mary as Mediatrix of graces. Emphasizing that Mary's role depends for its existence and efficacy on the wisdom and good pleasure of God, the key passage read:

> Therefore, when this humble "Handmaid of the Lord" for whom "He who is mighty has done great things" (Lk 1:49) is formally named Mediatrix of all graces, because she was associated with Christ in acquiring them; and when too, remaining an associate with Christ now glorious in heaven, she is invoked by the Church as our Mediatrix and our Advocate, because she intercedes for all through Christ in such a way that the maternal charity of the Blessed Virgin is present in the conferring of all graces to human beings; then in no way is the unique mediation of our Mediator, in the absolute sense spoken of by the Apostle who said: "For there is one God, and one Mediator between God and human beings, the human being Jesus Christ" (1 Tim 2:5), obscured or lessened; on the contrary, this mediation of Christ is enhanced and honored. For Mary is Mediatrix in Christ, and her mediation arises not from any necessity but from divine good pleasure and the superabundance and excellence of the merits of Jesus.[25]

A note appended to this draft pointed out that, in the intent of the authors, calling Mary "Mediatrix of all graces" meant that she could petition all graces for us. As to the question of whether all graces were given to us through her, that was a question left open for the exploration of theologians.

This draft was not discussed during the first session due to the pressure of other business. Nor was it discussed during the second session when debate centered on the more fundamental question of whether the document on Mary should stand separately or be incorporated into the teaching on the church. After the close vote to incorporate, the first draft was sent back to committee to be reworked in the light of its new context. The debate over incorporation had shown the strong preference of a number of bishops for a more biblical, pastoral, and ecumenical statement, while an almost equal number had supported the original text. Consequently a new, second draft was drawn up with an eye to reconciling the two opposing tendencies.

This was the text submitted for discussion at the Council's third session in 1964. Bishop Maurice Roy of Ottawa, its presenter, noted that the title of Mediatrix had been included over the objections of a number (*pluribus*) of members of the Theological Commission even though the text explained that it did not impair the sole mediatorship of Jesus Christ. Speeches were given pro and con.[26] Speaking in favor of "Mediatrix" were bishops such as Ruffini, Gasbarri, and Rendiero, the latter speaking for ninety-eight others. Their principal arguments included the points that it was an ancient title, used in numerous papal encyclicals, and its omission would scandalize the faithful. Others such as Bea, Léger, and Alfrink, the latter speaking for 129 others, insisted that the title should be suppressed. They argued that it was not biblical, appearing to contradict the one Mediator (1 Tim 2:5); that it was ambiguous and thus susceptible to being poorly preached by the clergy and poorly understood by the faithful; and that it was a point of discord with Protestants, likely to cause more divisiveness. After the speeches the text was withdrawn from the floor to be reworked, at which point several hundred bishops submitted written observations and amendments: 191 to keep the title Mediatrix, 196 to delete it, and 34 to keep it within the relativizing context of other titles.[27]

In the next draft the title of Mediatrix was kept, while other changes modulated its meaning. The germane emendations included:

(1) the addition of other titles (Advocate, Auxiliatrix, Adjutrix) in a row with Mediatrix. Roy explained that this was a way to relativize the title because it was only one approximation among others to express Mary's role in the church.

(2) the change of the verb in the sentence in which Mediatrix appeared from "adored" to "invoked." Thus the title was set within the context of piety and prayer, not official doctrine.

(3) repetition of the point that Christ is the sole Mediator and that Mary's role is but a participation in Christ.

(4) the addition of the word "subordinate" to clarify Mary's relation to Christ, and emphasis through various phrasings that Mary's role is not to be envisioned alongside of, parallel to, or in addition to Christ, "for no creature could ever be classed with the Incarnate Word and Redeemer."

(5) the addition of analogies from the priesthood of Christ and the goodness of God, both of which are shared in by others, to show how Mary's mediation is but a sharing in the one source of mediation who is Christ.

The bishops voted positively for this revised text: yes, 1,559; no, 10; and *Placet juxta Modum*, 521, a position that indicated a desire for further particular revisions. A number of these requested *modi* concerned the question of mediation. Stronger affirmation of Mary's mediation was asked for by 121 bishops; 61 called for deletion of the term since it was unbiblical, ambiguous, and ecumenically problematic. Still others affirmed the compromise solution whereby the title was kept in a row with the others, but asked for more clarification of Christ's role.

The final draft was voted on a month later (November 1964). As Roy explained, the committee had decided for the compromise option in hopes that the opposing parties would be resigned, if not happy. The relevant section of the final text opens with an affirmation of the sole mediatorship of Jesus Christ, quoting the words of 1 Tim 2:5. It then continues:

> The maternal duty of Mary toward men in no way obscures or diminishes this unique mediation of Christ, but rather shows its power. For all the saving influences of the Blessed Virgin on men originate not from some inner necessity, but from the divine pleasure. They flow forth from the superabundance of the merits of Christ, rest on his mediation, depend entirely on it, and draw all their power from it. In no way do they impede the immediate union of the faithful with Christ. Rather, they foster this union.[28]

After reviewing her role from the incarnation of Christ to her present prayer in heaven, the text continues:

> By her maternal charity Mary cares for the brethren of her Son who still journey on earth surrounded by dangers and difficulties, until they are led to their happy fatherland. Therefore the Blessed Virgin is invoked in the Church under the titles of Advocate, Auxiliatrix, Adjutrix, and Mediatrix. These, however, are to be so understood that they neither take away from nor add anything to the dignity and efficacy of Christ the one Mediator. For no creature could ever be classed with the Incarnate Word and Redeemer.[29]

In the end, it is declared that "The Church does not hesitate to profess this subordinate role of Mary."[30]

After minor modifications the final vote on the document was: yes, 2,096; no, 23 (representing hardliners of both sides). It is no secret that while they voted for the document, many of those who had borne into the Council the preconciliar mariological current felt that they had suffered a setback.

From first to last drafts of the document on Mary there had been major changes. Successive reductions relativized the importance of the theme of Mary's mediation and clarified its theological meaning in relation to Christ. The first text had been a virtual collation of excerpts from papal encyclicals, 117 citations compared with 14 in the final version. With greater use of biblical and patristic sources and with the onset of ecumenical sensitivity, later drafts tried to avoid what was propounded by only one school of thought and to affirm what was commonly held to be basic. As a result, the final document carries a strong stress on the centrality of Christ the sole Mediator, with Mary's role being affirmed as a participation in Christ.

It is important to note what in the end the Council did not say regarding Mary. Since these things had been proposed, the omission was conscious and deliberate. Furthermore, the intensity of the debate made it highly unlikely that points considered essential would have been omitted. Hence the silence has a certain significance that bears upon the interpretation of the text. The Council did not define Mary's mediation as a dogma. Neither did it unequivocally endorse the preconciliar understanding of this theme. It refused to use the title Mediatrix of grace or of all graces and relativized the term Mediatrix by setting it with others. These titles of praise are referred to within the context of prayer in such a way as to be descriptive rather than prescriptive. There is no precise statement regarding Mary's mode of action in the communication of grace. Likewise omitted are the traditional images of the aqueduct, neck, minister, treasurer, or dispensatrix of grace, as well as the title of Co-redemptrix. On balance the final text affirms Mary's special participation in the saving mystery wrought by the one Mediator Jesus Christ while braking the particular preconciliar way of developing this theme.

Since the Council and due largely to its deliberations, the term Mediatrix with its attendant neo-Scholastic precisions has been little used in theology as a whole. As a Marian title it has virtually disappeared from the vocabulary of preaching and popular piety, at least in the United States.[31] The revised Roman liturgy has dropped the optional feast of Mary as Mediatrix (*Calendarium Romanum* 1969), although the theme reappears as one of forty-six votive masses approved in 1987 for use at Marian shrines, with a covering instruction that it should be interpreted according to the teaching of *Lumen Gentium*.

The idea of Mary's mediation comes to the fore in John Paul II's Marian year encyclical (1987), but in a way clearly influenced by the Council, which is quoted liberally.[32] Christ alone is the one

Mediator between God and human beings, while Mary shows forth the efficacy of Christ's mediation by sharing in this unique source. Her mediation consists of her prayer offered in burning love of God and care for all the pilgrim people. "Her mediation is thus in the nature of intercession" (§21). As such, "It is mediation in Christ" (§38). In a series of theological meditations on key biblical scenes such as the Annunciation, Cana, and the cross, John Paul II then gives this conciliar insight an interpretation that heavily stresses the maternal character of Mary's intercession, which makes her unique among others who also share in the one mediation of Christ.

INTERPRETATIONS

The question becomes: What are we to make theologically of this theme of Mary's mediation? Those relatively few Catholic theologians who have addressed the issue since the Council have ventured critical interpretations of older understandings and have suggested ways in which the theme might be suitably reappropriated in the theology and piety of our own age.

Even before the Council Yves Congar, with particular reference to the preaching of Bernard and its use by later devotional writers, critically analyzed the theme of Mary's mediation.[33] In his judgment its growth stemmed in some measure from a deficient Christology. Under the pressure of a monophysite tendency, the divinity of Jesus Christ had been stressed to the point where his real humanity slipped from view or seemed unreal. In this situation the simply human Mary seemed more approachable. In addition, the gracious mercy of God in Christ had been partially eclipsed by emphasis on God's just judgment. The maternal figure of Mary assumed the role of mercifully interceding for sinners and even of turning away Christ's wrath. Thus a christological problem lay behind the overenthusiasm for Mary's mediation.

A more recent line of interpretation has attributed the post-Reformation growth of the theme of Mary's mediation to a deficient pneumatology. Theologians such as René Laurentin, Yves Congar, Heribert Mühlen, and Leon Joseph Suenens have found substantially correct the observation of Protestant student Elsie Gibson, who wrote of her studies in Catholic theology:

> every place I expected to find an exposition of the Holy Spirit, I found Mary. What Protestants universally attribute to the action of the Holy Spirit was attributed to Mary.[34]

René Laurentin, for example, has noted how Catholics have said of Mary that she forms Christ in them; that she is spiritually present to guide and inspire; that one goes to Jesus through her. But are not these precisely the roles of the Spirit of Christ? Biblically it is the Spirit who makes Christ present, forms Christ in believers, guides, and inspires. Such Marian phrases are an indication of an underdeveloped understanding of the third person of the Trinity.[35] In his trilogy on the Holy Spirit Yves Congar develops the intriguing point that the substitution of Mary for the Spirit is more understandable if one sees the Spirit as the "feminine" person in God, who in fact was called "Mother" in the early Syriac church. Mary's maternal characteristics have an affinity with the character of the Spirit.[36] This line of interpretation shows no sign of abating as more theologians explore the relation between the roles of Mary and the Spirit.

In addition to christological or pneumatological aspects, a third postconciliar approach has been linguistic, analyzing the nature of the language used in speaking of Mary as Mediatrix. One preconciliar writer had already opened this door:

> When Tradition tells us that Mary's position in the Mystical Body is comparable to that of the neck which unites the Head to the members and transmits the vital impulse to them, at the very least the metaphor it uses is an expressive one, but we cannot affirm with certainty that it is more than a metaphor.[37]

Laurentin has observed that much difficulty has resulted from the precise mentality of recent centuries which took symbolic images of the Greek Fathers and medieval preachers and interpreted them literally.[38] Such expressions should rather be seen as analogical, symbolic, or metaphorical. Again, Michael Schmaus has argued that enthusiastic Marian expressions are not meant to be theological assertions. They are pieces of poetry and should be interpreted by a hermeneutic suitable to the literary genre of poetry, not a hermeneutic of dogmatic statements.[39] Karl Rahner has written in a similar vein:

> Vatican II by no means ascribes to Mary the title and function of a Mediatrix in the strict theological sense, but rather takes the freer language of pious affection under its protection when the latter has recourse to the title "Mediatrix."[40]

In any event, there is unanimity today among those relatively few theologians who address the topic that Mary's mediation is to be interpreted as a participation in the saving work of Christ the sole Mediator. In the Catholic perspective Christ alone is not simply alone, but his saving power shows its efficacy by giving rise to manifold participation by others.[41] Thus it is not the case that Mary takes the initiative to gain Christ's favor or mercy, but that Jesus Christ involves Mary and all others in his own saving care for the world. Everyone benefits from the mystery of salvation being accomplished in everyone else. Commentaries on Vatican II, dogmatic treatises, the 1974 Pastoral Letter of the U.S. Catholic Bishops on Mary, and occasional theological pieces all reflect this interpretation of the meaning of Mary's mediation.[42] In addition, there is agreement that what Mary does to participate in Christ's saving work is to pray for the church. The general silence of the postconciliar church about Mary as Mediatrix does not mean that her reality or that of other saints has been disavowed. Rather, language and conceptualities of the past are being adapted to express the importance of Mary and the saints in a more christocentric and pneumatologically oriented vision.

GERHARD O. FORDE

15

Is Invocation of Saints an Adiaphoron?

The Lutheran Understanding of Adiaphoron

Prayer requesting departed saints to intercede for saints still on earth, it can be said, is neither explicitly commanded nor forbidden in the Scriptures. Since such a circumstance corresponds to a possible definition of an adiaphoron, the question naturally arises whether invocation of the saints and Mary might be classified as an adiaphoron. Could such invocation be considered a genuine adiaphoron, i.e., acceptable in a future unified church as long as it was not made mandatory? The purpose of this essay is to explore that question.

From a Lutheran perspective the question can most helpfully be addressed from two vantage points. First, from that of Lutheran history and experience, especially in the Confessional generation: Does Lutheran tradition seem open to considering the invocation of saints as an adiaphoron? Second, from the more internal perspective of Lutheran theological understanding itself: Is there something at stake in the issue that automatically lifts it out of the sphere of adiaphora? The two questions are of course intimately related, but for analytical purposes it is useful to look at them separately before we venture a judgment.

Before turning to Lutheran history and experience on the matter, we should attempt something by way of a definition. The term "adiaphoron" as used in church theology and practice is elusive because so much depends on the context. To get our bearings, it is helpful to distinguish between the general definition of the word and more specific usage in theological circles. According to its root meaning, it designates things "indifferent" or "which make no difference," i.e., teachings, practices, and rites that in themselves are never of such value or disvalue as "not to be able to be rendered either good or evil in the concrete by the human intention."[1] In theological circles it means such teachings, practices, or rites that are neither commanded nor prohibited by the external operations of divine law as revealed in the New Testament.[2] Lutherans, operating from the gospel of justification by faith alone, usually find it necessary to hone this general definition in order to give it a sharper edge and to speak of adiaphora as "those things 'not necessary' to be done by the church in its task of doing good for the neighbor by proclaiming and enacting the gospel, or in its privilege of obeying God's contingent commands about that task."[3] In this Lutheran sense adiaphora are those things not strictly necessary to the communication of the gospel and caring for the neighbor. Mostly, in Lutheran circles, the term has been used in connection with forms of church order and liturgy. If applied at all to matters involving doctrinal decisions, it has been done only by extension.

First, then, to history and Lutheran experience with the problem. The use of the term "adiaphoron" is heavily affected, not to say determined, by the actual controversy over adiaphora in the mid-sixteenth century. The problem arose then because of the reintroduction of Roman Catholic practices and rites by political force after the military defeat of the Protestant forces. At stake was the survival of the Lutheran and Protestant cause. The question was not so much about what may be considered "not necessary" but rather about how much is allowable to preserve the cause of the gospel: What price survival? None of the Lutherans were in favor of the rites and none of them thought it right to reintroduce the rites by political force. But the Lutherans split over whether certain practices that had been discontinued could be tolerated for the sake of the survival of the Lutheran cause.

A soft (Philippist—so called for Philipp Melanchthon) and a hard (Gnesio-Lutheran) line resulted and they caused a more or less permanent rift among the Confessors. Melanchthon and his supporters argued that if the gospel of justification by faith was preserved and the canon of the Mass excised, other rites and practices could be allowed on the grounds that they were adiaphora, "i.e., matters of indifference (*Mitteldingen*) which may be held without injury to the Divine Scriptures. . ." (Leipzig Interim, 1548).[4] The soft line was that adiaphora could be allowed in the face of persecution to preserve the gospel. They said they would bear this harsh servitude, but they would not say it was right.[5] Thus even for the soft-liners it would not be fair to say it was a matter of indifference, but a question of how much they would suffer, how high a price they were willing to pay for survival.

The hard line drawn by Matthias Flacius and the Gnesio-Lutherans was that precisely in the face of such force and persecution one could not surrender anything. To do so was simply to surrender the evangelical freedom one was supposed to confess. One might indeed survive by submitting to such "adiaphora," but one would have lost that for which one was seeking to survive. In such times, therefore, the very substance and clarity of the confession was at stake. When one finds oneself in such a situation (*in statu confessionis*), one cannot give into what is being forced upon one because the freedom of "indifference" is surrendered. When adiaphora are forced upon one, they are no longer adiaphora. The freedom of the gospel is lost, and one cannot give in.

While the compromise of the soft line probably enabled Lutheranism to survive until political fortunes changed, it was the hard line that largely won the Confessional battle and became official in the Formula of Concord.[6] Important for our consideration is the fact that Flacius and the Gnesio-Lutherans had a keener sense for the relationship between liturgical rites and the theology expressed in them—supposedly adiaphoristic actions and the beliefs mirrored in them—as well as the political significance of such practices.[7] Perhaps in this respect they were closer to the Thomists who held that no ceremony or rite could really be an adiaphoron since all conscious, concrete actions have ends and "would be integrally bound up with and expressive of the beliefs undergirding worship."[8]

Against this historical background the Lutheran Confessional position has been that while there are such things as adiaphora that one may or may not espouse in freedom, the matter is substantively altered when an adiaphoron is forced upon one. *In statu confessionis* one can only resist. One cannot allow an adiaphoron to be made a necessity.

The Invocation of Saints—an Adiaphoron?

How might this bear upon our discussion about invocation of the saints? First of all, it is worth noting that the question per se seemed to have played no part in the controversies of the time. The rites and practices imposed were such things as episcopal authority, baptismal ceremonies, confirmation, auricular confession and absolution prior to communion, unction, episcopal ordination, marriage, Mass (with bells, lights, vessels, chant, vestments, and the like but without the canon), images (here one comes closest to the question of the saints: images are to be only remembrances and no divine honor is to be attached to them; no superstitious resort should occur or be encouraged), singing, holidays, fasts, and distinctive pastoral attire.[9] No mention is made of the invocation of saints. Does this mean that it was at that time truly an adiaphoron—for both sides? Or does it mean that given the Lutheran stand in the Augsburg Confession, its Apology, and the Smalcald Articles, it was simply out of the question and that Lutherans would not have tolerated it at all? Or was the canon of the Mass the only instance in which invocation of saints would have been forced upon them and thus no longer a problem since the canon was excised? More research would have to be done to answer such questions.

The Augsburg Confession

Obviously the question is no longer so politically charged. Could the invocation of saints be considered an adiaphoron today? Now it is more a doctrinal and liturgical question than a political one. But before moving to those questions, it is useful to recall the original setting of the question in the movement from the Augsburg Confession through the reply of Catholic theologians in the Confutation requested by Charles V to the Lutheran Apology. The Augsburg Confession rather mildly asserted that the invocation of the saints could not be proved from Scripture and therefore could not be required. The Confutation then rejects this position "utterly" and condemns it as an error, claiming in this to be "in harmony with the whole universal church" and calls upon the princes to see to it that "the practice continue."[10] The Apology then takes this utter rejection and call to the princes to mean that the practice is mandatory. Thus the first sentence of the Apology: "They [the Confutators] absolutely condemn Article 21 because we do not require the invocation of saints."[11] And later: "Not only do our opponents require invocation in the veneration of saints; they even apply the merits of the saints to others."[12] Did Melanchthon mishear the Confutation—given the fact that he was not allowed to have a copy of it? In any case, the move from the Augsburg Confession to Confutation to Apology raises the question of what constitutes requirement in this matter. Certainly political enforcement would violate freedom. But would just prescribed practice in liturgical matters constitute a breach of adiaphoristic freedom? Would, for example, a contemporary Mass canon—officially recommended or prescribed—with invocation of saints be a form of requirement? The Apology understands the Confutation to move in that direction and is adamant in refusing to accept such requirement in any form. The formal reason for this is simply that it is not required, commanded, or even taught in the Scriptures. More materially, faithful prayer depends upon a promise. There is, in this case, no promise that departed saints will hear invocations addressed to them.[13] Thus the practice has not only no formal command, but no material basis.

These opening stages of the debate surrounding the stance of the Augsburg Confession do not, to be sure, raise the question of adiaphora explicitly. At the very least, however, the Lutherans were quite clear and adamant that the invocation of saints, while perhaps neither commanded nor forbidden by Scriptures, could not be required of Lutherans and that to do so in any way would be met by firm resistance. One might say that the germ of the stance taken later in the adiaphoristic controversies is already present. The practice is not formally, at least, rejected, but it cannot be required. If it is required, the situation is radically altered.

This brings us to the second vantage point from which to address the question, that of Lutheran theological understanding itself. No doubt this is more crucial for contemporary discussion. Does Lutheran doctrine lead in the direction of a theological critique so severe as to remove invocation of saints from the category of an adiaphoron altogether? One should first mention the positive attitude of the Lutherans expressed in the Augsburg Confession and also in the Apology. Saints should be remembered so faith can be encouraged and strengthened by their faith, by seeing what grace they received, and by the example they leave for the faithful. However, this does not ameliorate the critique of the practice of invocation. Primary and persistent is the contention that such invocation detracts from what belongs only to God and his Christ. Thus the Apology: "To put it mildly, . . . this obscures the work of Christ and transfers to the saints the trust we should have in Christ's mercy. Men suppose that Christ is more severe and the saints more approachable."[14] One should no doubt take Melanchthon at his word when he said this was to put the matter mildly. It was and is, for Lutherans, the most serious consideration. Lutherans find it difficult to understand why one should find a departed saint closer or more approachable than Christ.

The Smalcald Articles

In the Smalcald Articles Luther was not so mild, though the argument is essentially the same. He deals with the invocation of saints under a heading of its own in the list of abuses spawned by the misuse of the Mass. For Luther it is "in conflict with the first, chief article and undermines knowledge of Christ." It is "idolatry" to invoke saints, keep fasts and festivals for them, say Masses for them, regard them as helpers in time of need, assign them special functions, etc., because "such honor belongs to God alone."[15] The Confessional concern is that whatever honor is to be accorded the saints cannot be such as to put them in the position of being more accessible than Christ. They cannot be considered mediators who compete with the one and only Mediator, Jesus Christ. Such a matter is not an adiaphoron, and the practice could only be rejected.

The question of invocation therefore inevitably turns to the understanding of mediation. In what sense could departed saints be said to stand between the saints yet living and Christ? What sort of a mediatorial role do they play? In the Apology Melanchthon objects that his Catholic opponents make saints out to be not only mediators of intercession but mediators of propitiation and redemption because the merits of saints are supposedly available to others.[16] For Lutherans this inevitably raises the question of the relation between invocation of saints and the merits of the saints. Do the merits of the saints, perhaps, qualify them to be ones who may be invoked? Such questions lead to two further considerations that must be addressed before we can decide whether the theological critique is such that it lifts the invocation out of the category of adiaphoron: What is a saint and what is the nature of the mediation in question? In other words, is the understanding of saints and their merits as well as the mediation they can be said to proffer such that it conflicts with the Lutheran understanding?

Lutheran Understanding of Saints

What is a saint according to Lutheran understanding? Even though in popular parlance Lutherans continued to follow the traditional practice of calling some of the departed heroes of the faith saints, continued to name churches after them, etc., they set out intentionally to reclaim the title for the living. Thus the Reformers insisted that the title was to be brought back from heaven down to earth. A saint is one who has been justified by faith alone and who lives and acts on that basis. Since they are justified *sola gratia*, they are simultaneously saints and sinners. Thus they should not, out of false humility, hesitate to claim the title.

> How could anyone be so arrogant as to let himself be called holy? After all, we are nothing but poor sinners. Answer: All this stems from the old notion that when we hear of saintliness, we must look for only great, splendid works and gaze at the saints in heaven, as if they had earned and merited it. But we say that the real saints of Christ must be good, stout sinners and remain saints who are not ashamed to pray the Lord's Prayer.[17]

> To call yourself a saint is, therefore, no presumption but an act of gratitude and a confession of God's blessings.[18]

> Scripture calls us holy while we still live on earth—if we believe. But this name the papists have taken away from us; they say that we are not to be considered holy, that the saints in heaven alone are holy. Therefore we are compelled to reclaim the noble name. Holy you must be, but you must also guard against imagining that you are holy of yourself or by your own merit.[19]

The import of passages like these is clear. Not only is it an attempt to reclaim the name for the living, but it is also a critique of the system of merit which reserves the name for the most successful. Holiness is a gift, the result of a relation, not an achievement—even if with the help of grace. A saint, in this light, is one who claims nothing for self, but lives in the light of the divine grace, justified by faith alone.

The reclaiming of the name of saint for the living and the consequent critique of the merits of the saints also shapes the understanding of the "communion of saints." Participation in the communion of saints does not mean sharing the merits of those who may have gained such, but rather sharing the burdens and blessings of the living. A saint is one who because of the sheer gift of alien righteousness and holiness is to turn about and serve the living, not the dead.

> Whatever it is that you want to do for the saints, turn your attention away from the dead toward the living. The living saints

> are your neighbors, the naked, the hungry, the thirsty, the poor people who have wives and children and suffer shame. Direct your help toward them, begin your work here, use your tongue in order to protect them, your coat in order to cover them and to give them honor.[20]

In fact, the life of the departed is hidden from us. Death represents a barrier we cannot penetrate. Thus we should turn our attention to the service of the living.

> Let the dear saints rest where they are and take care of those whom we have with us; for we have enough to take care of with ourselves if we are to live as Christians should. Therefore let them be, and let God take care of them. We can neither know nor understand how they live in the world beyond. That world is quite different from this one.[21]

Departed saints who are remembered for their faithful service thus play a role in the communion of saints as encouraging examples of faith and obedience. Their significance does not lie in their moral achievements, however, nor can their "merits" be summed up or exchanged. They are examples of how faith perseveres in suffering and trial and thus strengthen and encourage believers after the model of Hebrews 11. They serve the body in that manner. Their works cannot be substituted for those of the living in any way. That could mean that the merits of the saints might be used to avoid rather than foster service to the living. Saints are respected and properly venerated when their example in the life of faith is followed, not when their works are substituted for the shortcomings of the living.

Given this understanding of what makes a saint, the practice of invoking departed saints is highly questionable. Rejection of the idea of the merits of the saints carries with it negative consequences for the practice of invocation as well. If there are no saints who have merited higher status or who could be said to have enjoyed the beatific vision, to whom should one direct the invocations? One may, of course, ask living saints to intercede for oneself and others, but there is no indication or promise that the departed can or will hear us. While the Reformers were willing to grant that Mary and the saints in heaven perhaps pray for us, they saw no reason to promote or encourage the practice of invocation by saints on earth. Since Christ is the giver of all righteousness, holiness, and every gift, the Reformers found it difficult to understand why one should turn elsewhere. The presuppositions on which the practice of invocation depended had been removed. Thus Luther never thought it necessary to polemicize directly against the practice of invocation, but believed that under the effect of evangelical preaching it would simply die out.[22] And so it did in Lutheran churches.

Mediation and Sainthood

It seems obvious that this discussion about what a saint is depends on our second question about mediation. A saint is made by the "mediation" of Christ. If his mediation is such that his saints are inspired to turn solely to him and give all glory to him—in such a way that the invocation of saints seems to detract from the honor due him—then we must inquire more closely about this mediation before we bring this essay to a close.

What sort of "mediation" is this and is it such that the invocation of saints would necessarily pose a threat serious enough to render such invocation more than an adiaphoron? The Roman Catholic argument is that since saints are born and carried by the grace of Christ, their role as intercessors in the hereafter need not, in a properly ordered faith, compete with Christ's role as sole Mediator of such grace. The practice of venerating the saints may in fact be subject to abuse. But abuse does not abrogate proper use. Properly understood, the saints may be taken as prominent examples of the "success" of Christ's mediation. If we can ask living saints to intercede for us, there should be no reason why we cannot ask those hereafter who already share Christ's victory over death to continue to do so. Why should a Lutheran object to this or hold that it is more than an adiaphoron?

The key issue is the subtle one of mediation itself. For Lutherans the word itself tends to lead astray. Perhaps that is why it has never figured as a prominent category in Lutheran Christology. It suggests the idea of a "go-between," an arbiter between parties that have fallen out, a medium between two extremes. Christologically this suggests that Christ is a go-between, one who perhaps conveys divine favors to humans or human requests to God. The tendency then is to think of mediation as the act of interceding for and delivering divine grace to those who otherwise would have no access to it.

Judgment as to the theological appropriateness of such a view will depend, no doubt, on one's view of what salvation means and how it is granted. In what we called in the previous round of dialogue a "transformationist" model, one could think of Christ as mediating transforming grace and saints as the evidence of the effectiveness of such mediation. It could then be held that asking such saints to intercede in the hereafter is simply an indication of one's faith and confidence in the grace of Christ.

Lutheran and Catholic Views of Mediation

Lutheran difficulties with such a view of mediation stem, as in the previous round of dialogue on justification, from difficulties with the model itself. Where justification is by faith alone, creating the situation in which one is simultaneously just and sinner, what is mediated is not some intermediate thing or power but Christ himself through the word of the cross and the sacraments. The only mediation that occurs happens in the event itself and the proclamation of it. Christ becomes sin for us and bears the curse even until death. If there is no resurrection and consequently no proclamation, there is no mediation. Since he is raised, he is now our life. The mediation, if one is to use the word, occurs through what Luther called "the happy exchange and struggle." Christ takes our sin and gives us the righteousness that emerges from his struggle with that sin and death. Thus he alone is the "Mediator." As such, he is not a go-between, he is God for us. Subsequent mediation takes place through the word of this victory in which he gives himself to us. The "real presence" of Christ is mediated through word and sacrament. What takes place for the sinner is not, therefore, a transformation as such, but a death and a resurrection in Christ. In this life we are simultaneously just and sinner, dead and alive, in faith, until the end.

Given this view, Lutherans find it difficult to understand why it is necessary or advantageous to appeal to someone other than Christ to intercede for us or to grant favor of any sort. The idea that someone other than Christ may, due to the merit gained by cooperation with grace, be so placed as to be such an intercessor is simply foreign if not inimical to a piety nourished on justification by faith alone. Such piety is grasped and shaped by what is revealed rather than what is hidden and thus not open to speculation. Moreover, speculation about saints in the hereafter can create problems for the conscience if it suggests that to become a "real" saint one must somehow attain such status—even if with the aid of grace.

Perhaps it is the case here that we come up against a fundamental difference in understanding the mediation and its effects. As Carl Peter has put it:

> There are, as I see it, genuine differences between Lutheran and Roman Catholic members of the dialogue when it comes to assessing creaturely mediation and cooperation in the ways in which Christ's grace reaches human beings. Two different approaches are taken—motivated at least in part by diverse hopes and fears. Lutherans have a fear that the truth of Christ's unique mediation will be compromised and hope to avoid this by criticizing any function, form of worship or piety, office or person that looks like a pretender in this context. Roman Catholics fear that Christ's unique mediation will thus be made needlessly fruitless and hope to avoid this by stressing the truth of the manifold cooperation to which that mediation gives rise as his grace is communicated to those in need of it.
>
> I suspect that we are dealing here with what ecumenists today might call a fundamental difference. I doubt that it will ever be completely eliminated. But could such a difference exist in a more united church—could it be a difference within one faith rather than of diverse faiths?[23]

If it is the case—and I expect I would agree with Carl Peter here—that we have to do with a fundamental and thus deeply held difference, it does not appear that the category of adiaphoron is very useful in working toward a resolution of the problems surrounding the invocation of saints. Lutheran attitudes about the kind of mediation available in the saints should not, I expect, simply be a matter of indifference to Roman Catholics. Likewise, Roman Catholic theology and practice in this regard cannot be a matter of indifference to Lutherans. We face a fundamental difference in the understanding of mediation. The question then is, as Carl Peter put it, whether we can find ways to live with this difference.

If there is a way ahead together, perhaps it lies in the fact that both Roman Catholics and Lutherans are concerned about the concrete and objective nature of the mediation given in Christ. Roman Catholics tend to find this concretion and objectivity in the church, its priesthood, and the saints. Lutherans find this objectivity in the preached word, a word that comes from without and maintains its objectivity precisely by putting the old subject to death and raising up a new one in faith. Perhaps one can say that only in death and the promise of new life do we come up against that which is truly and irreducibly from without. The common concern for the concrete mediation of Christ's gifts, it is to be hoped, can draw us together even as we seek to understand the differences between us.

Notes

COMMON STATEMENT: THE ONE MEDIATOR, THE SAINTS, AND MARY

Introduction

1. Lutherans and Catholics in Dialogue, 6 vols. 1. *The Status of the Nicene Creed as Dogma of the Church* (1965); 2. *One Baptism for the Remission of Sins* (1966); 3. *The Eucharist as Sacrifice* (1967); 4. *Eucharist and Ministry* (1970); 5. *Papal Primacy and the Universal Church* (Minneapolis: Augsburg, 1974); 6. *Teaching Authority and Infallibility in the Church* (Minneapolis: Augsburg, 1980). Vols. 1–4 were originally published by the Bishops' Committee for Ecumenical and Interreligious Affairs, Washington, D.C., and the U.S.A. National Committee of the Lutheran World Federation, New York, N.Y. Vols. 1–3 have been reprinted together in one volume by Augsburg Publishing House (n.d.), as has vol. 4 (1979).
2. *Origins* 13:17 (Oct. 6, 1983) 277, 279–304 (preliminary text); L/RC 7 (final, official text).

Part One: Issues and Perspectives

I. The Problem in the Sixteenth Century

3. See the historical sketch by Karl Hausberger, "Heilige/Heiligenverehrung. Abendländisches Mittelalter," TRE 14 (1985) 652. The Greek terms "*latreia*" and "*douleia*," Latinized as *latria* and *dulia*, referred, respectively, to the fullness of divine worship accorded to God alone and the reverence which may be paid to the saints. The term "*hyperdouleia*" (Latin: *hyperdulia*) was used with reference to Mary.
4. DS 812–14.
5. For church teachings on indulgences during the Middle Ages, cf. DS 819, 868, 1025–27, 1447–49.
6. Eric W. Gritsch, "The Origin of the Lutheran Teaching on Justification," L/RC 7: pp. 164–67.
7. Andreas Bodenstein of Karlstadt, dean of Wittenberg University, was an iconoclast who succeeded in establishing a new "church order" in Wittenberg in

1521. Luther modified this order in 1523. See James H. Preus, *Carlstadt's Ordinances and Luther's Liberty* (Cambridge MA: Harvard University Press, 1974).

8. One example of Luther's modification of tradition is his *Fourteen Consolations*, 1520. WA 6:104–34; LW 42:119–66. On Martin Bucer, see Frieder Schulz, *TRE* 14 (1985) 664.
9. Thomas de Vio of Gaeta (known as Cajetan), general of the Dominican order and cardinal, conducted the first hearing of Luther in Augsburg in 1518.
10. Thomas de Vio Cardinal Cajetan, *Opuscula Omnia. Tractatus de Indulgentiis* (Venice: Apud Haeredêm Hieronymi Scoti, 1580) q.1, 51, v, 1 G.
11. See Carl J. Peter, "The Church's Treasures (*Thesauri Ecclesiae*) Then and Now," *Theological Studies* 7 (1986) 251–72.
12. DS 1492.
13. *Sermon on the Birth of Mary*, 1522. WA 10/3:317, 4–318, 7. See also Luther's critique in the context of his view of *communio sanctorum* in Paul Althaus, *The Theology of Martin Luther* (tr. Robert C. Schultz; Philadelphia: Fortress, 1966) 298–300. Luther's movement toward rejection of the cult of the saints has been analyzed by Lennart Pinomaa, "Luthers Weg zur Verwerfung des Heiligendienstes," *Lutherjahrbuch* 29 (1962) 35–43. See also *idem*, *Die Heiligen bei Luther* (Helsinki: Luther-Agricola-Gesellschaft, 1977). Very helpful is also the detailed analysis of Luther's view by Peter Manns, "Luther und die Heiligen," *Reformatio Ecclesiae. Beiträge zu kirchlichen Reformbemühungen von der Alten Kirche bis zur Neuzeit* (FS. E. Iserloh; ed. R. Bäumer; Paderborn, Munich, Vienna, Zurich: Schöningh, 1980) 535–80; cf. Horst Gorski, *Die Niedrigkeit seiner Magd*. Darstellung und theologische Analyse der Marientheologie Luthers als Beitrag zum gegenwärtigen lutherisch/römisch-katholischen Gespräch (Europäische Hochschulschriften 23; Berlin, New York: Lanning, 1987).
14. *The Bondage of the Will*, 1525. WA 18:778, 8–13; LW 33:280.
15. *Concerning Rebaptism*, 1520. WA 26:168, 12–16; LW 40:256. Luther's concept of example is closely related to Augustine's concept of *sacramentum et exemplum*; cf. Kenneth Hagen, *A Theology of Testament in the Young Luther. The Lectures on Hebrews* (Studies in Medieval and Reformation Thought 12; Leiden: Brill, 1974) 114–15.
16. *Lectures on Genesis*, 1539. WA 43:108, 24–31; LW 3:325. On *Divum Bernardum veneror*, see *Leipzig Disputation*, WA 59:445, 410–14; cf. Franz Posset, "Bernard of Clairvaux as Luther's Source: Reading Bernard with Luther's 'Spectacles,' " *Concordia Theological Quarterly* 54 (1990) 281–304.
17. *The Burning of Brother Henry*, 1525. WA 18:224–40; LW 32:265–86. How Luther and other reformers continued the patristic and medieval martyriological tradition has been demonstrated by Robert Kolb, *For All the Saints. Changing Perceptions of Martyrdom and Sainthood in the Lutheran Reformation* (Macon GA: Mercer University Press, 1987); on Henry of Zutphen, 21, 66.
18. *Vorrede . . .* , 1544. WA 54:109–11.
19. Sermon on May 13, 1526. WA 20:390, 6–8. Sermon on June 17, 1526. WA 20:444, 1–2. Wilhelm Maurer, *Historical Commentary on the Augsburg Confession* (tr. H. G. Anderson; Philadelphia: Fortress, 1986) 371–75, has shown how Luther linked the veneration of saints to Christ and the "Word." Maurer concludes that CA 21 discloses Melanchthon's concern about abuses more than the depth of Luther's thought (ibid., 375).
20. With regard to the Immaculate Conception, Luther taught that Mary had been conceived in sin but her soul had been purified by infusion after conception.

Sermon on the Feast of the Immaculate Conception, 1527. Festival Postil (*Festpostille*). WA 17/2:288, 17–34. In 1518 Luther declared that, even though the Immaculate Conception of Mary was an opinion asserted by the Council of Basel (1431–49), a contrary opinion need not be considered heretical unless it is disproved. *Explanations of the Ninety–Five Theses*. 1518. WA 1:583, 8–12; LW 31:173. See also Hans Düfel, *Luthers Stellung zur Marienverehrung* (Kirche und Konfession, Veröffentlichungen des konfessionskundlichen Instituts des Evangelischen Bundes 13; Göttingen: Vandenhoeck and Ruprecht, 1968) 169–70. That Christ should be born of a virgin who was "immaculate" is "a pious and pleasing thought" (*haec pia cogitatio et placet*) which need not be imposed on the faithful (*Exposition of the Ninth Chapter of Isaiah*, 1543/44. WA 40/3:680, 31–32). Luther taught that Mary remained a virgin before the birth of Christ (*ante partum*), at the birth (*in partu*), and after his birth (*post partum*) (*That Jesus Was Born a Jew*, 1523. WA 11:320, 1–6; LW 45:206). Further evidence in William J. Cole, "Was Luther a Devotee of Mary?" *Marian Studies* 21 (1970) 119–20; on the Immaculate Conception, ibid., 120–23.

21. In the sixteenth century most Lutheran territories celebrated the Marian festivals of purification (February 2), of the Annunciation (March 25), and of the Visitation (July 2). See Walter Delius, "Luther und die Marienverehrung," *Theologische Literaturzeitung* 79 (1954) 414.
22. "Like Mary's virginity, the church will not be destroyed (*vertilgt*)" (*Sermon on the Sunday After Christmas on Luke 2:23–40*. Church Postil [*Kirchenpostille*], 1522. WA 10/1/1:405, 13–16). Luther interpreted Luke 1:48b ("All generations call me blessed"): "Not *she* is praised thereby, but God's *grace* towards her" (WA 7:568,4; LW 21:321). Here he learned from, and resonates to, Nicholas of Lyra; see Kenneth Hagen, "Lyra and Luther on Luke 1:26-55," p. 3 (unpublished; Sept. 1983); see also Eric W. Gritsch, "Embodiment of Unmerited Grace. The Virgin Mary According to Martin Luther and Lutheranism" in *Mary's Place in Christian Dialogue* (ed. A. Stacpoole; Wilten CN: Morehouse-Barlow, 1983) 133–41. On "*typus ecclesiae*," see Heiko A. Oberman, "The Virgin Mary in Evangelical Perspective," *Journal of Ecumenical Studies* 1 (1964) 13; reprinted in Facet Books, Historical Series 20; Philadelphia: Fortress, 1971.
23. *Sermon on the Festival of the Assumption*, August 15, 1522. WA 10/3:269,12–13; also the sermon on August 15, 1544. WA 52:681, 27–31.
24. Most of Luther's hymns originated in 1523 and 1524. (Thirty-six hymns are listed in WA 35:411–73; English translations in LW 53:211–309.) It is mostly the festival hymns that refer to Mary, especially Advent and Christmas hymns. See Karlfried Froehlich, "Mary in the Hymns of Martin Luther" (unpublished; Sept. 1983).
25. *Confession Concerning Christ's Supper*, 1528. WA 26:508, 14–15; LW 37:370.
26. *Instructions for the Visitors of Parish Pastors in Electoral Saxony*, 1528. WA 26:224, 26–31; LW 40:300.
27. The significance of this step is stressed by Georg Kretschmar and René Laurentin, "The Cult of the Saints," *Confessing One Faith. A Joint Commentary on the Augsburg Confession by Lutheran and Catholic Theologians* (ed. G. W. Forell and J. F. McCue; tr. R. Gehrke; Minneapolis: Augsburg, 1982) 276; recall as well the teachings of the Second Council of Nicaea (DS 600–601).
28. *CA* 21:2; *BS* 83b–c; *BC* 47.
29. Reference will be to the German and Latin text as found in Herbert Immenkötter, *Die Confutatio der Augustana vom 3. August 1530* (Corpus Catholicorum 33: Münster: Aschendorff, 1979); English translation in J.M. Reu (ed.), *The Augsburg*

Confession: A Collection of Sources with an Historical Introduction (Chicago: Wartburg Publishing House, 1930; reprinted, St. Louis: Concordia Seminary Press, 1966).

30. *Die Confutatio* 21:124, 11–12 (German); 125, 10 (Latin).
31. *Contra Faustum* 20:21; *CSEL* 25:562, 8–10.
32. *Die Confutatio* 21:130, 3–4 (German); 131, 3–4 (Latin).
33. *Die Confutatio*, 21:129, 14–16: "Nam etsi fatetur unum esse mediatorem redemptionis Caesarea majestas cum tota ecclesia, tamen multi sunt mediatores intercessionis" (Reu 361).
34. Ap 21:8–9; *BS* 318; *BC* 230.
35. Ap 21:10; *BS* 318; *BC* 230.
36. Ap 21:3; *BS* 317; *BC* 229.
37. *Die Confutatio*, 21:129, 14–16 (Reu 361).
38. Ap 21:29; *BS* 322; *BC* 233.
39. Ap 21:17–32; *BS* 320–23; *BC* 231–33.
40. Ap 21:38–44; *BS* 325–28; *BC* 234–36.
41. See Kenneth Hagen, "The Historical Context of the Smalcald Articles," *Concordia Theological Quarterly* 51 (1987) 245–53.
42. SA 2:25; *BS* 424; *BC* 297.
43. SA 2:28; *BS* 425; *BC* 297.
44. CR 4:369–70.
45. For the complete texts, *C.O.D.* 750–52; 772–73; see also below, Carl J. Peter, "The Communion of Saints in the Final Days of the Council of Trent."
46. *LG* 50–51.
47. *C.O.D.*, 750–51.
48. *C.O.D.*, 751; DS 1822.
49. *C.O.D.*, 751.
50. *C.O.D..*, 751–52.
51. See above, CS §§28–29.
52. Martin Chemnitz, *Examination of the Council of Trent* (tr. Fred Kramer; St. Louis: Concordia, 1986) 2:353–507.
53. FC Ep 8:12; *BS* 806; *BC* 488; *FC SD* 8:24; *BS* 1024; *BC* 595.
54. Rabus's work has been analyzed and evaluated by Kolb (n. 17 above).

II. Perspectives on Critical Issues

A. Lutheran Perspectives

55. See Robert Bertram, "Luther on Christ as the Sole Mediator" 249–62 below.
56. L/RC7 24:25; 70:154.
57. Ap 21:4–7; *BS* 317–18; *BC* 229–30.
58. SA 2:3:26; *BS* 425; *BC* 297.
59. Ap 21:27; *BS* 322; *BC* 232.
60. The Magnificat, 1521. WA 7:561; LW 21:314.
61. Cf. Arthur C. Piepkorn, "Mary's Place within the People of God according to non-Roman Catholics," *Marian Studies* 18 (1967) 46–86, esp. 73–78.
62. *CA* 1–17; *BS* 50–73; *BC* 27–39.
63. Cited in a note in *LG* 50.

B. Catholic Perspectives

64. *LG* 1.
65. For the background regarding the conciliar debate leading up to this decison, see Carl J. Peter, "The Eschatology of *Lumen Gentium*" and S. C. Napiorkowski, "Marie dans la piété Catholique," *Collectanea Theologica* 56 (1986) 69–84.
66. *LG* 61.
67. Augustine, *De Praedestinatione Sanctorum* 15:30–31; *PL* 44:981–82; Aquinas, *Super Epistolam ad Romanos*, I Lect. 3, 48–49.
68. *The Church's Confession of Faith: A Catechism for Adults* (ed. M. Jordan; tr. S. Arndt; San Francisco: Ignatius, 1987) 348.
69. Carl J. Peter, "A Moment of Truth for Lutheran-Catholic Dialogue," *Origins* 17 (1988) 541; reprinted, *One in Christ* 24 (1988) 151.
70. Medieval theologians rather commonly held that in seeing the eternal God, to whom all is present, the saints in heaven see as well whatever is of legitimate concern and interest to them on earth. For Thomas Aquinas, cf. *In IV Sent.*, d. 45, 1. 3, a. 1, sol. and *S.T.* III, q. 10, a. 2, c. Melanchthon referred to a dispute that had arisen precisely because this was taken as a given (Ap 21:11).

III. The Problem Reexamined

A. Dimensions of the Problem

71. L/RC 7:152; cf. 121.
72. L/RC 7:91.
73. Ibid.
74. Carl J. Peter, "The Need of Another Principle," L/RC 7: p. 309; cf. 314; also L/RC 7:118.154.

B. Divergences

75. Vatican II is here quoting the "*Decretum pro Graecis*" of the Council of Florence (DS 1305).
76. CS §§159, 165, 166, and 177; also 50 and 51.
77. For some evidence, see Robert Eno, *St. Augustine and the Saints* (The Saint Augustine Lecture for 1985; Philadelphia: Villanova University Press, 1989) 29–48.
78. For an example of how the term "divine motherhood" took on a more-than-physical meaning, see the work of Scheeben as summarized in CS §189.
79. On the debate about Mary as Mediatrix at Vatican II, see the literature cited in n. 261; also Elizabeth A. Johnson, "Mary as Mediatrix," 311–26 below. In the 1962 schema *De beata Maria Virgine matre Dei et matre hominum*, no. 3, it had been stated that "the most blessed Virgin is not undeservedly called Mediatrix of graces." Note that in the final text the only mention of Mary as Mediatrix, made in passing, is in the context of her maternal intercession in heaven. For further discussion, see Guilherme Baraúna, "Le très sainte Vierge au service de l'économie du salut," *L'Eglise de Vatican II* (Unam Sanctum 51c; ed. G. Baraúna; Paris: Cerf, 1966) 1226–30.
80. Pius IX, *Ineffabilis Deus* (December 8, 1854), DS 2803.
81. See Frederick M. Jelly, "The Roman Catholic Dogma of Mary's Immaculate Conception," 263–78 below.

82. In the apostolic constitution, *Munificentissimus Deus* (November 1, 1950), Pius XII, defining the dogma, pointed out that many Scholastic theologians made the connection between Mary's absolute sinlessness and her Assumption. Summarizing the theological arguments, the pope presented the Assumption as the crowning privilege that follows upon, and is the appropriate complement to, four other privileges: Mary's connection with Christ in one and the same decree of predestination; her Immaculate Conception; her virginal motherhood; and her intimate association with Christ's redemptive work. In this connection the text speaks explicitly of Mary's having been "preserved from the corruption of the tomb," though the concluding paragraph containing the binding definition states only that Mary, "having completed the course of her earthly life, was assumed body and soul into heavenly glory." See the text of the bull in *Papal Documents on Mary* (ed. W. J. Doheny and J. P. Kelly; Boston: St. Paul Editions, 1981) 299–320, esp. 318, corresponding to DS 3902; also Avery Dulles, "The Dogma of the Assumption," 279–94 below.
83. Valerius Herberger, "Am Tage Mariae Himmelfahrt," *Evangelische Herz–Postilla*, Ander Theil (reprinted Leipzig: Gleditsch, 1687) 200–204.
84. In some instances Lutherans contended that the Assumption had its roots in pagan polytheism and raised Mary to quasi-divine status; see Eric W. Gritsch, "The Views of Luther and Lutheranism on the Veneration of Mary," 235–48 below.

C. Need the Divergences Be Church-Dividing?

85. Cf. *Facing Unity: Models, Forms and Phases of Catholic-Lutheran Church Fellowship* (Geneva: Lutheran World Federation, 1985) §§47–49.
86. DS 1821. For discussion see Carl J. Peter, "The Communion of Saints in the Final Days of the Council of Trent," esp. 230–31 below. For a more general statement on the obligation of invoking saints, see Karl Rahner and Johann B. Metz, *The Courage to Pray* (New York: Crossroad, 1981) 33–34.
87. The five principles set forth by Paul VI to guide proper Marian devotion (§§ 25 to 37 of the text *AAS* 64 [1974]) are discussed in detail in the Roman Catholic Reflections below.
88. See the quotations from Karl Rahner and other contemporary Catholic theologians in Elizabeth A. Johnson, "Mary as Mediatrix," pp. 324–26 below. On Vatican II, see n. 79 above.
89. L/RC 6:50; emphasis added; consult also the further clarifications in "Observations on the Critique Submitted by the Committee on Doctrine of the National Conference of Catholic Bishops," *Lutheran Quarterly*, ns 1 (1987) 151–58.
90. The conditions under which eucharistic sharing with Protestants may be permitted are spelled out in the *Code of Canon Law* (1983), canon 844, which permits Catholic ministers under some circumstances to administer Holy Communion to Protestants. Canon 908 forbids concelebration of the Eucharist with ministers of churches not in full communion with the Catholic Church.
91. L/RC 6:50.
92. In *Christian Unity and Christian Diversity* (Philadelphia: Westminister, 1975) 90–96, John Macquarrie proposed an ecumenical reinterpretation of the dogma of the Immaculate Conception. Joseph Ratzinger, *Church, Ecumenism and Politics* (New York: Crossroad, 1988) 82–83, speaks of a "hermeneutics of unity" for dogmas defined in separation. For discussion of Ratzinger's position in light

of similar proposals by Yves Congar and others, see Avery Dulles, *The Reshaping of Catholicism* (San Francisco: Harper & Row, 1988) 238–41.

Part Two: Biblical and Historical Foundations

I. Scripture on Christ, the Saints, and Mary

93. Cf. Josef Hainz, *Koinonia: "Kirche" als Gemeinschaft bei Paulus* (Biblische Untersuchungen 16; Regensburg: Pustet, 1982) 232–72, for ecumenical development of the term in Roman Catholic, Reformation, and Orthodox Churches.
94. A. Oepke, *TWNT* 4 (1942) 618; *TDNT* 4 (1967) 614.
95. Thus Mithra, the mediator between Persian Ahuramazda and Ahriman (Plutarch, *Is. et Os.* 46 [2.369e]), and various cosmic beings and spirits.
96. For exegetical details on a and b, see respectively the papers by J. A. Fitzmyer, "Biblical Data on the Veneration, Intercession, and Invocation of Holy People," 135–47 below; and J. Reumann, "How Do We Interpret 1 Timothy 2:5 (and Related Passages)?" 149–57 below.
97. Other Greek nouns for prayer in the New Testament include *aitēma* ("request," Phil 4:4); *hiketēria* ("supplication," Heb. 5:7); and *eperōtēma* ("appeal," 1 Pet 3:21), not to mention the related verbs.
98. The verb *epikaleisthai*, "call upon," is also used in this sense at Rom 10:12, 13, 14; 1 Cor 1:2; 2 Cor 2:23; 2 Tim 2:22; Acts 2:21; 9:14, 21; 22:16; believers are "those who call on the name of the Lord"; cf. also Heb 11:20) and 1 Chron 16:4 (to invoke, thank, and praise the Lord; hiphil *zakar*). In the Latin Vulgate *invoco* is employed for *epikaleisthai* in all the above New Testament passages, but *invocatio* only at 2 Macc 8:15 ("on account of invocation of [the Lord's] holy and magnificent name over them").
99. L/RC 7:132.
100. Understood as a translation of the Hebrew, *ḥeblo šel-māšîah*, "the travail of the messiah," the phrase would refer to woes such as rebellion, war, pestilence, drought, crop failure, inflation, penury, apostasy, and cosmic cataclysms, expected to precede the end-time when God will send an appointed agent to deliver his people.
101. The Luther Bible includes Sirach (Ecclesiasticus or The Wisdom of Jesus the Son of Sirach) and 2 Maccabees in the Apocrypha, with the comment "good and useful for reading" but not on a par with the canonical books for the purposes of doctrine. The Council of Trent included them as part of its listing of the canon of holy Scriptures; they are sometimes termed by Catholics "deuterocanonical." 4 Maccabees, though in important Greek manuscripts of the Bible and revered in Eastern churches, has never been canonized. All three books are in the RSV Apocrypha, Expanded Edition, 1977.
102. For surveys of the biblical data, see J. Reumann "Death," and Osmo Tiililae, "Resurrection," in *The Encyclopedia of the Lutheran Church* (ed. J. Bodensieck; Philadelphia: Fortress; Minneapolis: Augsburg, 1965) 1:667–71 and 3:2048–50; P. Benoit and R. Murphy (eds.), *Immortality and Resurrection* (Concilium 60; New York: Herder and Herder, 1970); Günter Kegel, *Auferstehung Jesu—Auferstehung der Toten: Eine traditionsgeschichtliche Untersuchung zum Neuen Testament* (Gütersloh: Gütersloher Verlagshaus Gerd Mohn, 1970); L. Coenen and C. Brown, "Resurrection," *NIDNTT* 3 (1978) 259–309; G. Stemberger and P. Hoffmann, "Auferstehung der Toten I/2. Judentum," "I/3. Neues Testament," "Auferstehung Jesu Christi II/1. Neues Testamentum," *TRE* 4 (1979) 443–67, 478–513; H.

C. Cavallin, "Leben nach dem Tode im Spätjudentum und im frühen Christentum," *Aufstieg und Niedergang der römischen Welt* II 19/1 (1979) 240–345; P. Hoffmann, *Die Toten in Christus: eine religionsgeschichtliche und exegetische Untersuchung zur paulinischen Eschatologie*, Neutestamentliche Abhandlungen, Neue Folge 2; (Münster: Aschendorff, 1966); Pheme Perkins, *Resurrection: New Testament Witness and Contemporary Reflection* (Garden City: Doubleday, 1984); R. Martin-Achard,"Resurrection (A.T.; Judaisme)," *Dictionnaire de la Bible*, Supplement 10 (1985) 437–87; Gisbert Greshake and Jacob Kremer, *Resurrectio Mortuorum: Zum theologischen Verständnis der leiblichen Auferstehung* (Darmstadt: Wissenschaftliche Buchgesellschaft, 1986); Julien Ries, "Immortality," and Helmer Ringgren, "Resurrection," *ER* 7:123–45; 12:344–50.

103. Cf. Isa 25:8; Hos 6:1-3; Job 19:26; Ps 49:15; 73:23-28; 22:30; Isa 65:17; 66:22-24. J. L. McKenzie, *JBC* 77:168, has written, "It is generally held by scholars that no hope of individual survival after death is expressed in the OT before some of its latest passages, which were probably written in the 2nd cent B.C." M. Dahood, *Psalms I* (AB 16; Garden City NY: Doubleday & Co., 1966) vi and passim, has, however, on the basis of Canaanite motifs in the Psalter, argued for references to resurrection and even "Elysian Fields" there.

104. See especially A. M. Dubarle in Concilium 60:34–45 (n. 102 above); G. Stemberger, *TRE* 4:446–51 (n. 102 above); Cavallin (n. 102 above); Martin-Achard (n. 102 above); George W. E. Nickelsburg, *Resurrection, Immortality, and Eternal Life in Intertestamental Judaism* (Harvard Theological Studies 26; Cambridge: Harvard University Press, 1972); Kremer, *Resurrectio*, 60–76 (n. 102 above).

105. For the Eighteen Benedictions (*Sh[e]moneh ʿEsreh*), see Simeon Singer, *The Authorized Daily Prayer Book of the United Hebrew Congregations of the British Empire* (15th ed. rev.; London: Eyre & Spottiswoode, 1935) 158–64; further, C. G. Montefiore and H. Loewe, *A Rabbinic Anthology* (Cleveland and New York: World Publishing Company; and Philadelphia: Jewish Publication Society of America, 1960), "Life to Come: Resurrection and Judgment," 580–608, esp. 599–600. For *m. Sanhedrin* 10.1a, see Herbert Danby, *The Mishnah* (Oxford: Clarendon, 1933) 397; the bracketed phrase is lacking in some texts. For resurrection, in addition to passages already cited in 2 Maccabees and 2 Esdras, see 2 Macc 12: 43-45; 1 (Ethiopic) Enoch 22; 51; 91; 10; 92:3; 2 (Syriac Apocalypse of) Baruch 21:23-24; 42:7-8; 50:2; 2 Esdras 7:88-99 [v. 97, cf. Dan 12:3]; and Pseudo-Philo, *Biblical Antiquities* 3.10; 19.12; 32.13. For Enoch references, see *Old Testament Pseudepigrapha* (ed. J. H. Charlesworth; Garden City NY: Doubleday & Co., 1983–85) 1:24-25, 36-37, 72, 74; 2 Baruch, ibid. 1:628, 634, 638; for the *Liber Antiquitatum Biblicarum*, ibid. 2:307, 328, 346–47; Kremer, *Resurrectio*, 60–70 (n. 102 above).

106. 2 Macc 12:39-45 describes how it was discovered that all the Jews who died in a battle had amulets of idols under their tunics. Supplication was made that this sin might be blotted out, and Judas took up a collection for an expiatory sacrifice at the Jerusalem temple, that "they might be delivered from their sin." Vv. 44 and 45 seek to justify Judas's belief in the resurrection: "if he were not expecting that those who had fallen would rise again, it would have been superfluous and foolish to pray for the dead. But if he was looking to the splendid reward that is laid up for those who fall asleep in godliness, it was a holy and pious thought." T. Corbishley, S.J., in *A New Catholic Commentary on Holy Scripture* (London: Thomas Nelson, 1969) 599d (p. 758) sees here "a clear-cut and confident belief in personal immortality and in the value of intercessory prayer for the dead," even though "such an idea is unparalleled in

Jewish Literature"; Judas's gesture strengthened the faith presupposed but then under debate among Jews. The note in the NAB views the statement about prayers and sacrifices as made "only for the purpose of proving that Judas believed in the resurrection of the just," the expiation here being "similar to, but not quite the same as, the Catholic doctrine of purgatory." Jonathan A. Goldstein, *II Maccabees* (AB 41A; Garden City: Doubleday, 1983) 449–51, thinks the author "has engaged in a complicated piece of logical gymnastics to prove that Judas believed in the resurrection of the dead." Judas and his soldiers were probably following Lev 4:13-21, about a sin that taints the community; there one sin offering, a bull, is called for, to take away the corporate guilt in the surviving community, not offerings for each dead soldier (in rabbinic law, "sacrifices do not secure expiation for the dead"). G. Stemberger, in *TRE* 4 (1979) 447, suggests one early scribe wrote in the margin that to pray for the dead is foolish, but another that atonement for the dead is good; a copyist harmonized both ideas in vv. 44-45.

107. "The dead of Israel" is explained in 3:10-11 to refer to Israel "in the land of your enemies, . . . defiled with the dead, . . . counted among those in Hades"; cf. Isa 59:10; Lam 3:6 in its context of 3:1ff. *A New Catholic Commentary* (n. 106 above; 505i, p. 630; P. P. Saydon and T. Hanlon) points out that "a desperate condition is sometimes compared to death; cf. Is 26:19." The NAB takes the Hebrew underlying the Greek *tōn tethnēkotōn* to be, not *mêtê* "dead," but *m^{e}tê* "the few of Israel" (cf. Isa 41:14: [New International Version] "O little Israel"; [Luther] *"du armer Haufe Israel"*).

108. References like 1QH 6.29–30, that the sons of truth "shall awake and the sons of iniquity shall be no more" (cf. 6.34), or 7.31, the sons of truth shall be established before God for ever (cf. 11.12–14), may simply be metaphors for deliverance from dangers. Belief in immortality and/or resurrection seems to be absent. So Helmer Ringgren, *The Faith of Qumran* (Philadelphia: Fortress, 1963) 148–51; *ER* 12:346; H. Braun, *Qumran und das Neue Testament* (Tübingen: Mohr [Siebeck], 1966) 2:270–72; Kremer, *Resurrectio*, 61–63 (n. 102 above); Stemberger, *TRE* 4 (1979) 447.

109. Cf. David Winston, *The Wisdom of Solomon* (AB 43; Garden City: Doubleday, 1979) 25–33 and 125–27 (further references) on "the souls of the just" and "immortality"; this book in the Apocrypha, likely first century B.C., reflects a new emphasis in Jewish sources on a preexistent and immortal soul; cf. 2:23–3:9; Kremer, *Resurrectio*, 71–76 (n. 102 above).

110. See esp. F. Mussner, in Concilium 60:46–53 (n. 102 above); P. Hoffmann, *TRE* 4 (1979) 452–54 (n. 102 above); Perkins, *Resurrection*, 71–112 (n. 102 above); Kremer, *Resurrectio*, 50–59 (n. 102 above). It must be remembered that, while today we distinguish "levels of meaning"—the evangelist, the source, and Jesus, respectively—Christians until the nineteenth century by and large took all gospel accounts as historical fact, on the "Jesus level."

111. B. van Iersel, in Concilium 60:54–67 (n. 102 above); *NIDNTT* 3:276–77, 281--302 (n. 102 above); Perkins, *Resurrection*, 113–292 (n. 102 above); E. Käsemann, "The Beginnings of Christian Theology," *New Testament Questions of Today* (Philadelphia: Fortress, 1969) 82–107 ("in post–Easter apocalyptic" there was "a new theological start," 102).

112. See the examples wrought by Elijah (1 Kings 17:17-24), Elisha (2 Kings 4:18-37), Jesus (Mark 5:35-43; John 11) or the apostles (Acts 9:36-42; 20:9-12).

113. Examples: "make alive" (*zōopoieō*), John 5:21; Rom. 8:11; 1 Pet 3:18; "live" (*zaō*), Rom 14:9 RSV "Christ died and lived again"; 2 Cor 13:4; John 6:51, 58 "live for

ever"; Rom 1:17, the person who is "righteous by faith will have life." In addition to the older articles in the *TDNT* on all these terms, see also J. Kremer, "*anastasis,* etc." and "*egeirō*" in *EWNT* 1 (1980) 210–21 and 899–910.

114. Kremer, *Resurrectio,* 42 (n. 102 above).
115. Ibid. 43–50 on these letters and the rest of the New Testament. The later (deutero-)Pauline writings incline more to the present side of redemption, but even here the future aspect of fulfillment when Christ comes is not lost (Col 3:1-4; Eph 2:5-6, cf. 1:13-14, 4:30, and 6:11-15), though the emphasis is on "the presence of the future" in the church (cf. M. Barth, *Ephesians* [AB 34; Garden City: Doubleday, 1974] 115). The Pastoral Epistles emphasize more emphatically the future appearing of Christ (1 Tim 6:14; 2 Tim 1:18; 4:1, 8, yet *epiphaneia* is used also of Christ's past appearing, 1:10). In Hebrews, resurrection of the dead is regarded as one of the "elementary doctrines" (6:2), already known to Abraham (11:19) and to women in the Elijah, Elisha, and Maccabees stories (11:35). In John "eternal life," as is well known, becomes a present gift (e.g., 5:24-27, cf. 3:15-16), but the future aspect at the resurrection of the dead is preserved in the final form of the Fourth Gospel (e.g., 5:28-29; 6:39-40). Luke uses Jesus' resurrection to ground a teaching for his Gentile audience about the general resurrection (cf. Acts 26:23; 5:31; 3:15), in contrast to the Jewish, Pharisaic expectation of a general resurrection, at least of the righteous, of which Jesus' resurrection is the initial, significant exemplar (cf. P. Hoffmann, *TRE* 4 [1979] 463–64 [n. 102 above]; Kegel, *Auferstehung Jesu,* 81–100 [n. 102 above]).
116. Ibid 464; E. Earle Ellis, *Eschatology in Luke* (Facet Books. Biblical Series 30; Philadelphia: Fortress, 1972) 9 n. 16.
117. See Acts 10:42; 24:15; John 5:28-29; cf. also vv. 24 and 27; Matt 19:28; 25:31-46; Heb 9:27.
118. Cf. the literature cited in n. 102, especially in *The Encyclopedia of the Lutheran Church;* Concilium 60; Perkins; and Kremer, *Resurrectio.*
119. In addition to references cited above, see also 2 Esdras 7:88-99 ("when they shall be separated from their mortal body," v. 88; "they hasten to behold the face of" God, v. 98), and the martyr Eleazer in 4 Macc 7:13, 19. Jesus' words to the Sadducees suggest the patriarchs were each already alive and with God (Mark 12:18-27 par.).
120. See also Isa 26:19 in the context of 26:1 and 27:1, 2, and 6. For Paul, see 1 Cor 15:23-28, 49-55; 2 Cor 4:14; Phil 3:20-21. Further, Col 3:3-4; Eph 4:30; John 5:28-29; 6:39, 40, 44, 54; 1 John 3:2.
121. If, as the Hebrew Scriptures say, the Lord "kills and brings to life" or "brings down to Sheol and raises up," God may then do this already in one's present existence; cf. Deut 5:2-3; Ps 68:20; or passages where God's kingship is regarded as already in place over all the world (Ps 47); perhaps also 2 Macc 7:36. The connection may be made via conversion, faith, or baptism: now the person "lives."
122. For Paul, see also Rom 6:4; 8:1, 11; 2 Cor 5:15, 17. Cf. further Col 2:11-13; 3:1-2, 4.
123. Cf. Kremer, *Resurrectio,* 158–61 (n. 102 above): The New Testament provides no basis for notions of a bodiless soul or an immortal soul (159, 161, and passim). See also P. Benoit, "Resurrection: At the End of Time or Immediately after Death?" Concilium 60:103–14 (n. 102 above). T. Francis Glasson, *Greek Influence in Jewish Eschatology* (SPCK Biblical Monographs 1; London: SPCK, 1961), ar-

gued, however, for reincarnation as well as immortality of the soul as a Greek influence in Jewish apocalypses and pseudepigraphs (28–32, 38–45, 82–83).

Though the idea of an "immortal soul" and the expression *psychē athanatos* appear in Greek literature as early as Plato (*Phaedo* 28 [80b]; *Meno* 81b; *Ep.* 7 [335a]), the expression occurs in the LXX only in the apocryphal 4 Macc 14:6 and possibly 18:23 (with a variant in ms. S). It is not found in the New Testament. *Athanasia*, "immortality," begins to surface in the deuterocanonical Book of Wisdom (3:4; 4:1; 8:13, 17; 15:3) and in the apocryphal 4 Macc (14:5; 16:13)—along with a denial of it: "a son of man is not immortal" (Sir 17:30). In 1 Cor 15: 53-54, "What is mortal" (*to thnēton*) is said to "don immortality" (*endysasthai athanasian*), "at the last trumpet," when "the dead will be raised imperishable," but it is not stated how this is to be understood.

124. In Matt 10:28 Jesus warns his disciples about persecution: "Do not fear those who kill the body, but cannot kill the soul; fear rather him who can destroy both soul and body in gehenna." Apropos of this saying, three things should be noted.

(1) Scholars usually view it as derived from "Q," and its Lucan form runs: "To you my friends I say, Do not fear those who kill the body and afterward can do no more. I shall show you whom you should fear: Fear him who after killing has authority to hurl you into gehenna" (12:4-5). Though M.-J. Lagrange (*Evangile selon Saint Matthieu* [3d ed.; Paris: Gabalda, 1927] 208) regards the phrase "kill the soul" as "surely original," the Hellenistic dualism of *sōma* and *psychē* would argue against its originality. Matthew, who uses it also in 6:25, has adopted the distinction here (so J. P. Meier, *Matthew* [New Testament Monographs 3; Wilmington: Glazier, 1980] 112), possibly under the influence of the Hellenistic synagogue (W. Grundmann, *Das Evangelium nach Matthäus* [Theologischer Handkommentar zum Neuen Testament 1; 5th ed.; Berlin: Evangelische Verlagsanstalt, 1981] 297).

(2) "Fear rather him who can destroy both soul and body in gehenna" (10:28b) is to be understood neither of Satan or the Evil One (so Meier, ibid.; K. Stendahl, "Matthew," *Peake's Commentary on the Bible* [ed. M. Black and H. H. Rowley; London: Nelson, 1962] 783) nor of an avenging angel (Rev 9:11), but of God himself, as did many church fathers and as do the majority of modern commentators (Allen [see below, n. 124, §3]; John C. Fenton, *The Gospel of St. Matthew* [Baltimore: Penguin Books, 1963]; Floyd V. Filson, *A Commentary on the Gospel according to St. Matthew* [Black's New Testament Commentary; 2d ed.; London: A. & C. Black, 1971]; M.-J. Lagrange [see above, n. 124, §1]; Leopold Sabourin, *The Gospel according to St. Matthew* [2 vols.; Bandra (Bombay, India): St. Paul Publications, 1962]; Eduard Schweizer, *The Good News according to Matthew* [tr. D.E. Green; Atlanta: Knox, 1975]; Wansbrough [see below, n. 124, §3]). Disciples sent forth to preach the gospel are not to fear human persecutors, but rather God himself, who can subject the whole person of the faithless disciple to the destruction of gehenna.

(3) Commentators disagree about whether 10:28a adopts the "Hellenistic" distinction between body and soul not present in the Lucan parallel. Among those who find the Hellenistic position in this text are J. L. McKenzie (*JBC* 43:70, "unusual in the NT"), Benedict Viviano (*NJBC* 42:70, "seems Hellenistic"), and J. Meier (*Matthew*, 112). These commentators do not deny that in 10:28a, "the seeming opposition is between the body and the whole person (*nepes*, translated into Gr. *psuche*)" (H. Wansbrough, "St. Matthew," *New Catholic Commentary on Holy Scripture* [ed. R. C. Fuller *et al.*; London: Nelson, 1969]). Cf.

NJBC 33:12, 13, 28, and 77:66. Hence the sense of "life" is preferred by some for *psychē*, as at Luke 21:19 (RSV, JB), on the grounds that it is "dangerous . . . for the understanding of Old Testament psychology to translate *nepes* as 'soul' *tout court*. First and foremost the word means 'life,' . . . *life bound up with a body*" (W. Eichrodt, *Theology of the Old Testament* [Philadelphia: Westminster, 1967] 2:135). Indeed according to E. Schweizer ("*Psychē* . . . ," *TWNT* 9 [1973] 645; *TDNT* 9 [1974] 646), "the reference to God's power to destroy the *psychē* and *sōma* in Hades is opposed to the idea of the immortality of the soul." Though BAGD (893) lists Matt 10:28 under *psychē* meaning "the soul as seat and center of life that transcends the earthly," it comments further: "Men cannot injure it, but God can hand it over to destruction." A classic commentator, W. C. Allen, paraphrases: " 'In your work of making my teaching public you will meet with persecution. Fear not physical death. But fear the wrath of God against unfaithfulness to Him, for He can destroy soul and body together in Gehenna' " (*A Critical and Exegetical Commentary on the Gospel according to S. Matthew* [International Critical Commentary; New York: Scribner, 1907] 109).

Once the idea of *psychē athanatos* became rooted in the Christian tradition, the Matthean phrase "cannot kill the soul" was explained in terms of that idea. Indeed, it may be a legitimate conclusion from that Matthean phrase, but it is not yet explicit in Matt 10:28. Since we are dealing with texts that are on the borderline between the implicit and the formal expression of the "immortality of the soul," there is the danger of reading back into the Matthean formulation an interpretation that eventually enters the tradition. It is precisely this borderline situation that commentators on Matthew have been trying to respect.

125. For further treatment see the study prepared previously for this dialogue, *Mary in the New Testament: A Collaborative Assessment by Protestant and Roman Catholic Scholars* (ed. R. E. Brown, K. P. Donfried, J. A. Fitzmyer, and J. Reumann; Philadelphia: Fortress; New York: Paulist, 1978).

126. The technique is sometimes called "sandwiching," to begin one story, tell another, and then return to the first one. See further 4:21-22 (4:23) 4:24-25; 5:21-24 (5:25-34) 5:35-43; 6:6b-13 (6:14-29) 6:30-34; 11:2-14 (11:15-19) 11:20-21; 14:53-54 (14:55-65) 14:66-72. Others speak of a chiastic structure in 3:20–35; see John McHugh, *The Mother of Jesus in the New Testament* (Garden City: Doubleday, 1975) 235-39, especially n. 3. See further Rudolf Pesch, *Das Markusevangelium, I. Teil* (Herders Theologischer Kommentar zum Neuen Testament II/1; Freiburg: Herder, 1976) 209–25, esp. n. 4.

127. Instead of *akousantes hoi par autou*, "his own having heard" (3:21), mss. D and W and the Old Latin version read rather *akousantes peri autou hoi grammateis kai hoi loipoi*, "the scribes and the others, hearing about him, came out. . . ." But this reading cannot be preferred to that of the best Greek mss. (used above) since it is clearly the correction of a later Christian copyist who sought to tone down the pejorative connotation of v. 21 ("He is beside himself") and to dissociate Jesus' family (mother and brothers) from it.

128. See 6:6b–8:21; 8:32-33; 9:32-37; 10:35-45. E. Best, *Disciples and Discipleship: Studies in the Gospel according to Mark* (Edinburgh: Clark, 1986); cf. *Following Jesus: Discipleship in the Gospel of Mark* (Journal for the Study of the New Testament, Supplement 4; Sheffield: Journal for the Study of the Old Testament, 1981). Other commentators interpret Mary in Mark's Gospel in more positive terms.

129. *Mary in the NT,* 241–82. See below, CS §§162, 164.

II. From the Second to the Sixteenth Century

130. E.g., Robin Lane Fox, *Pagans and Christians* (New York: Knopf, 1987); R. A. Markus, *Christianity in the Roman World* (London: Scribner, 1974); S. Benko and J. J. O'Rourke, (eds.,), *The Catacombs and the Colosseum* (Valley Forge; Judson Press, 1971); with reference to the cult of saints: Peter Brown, *The Cult of the Saints: Its Rise and Function in Latin Christianity* (Chicago: Chicago University Press, 1981). Relevant work is carried on by the Franz-Josef-Dölger Institute for the Study of Early Christianity at the University of Bonn under whose auspices one of the major tools in the field is being published: *Reallexikon für Antike und Christentum* (ed. by T. Klauser *et al.*; vol. 1–13 ["Heilgötter"]; Stuttgart: Hiersemann, 1950–1986).
131. See H. Koester, *Introduction to the New Testament History, Culture, and Religion of the Hellenistic Age* (Philadelphia: Fortress, 1982) 1:32–36 and 366–71.
132. The degree of Christian borrowing, and especially the evaluation of the phenomenon as licit or illicit, is much debated. Robert Eno, *St. Augustine and the Saints* (The Saint Augustine Lecture for 1985; Philadelphia: Villanova University Press, 1989) 1–10, surveys the scholarly debate about the roots of the Christian devotion to the saints since Lucius and Anrich. His summary remarks emphasize that, while being much closer to each other today in their assessment of the literary and archeological evidence, Protestant and Catholic scholars still view the same phenomena with a different agenda in mind and with very different value judgments.
133. Greek-English in *The Apostolic Fathers* (*LCL;* ed. and tr. K. Lake; London: Heinemann; Cambridge: Harvard University Press, 1965 [1913]) 2:6–305. The subject of mediating powers in the Shepherd is discussed by J. Danielou, *The Theology of Jewish Christianity* (Philadelphia: Westminster, 1964) 37–38; 119–27, esp. 122 (Sim. 9.12:7–8, the son as sole Mediator, in "an attack on the cult of angels"), and 125 (Michael the Word); cf. Test. Div. 6.2, "the angel that intercedes for you, for he is a mediation between God and man." Cf. also H. Moxnes, "God and His Angel in the Shepherd of Hermas," *Studia Theologica* (Oslo) 28 (1974) 49–56.
134. Acts 17:32; Acts of Paul and Thecla 5, 12, 14; III Cor 24; Martyrdom of Paul 2, 4; Acts of Peter 7–8. See *New Testament Apocrypha* (ed. W. Schneemelcher; English ed. R. McL. Wilson; Philadelphia: Westminster, 1963–64) 2:354, 356, 357; 376; 384; 288–90.
135. W. C. Van Unnik, "The Newly Discovered Gnostic 'Epistle to Rheginos' on the Resurrection," *Journal of Ecclesiastical History* 15 (1964) 141–52; 153–67; esp. 141–43; 153–55; Perkins, *Resurrection*, 331–90 (n. 102 above).
136. Eusebius, *Church History* 6. 37. Origen discusses the topic in his "Dialogue with Heraclides," which was discovered among the Toura papyri in 1941; English translation: *Alexandrian Christianity* (Library of Christian Classics; tr. J. E. C. Oulton and H. Chadwick; Philadelphia: Westminster, 1954) 2:437–55. The discussion focuses here on the interpretation of Lev 17:11; Deut 12:23; and Luke 23:46.
137. DS 403–11.
138. Acts of the Scillitan Martyrs 15 (ed. H. Musurillo [see below, note 145] 86–89); Tertullian, *De resurrectione* 23; Cyprian, *Epist* 31:3; Ps. Cyprian, *De laude martyrii* 14. See Eno, *St. Augustine* 11; 16–17 (n. 132 above).

139. See Eno, ibid., 20–24.
140. Eno, ibid., 25–27. Many of these practices are described in the *Carmina natalicia* celebrating St. Felix, the patron saint of Nola, written in 410/30 by Paulinus of Nola. See Eno, ibid., 29–35.
141. Smyrn 1:1; Trall 9:1; Eph 7:2; 18:2; 19:1.
142. English translation: *New Testament Apocrypha*, 1:370–88 (see n. 134 above); M. R. James, *The Apocryphal New Testament* (Oxford: Clarendon, 1953) 38–49. Commentary: H. R. Smid, *Protevangelium Jacobi, A Commentary* (Assen: Van Gorcum, 1963). See also *Mary in the New Testament*, 247–49; 258–61.
143. Cf. the apocryphal Apocalypses of Peter, Paul, John, James, and the "Questions of Bartholomew," as well as several Gnostic writings found among the Nag Hammadi codices. James, *The Apocryphal New Testament*, 563–64 (n. 142 above), reports on two forms of an Apocalypse of Mary; on these and other Marian apocalypses, see A. Wenger, "Marie, mère de miséricorde; les apocalypses de la Vierge," in: *Maria, Etudes sur la sainte Vierge* (ed. H. du Manoir; Paris, 1961) 5:956–62. On the traditions concerning Christ's descent into hell, see E. Koch, "Höllenfahrt Christi," *TRE* 15 (1986) 455–61 (bibliography).
144. Erwin Preuschen, *Analecta: Kürzere Texte zur Geschichte der Alten Kirche und des Kanons*. 2: *Zur Kanonsgeschichte* (2d ed.; Tübingen: Mohr, 1910) 59, no. 15: "Liber de natiuitate saluatoris et de Maria uel obstetrice, apocryphus," *New Testament Apocrypha* 1:22 (see n. 134 above); see also Jerome's sharp criticism: *Adversus Helvidium* 8 (*PL* 23:192).
145. "Acts" or "Deeds" of the Martyrs constituted a literary genre in which the suffering and triumph of the Christian martyrs were told in a form suitable for congregational reading. Such "Acts" were often based on court records, eyewitness reports, and other contemporary sources. The standard edition by H. Musurillo, *The Acts of the Christian Martyrs* (Oxford: Clarendon Press, 1972), gives texts and English translations of twenty-eight such documents from the second and third centuries.
146. Origen, *On Prayer* 11.1. A prayer to the three young men in the fiery furnace found in Hippolytus's *Commentary on Daniel*, II. 30 (*GCS* Hippolyt 1; ed. N. Bonwetsch and H. Achelis; Leipzig: Hinrich, 1897) 98:21–22, is sometimes regarded as the first literary instance of an "invocation" of saints; see Eno, *St. Augustine*, 20–25 (n. 132 above).
147. Justin Martyr, *Dialogue with Trypho the Jew* 100.4f. *Die ältesten christlichen Apologeten* (ed. E. J. Goodspeed; Göttingen: Vandenhoeck & Ruprecht, 1914) 215; Irenaeus, *Adversus Haereses* III.22.4; 32.1; V.19.1; *Demonstr*. 33; cf. Tertullian, *De carne Christi* 7. A sentence in the *Epistle to Diognetus* 12:7 is sometimes thought to be the first occurrence of the theme: "Then Eve is not seduced, and the virgin is trusted," but the date of this writing is uncertain (*Mary in the New Testament*, 255, notes 563–64). On the comparison between Eve and Mary and the theme of the "New Eve" in patristic times, see W. Burghardt, in: *Mariology* (ed. J. B. Carol; Milwaukee: Bruce) 1(1955) 110–17; 2(1957) 88–100.
148. Jerome, *Epistula* 22.21 (*CSEL* 154:173), quoted in *LG* 56, note 180. The Early Syrian tradition seems to have been particularly fond of this theme; see R. Murray, "Mary the Second Eve in the Early Syrian Fathers," *Eastern Churches Quarterly* 3 (1970–71) 372–95.
149. *C.O.D.* 39:2; 48:1; cf. DS 252. While the church historian Socrates (early fifth century) says that Origen already used the term *Theotokos* (7.32), and a fragment of Hippolytus (c. A.D. 220) has been adduced for its earlier occurrence (H. Rahner, "Hippolyt von Rom als Zeuge für den Ausdruck *Theotokos*," *Zeitschrift*

für katholische Theologie 59 [1935] 73–81; cf. also H. Vorgrimler, "*Theotokos*," *LThK* [2d ed.; Freiburg: Herder, 1965] 10:95), the first undisputed literary occurrence is in the letter of Bishop Alexander of Alexandria to Alexander of Thessalonica 1.12 (*GCS* 44 [19] 23; *PG* 18: 568C), written in A.D. 324; cf. also n. 156 below.

150. The earliest literary and archeological evidence for churches dedicated to the Virgin Mary in Palestine and Constantinople is discussed by M. Jugie, *La mort* (see n. 152 below), 89–95. According to contemporary sources, the Council of 431 met in the main church of the city which was named after "John the Theologian" and "the Virgin *theotokos*, Saint Mary"; it is not known whether this designation was in use prior to the Council or was a result of it (Jugie, 96–98 [n. 152 below]).

151. On these traditions, see *Mary in the New Testament*, 267–78; R. Eno ("Mary and Her Role in Patristic Theology") 159–76 below, discusses the evidence for dissenting opinions in Origen and Tertullian.

152. See W. Burghardt, *The Testimony of the Patristic Age Concerning Mary's Death* (Westminster MD: Newman, 1957). The most comprehensive treatment of this question is found in the historical part of M. Jugie's book, *La mort et l'Assomption de la Sainte Vierge: Etude historico-doctrinale* (Studi e Testi 114; Vatican City: Biblioteca Apostolica Vaticana, 1944), which contributed significantly to the papal decision to define the dogma of the Assumption in 1950. The suggestion of a violent death was put forward as a possibility by Epiphanius, *Panarion* 78.11 (*PG* 42:716) on the basis of the mention of the "sword" in Luke 2:35; it was explicitly rejected by Ambrose, *Commentary on the Gospel of Luke* II.61. For a brief report on the modern controversy about Mary's death in connection with the papal definition, see Michael O'Carroll, *Theotokos* (rev. ed.; Wilmington DE: Glazier, 1983) 17–118 ("Death of Mary").

153. The most common delay is three days, but the Coptic and Ethiopic tradition also reckons with a much longer time span. For an informative survey of the "*transitus*" literature, see the article on "Assumption Apocrypha" in O'Carroll, *Theotokos*, 58–61 (with literature) (n. 152 above).

154. "Anaphora Syriaca XII Apostolorum," *Anaphorae Syriacae* (ed. A. Raes; Vatican City: Pontifical Institute of Oriental Studies, 1939–44) 222. G. Frenaut, "De intercessione B.V.Mariae in Canone Missae Romanae et in Anaphoris Liturgiarum Orientalium ante VII saec.," in *De primordiis cultus mariani. Acta congressus mariologici-mariani in Lusitania anno 1967 celebrati* (Rome: Academia Mariana Internationalis, 1970) 2:459–62, interpreted this instance as "invocation." On Mary in early Syrian poetry see K. McVey, Introduction to *Ephrem the Syrian; Hymns* (Classics of Western Spirituality; New York: Paulist Press, 1989) 30–34.

155. For a survey of the development of Marian feasts in the early and medieval church, see O'Carroll, *Theotokos*, 220–24 (n. 152 above). Also K. McDonnell, "The Marian Liturgical Tradition," 177–91 below.

156. "God-bearer, [hear] my supplications; do not allow us [to be] in adversity, but deliver us from danger. Thou alone. . . ." The text is found on a papyrus fragment now in the John Rylands Library in Manchester and first published in 1938. On the debate concerning the date, see O. Stegmüller, "Sub Tuum Praesidium. Bemerkungen zur ältesten Überlieferung," *Zeitschrift für katholische Theologie* 74 (1952) 76–82.

157. On the options in interpreting the meaning of the phrase "communion of *sancti/sancta*," see J. P. Kirsch, *The Doctrine of the Communion of Saints in the Ancient Church* (London: Sands, 1910); A. Michel, "La communion des saints," *Doctor*

Communis 9 (1956) 1–125. Sharply critical of the tendency to minimize the difference: Ernst Wolf, "Sanctorum Communio. Erwägungen zur Romantisierung des Kirchenbegriffs," *Peregrinatio* (2d ed.; Munich: Kaiser, 1962) 1:279–301.

158. As a title for Mary, the term seems to occur for the first time in Origen's *Homilies on the Gospel of Luke*, Hom. 6 and 7 (*GCS* 35, Origenes Bv. 9; ed. M. Rauer, 1930) 44 and 50. It was generally accepted in Byzantine theology from the sixth century on. See W. Burghardt, "Our Lady's Holiness," in *Mariology*, 2:125–139 (n. 147 above).
159. Augustine, *De natura et gratia* 36.42 (*CSEL* 60:263f.); but cf. *Opus imperfectum contra Iulianum* 4.122 (*PL* 45:1418). See also Ch. Boyer, "La controverse sur l'opinion de s. Augustin touchant la conception de la Vierge," in: *Virgo Immaculata, Acta congressus mariologies ariologici-mariani, Romae anno 1954 celebrati* (Rome: Academia Mariana Internationalis, 1955) 4:48–60. Eno ("Mary and Her Role in Patristic Theology, "159–76 below) is more cautious in his conclusions.
160. "Veneramini martyres, . . . Deum martyrum colite" *Sermo* 273.9 (*PL* 38:1252B). For other texts see Eno, *St. Augustine and the Saints*, 29–48 (n. 132 above).
161. See Guy Lapointe, *La célébration des martyrs en Afrique d'après les sermons de saint Augustin* (Cahiers de communauté chrétienne 8; Montreal: Communauté chrétienne, 1972).
162. The central texts come from the later works: *Enchiridion* 18.68–69; *De civitate Dei* 21.26f. Augustine, however, polemicized in these instances against the notion that there is *only* a purgatorial, that is, a temporary fire and not also an eternal one. To him such a Christian "universalism" seemed dangerous because it might lead to a lack of pious zeal in this life. On the development of Augustine's thought on this theme and earlier notions of a cleansing fire, see R. Eno, "The Fathers and the Cleansing Fire," *Irish Theological Quarterly* 53 (1987) 184–202. Jacques Le Goff, *The Birth of Purgatory* (Chicago: Chicago University Press, 1984) 61–85, quotes the relevant passages at length. See also below, n. 196.
163. *De civitate Dei* 22.10. The theme became prominent with the arrival of the relics of St. Stephen at Hippo: cf. Eno, *St. Augustine* (note 132 above) 74–82. On the miracles connected with the discovery of the bones of Saints Gervase and Protase at Milan, see the *Confessiones* 9.7.16.
164. *Vita sancti Ambrosii* 10.48–11.56 (ed. Sister M. S. Kaniecka; Patristic Studies 16; Washington DC: Catholic University Press, 1928) 93–101.
165. *De civitate Dei* 20.9 and 13.
166. Gregory the Great, *Dialogues* 4.29.1; 45.1–2 (*SC* 265; ed. de Vogue and Antin; Paris: Cerf, 1980) 99; 169–71. Also *Moralia in Job*, 9.98 (*CCL*, 143; Turnhout: Brepols, 1979) 526–27.
167. Gregory the Great, *Dialogues* 4.40.13; 41.3–4; 57.1–17 (*SC* 265:147, 149, 185–95). Regarding Gregory's views on the afterlife see G. R. Evans, *The Thought of Gregory the Great* (Cambridge, England: Cambridge University Press, 1986) 13–15; Le Goff (above, note 162), 88–95.
168. A well–known text is the *megalynarion*, a brief praise of Mary sung by the choir in the Divine Liturgy after the censing of the gifts and elsewhere: "More honorable than the cherubim and infinitely more glorious than the seraphim, who didst bear the Word of God without stain, true *theotokos*, we magnify Thee" (Isabel F. Hapgood, *Service Book* [5th ed.; Englewood NJ: Antiochian Orthodox Christian Archdiocese of New York and All North America, 1975] 14; 108).

169. J. Pelikan, *The Growth of Medieval Theology (600–1300)* (The Christian Tradition 3; Chicago: Chicago University Press, 1978) 116–19 and 133–44.
170. See A. E. McGrath, *Iustitia Dei: A History of the Christian Doctrine of Justification. I. Beginnings to 1500* (Cambridge, England: Cambridge University Press, 1986) 74f., who refers to the discovery of this curious fact by H. Bouillard, *Conversion et grâce chez S.Thomas d'Aquin* (Paris: Aubier, 1944) 90–133.
171. The revision was undertaken at Vivarium in the sixth century by Cassiodorus and his pupils. It was known under the names of Jerome (*PL* 30:669–746) and, in a different version, Primasius of Hadrumetum (*PL* 68:413–686).
172. Th. Zwoelfer, *Sankt Peter, Apostelfürst und Himmelspförtner: Seine Verehrung bei den Angelsachsen und Franken* (Stuttgart: Kohlhammer, 1929); J. van den Bosch, *Capa, basilica, monasterium et le culte de Saint Martin de Tours* (Nijmegen: Dekker & Van de Vegt, 1959).
173. Rupert of Deutz interpreted Jesus' word, "O woman, what have you to do with me?" (v. 4), as a rebuke of the mother who did not yet understand. The patristic precedents are described in A. Smitmans, *Das Weinwunder von Kana* (Beiträge zur Geschichte der biblischen Exegese 6; Tübingen: Mohr, 1966) 97–124.
174. On Anselm's Mariology, see J. Bruder, *The Mariology of St. Anselm of Canterbury* (Dayton OH: Mount St. John's Press, 1939), and several articles in the work: *De cultu Mariano saeculi VI–XI. Acta congressus mariologici-mariani in Croatia anno 1971 celebrati* (Rome: Academia Mariana Internationalis, 1972) 3:597–664. The Cathedral of Chartres housed a celebrated Marian relic, the tunic of the Virgin, which had been given to the bishop by King Charles the Bald (840–77).
175. DS 600–603; *C.O.D.* 111–13.
176. See H. G. Thümmel, "Bilder, V.1 Byzanz," *TRE* 6 (1980) 532.
177. The text of the *Libri Carolini* is found in the *Monumenta Germaniae Historica, Legum Sectio III, Concilia II, Supplementum* (ed. H. Bastgen; Hannover and Leipzig: Hahnsche Buchhandlung, 1924); the two letters of Gregory the Great to Serenus of Marseille in: *Gregorii Magni Registrum Epistularum Libri VII–XIV* (*CCL* 140A; ed. D. Norberg; Turnhout: Brepols, 1982), 768 (9.209) and 873–76 (11.10). See K. Froehlich, "The *Libri Carolini* and the Lessons of the Iconoclastic Controversy," 193–208 below.
178. This accusation was probably grounded in a faulty Latin translation of the original Greek terms employed at Nicaea II.
179. Agobard of Lyon, *Liber de imaginibus sanctorum* (*PL* 104:199–228). Agobard's central point is that, whatever they represent, pictures and statues are only the works of human hands. Claudius, a Spaniard who became bishop of Turin, rejected the cult of relics and the invocation of saints as well as the veneration of images; his *Apologeticum atque rescriptum adversus Theodemirum abbatem*, written in 823, is known chiefly through long quotations in a refutation by Jonas of Orleans, *De cultu imaginum* (*PL* 106:306–88); the beginning of Claudius's book is in *PL* 104:615–20. The attitude of the Frankish theologians was not unlike that of many of the Protestant reformers.
180. Already Hadrian I (772–795) formally endorsed Nicaea II, rejecting the doctrine of the *Libri Carolini: Epistola ad Carolum Regem de imaginibus* (*PL* 98:1247–92). This attitude prevailed under his successors as well; none of them showed sympathy for the Frankish theologians. On the attitudes of Eugenius II, Nicholas I, and especially John VIII, see G. Haendler, *Epochen karolingischer Theologie* (Theologische Arbeiten 10; Berlin: Evangelische Verlagsanstalt, 1958).

181. K. McDonnell, "The Liturgical Veneration of the Saints. A Note" (unpublished). See also R. Kieckhefer, "Major Currents in Late Medieval Devotion," *Christian Spirituality, High Middle Ages and Reformation* (ed. J. Raitt; New York: Crossroad, 1987) 93–96; Patrick Geary, *Furta Sacra: Thefts of Relics in the Central Middle Ages* (Princeton: Princeton University Press, 1978).
182. See, e.g., the collection of Marian poetry made by Alphonsus X the Wise, King of Castile and Leon, *Cantigas de Maria*, on the model of the popular *Cantigas de amiga* that were sung by the troubadours. The collection contains more than four hundred *cantigas* for the Virgin; these are of two kinds: some forty *cantigas de loor* (of praise), all the others being *cantigas de miragros* (of miracles). See P. Droncke, *The Medieval Lyric* (2d ed.; New York: Cambridge University Press, 1977) 70–72.
183. Elizabeth Johnson, "Marian Devotion in the Western Church," *Christian Spirituality*, 392–414 (n. 181 above).
184. On the emergence of the important collections of Marian miracles, see Benedicta Ward, *Miracles and the Medieval Mind* (Philadelphia: University of Pennsylvania Press, 1982) 132–65.
185. See K. McDonnell, "The Liturgical Veneration of the Saints. A Note," and "Extended Memo on the Veneration of the Saints" (unpublished).
186. Elizabeth Johnson (n. 183 above); see the prayer of St. Francis of Assisi in G. Tavard, *The Forthbringer of God. St. Bonaventure on the Virgin Mary* (Chicago: Franciscan Herald Press, 1989) 149–50. Theologians often invented new Marian titles; Alan of Lille invoked Mary, among other titles, as *virtutum gazophylacium*, "treasure–keeper of the virtues" (*In Cantica Canticorum elucidatio*, *PL* 210:53). Enthusiastic Marian titles abound in the sermons of St. Bonaventure.
187. Elizabeth Johnson, 403 (n. 183 above).
188. Among the first commentators who identified Mary as the bride of the Song of Songs were Rupert of Deutz (d. 1130), *In Cantica Canticorum de incarnatione Domini commentarium* (*PL* 168:839–962), and Alan of Lille (*PL* 210:51–110). According to Alan the Song refers *specialiter et spiritualiter* to the church, *specialissime et spiritualissime* to the glorious Virgin (*PL* 210:53). In the fifteenth century Dionysius the Carthusian (d. 1471) explained in his *Enarratio in Cantica Canticorum Salomonis* that each verse of the Song of Songs refers to the bridegroom's *sponsa generalis*, which is the church, to his *sponsa specialis*, which is the faithful soul, and to his *sponsa singularis*, the Virgin Mary. A detailed account of the new mariological commentaries is given by H. Riedlinger, *Die Makellosigkeit der Kirche in den lateinischen Hoheliedkommentaren des Mittelalters* (Beiträge zur Geschichte der Philosophie und Theologie des Mittelalters 38.3; Münster: Aschendorff, 1958) 202–33.
189. Quoted by Elizabeth Johnson, 408 (n. 183 above).
190. "Virgo de cuius utero quasi de quodam diuinitatis oceano rivi et flumina emanabant omnium gratiarum," St. Bernardine of Siena, *Sermo* 61.8, *Opera Omnia* (Quaracchi: Collegio S.Bonaventura, 1950) 2:378.
191. John Johnson, "Anselm on the Virgin Birth. A Reflection on Mary" (unpublished).
192. Elizabeth Johnson, 397 (n. 183 above).
193. Tavard, "Bonaventure" (n. 186 above).
194. He agreed with [Ps.] Augustine that the Assumption can be reasonably argued even though it cannot be derived from Scripture: *S.T.* III, q. 27, a.1, c; on the Immaculate Conception: a.2.

195. That the soul is the "form" of the body was even the object of a decree at the Council of Vienne in 1312; the opposite opinion was declared to be heretical (DS 902; *C.O.D.* 336–37). This declaration was solemnly repeated by the Fifth Lateran Council in 1513 (DS 1440; *C.O.D.*, 581). Albert Lang, in his study, "Der Bedeutungswandel der Begriffe 'fides' und 'haeresis' und die dogmatische Wertung der Konzilsentscheidungen von Vienne und Trient," *Münchener Theologische Zeitschrift* 4 (1953) 133–46, shows that medieval councils did not use terms such as "de fide," "anathema," "heretical" in the sense of a dogmatic definition as understood after the First Vatican Council.
196. In his *Vita Odilonis* St. Peter Damian records that Abbot Odilo of Cluny (962–1049) ordered all Cluniac monks to devote November 2, the day after the feast of All Saints, to prayers for the dead; this was done around 1030 at the request of a hermit in Sicily who had told the abbot that he could hear the cries of the souls being tormented in a nearby volcano (*PL* 144:935–37); from Cluny the custom spread to the whole Western church. There were antecedents. Amalarius of Metz had devoted three chapters of his *De ecclesiasticis officiis libri IV* to the liturgical care of the dead (Book II, ch. 44: *De missa pro mortuis* [*PL* 105:1161–64]; Book IV, ch. 41: *De exsequiis mortuorum* [*PL* 105:1236–38]; ch. 42: *De officiis mortuorum* [*PL* 105:1238–40]). Among other points he explained that it is proper *orare et sacrificare pro mortuis* every day, but especially on the third day (for the three aspects of the soul: *ex toto corde, ex toto anima, et ex toto virtutue*), on the seventh (for the four elements of the body, three plus four being seven), and on the thirtieth (for this is the end of the month, and the month represents *curriculum praesentis vitae, ut ex statu lunae facile dignoscitur*) [*PL* 105:1162]; in this way Gregory the Great's series of thirty Masses for the deceased was justified. A liturgical commemoration of all the dead is featured in many places in the ninth and tenth centuries, though at varying dates in the calendar (*Dictionnaire d'Archéologie et de Liturgie* [Paris: Letouzey, 1953] 15/2:2677–82). Peter Damian himself reports someone else's claim that Mount Vesuvius is one place where the souls are tormented by demons; popes and bishops are among them, notably Benedict (presumably Benedict VIII [1012–24], since Peter reports an alleged message from him addressed to his successor, John XIX [1024–32]). Some of these souls may be seen in the late afternoon on Saturdays in the shape of birds (*Opusculum* XIX: *De abdicatione episcopatus ad Nicolaum II*; *PL* 145:427–30).
197. The poem *Dies irae* was composed in Italy in the twelfth or thirteenth century; see Pierre Adnes, "Liturgie de la mort," in *Dictionnaire de Spiritualité* (Paris: Beauchesne, 1980) 10:1773–74. Numerous confraternities were devoted to preparing their members for a good death (Kieckhefer, 77 [n. 181 above]). At the end of the Middle Ages, a new literary genre of "guides for dying" (*Ars Moriendi*) had considerable success. Much of its inspiration derived from the writings of the Paris chancellor Jean Gerson, especially his *Opus tripartitum de praeceptis decalogi, de confessione, et de arte moriendi*, *Opera Omnia* (2d ed.; ed. E. L. DuPin; Hagae Comitum: apud Petrum De Hondt, 1728) 425–30. See Mary Catherine O'Connor, *The Art of Dying Well: The Development of the Ars Moriendi* (Columbia Studies in English and Comparative Literature 156; New York: Columbia University Press, 1942).
198. The word, *purgatorius*, was first used as an adjective, with the meaning of "purgatorial, cleansing," in such expressions as *ignis purgatorius*; in the Profession of Faith of Emperor Michael Palaeologus it was equivalent to *catharterius*

(καθαρτήριος): DS 856. In the neuter form, *purgatorium*, it was used later as a substantive, meaning "purgatory." The first use of the noun seems to go back to Odo of Soissons (d. 1171) or Peter Comestor (d. 1178/79) in a *Sermo* 85 formerly attributed to Hildebert of Mans (*PL* 171:739); see J. Le Goff, *The Birth of Purgatory* (n. 162 above), 158–59, and Appendix II, 362–66. In papal documents the substantive appears for the first time in a letter of Pope Innocent IV to his legate in Constantinople. Innocent urges the legate to impose this term on the Greeks *iuxta traditiones et auctoritates sanctorum patrum* in spite of the Greeks' objection that the word has not been received from their own doctors (*ex eorum doctoribus*): DS 838.

199. DS 856–59. This Confession of Faith had been proposed to the Emperor by Pope Clement IV in 1267. It was read at the fourth session of the Council in the presence of Pope Gregory X, though it was not included in a conciliar decree. The Confession of Faith distinguishes among three categories of souls: first, those that still need to be cleansed because they did not fully satisfy the divine justice in this life; second, those that need no cleansing, either because they died just after baptism, or because, although they have sinned, they have also "repented and been cleansed, in this life or in the next"; third, those "who die in sin, whether this is original sin or mortal sin." The first go to the place of "purgatorial pains," the second to heaven, the third to hell. All of them will stand before Christ in their risen bodies on the Day of Judgment.
200. See M. Dykmans, *Les sermons de Jean XXII sur la vision béatifique* (Rome: Gregorian University Press, 1973). The second sermon lays out the authorities from Scripture and tradition. Before preaching these sermons John XXII had endorsed the doctrine of the Confession of Faith of Michael Palaeologus on the three categories of souls; see his letter, *Nequaquam sine dolore* to the Armenians, dated 1321 (DS 925–26). The contradiction between this and the view expressed in his later sermons did cause some consternation and occasioned the polemic that led to the pope's retraction.
201. See the retraction in DS 990–91.
202. DS 1000–1001.
203. Session VI, "Decree for the Greeks": DS 1304–1306; cf. *C.O.D.* 503–504.
204. C. Peter, "The Communion of Saints in the Final Days of the Council of Trent," 219–33 below.
205. Elizabeth Johnson, "Mary as Mediatrix," 311–26 below.
206. K. McDonnell, "Liturgical Veneration" (n. 181 above). On the critical attitude of the Holy See before alleged miracles, see André Vauchez, *La sainteté en occident aux derniers siècles du moyen age, d'après les procès de canonisation et les documents hagiographiques* (Rome: Ecole française, Palais Farnese, 1981) 559–82.
207. The institutionalization of the process for the canonization of saints began in the tenth century; the first official canonization by "regular procedure" was that of Bishop Ulrich of Augsburg on January 31, 993 (Vauchez, *La sainteté*, 39–120).
208. Devotion to the "fourteen auxiliary saints" was based on a fifteenth-century legend. Luther drew on it by way of contrast in his booklet *Fourteen Consolations*; see G. Tavard, "Luther's Teaching on Prayer," *Lutheran Theological Seminary Bulletin*, Gettysburg PA, 67 (1987) 7–8.
209. Elizabeth Johnson, "Mary as Mediatrix," 311–26 below.
210. Text in Hyacinthus Ameri, O.F.M., *Doctrina Theologorum de Immaculata B. V. Mariae Conceptione Tempore Concilii Basiliensis* (Bibliotheca Immaculatae Conceptionis; Rome: Academia Mariana Internationalis, 1954) 4:216–17, n. 6.

211. See Tavard, *Bonaventure* (n. 186 above); F. Jelly, "The Roman Catholic Dogma of Mary's Immaculate Conception," 263–78 below. King Alphonse V of Aragon (1416–58) made it an official Spanish policy to promote the doctrine of the Immaculate Conception (see n. 210 above).

III. From the Reformation to the Present

212. In his *Catechismus maior seu summa doctrinae christianae* (1556), Peter Canisius insists that the communion of saints includes not only members of the pilgrim church on earth but also the pious souls in purgatory and the blessed who are with Christ in heaven (chapter 1, art. 18). In his explanation of the angelic salutation, he holds that Gabriel provides a model for the way Christians should greet Mary; he adds a series of testimonies to the holiness of Mary from the Greek and Latin Fathers (chapter 2, part 2); see P. Canisius, *Catechismi Latini* (Rome: Gregorian University, 1933) 1:89, 95–97.
213. In his *De virtute et statu religionis, Tractatus* I and III, Suarez explains the distinction between the adoration (*latria*) due to God and the honor (*dulia*) due to the saints. While defending the veneration of the saints, he holds that it would be sacrilegious to adore them. See F. Suarez, *Opera omnia* (Paris: Vives, 1853) 13:10–14, 616–19.
214. Robert Bellarmine has a very thorough discussion of the veneration and invocation of saints in his *Disputationes de controversiis christianae fidei*, Controversy III, *De Ecclesia triumphante*, Book I, 141–97. He holds that the saints are not immediate intercessors with God, but that whatever they ask from God they ask through Christ (179). In Book II he has a full discussion of the relics and images of the saints (199–266). See Robert Bellarmine, *Opera omnia* (Paris: Vives, 1870), vol. 3.
215. Ingolstadt: excudebat David Sartorius, 1577.
216. Cf. René Laurentin, *Maria, Ecclesia, Sacerdotium* (Paris: Nouvelles Editions Latines, 1953) 211. For a history of Mariology see Hilda C. Graef, *Mary, A History of Doctrine and Devotion* (2 vols.; New York: Sheed & Ward, 1963); reprint, Westminster MD: Christian Classics, 1985.
217. The purpose of the Sodality was the practice of devotion to Our Lady, which was accomplished by the pursuit of personal perfection according to the Sodality's way of life, and by engaging in apostolic works. Cf. Elder Mullan, *The Sodality of Our Lady Studied in the Documents* (New York: P. J. Kenedy and Sons, 1912) 9. A detailed description of the history, goals, and rules of the Sodality can be found in this work.
218. Cf. William V. Bangert, *A History of the Society of Jesus* (St. Louis: The Institute of Jesuit Sources, 1972) 56. For further information on the spread of the Sodality, cf. ibid., 106–107.
219. For statistics see Pierre Delooz, *Sociologie et canonisations* (The Hague: M. Nijhoff, 1969). For canonizations by pontifical power prior to 1662 he lists eighty-eight religious, twenty diocesan clergy, eleven laity, and six of unknown status. For canonizations by formal procedures before the Congregation of Rites since 1662 (to 1967) he lists: 129 religious men (including twenty-four founders), forty religious women, fifteen diocesan clergy, and fifty-six laity.
220. Accessible in Benedict XIV, *Omnia Opera* (Prati: Aldina, 1839–47), vols. 1–7.
221. Their work is found in *Acta Sanctorum* (Paris: Victor Palmé, 1863ff.). For an account of the Bollandist movement, cf. Hippolyte Delehaye, *A travers trois*

siècles, l'oeuvre des Bollandistes (Brussels: Bureaux de la Sociétés Bollandistes, 1920); English tr. *The Work of the Bollandists through Three Centuries, 1615–1915* (Princeton: Princeton University Press, 1922).

222. For detailed references and more extensive coverage of the Mariology of this period, see René Laurentin, *Queen of Heaven* (tr. G. Smith; London: Burns, Oates & Washbourne, 1956); and Hilda Graef, *Mary: A History of Doctrine and Devotion* (New York: Sheed and Ward, 1965), vol. 2.
223. *The Admirable Heart of Mary* (tr. C. DiTargiani and R. Hauser; New York: P. J. Kenedy & Sons, 1948).
224. *A Treatise on the True Devotion to the Blessed Virgin* (tr. F. W. Faber; London: Burns & Oates, Limited, 1888).
225. English tr. *The Glories of Mary* (Baltimore/Dublin: Helicon, 1963; New York: P. J. Kenedy & Sons, 1948).
226. F. W. Faber, who had edited a controversial series of lives of English saints as a Tractarian in 1844, undertook as a Catholic in 1846 to publish a series of lives of the modern saints, translated from other languages. The first biographies, which appeared in 1847, were criticized by some Catholics as unsuited for English readers. Thereupon Newman, as Faber's religious superior, wrote to him communicating the decision that the series should be suspended. But in the following year, 1849, the series was resumed with Newman's agreement, and in 1851 Cardinal Wiseman approved and sanctioned the series; see John E. Bowden, *The Life and Letters of Father William Faber* (London: Burns and Oates, 1969).
227. J. H. Newman, "A Letter Addressed to the Reverend E. B. Pusey, D.D., on the Occasion of His *Eirenicon*," reprinted in *Certain Difficulties Felt by Anglicans in Catholic Teaching* (Vol. 2; London: Longmans, Green, 1907).
228. Ibid., 101.
229. Cf. vol. 5, reprinted Freiburg: Herder, 1954.
230. E.g., Karl Rahner, "Le Principe fondamental de la théologie mariale," *Recherches de science religieuse* 42 (1954) 481–522.
231. See Elizabeth Johnson, "Mary as Mediatrix," 311–26 below.
232. Cf. Giuseppe M. Besutti, *Bibliografia Mariana*, Vol. 3 (1952–57) (Rome: Edizioni "Marianum," 1959). Besutti has compiled five other volumes of Marian bibliographical information; these span the years 1948–77.
233. *La Question Mariale* (Paris: Editions du Seuil, 1963), 117–18. *Mary's Place in the Church* (tr. I. Pidoux; New York: Holt, Rinehart and Winston, 1965) 99; translation adapted.
234. See above, CS §175, nn. 192–94.
235. See George Tavard, "John Dun Scotus and the Immaculate Conception," 209–17 below.
236. DS 2803.
237. *Munificentissimus Deus*, 1950; DS 3903.
238. Gottfried Maron, "Mary in Protestant Theology" in: *Mary in the Churches* (ed. H. Küng and Jürgen Moltmann; Marcus Lefebure [English ed.]; Concilium 168; Edinburgh: Clark; New York: Seabury, 1986) 42. Maron refers to Gerhard's *Confessio Catholica* (1634–37). Pertinent text in *TRE* 14 (1985) 664.
239. Quoted in Maron, 42 (n. 238 above).
240. Ibid., 43.
241. Quoted in Maron, 43 (n. 238 above).

242. Frieder Schulz, "Heilige/Heiligenverehrung," VII: "Die protestantischen Kirchen," *TRE* 14 (1985) 664.
243. Ibid; quoted from Schleiermacher's *Weihnachtsfeier* (1806).
244. Maron, 43 (n. 238 above).
245. The sharpest Lutheran reaction came from the theologian Eduard Preuss, *Die römische Lehre von der unbefleckten Empfängnis aus den Quellen dargestellt und aus Gottes Wort widerlegt* (Berlin: Schlawitz, 1865). See also Eric W. Gritsch, "The Views of Luther and Lutheranism on the Veneration of Mary," 235–48 below.
246. Wilhelm O. Dietlein, *Evangelisches Ave Maria. Ein Beitrag zur Lehre von der selig zu preisenden Jungfrau* (Halle: Fricke, 1863). The work is summarized in Walter Delius, *Geschichte der Marienverehrung* (Munich and Basel: Reinhardt, 1963) 302–303.
247. When Heiler received communion at the Lord's Supper at Vadstena, Sweden, in 1919, he was given assurances by his host, Archbishop Söderblom, that no formal repudiation of Catholicism would be required of him. "As entries in his diary indicate, he himself saw it less as a conversion (*Übertritt*) than as an ecumenical act" (Günther Lanckowski, "Friedrich Heiler," *TRE* 14 [1976] 539). Annemarie Schimmel speaks of "Heiler's double allegiance to the Catholic church and his new Lutheran affiliation" as "never resolved" ("Friedrich Heiler," *ER* 6 [1987] 250). Instead, he became "a wanderer between two worlds, Catholic and Protestant, fully at home in neither in their present state, but living out a vocation in aid of their eventually coming to terms with one another" (Paul Misner, "*Religio Eruditi*: Some Letters of Friedrich Heiler," *Journal of the American Academy of Religion* 45 [1977] 842).
248. See Karlfried Froehlich, "Report: Modern Liturgical Movements, The Saints, and Mary in Protestantism (Germany Only)" 1–2 (unpublished; February 1986).
249. Hans Asmussen, *Maria die Mutter Gottes* (Stuttgart: Evangelisches Verlagswerk, 1950).
250. *Evangelisches Gutachten zur Dogmatisierung der leiblichen Himmelfahrt Mariens* (Munich: Kaiser, 1950). See also the summary and discussion of this *Gutachten* in "Zur Dogmatisierung der Assumptio Mariae. Ein Gutachten evangelischer Theologen," *Theologische Literaturzeitung* 75 (1950) 578–85.
251. Walter Künneth, *Christus oder Maria? Ein evangelisches Wort zum Mariendogma* (Berlin: Wichern: 1950) 10.
252. The Transitus legend. See "Das neue Mariendogma im Lichte der Geschichte und im Urteil der Ökumene," *Ökumenische Einheit* 2 (1950), Fascicles 2 and 3. These and other reactions to the dogma of 1950 are summarized in Friedrich Heiler, "*Assumptio.* Zur Dogmatisierung der leiblichen Himmelfahrt Marias," *Theologische Literaturzeitung* 79 (1954) 45.
253. Hans Asmussen, *The Unfinished Reformation* (tr. R. J. Olsen; Notre Dame: Fides, 1961) 127.
254. Max Thurian, *Mary, Mother of All Christians* (tr. N. B. Cryer; New York: Herder and Herder, 1963). Thurian is a Reformed theologian who converted to Catholicism.
255. Max Lackmann, *Verehrung der Heiligen, Versuch einer lutherischen Lehre der Heiligen* (Stuttgart: Schwabenverlag, 1958). Although his position was widely rejected, it was cautiously supported by some. See Adolf Köberle and Reinhard Mumm, *Wir gedenken der Entschlafenen* (Kassel: Staude, 1981) 63–67.
256. The Prefaces end with "And so with the Church on earth and the hosts of heaven, we praise your name and join their unending hymn. . . ." See, for example, *LBW, Ministers Desk Edition* (1983) 208–20.

257. For example, "Into your hands, O merciful Savior, we commend your servant, ___*name*___. Receive *him/her* into the arms of your mercy, . . . and into the glorious company of the saints in light," Service for the "Burial of the Dead," *LBW* (1978) 211.
258. *LBW. Ministers Desk Edition* (1983) 44.
259. For background history of the chapter on Mary, cf. René Laurentin, *La Vierge au Concile* (Paris: Lethielleux, 1965) 8–50. *Marian Studies* 37 (1986) is also devoted to this chapter and contains much material on textual evolution; contributing authors include: Frederick M. Jelly, James T. O'Connor, Charles W. Newman, George F. Kirwin, and Eamon R. Carroll.
260. Translations in the main taken from *The Documents of Vatican II* (ed. W. M. Abbott; New York: America Press, 1966); Arabic numbers in the text of this paper refer to articles of the Dogmatic Constitution on the Church.
261. According to the *Relatio* of November 14, 1964, "132 Fathers propose that, instead of 'Propterea B. Maria *in* Ecclesia . . .' [the text] should say 'Propterea B. Maria *ab* Ecclesia . . . ,' for these titles [advocata, auxiliatrix, adiutrix, mediatrix], they say, occur very frequently, even in pontifical documents." But since difficulties were raised also from the other side, with sixty-one Fathers requesting the deletion of the title "mediatrix," the Theological Commission retained the reading "in Ecclesia" as representing a middle path, likely to win acceptance by a larger group. See *A.S.V.* (1976) 2:8:163–64. The whole debate is thoroughly described in Michael O'Carroll, "Vatican II and Our Lady's Mediation," *Irish Theological Quarterly* 37 (1970) 24–55, esp. for the present question at 49–52.
262. See *Sacrosanctum Concilium* 108 and 111. See also *Documents on the Liturgy 1963–1979: Conciliar, Papal, and Curial Texts* (Collegeville: Liturgical Press, 1982).
263. Statistics in *Index ac status causarum* published by the Sacred Congregation for the Causes of the Saints, editions of 1975, 1985, and 1988.
264. Apostolic Constitution, *Divinus perfectionis magister*, of January 23, 1983, *AAS* 75 (1983), and Norms published by the Congregation for the Causes of the Saints, February 7, 1983, *AAS* 75 (1983) 396–404.
265. Yvon Beaudoin, "Le Processus de canonisation dans l'Eglise Catholique Romaine," a paper on "Saints and Models" presented at the 21st International Ecumenical Seminar, Institute for Ecumenical Research, Strasbourg, 1987.
266. *AAS* 64 (1974); English tr., Washington, D.C.: United States Catholic Conference, 1974.
267. Text in *Catholic Mind* 72 (1974) 26–64; *Behold Your Mother: Woman of Faith* (Washington DC: United States Catholic Conference, 1973).
268. *AAS* 69 (1987) 361–433; English tr. *Origins* 16 (1987) 745–66.
269. Stephano de Fiores, "Mary in Postconciliar Theology," *Vatican II: Assessment and Perspectives* (Vol. 1; ed. R. Latourelle; New York: Paulist, 1988) 469–539.

Catholic Reflections

1. *LG* 67.
2. Such reservations on the suppression of superstitions are eloquently expressed by John Henry Newman in his 1877 Preface to *The Via Media of the Anglican Church* (Vol. 1; new ed.; London: Longmans Green & Co., 1897) lii to lxxvi.
3. John Paul II, *Ad Limina* address to the Bishops of the Episcopal Conference of Abruzzo and Molise (Italy), April 24, 1986, *L'Osservatore Romano* (Weekly Edition), May 12, 1986, 8–9.

4. The Apostolic Exhortation *Marialis Cultus*, issued Feb. 2, 1974; English tr., *True Devotion to the Blessed Virgin Mary* (Washington DC: United States Catholic Conference, 1974); for what follows, see especially §§25–39.
5. In the pastoral letter *Behold Your Mother: Woman of Faith, Catholic Mind* 72 (1974) 26–64; §100.
6. Karl Rahner, *Visions and Prophecies* (tr. E. Henkey and R. Strachan; New York: Herder and Herder, 1963); Edward Schillebeeckx, *Mary, Mother of the Redemption* (tr. N. D. Smith; New York: Sheed & Ward, 1964) 131–75; Virgil Elizondo, "Our Lady of Guadalupe as a Cultural Symbol: The Power of the Powerless," *Liturgy and Cultural Religious Traditions* (ed. H. Schmidt and D. Power; New York: Seabury, 1977) 25–33.
7. See Vatican Council II, Decree on Ecumenism, no. 3; cf. Extraordinary Synod of Bishops, 1985, Final Report, II C 7; *LG* 15; we take this as applying to the Lutheran churches.
8. This possibility was discussed in the Catholic Reflections in our earlier volume on teaching authority, with some explanations that apply to the present recommendation; L/RC 6:II, §§42–50; cf. CS §100 above.
9. *Lectionary for Mass*. Translation of the Roman Missal by the International Committee on English in the Liturgy (Washington DC: United States Catholic Conference, 1969).

Lutheran Reflections

1. That Mary was "always virgin" (*semper virgine;* SA 1:4; *BS* 414; *BC* 292), though not directly asserted in the biblical canon, was often an aspect of sixteenth-century spirituality.
2. Cf. John Stroup, *The Struggle for Identity in the Clerical Estate* (Studies in the History of Christian Thought 33; Leiden: Brill, 1984).
3. Cf. Karl Rahner, "The Church of the Saints," *Theological Investigations* (Baltimore: Helicon, 1967) 3:100, n. 6; *idem*, "Why and How Can We Venerate the Saints?" *Theological Investigations* (New York: Herder and Herder, 1971) 8:23; *idem*, "The Life of the Dead," *Theological Investigations* (Baltimore: Helicon, 1966) 4:352; cf. *idem*, "Gebet. IV. Dogmatisch," *LThK* (2d ed.; 1960) 4:545.
4. Luther accepted the practice as a "free devotion" to be done "once or twice" apart from funerals. See "Confession Concerning Christ's Supper" (1528), WA 26:508; *LW* 37:369. The Lutheran Confessions honor such prayer as an ancient custom that need not be forbidden as long as the Lord's Supper is not transferred to the dead (Ap 24:94, 96; *BS* 375, 376; *BC* 267). See also *LBW*, 211, Commendation (18).
5. The faith of the saints is to be imitated, as are "their other virtues" (Latin text only) in accordance with one's calling (Ap 21:6; *BS* 318; *BC* 230). But faith "which takes hold of Christ" is the only "virtue that justifies" (Ap 4:227; *BS* 203; *BC* 138).
6. Typical for Lutherans in this process of discernment is that we avoid making infallible pronouncements because we find the language of infallibility "dangerously misleading" (L/RC 6:III, §16, p. 65); cf. the cases of Richard Baumann and Paul Schulz, where the German regional churches refused to make decisions about dogma ("Entscheid des Spruchkollegiums in Lehrzuchverfahren betreffend Pfarrer i. W. Richard Baumann. Erlass des Ev. Oberkirchenrats vom 7. August, 1953, Nr. A 9609," *Amtsblatt der Evangelischen Landeskirche in Württemberg* 35, Nr. 36 [1953] 445–54, esp. 453; *Nachdruck der Niederschrift über das*

Feststellungsverfahren nach dem Kirchengesetz der Vereingten Ev. Luth. Kirche Deutschlands über das Verfahren bei Lehrbeanstandungen gegen Pastor Dr. Paul Schulz, Hamburg [ed. Lutherisches Kirchenamt, Hannover; Hamburg: Lutherisches Verlagshaus, 1979] passim).

7. *CA* Conclusion of Pt 1:1; *BS* 83d; *BC* 47; *CA* Conclusion of Pt 2:5; *BS* 134; *BC* 95; cf. Martin Chemnitz, *Examination of the Council of Trent* (tr. F. Kramer; St. Louis: Concordia, 1971) 1:215–307; David Hollaz, *Examen Theologicum Acroamaticum* (ed. R. Teller; Leipzig: Kiesewetter, 1750), De Sacra Scriptura, q. 51; 177–82.

BACKGROUND PAPERS

1. Fitzmyer

1. R. E. Brown, et al. (eds.), *Mary in the New Testament: A Collaborative Assessment by Protestant and Roman Catholic Scholars* (Philadelphia: Fortress; Ramsey NJ: Paulist, 1978).
2. R. Otto, *Idea of the Holy* (London: Oxford University, 1931); O. R. Jones, *Concept of Holiness* (New York: Macmillan, 1961). Cf. O. Procksch and K.-G. Kuhn, "Hagios, etc.," *TWNT* 1 (1933) 87–116; *TDNT* 1 (1964) 88–115; H. Balz, "Hagios, etc.," *EWNT* 1 (1980) 38–48.
3. See also Sir 42:7, "even God's holy ones must fail in recounting the wonders of the Lord" (NAB). Cf. *1 Enoch* 1:9, "He comes with ten thousand holy ones to execute judgment upon them" (M. A. Knibb, *The Ethiopic Book of Enoch* [2 vols.; Oxford: Clarendon, 1978] 2:60).
4. See BAGD 10; cf. *TWNT* 1 (1933) 14; *TDNT* 1 (1964) 109. L. Morris (*First and Second Epistles to the Thessalonians* [Grand Rapids: Eerdmans, 1959] 114) notes that *hagioi* scarcely means "believers on earth," but queries whether it means "angels" or "Christians who have departed this life." So too K. Staab, *Die Thessalonicherbriefe* (5th ed.; Regensburg: Pustet, 1969) 25. But cf. J. M. Reese, *1 and 2 Thessalonians* (Wilmington DE: Glazier, 1980) 41: since "Paul never uses the term 'saints' for angels elsewhere, the presumption is that he is describing the heroes of sacred history as coming with the glorified Jesus."
5. See P. Bonnard, *L'Evangile selon Saint Matthieu* (Commentaire du Nouveau Testament 1; Neuchâtel: Delachaux & Niestlé, 1963) 407. Cf. M.-J. Lagrange, *L'Evangile selon Saint Matthieu* (Etudes bibliques; 4th ed.; Paris: Gabalda, 1927) 532–33.
6. (1) "descent from heaven" (cf. 2 Thess 1:7; *1 Enoch* 1:3); (2) "cry of command" (Dan 10:11; Rev 4:1); (3) "archangel's call" (Jude 9; Rev 5:2-12); (4) "sound of God's trumpet" (Joel 2:2; Rev 1:10; 4:1; 1 Cor 15:52); (5) rapture or lifting up (Dan 7:13; Acts 1:9; Rev 4:1); (6) "clouds" (Zeph 1:15; Dan 7:13; Acts 1:9); and (7) "meeting in the air" (conjectured—cf. Eph 2:2).
7. Cf. 1 Thess 5:10; 2 Cor 5:8; Rom 6:8; Luke 23:43; Matt 19:28.
8. See *Jub.* 23:31; *1 Enoch* 91:10; Wis 1:15; 3:4; 8:13; 15:3; 2 Macc 7:9. Cf. H. Buckers, *Die Unsterblichkeitslehre des Weisheitsbuches* (Münster: Aschendorff, 1938); O. Cullmann, *Immortality of the Soul or Resurrection of the Dead? The Witness of the New Testament* (London: Epworth, 1958).
9. RSV takes *rî'šônîm, 'aharônîm* as neuter, "former things." Commentators differ; Qoh 2:16 mentions no remembrance of "wise man" or "fool," hence of bygone persons.
10. See J. L. Duhaime, "El elogio de los padres de Ben Sira y el cantico de Moisés (Sir 44–50 y Dt 32)," *Estudios Biblicos* 35 (1976) 223–28; E. Jacob, "L'Histoire d'Israël vue par Ben Sira," *Mélanges bibliques rédigés en l'honneur de André Robert*

(Paris: Bloud & Gay, 1957) 288–94; R. T. Siebeneck, "May Their Bones Return to Life—Sirach's Praise of the Fathers," *Catholic Biblical Quarterly* 21 (1959) 411–28; J. G. Snaith, *Ecclesiasticus or the Wisdom of Jesus Son of Sirach* (Cambridge: University Press, 1974) 214–53; C. Spicq, "L'Ecclésiastique," *La sainte Bible* (ed. L. Pirot and A. Clamer; Paris: Letouzey et Ané) 6 (1946) 799–843.

11. But it is used of the temple and its altar (49:20; 50:11).
12. See J. Reumann, *"Righteousness" in the New Testament: "Justification" in the United States Lutheran–Roman Catholic Dialogue* (Philadelphia: Fortress; New York/Ramsey NJ: Paulist, 1982) 222–23.
13. See M. M. Bourke, "The Epistle to the Hebrews," *NJBC*, art. 60, §§62–66; F. F. Bruce, *Epistle to the Hebrews* (Grand Rapids MI: Eerdmans, 1964) 277–344; J. Héring, *L'Epître aux Hébreux* (Commentaire du Nouveau Testament 12; Neuchâtel: Delachaux et Niestlé, 1954) 103–12; P. E. Hughes, *Commentary on the Epistle to the Hebrews* (Grand Rapids MI: Eerdmans, 1977) 437–518; F. J. Schierse, *Epistle to the Hebrews* (New York: Herder and Herder, 1969); C. Spicq, *L'Epître aux Hébreux* (Sources bibliques; Paris: Gabalda, 1977) 181–99.
14. *Heiligengräber in Jesu Umwelt (Mt. 23,29; Lk 11:47): Eine Untersuchung zur Volksreligion der Zeit Jesu* (Göttingen: Vandenhoeck & Ruprecht, 1958).
15. Ibid., 11–17. E.g., the tomb of the Maccabees (ibid., 49–50, 120); the tomb of Zechariah (ibid., 67–72); the tomb of the Davidic dynasty (ibid., 53–61); Rachel's tomb (ibid., 75–76).
16. *Jérusalem II* (Paris: Gabalda, 1926).
17. *Heiligengräber*, 121 n. 5 (n. 14 above).
18. Ibid., 127. See A. Schlatter, *Der Märtyrer in den Anfängen der Kirche* (Gütersloh: Bertelsmann, 1915) 28.
19. See F.-M. Abel, *Les livres des Maccabées* (2d ed.; Paris: Gabalda, 1949) 365–84; C. Habicht, *2. Makkabäerbuch: Historische und legendarische Erzählungen* (Jüdische Schriften aus hellenistisch–römischer Zeit 1/3; Gütersloh: Mohn, 1976) 229–38; U. Kellermann, *Auferstanden in den Himmel: 2 Makkabäer 7 und die Auferstehung der Märtyrer* (Stuttgart: Katholisches BibelWerk, 1979). For later Jewish legends about the mother and her sons, see G. D. Cohen, "Hannah and Her Seven Sons," *Encyclopaedia Judaica* (16 vols.; New York: Macmillan, 1971) 7:1270–72.
20. 4 Macc 17:9–10. See *The Old Testament Pseudepigrapha* (ed. J. H. Charlesworth; Garden City NY: Doubleday, 1983, 1985), 2:562.
21. The Seven were honored as "Septem Fratres Machabaei, et horum Mater" in the Roman Martyrology. See *Acta Sanctorum* (ed. Bollandists; Paris: Palme) 35 (1867) ad diem primam Augusti, 5–15.
22. Gregory of Nyssa, *Steph.* 2 (*PG* 46:725B); *Const. Apost.* 2.49,3 (ed. F. X. Funk, 147); cf. Gregory Nazianzen, *Hom. 15 in Macc.* 3 (*PG* 35:913); Acts 22:20 (mss. L, 614, 945).
23. See N. Brox, *Zeuge und Märtyrer* (Munich: Kösel, 1961); H. von Campenhausen, *Die Idee des Märtyriums in der alten Kirche* (2d ed.; Göttingen: Vandenhoeck & Ruprecht, 1964); M. Lods, *Confesseurs et martyrs* (Neuchâtel: Delachaux et Niestlé, 1958).
24. See F. F. Bruce, *Epistle to the Hebrews*, 346.
25. See H. Ridderbos, *Paul: An Outline of His Theology* (Grand Rapids MI: Eerdmans, 1975) 362–95; H. Schlier, *Der Brief an die Epheser* (Düsseldorf; Patmos, 1957) 90–96 (excursus *to sōma tou Christou*); E. Schweizer, *TWNT* 7 (1964) 1066–77; *TDNT* 7 (1971) 1068–81.
26. *Heiligengräber*, 133–34 (n. 14 above).

27. F. Mussner, *Der Jakobusbrief* (Freiburg: Herder, 1964) 227–29; M. Dibelius and H. Greeven, *James* (Philadelphia: Fortress, 1976) 255–56.
28. Many do not even discuss the problem of *touto*, taking it for granted that its antecedent is the prayers and supplications: so N. Brox, *Die Pastoralbriefe* (4th ed.; Regensburg: Pustet, 1969) 122–29; M. Dibelius, *The Pastoral Epistles* (Philadelphia: Fortress, 1972) 35–43; P. Dornier, *Les épîtres pastorales* (Paris: Gabalda, 1969) 47–53; J. L. Houlden, *The Pastoral Epistles: I and II Timothy, Titus* (Harmondsworth: Penguin, 1976) 65–68; J. Jeremias, *Die Briefe an Timotheus und Titus*, 15–16; J. N. D. Kelly, *A Commentary on the Pastoral Epistles* (London: Black, 1963) 59–64; W. Lock (*The Pastoral Epistles* [New York: Scribner's, 1924] 23–28); C. Spicq (*Les épîtres pastorales* [4th ed.; Paris: Gabalda, 1969] 1:356–66); and C. K. Barrett (*The Pastoral Epistles* [Oxford: Clarendon, 1963] 49–51) consider the antecedent to be both the prayers and the living of a tranquil life. Only G. Holtz (*Die Pastoralbriefe* [Berlin: Evangelische V., 1965] 52–61) limits the antecedent to tranquil life.
29. See N. Brox, *Die Pastoralbriefe*, 127.
30. R. J. Bauckham, "Colossians 1,24 Again: The Apocalyptic Motif," *Evangelical Quarterly* 47 (1975) 168–70; M. Carrez, "Souffrance et gloire dans les épîtres pauliniennes (Contribution à l'exégèse de Col. 1, 24–27)," *Revue d'histoire et de philosophie religieuses* 31 (1951) 343–53; J. Ernst, *Die Briefe an die Philipper, an Philemon, an die Kolosser, an die Epheser* (Regensburg: Pustet, 1974) 182–87; J. Gnilka, *Der Kolosserbrief* (Freiburg: Herder, 1980) 93–101; J. Kremer, "Thlipsis, etc." *EWNT* 2 (1981) 375–79; *idem, Was an den Leiden Christi noch mangelt* (Bonn: Hanstein, 1956); E. Lohse, *Colossians and Philemon* (Philadelphia: Fortress, 1971) 68–75; G. H. P. Thompson, "Ephesians iii.13 and 2 Timothy ii.10 in the Light of Colossians i.24," *Expository Times* 71 (1959–60) 187–89.
31. Five interpretations may be mentioned: (a) "Filling up what is lacking in the afflictions of Christ" might seem to mean that there is something still lacking in the vicarious sufferings of Christ himself. But such an interpretation would run counter to the normal NT understanding of Christ's vicarious death; cf. 1 Tim 2:5 (sole mediator); Rom 6:10a (Christ having died "once for all"); even Col 2:13–14 (nailing of the bond that stood against us to the cross). Also, *thlipsis* is not otherwise used in the NT for the sufferings of Jesus (see G. Delling, *TWNT* 6 [1959] 305 n. 3; *TDNT* 6 [1968] 307 n. 3). (b) The clause has been understood in a mystical sense, of a union of the "saints" with Christ that permits the whole body to benefit from sufferings experienced in corporate apostolic activity. But this interpretation imports into a difficult text a notion of mystic co-suffering otherwise foreign to it. Suffering with or like Christ is found in the NT (2 Cor 1:5-7; 4:10; 1 Thess 3:3), but a mystic meaning is not clearly intended. (c) The clause has been given a gnostic interpretation: the vicarious suffering of Christ is complete only when gnostic souls have suffered as did the crucified Christ. This imports a notion that is not certainly current in the first century. (d) The clause has been understood of the "woes of the Messiah"; *hai thlipseis tou Christou* is said to be the translation of Hebrew *ḥeblô šel māšîaḥ*, "the travail of the Messiah." The woes are the rebellion, war, pestilence, drought, and cosmic cataclysms that are expected to precede the end time, when God will send an anointed agent to deliver his people. Justification for this interpretation is sought in the mention of the "secret" now "made manifest" and in the apocalyptic stage props in the passage said to be similar to those in the Marcan eschatological discourse (13:8, 19-20, 24, 27). Those who

use this interpretation appeal to H. Strack and P. Billerbeck, *Kommentar zum Neuen Testament aus Talmud und Midrasch* (6 vols.; Munich: Beck, 1922–61) 4/2:977–86, where passages from intertestamental and rabbinic literature are cited describing the woes. But none of the intertestamental passages (*1 Enoch, Jubilees, 4 Ezra, Sibylline Oracles*) mentions a Messiah, save *2 Apoc. Bar*. 25:1–29:3; 70:2-10. As for the rabbinic sources, they are all of late vintage (Babylonian Talmud or later midrashim). (e) The best interpretation of the clause sees it as an expression of the sufferings that the author vicariously endures for the "saints" or the "church," which unites them or it with Christ, as the author supplies in his apostolic preaching and suffering whatever may still be lacking in their/its share of the sufferings that all are called on to endure for the sake of completing the preaching of the word of God (cf. 2 Cor 1:4-6; 4:10).

32. See M. A. Knibb, *The Ethiopic Book of Enoch*, 2:126 (n. 3 above).
33. *Heiligengräber*, 133–43 (n. 14 above); H. Delehaye, *Les origines du culte des martyrs* (2d ed.; Brussels: Société des Bollandistes, 1933) 120–27.

2. Reumann

1. Cf. J. Fitzmyer, "Biblical Data on the Veneration, Intercession, and Invocation of Holy People," 146–47 above; bibliography in n. 30; five possible interpretations in n. 31.
2. An overview, originally presented to the dialogue as part of this paper in 1986, has been published in *Currents in Theology and Mission* 17 (1990) 454–61.
3. Fitzmyer, "Biblical Data," 147 above.
4. *PG* 101:711.
5. In *Was an den Leiden Christi Noch Mangelt: Eine Interpretationsgeschichtliche und Exegetische Untersuchung zu Kol. 1, 24b* (Bonner biblische Beiträge 12; Bonn: Hanstein, 1956).
6. Cf. C. F. D. Moule, *The Epistle of Paul the Apostle to the Colossians and to Philemon* (Cambridge Greek Testament Commentary; New York: Cambridge University Press, 1957) 76; Eduard Lohse, *Colossians and Philemon* (German 1968; Hermeneia; trans. W. R. Poehlmann and R. J. Karris; Philadelphia: Fortress, 1971) 70; Peter T. O'Brien, *Colossians, Philemon* (Word Bible Commentary; Waco: Word Books, 1982) 79–80; J. D. G. Dunn, *Jesus and the Spirit: A Study of the Religious and Charismatic Experience of Jesus and the First Christians as Reflected in the New Testament* (New Testament Library; London: SCM, 1975) 113, 332–33, cf. n. 157.
7. Cf. J. Reumann, *Colossians* (Augsburg Commentary on the New Testament; Minneapolis: Augsburg, 1985) 133–34.
8. "Biblical Data," n. 1 above.
9. *The Old Testament Pseudepigrapha* (ed. J. H. Charlesworth; Garden City NY: Doubleday, 1983) 1:617.
10. P. Billerbeck, *Kommentar zum Neuen Testament aus Talmud und Midrasch* (Munich: C. H. Beck) 1 (1926) 950; E. Schweitzer, *The Good News According to Mark* (Richmond: John Knox, 1970) 269; C. S. Mann, *Mark* (AB 27; Garden City NY: Doubleday, 1986) 515 (date in rabbinic sources uncertain).
11. "The Church as the Missionary Body of Christ," *New Testament Studies* 8 (1961–62) 1–11, reprinted in Schweizer's *Neotestamentica: Deutsche und Englische Aufsätze 1951–63* (Zurich: Zwingli, 1963) 317–29; cf. his *The Letter to the Colossians* (Minneapolis: Augsburg, 1982) 98–114. Maurya P. Horgan, *NJBC* 54:16, takes *tou Christou* to mean "Christian sufferings"; cf. 2:11.

12. Erhardt Guttgemanns, *Der leidende Apostel und sein Herr* (Forschungen zur Religion und Literatur des Alten und Neuen Testaments 90; Göttingen: Vandenhoeck & Ruprecht, 1966) 126–35, 195–98, 323–28.
13. Verse 4, God "desires all men to be saved and to come to the knowledge of the truth" (RSV), was a battleground for Calvinists and Arminians. Tertullian had long before taken *pantas anthrōpous* as "all whom God adopted," Augustine as "all the predestined," every type of humankind among them, and the Greek Fathers and Aquinas as well dealt with the problem; cf. C. Spicq, *Les épîtres pastorales* (Etudes bibliques; 4th ed.; Paris: Gabalda, 1969) 57–58; J. N. D. Kelly, *A Commentary on the Pastoral Epistles* (Harper's/Black's New Testament Commentaries; New York: Harper & Row, 1963) 62–63.
14. Fitzmyer, "Biblical Data," 146 above. I omit the references cited, which differ slightly from those in Immenkötter's margin or Reu's translation, *361; whether Deut 5:5, 27, or 31, Moses is no saving mediator.
15. Cf. A. Oepke, e.g., in *TDNT* 4 (1967) 598–624; *TWNT* 4 (1942) 602–29. O. Becker, *engyos, mesitēs*, under "Covenant," *NIDNTT* 1 (1975) 372–75.
16. Oepke, *TDNT* 4 (1967) 620–24; *TWNT* 4 (1942) 624–28, in this way finds "NT religion . . . exclusively oriented to the mediator concept" and, citing *CA* 21, argues that "in Roman Catholicism the Church and its agents took over the mediatorial function" whereas the Reformation outlook is reasserted in Emil Brunner's *Der Mittler* (1930; trans., *The Mediator* [New York: Macmillan, 1934]).
17. *A Greek Patristic Lexicon* (ed. G. W. H. Lampe; Oxford: Clarendon, 1961–68) 846.
18. *TDNT* 4 (1967) 620; *TWNT* 4 (1942) 624. Cf. H. Preisker, "*engyos*," *TDNT* 2 (1964) 329; *TWNT* 2 (1935) 329.
19. Gottfried Holtz, *Die Pastoralbriefe* (3d ed.; Theologischer Handkommentar zum Neuen Testament 13; Berlin: Evangelische Verlagsanstalt, 1980) 52–65.
20. Thus G. Denzer, *JBC* 57:18; Kelly (n. 13 above) 60; M. Dibelius and Hans Conzelmann, *The Pastoral Epistles* (Hermeneia; Philadelphia: Fortress, 1972) 36.
21. BAGD 726, s.v. *prōtos* 2c.
22. There is ample later illustrative material in the excursus, "Prayer for the Proper Authorities," Dibelius-Conzelmann (n. 20 above) 37–38.
23. Thus Kelly (n. 13 above) 61–62.
24. BAGD 798, *sōzō* 1.
25. E. K. Simpson, *The Pastoral Epistles* (London: Tyndale, 1954) 41–42.
26. Cf. BAGD, *houtos*, 1aß, and 2 Tim 2:2; 3:5, 6, 8 for examples where the term points back; BAGD 1bß, and 1 Tim 1:9, 16, and, better, 2 Tim 3:1, for examples pointing to what follows.
27. Cf. Fitzmyer, "Biblical Data," n. 28 above.
28. Large Catechism, Third Part; *BC* 424, 28; *BS* 668–69, 28.
29. Fitzmyer, "Biblical Data," 146 above. An additional factor may be the presence of a chiastic structure running through the passage; which can be outlined thus:

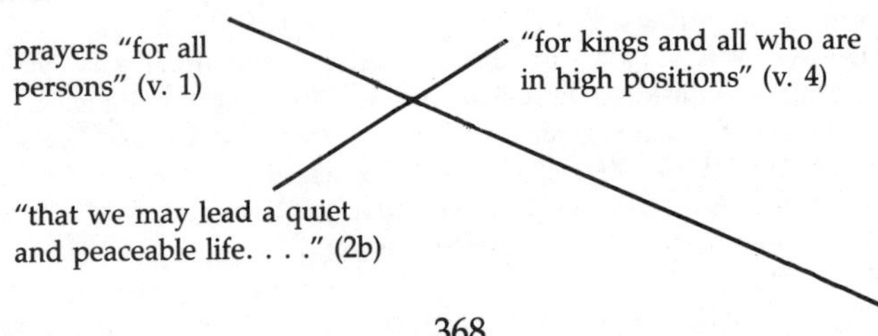

This is good and is acceptable in the sight of God our Savior (v. 3)		who desires all persons to be preserved or saved and come to the knowledge of the truth (v. 4).
One God	and	One Mediator between God and human beings, the man Christ Jesus (v. 5), who gave himself a ransom for all . . . (v. 6), for which I was appointed as preacher and apostle (v. 7)

30. *BC* 39, n. 3; *BS* 72, n. 3.
31. E. Lohse, *Die Offenbarung des Johannes* (Das Neue Testament Deutsch 11; Göttingen: Vandenhoeck & Ruprecht, 1966) 46.
32. Cf. *Aboth, Rabbi Nathan*, 26; *Shabbath* 152b; *Deut. Rabbah* 11.10; *Gittin* 57b; so R. H. Charles, *The Revelation of St. John* (International Critical Commentary; Edinburgh: T. & T. Clark, 1920) 1:173–74; J. Massyngberde Ford, *Revelation* (AB 38; Garden City NY: Doubleday, 1975) 110.
33. Ford (n. 32 above) 100.
34. Charles (n. 32 above) 174–75.

3. Eno

1. A visual impression of the relative importance of this topic for the Catholic and Protestant traditions may be gained by considering two collections of texts. The collection by Walter Delius, revised by Hans-Udo Rosenbaum, *Texte zur Geschichte der Marienverehrung und Marienverkündigung in der alten Kirche* (New York & Berlin: de Gruyter, 1973) contains 47 pages. It is appropriately part of a collection of "Kleine Texte." On the Roman Catholic side there is the eight-volume *Corpus Patristicum Marianum* by Sergio Alvarez Campos (Burgos: Aldecoa, 1970–85).

   There are several surveys of this material available. Some of these are: George Söll, *Mariologie, Handbuch der Dogmengeschichte* (Freiburg: Herder, 1978) vol. 3, fascicle 4.

   W. Delius, *Die Geschichte der Marienverenhrung* (Munich: Reinhardt, 1963).

   H. Graef, *Mary: A History of Doctrine and Devotion* (vol. 1; New York: Sheed & Ward, 1963).

   W. J. Burghardt, "Mary in Western Patristic Thought," *Mariology* (ed. J. Carol; Milwaukee: Bruce, 1955) 1:109–55; *idem*, "Mary in Eastern Patristic Thought," *Mariology* (1957) 2:88–153.

   On the issue of the virginal conception, one recent work is: Suso Frank, "Geboren aus der Jungfrau Maria—Das Zeugnis der alten Kirche," *Zum Thema Jungfrauengeburt* (Stuttgart: Katholisches BibelWerk, 1970) 91–120.
2. Jerome, *ep*. 22.21; *CSEL* 154:173 ed. I. Hilberg (1910).
3. H. R. Smid, *Protevangelium Jacobi: A Commentary* (Assen: van Gorcum, 1965). Text in: *New Testament Apocrypha* (ed. E. Hennecke; rev. W. Schneemelcher; Philadelphia: Westminster, 1963) 1:370–88.
4. Clement of Alexandria, *Stromata* 7.16; *GCS* 17:66, ed. O. Stählin (1909).
5. Jerome, *Adversus Helvidium* 8; *PL* 23:192.

6. Ignatius of Antioch, *Smyrn.* 1.1; *Apostolic Fathers, LCL* 1: 252, ed. K. Lake (1965, [orig. 1912]).
7. Justin, *Dialogue with Trypho the Jew* 100.2; *PG* 6:712.
8. Irenaeus, *Adversus haereses* 3.22.4; *SC* 211:438–44, ed. A. Rousseau and L. Doutreleau (1974).
9. *Adv. haer.* 5.19.1; *SC* 153:248–50 (1969): *Démonstration* 33; *SC* 62:85, ed. L. Froidevaux (1959).
10. *Adv. haer.* 3.16.7; *SC* 211:314.
11. Origen, *Contra Celsum* 1.32; *SC* 132:162–64, ed. M. Borret (1967).
12. Origen, *Hom. in Lc.* 6.7; *SC* 87:148, ed. H. Crouzel, F. Fournier, and P. Périchon (1962). For a study, see H. Crouzel, "La Théologie mariale d'Origène," *SC* 87:11–64. Another text: Fragment 20; *SC* 87:478.
13. Socrates, *Hist. eccl.* 7.32; *PG* 67:812.
14. Origen, *Hom. in Lc.* 7.4; *SC* 87:158. Cf. also Fragment 31 in the *Commentary on John, GCS* 10:506–507, ed. E. Preuschen (1903).
15. Origen, *Comm. in Joann.* 1.23; *SC* 120:70, ed. C. Blanc (1966).
16. Origen, *Hom. in Lc.* 14.3; *SC* 87:218.
17. Origen, *Hom in Lc.* 14.8; *SC* 87:226. Cf. also *Hom. in Lev.* 8.2; *SC* 287:12, ed. M. Borret (1981).
18. Origen, *Ser. Comm. Matt.* 25; *GCS* 38:42–43, ed. E. Klostermann & E. Benz (1933).
19. Origen, *Comm. in Matt.* 10.17; *SC* 162:216, ed. R. Girod (1970).
20. Origen, *Hom. in Lc.* 17.6; *SC* 87:256–58.
21. Origen, *Hom. in Lc.*, Fragment 30; *SC* 87:484.
22. Origen, *Hom. in Lc.* 20.4; *SC* 87:282–84.
23. Tertullian, *De carne Christi* 19–20; ed. E. Evans (London: SPCK, 1956) 66, 68.
24. Ibid., 23; p. 76.
25. Ibid., 7; pp. 30, 32.
26. Tertullian, *Adversus Marcionem* 4.19.11–13; *Oxford Early Christian Texts* (ed. E. Evans; Oxford: Clarendon Press, 1972) 362; ibid. 4.26.13; 412.
27. See n. 19 above.
28. Athanasius, *Epistola ad Virgines, CSCO* 151:58–62, ed. L.-Th. Lefort (1955). Athanasius's authorship is generally accepted; see *CPG* 2, nr. 2147. The citation on p. 165 comes from a work whose authorship is uncertain: *Homilia adversus Arium, de s. genetrice dei Maria* (*CPG* 2, nr. 2187). Text in L.-Th. Lefort, "L'Homélie de S. Athanase du Papyrus de Turin," *Muséon* 71 (1958) 209–39; text cited on 217.
29. Athanasius, *Epistola ad Epictetum* 5, *PG* 26:1057.
30. Alexander, *Epistola ad Alexandrum* 1.12; *GCS* 44 (19)23 (1954).
31. Basil of Caesarea, *ep.* 260.9, *LCL* 4:70, 72, ed. R. Deferrari (1939).
32. Gregory of Nazianzus, *ep.* 101; *PG* 37:177; *Orat.* 45.9; *PG* 36:633.
33. Gregory of Nyssa, *Sermon on the Birth of Christ*; *PG* 46:1140.
34. Gregory of Nyssa, *Sermon on the Annunciation;* if the sermon is not authentically Gregorian, this obviously would be a good reason for its unusual style; *PG* 62:765–68. (It is listed in Migne among spuria attributed to Chrysostom.) Cf. *CPG* 2, nr. 4677: "still *sub iudice*."
35. Gregory of Nazianzus, *Orat.* 24.10–11; *SC* 284:58, 60, ed. J. Mossay (1981). Gregory of Nyssa, *Vita S. Greg. Thaumaturgi*; *PG* 46:912.
36. Gregory of Nazianzus, *The Greek Anthology*, Book 8: Epigrams of St. Gregory the Theologian, nr. 28; *LCL*, 412, ed. W. R. Paton (1917).

37. O. Stegmüller, "Sub tuum praesidium," *Zeitschrift für katholische Theologie* 74 (1952) 76–82. On Marian liturgy, see A. Baumstark, *Comparative Liturgy* (rev. ed.; B. Botte; Westminster MD: Newman Press, 1958) 186. The Hypapante at Jerusalem is mentioned in the *Peregrinatio Egeriae*, 26.
38. Epiphanius, *Panarion* Antidicomarianites 78; *GCS* 37:452–75, ed. K. Holl (1933). Collyridians 79; *GCS* 37:475–84. Fate of Mary 78.11; *GCS* 37:461–62.
39. John Chrysostom, *Hom. in Matt.* 1.6; *PG* 57:21. 4.5; *PG* 57:45. 5.2; *PG* 57:56.
40. John Chrysostom, *Hom. in Matt.* 8.4; *PG* 57:86.
41. John Chrysostom, *Hom. in Jn.* 21.2–3; *PG* 59:131–32. *Hom. in Jn.* 22.1 (Shame); *PG* 59:134.
42. John Chrysostom, *Hom. in Matt.* 44.1; *PG* 57:465–66.
43. John Chrysostom, *Hom. in Jn.* 85.2; *PG* 159:462.
44. Ephrem, *Comm. in Diatessaron* 2.17; *SC* 121:74–75, ed. L. Leloir (1966). 21.26; *SC* 121:388–89. 5.5; *SC* 121:109. On Mary and the church in Ephrem, see R. Murray, *Symbols of Church and Kingdom* (Cambridge: Cambridge University Press, 1975) 144–50.
45. Ephrem, *Carmina Nisibena* 27.8; *CSCO* 219:76, ed. E. Beck (1961). *Hymni de Nativitate* 28.7; *CSCO* 187:129, ed. E. Beck (1959).
46. Ambrose, *De officiis* 1.69; *PL* 16:44. *Exp. in Lc.* 2.8–9; *SC* 45:75, ed. G. Tissot (1956).
47. Ambrose, *Exp. in Lc.* 2.19–20; *SC* 45:81.
48. Ibid., 2.1; *SC* 45:71.
49. Ambrose, *ep.* 63.33; *PL* 16:1198. *ep.* 43.6; *PL* 16:1126. *De institutione virginis* 52; *PL* 16:319–20.
50. Ambrose, *Exp. in Lc.* 2.4; *SC* 45:73.
51. Ibid., 2.17; *SC* 45:80; On Mary in Ambrose, see C. W. Neumann, *The Virgin Mary in the Works of Saint Ambrose* (Fribourg: University Press, 1962). Ambrose, *De obitu Theodosii* 44, *CSEL* 73:394, ed. O. Faller (1955).
52. Ambrose, *ep.* 49.2; *PL* 26:1154.
53. Ambrose, *Exp. in Lc.* 4.7; *SC* 45:153. Ibid., 2.28; *SC* 45:84.
54. Ibid., 10.132; *SC* 52:200 (1958).
55. Augustine, *Enarr. in Ps.* 67.21; *CCL* 39:884, ed. E. Dekkers and J. Fraipont (1956).
56. Augustine, *De Genesi ad litteram* 10.32; *CSEL* 28/1:320, ed. J. Zycha (1894).
57. Augustine, *ep.* 190.25; *CSEL* 57:161, ed. A. Goldbacher (1911).
58. Augustine, *Opus imperfectum contra Julianum* 4.87; *PL* 45:1387–88.
59. Augustine, *Enchiridion* 34; *CCL* 46:68, ed. E. Evans (1969). *Sermo* 196.1; *PL* 38:1019. *De peccatorum meritis et remissione* 1.57; *CSEL* 60:57, ed. K. Urba and J. Zycha (1913). *Sermo* 229 P; (Lambot 3), *PL* Supplementum 2:758, ed. A. Hamman (Paris: Garnier, 1960). *De Trinitate* 13.23; *CCL* 50A:413, ed. W. Mountain (1968).
60. Augustine, *De nuptiis et concupiscentia* 2.15; *CSEL* 42:267, ed. K. Urba & J. Zycha (1902). *Tract. in Joann.* 10.2; *CCL* 36:101, ed. R. Willems (1954). *De catechizandis rudibus* 40; *CCL* 46:164, "Virgo moriens."
61. Augustine, *Sermo* 191.2; *PL* 38:1010. *Tract. in Joann.* 121.4; *CCL* 38:667. *Sermo* 189; *PL* 38:1006. *epp.* 135, 137; *CSEL* 44:89–92, 96–125, ed. A. Goldbacher (1904). *ep.* 137.8; *CSEL* 44:107. *Sermo* 184.1; *Stromata patristica et mediaevalia. Sancti Aurelii Augustini sermones selecti duodeviginti* (ed. C. Lambot; Utrecht: Spectrum, 1950) 1:75.
62. Augustine, *Sermo* 191.3; *PL* 38:1010–11. *Sermo* 184.2; *Stromata patristica et mediaevalia* 1:75 (n. 61 above).

63. *Sermo* 291.5; *PL* 38:1318. *De sancta virginitate* 4; *CSEL* 41:238, ed. J. Zycha (1900).
64. E. Lamirande, "En quel sens peut–on parler de dévotion mariale chez Saint Augustin?" *De primordiis cultus mariani*. Vol. 3: *De Fundamento cultus B. V. Mariae in operibus sanctorum Patrum* (Acta congressus mariologici-mariani in Lusitania; Roma: Pontifica Academia Mariana, 1970) 17–35.
65. Augustine, *Sermo* 265D.7; (*Sermo* Morin 17) *Miscellanea Agostiniana. Sancti Augustini Sermones post Maurinos reperti* (ed. G. Morin. Roma: Tipografia Poliglotta Vaticana, 1930) 1:664.
66. Augustine, *De natura et gratia* 42; *CSEL* 60:263–64. *Enchiridion* 34, 36; *CCL* 46:68–70.
67. Augustine, *Opus imperfectum contra Julianum* 4.122; *PL* 45:1418.
68. Augustine, *De gratia Christi et de peccato originali* 2.45; *CSEL* 42:202–203. *De doctrina christiana* 1.13; *CCL* 32:14, ed. J. Martin (1962).
69. Augustine, *De agone christiano* 22.24; *CSEL* 41:125, ed. J. Zycha (1900).
70. Augustine, *Sermo* 190.2; *PL* 38:1008.
71. Augustine, *Sermo* 51.21, 26; *PL* 38:344–45, 348. *Contra Faustum* 3.1–2; *CSEL* 25.261–62, ed. J. Zycha (1891). Ibid., 23.1; *CSEL* 25:707.
72. Augustine, *Sermo*, 23.8; *CSEL* 25:713–14. *De nuptiis et concupiscentia* 1.13; *CSEL* 42:225.
73. Augustine, *Enarr. in Ps.* 104.13; *CCL* 40:1543.
74. Augustine, *Tract. in Joann.* 8; 119; *CCL* 36:86–89, 658–60. *De fide et symbolo* 9; *CSEL* 41:13.
75. Augustine, *De sancta virginitate* 3; *CSEL* 41:237. *ep.* 243.9; *CSEL* 57:576, ed. A. Goldbacher (1911). *Enarr. in Ps.* 127.12; *CCL* 40:1876–77.
76. Augustine, *Sermo* 72A.7 (*Sermo* Denis 25) *Miscellanea Agostiniana* 1:162–63 (n. 65 above).
77. Proclus, *Sermo* delivered in Constantinople on "the feast of Mary" 428 A.D. in the presence of Nestorius, Section 3; for text see: *Acta conciliorum oecumenicorum* (ed. Edward Schwartz; Berlin: de Gruyter, 1927) 1.1.1:104.
78. Mary as protectress: e.g., see articles by Norman Baynes, "The Finding of the Virgin's Robe" (1949) 240–47; "The Supernatural Defenders of Constantinople" (1949) 248–60; both in *Byzantine Studies and Other Essays* (London: University of London, The Athlone Press, 1960). Averil Cameron, "The Theotokos in 6th century Constantinople" (1978); "The Virgin's Robe: An Episode in the history of early 7th century Constantinople" (1979), essays 16 and 17 in *Continuity and Change in Sixth-Century Byzantium* (London: Variorum Reprints, 1981). On the origins of the Assumption, see W. J. Burghardt, *The Testimony of the Patristic Age Concerning Mary's Death* (Westminster MD: Newman Press, 1957).

4. McDonnell

1. J. Pelikan, "Voices of the Church," *Proceedings of the Catholic Theological Society of America* 33 (1978) 4.
2. A. Tegels, "Virginity in the Liturgy," *Marian Studies* 11 (1960) 113.
3. The prehistory and history of Marian feasts given here is little more than a conflation, sometimes verbatim, of two texts by B. Capell, to which I have made some additions of material pertinent to our discussions. "La liturgie mariale en Occident," *Maria: Etudes sur la Sainte Vierge* (5 vols.; ed. D'Hubert du Manoir; Paris: Beauchesne, 1952) 1:216–430; "Les fêtes mariales," *L'Eglise en prière* (ed. A. G. Martimort; Paris: Desclée, 1961) 747–65.

4. These texts have been gathered by J. Lebon, "L'apostolicité de la doctrine de la médiation mariale," *Recherches de théologie ancienne et médievale* 2 (1930) 135–49.
5. P. Jounel, "The Veneration of Mary," *The Church at Prayer* (ed. A. G. Martimort *et al.*; Collegeville: Liturgical Press, 1986) 131.
6. A. Fliche and V. Martin, *Histoire des Conciles* (Paris: Letouzey et Ané, 1908) II–I:243, n. 4.
7. "Hippolyt von Rom als Zeuge für den Ausdruck *theotokos*," *Zeitschrift für katholische Theologie* 59 (1935) 73–81. Other authors used *theotokos* before Ephesus. See A. Fliche and V. Martin, *Histoire des Conciles* (Paris: Letouzey et Ané, 1908) II–I:243, n. 4.
8. E. J. Goodspeed and R. M. Grant, *A History of Early Christian Literature* (Chicago: University of Chicago Press, 1966) 150; F. L. Cross, "Hippolytus and the Church of Rome," *The Early Christian Fathers* (London: Duckworth, 1960) 158.
9. A. Hahn, *Bibliothek der Symbole und Glaubensregeln der Alten Kirche* (Hildesheim: Olms, 1962) 22–29.
10. "Sub tuum praesidium confugimus sancta Dei Genetrix; nostras deprecationes ne despicias in necessitatibus se a periculis cunctis libera nos semper, Virgo gloriosa et benedicta."
11. F. Mercenier, "Le plus ancienne prière à la Sainte Vierge: le *Sub tuum praesidium*," *Les Questions Liturgiques et Paroissiales* 25 (1940) 33–36.
12. Ibid., 43.
13. J. Pelikan, *The Emergence of the Catholic Tradition (100–600)* (The Christian Tradition 1; Chicago: University of Chicago Press, 1971) 242, 270, 272.
14. H. Graef, "The Council of Ephesus and After," *Mary: A History of Doctrine and Devotion* (New York: Sheed and Ward, 1963, 1965) 101–61.
15. P. Jounel, "The Cult of Mary," 133 (n. 5 above); B. Botte, "La premiere fête mariale de la liturgie romaine," *Ephemerides Liturgicae* 47 (1933) 425–30; A. Chavasse, *Le sacramentaire gélasien* (Tournai: Desclée, 1958) 381–82.
16. Tegels, "The Virginity of Mary," 109 (n. 2 above).
17. Ibid., 108.
18. Ibid., 20.
19. Jounel, "The Veneration of Mary," 135 (n. 5 above).
20. "La liturgie mariale en Occident," *L'Eglise en prière*, 229 (n. 3 above).
21. "Rite of Baptism of Children," 48: *The Rites of the Catholic Church* (New York: Pueblo, 1983) 201; "Rite of Christian Initiation of Adults," 214; ibid., 95.
22. "Nuptial Blessings," 64–65 (n. 21 above); ibid., 576–77.
23. "Commendation of the Dying," 217 (n. 21 above); ibid., 694.
24. "Masses of the Dead," *The Roman Missal: The Sacramentary* (Collegeville: Liturgical Press, 1974) 857–89.
25. "Various Texts for Funerals of Baptized Children," 226; ibid., 814.
26. "Motu proprio: Approval of the General Norms for the Liturgical Year and the New General Roman Calendar," *The Roman Missal: The Sacramentary* (Collegeville: Liturgical Press, 1974) 56.
27. "Constitution on the Sacred Liturgy," 103.
28. *Marialis Cultus* (To Honor Mary) 4.
29. Ibid., 5.
30. Ibid.
31. *Roman Missal*, 504 (n. 24 above).
32. Tegels, "Virginity in the Liturgy," 113, 114 (n. 2 above).

33. *Ineffabilis Deus*, 8 December 1854; DS 2800.
34. *Marialis Cultus* 1.
35. Ibid., 25.
36. Ibid., 4.
37. M. Thurian, "Marie et l'église, à propos de l'exhortation apostolique de Paul VI *Marialis cultus*," *Maison Dieu* 121 (1975) 101.
38. Ibid., 32.
39. *LG*, articles 8, 14, 28, 41, 49, 60, and 62.
40. *Marialis Cultus* 24.
41. Ibid.
42. Ibid., 30.
43. Ibid.
44. "Constitution on the Sacred Liturgy," 13.
45. *Marialis Cultus* 31.
46. Ibid., 3.
47. Ibid., 32.
48. Ibid., 38.
49. A. Kavanagh, *On Liturgical Theology* (New York: Pueblo, 1984) 73–121; G. Wainwright, *Doxology: The Praise of God in Worship, Doctrine, and Life* (New York: Oxford University Press, 1980) 218–83.
50. Pelikan, "Voices of the Church," 4 (n. 1 above).
51. Obviously this is not a one-way road. Creed is also a norm for cult.
52. F. G. Holweck, *Fasti Mariani sive Calendarium Festorum Sanctae Mariae Virginis Deiparae* (Freiburg: Herder, 1892).
53. K. Rahner, *Mary the Mother of the Lord* (Edinburgh: Nelson, 1962) 42–52.
54. Ibid., 38.

5. Froehlich

1. The literature is boundless. For an excellent introduction to the context see Judith Herrin, *The Formation of Christendom* (Princeton: Princeton University Press, 1987) 307–476. The recent commemoration of the events surrounding the Second Council of Nicaea (787) yielded two important collections of essays: *Iconoclasm: Papers Given at the Ninth Spring Symposium of Byzantine Studies. University of Birmingham. March 1975* (ed. A. Bryer and J. Herrin; Birmingham: Centre for Byzantine Studies, 1977); *Nicée II, 787–1987: Actes du Colloque International Nicée II tenu au Collège de France, Paris, les 2, 3, 4 octobre 1986* (ed. F. Boespflug and N. Lossky; Paris: Cerf, 1987). On the issues see also Peter Brown, "A Dark Age Crisis: Aspects of the Iconoclastic Controversy," *The English Historical Review* 346 (January 1973) 1–34; and the thoughtful study by Patrick Henry, "What Was the Iconoclastic Controversy About?" *Church History* 45 (1976) 13–31; cf. Henry's other contributions: "Initial Eastern Assessments of the Seventh Ecumenical Council," *Journal of Theological Studies*, n.s. 25 (1974) 83–95; "Images of the Church in the Second Nicene Council and in the Libri Carolini," in: *Law, Church, and Society: Essays in Honor of Stephan Kuttner* (ed. K. Pennington and R. Somerville; Philadelphia: University of Pennsylvania Press, 1977) 237–52.
2. The spirited debate about Alcuin (Luitpold Wallach) or Theodulf (Ann Freeman) as the true author of the *Libri Carolini* has triggered a wealth of important observations and arguments but remains inconclusive. In her report on the

"Forschungsstreit," Elisabeth Dahlhaus-Berg suggests that Theodulf may well have been the main "author," Alcuin the "final redactor": *Nova Antiquitas et Antiqua Novitas: Typologische Exegese und isidorianisches Geschichtsbild bei Theodulf von Orléans* (Kölner historische Abhandlungen 23; Köln: Böhlau, 1975) 169–180, esp. 178. Wallach's pertinent studies are collected in his *Diplomatic Studies in Latin and Greek Documents from the Carolingian Age* (Ithaca: Cornell University Press, 1977) 1–297. For Freeman's analyses see "Theodulf of Orléans and the Libri Carolini," *Speculum* 32 (1957) 663–705; "Further Studies in the Libri Carolini: 1. Paleographic Problems in Vat.Lat.720; 2. Patristic Exegesis, Mozarabic Antiphones, and the Vetus Latina," *Speculum* 40 (1965) 203–89; "Further Studies in the Libri Carolini: 3. The Marginal Notes in Vat.Lat.7207," *Speculum* 46 (1971) 597–612; and her masterful synthesis: "Carolingian Orthodoxy and the Fate of the Libri Carolini," *Viator* 16 (1985) 65–108.

3. There seems to be general agreement on this point today. See Herrin, *Formation*, 330–37 (n. 1 above), who like other scholars points also to the natural disaster of an enormous volcanic eruption in the Aegean in 726.
4. The standard text of the *Acta Nicaena* is found in *Sacrorum conciliorum nova et amplissima collectio* (ed. J. D. Mansi; Florence: Antonio Zatta) 12 (1766) 985–1154 and 13 (1767) 1–758. A full English translation was published by John Mendham, *The Seventh General Council, the Second of Nicaea* (London: William Edward Painter, 1850). In the notes Mendham also translated copious excerpts from the *Libri Carolini*. Recently Daniel J. Sahas translated again and annotated the Sixth Session of the Council, which contains the *Horos* of 754 and its refutation: *Icon and Logos: Sources in 8th Century Iconoclasm* (Toronto: University of Toronto Press, 1985). See also the collection in English of miscellaneous materials concerning this Council in H. R. Percival, *The Seven Ecumenical Councils of the Undivided Church: Their Canons and Dogmatic Decrees* (A Select Library of Nicene and Post–Nicene Fathers of the Christian Church, Second Series; Grand Rapids: Eerdmans, 1974; reprint of 1890 edition) 14:523–87.
5. Herrin, *Formation*, 466–69 and 472–75 (n. 1 above). A critical edition of the *Synodicon* has been provided by H. Gouillard, "Le Synodikon d'orthodoxie: édition et commentaire," *Travaux et Mémoires* 2 (1967) 1–316.
6. Herrin, *Formation*, 415–21 (n. 1 above). The text of the *Synodica* is printed in Mansi, 12:1055–1076D (n. 4 above) and *PL* 96:1215–34C. On the textual transmission see Wallach, *Diplomatic Studies*, 1–42 (n. 2 above).
7. Ann Freeman, "Carolingian Orthodoxy," especially the pages entitled "New Chronology," 105–106 (n. 2 above). All of modern scholarship on this topic is indebted to the seminal studies of Wolfram von den Steinen in the early 1930s.
8. Text in Mansi 13:759–810 (n. 4 above); *PG* 98:1247C–92.
9. *PL* 98:941–1248B
10. Freeman, "Carolingian Orthodoxy," 65, unnumbered note (n. 2 above). For the history of the text, see also her earlier studies (n. 7 above). Our references to the *Libri Carolini* will be to Bastgen's edition: *Libri Carolini sive Caroli Magni Capitulare de Imaginibus* (Monumenta Germaniae Historica: Legum Sectio III Concilia; Tomi II Supplementum; Hannover and Leipzig: Hahn, 1924; reprint 1979).
11. S. Gero, "The Libri Carolini and the Image Controversy," *Greek Orthodox Theological Review* 18 (1973) 7–34, esp. 11–14. Freeman thinks that the authors did have the full text but rearranged the material in the final redaction.
12. *Monumenta Germaniae Historica: Epistolarum* (Berlin: apud Weidmannos, 1899) 2:270–71.

13. In a recent article Celia Chazelle has stressed the identity of the piety reflected in the *Libri Carolini* with the general Frankish piety of the age: "Matter, Spirit, and Image in the Libri Carolini," *Recherches Augustiniennes* 21 (1986) 163–84. When she identifies, however, as the two underlying principles an extreme Augustinian dualism of matter/spirit, earth/heaven, body/soul, and a strict application of Augustine's distinction between *imago, similitudo,* and *aequalitas,* she probably underestimates the biblical roots of this language (e.g., John 6:63; 2 Cor 3:6), which Augustine interpreted in light of an anagogical dynamic as the bridge between the two poles. The principles of biblical hermeneutics that form the basis of the argumentation are recognized by Dahlhaus-Berg (n. 2 above); she links them to Theodulf's view of two ages, prefiguration and fulfillment (190–201).
14. Especially Gert Haendler, *Epochen karolingischer Theologie* (Theologische Arbeiten, 10; Berlin: Evangelische Verlagsanstalt, 1958); also Gero, 84–101 and 144–48 (n. 11 above).
15. This is different from the arguments of the Eastern iconoclasts. See S. Gero, "The Eucharistic Doctrine of the Byzantine Iconoclasm and Its Sources," *Byzantinische Zeitschrift* 68 (1975) 4–22, esp. 7–8.

6. Tavard

1. This list is given in León Amorós, "Los Teólogos immaculistas del siglo XII y la Cuestión de San Buenaventura sobre la Immaculada," *Verdad y Vida* 16 (1958) 129–71.
2. See Fred Jelly, "The Roman Catholic Dogma of Mary's Immaculate Conception," 263–78 below.
3. The critical edition of Saint Francis's works recognizes as authentic a prayer where Mary is called *virgo ecclesia facta . . . in qua fuit et est omnis plenitudo gratiae et omne bonum. . . SC* 285 (1981) 274.
4. See my volume, *The Forthbringer of God. St. Bonaventure on the Virgin Mary* (Chicago: Franciscan Herald Press, 1989).
5. Scotus studies the question in *Opus Oxonense,* III, d. 3, q. 1, iii and *Reportata Parisiensia,* III, d. 3, q. 1, i. A critical edition of the relevant texts is included in Carolus Balič, *Johannes Duns Scotus, Doctor Immaculatea Conceptionis,* vol. 1, *Textus Auctoris* (Rome: Academia Mariana Internationalis, 1954). The quotations are from *Opus Oxonense.* The reference for Henry of Ghent is *Quodlibeta,* XV, q. 13.
6. For illustrations of this point, see G. Tavard, "The Coincidence of Opposites. A Recent Interpretation of St. Bonaventure," *Theological Studies* 41 (1980) 576–84, and the remarks in *idem, Poetry and Contemplation in St. John of the Cross* (Athens OH: Ohio University Press, 1988) 75–92.
7. The argument, *potuit, decuit, ergo fecit,* was used for the first time by Eadmer of Canterbury in his *Tractatus de conceptione, PL* 159:301.
8. *Opus Oxonense,* III, d. 18.
9. *De Conceptu virginali,* ch. 18.
10. See Ignatius Brady, "The Development of the Doctrine on the Immaculate Conception in the Fourteenth Century after Aureoli," *Franciscan Studies* 15 (1955) 192.
11. *Commentarium Sententiarum,* II d. 30–33, q. 2, a. 1.

12. The text of the definition is given in Hyacinthus Ameri, *Doctrina Theologorum de Immaculatae Beatae Virginis Mariae Conceptione Tempore Concilii Basiliensis* (Rome: Academia Mariana Internationalis, 1954) 216, n. 6.

7. Peter

1. *A Response to Justification by Faith* (New York: Dept. for Ecumenical Relations of the Lutheran Church in America, 1986) 6. Italics added.
2. "A Statement of Response of the Inter-Church Relations Committee of the American Lutheran Church to the Lutheran-Roman Catholic Dialogue on Justification," in: *The American Lutheran Church Thirteenth General Convention: Reports and Actions: Supplement: General Officers, Church Council, and Districts, Exhibit C* (Minneapolis: Office of the General Secretary of The American Lutheran Church, 1986) 831. Italics added.
3. See Harding Meyer, "The Ecumenical Unburdening of the Mariological Problem: A Lutheran Perspective," and Carl J. Peter, "The Ecumenical Unburdening of the Mariological Problem: A Roman Catholic Response," *Journal of Ecumenical Studies* 26 (1989) 681–703.
4. Donald Nugent, *Ecumenism in the Age of the Reformation: The Colloquy of Poissy* in: *Harvard Historical Studies* 89 (Cambridge: Harvard University Press, 1974). For a reaction, cf. the review by Jill Raitt, *Church History* 44 (1975) 19. See also: N. M. Sutherland, "The Cardinal of Lorraine and the Colloquy of Poissy, 1561: A Reassessment," *Journal of Ecclesiastical History* 28 (1977) 265–89; M. Turchetti, *Concordia o Tolleranza?: Francois Bauduin (1520–1573) e i "Moyenneurs"* (Geneva: Droz, 1984) 649, and the review-reply of Donald Nugent in the *Journal of Ecclesiastical History* 37 (1986) 171–72.
5. Hubert Jedin, *Crisis and Closure of the Council of Trent: A Retrospective View from the Second Vatican Council* (trans. N. D. Smith; London and Melbourne: Sheed and Ward, 1967) 15. For a more complete treatment, see Hubert Jedin, *Geschichte des Konzils von Trient: Dritte Tagungsperiode und Abschluss*; Erster Halbband: *Frankreich und der neue Anfang in Trient bis zum Tode der Legaten Gonzaga und Seripando* (Freiburg-Basel-Vienna: Herder, 1975) esp. 17–38. To the Jedin history of the final period of the Council of Trent the author is much indebted. Unfortunately its two volumes have not been translated into English.
6. Erwin Iserloh, Joseph Glazik, and Hubert Jedin, *Reformation and Counter Reformation* (trans. Anselm Biggs and Peter Becker; New York: Seabury, 1980) 490.
7. H. Jedin, *Crisis*, 28–29 (n. 5 above).
8. A. G. Dickens, *The Counter Reformation* (Norwich: Jarrold and Sons, Ltd., 1969) 121.
9. H. Jedin, *G.K.T.*, Zweiter Halbband: *Uberwindung der Krise durch Morone, Schliessung und Bestätigung* (Freiburg-Basel-Vienna: Herder, 1975) 176.
10. Donald Nugent, *Ecumenism*, 199–200 (n. 4 above); H. Jedin, *G.K.T.*, Zweiter Halbband, 180.
11. DS 1725–34.
12. DS 1738–59.
13. DS 1763–78.
14. DS 1797–1812.
15. *C.O.D.* 720–29. For a more extended exposition of what this debate involved, see Carl J. Peter, "The Office of Bishop and *Jus Divinum*: Trent and the Lutheran

Confessions: A Rereading with Ecumenical Possibilities," *Cristianesimo nella Storia* 8 (1987) 93–113.

16. H. Jedin, *G.K.T.*, Zweiter Halbband, 180, with explicit reference to the decrees on purgatory and the saints. The extension to the decree on indulgences is warranted.
17. Ibid. Here again Jedin is speaking directly only of the decrees on purgatory and the saints. What he says is at least as applicable to the decree on indulgences, which was presented even later.
18. For the treatment of purgatory and of sacred images that Cardinal Guise said was needed, see the report of his comments at the meeting of notables in the residence of Cardinal Morone on Sunday, November 28, 1563: *Concilium Tridentinum: Diariorum, Actorum, Epistularum, Tractatuum Nova Collectio* (ed. Societas Goerresiana; Freiburg im Breisgau: Herder, 1931), Tomus Tertius Diariorum Pars III, I:757. That reference gives as well the view of the emperor's representatives (expressed at the same meeting and to the effect that something should be said about indulgences).
19. Ibid., for Cardinal Guise. At that time it was agreed to try to close the Council on December 9; the date would be moved up when news of the pope's serious illness reached Trent.
20. H. Jedin, *G.K.T.*; Zweiter Halbband, 290.
21. Without attributing an explicit awareness of this to ecumenical councils, the Congregation for the Doctrine of the Faith seems to have "implied" that such phenomena have occurred with regard to dogmatic formulations. In *Mysterium Ecclesiae* (*AAS* 65 [1973] 402–403) it made, among others, the following two points. First, the meaning of the pronouncements of faith depends partly upon the expressive power of the language used at a certain point in time and in particular circumstances. Second, sometimes a dogmatic truth is first expressed incompletely but not falsely, and later more fully and perfectly in a broader context of faith and human knowledge. In the opinion of the author of this essay that is true of what Trent said in its decrees about purgatory and the saints in comparison with what Vatican II said of both in the seventh chapter of *Lumen Gentium*. It is also the case with the Tridentine decree on indulgences in comparison with Paul VI's Constitution *Indulgentiarum Doctrina* (*AAS* 59 [1967] 5–24), which took its origins from deliberations at the Second Vatican Council.
22. For the fate of the minutes of the Council of Trent and the Sarpi–Pallavicino controversy, see Owen Chadwick, *Catholicism and History: The Opening of the Vatican Archives* (Cambridge: Cambridge University Press, 1978) 46–71.
23. *Istoria del Concilio di Trento Parte Seconda Scritta dal Padre Sforza Pallavicino della Compagnia di Giesu* [sic] *Qui insieme rifiutati con autorevoli testimonianze un' Istoria falsa divolgata nello stesso argomento sotto nome di Pietro Soave Polano alla Santitá di Nostro Signore Papa Alessandro VII Parte Seconda con Tavola Universale delle cose piu notabili contenute in ambedue le Parti* (Rome: Nel Stamperia d'Angelo Barnabo dal Verme, 1657) Libro 34, capo 4, 1004. The translation and parentheses that have been added to it are mine.
24. Hubert Jedin, "Entstehung und Tragweite des Trienter Dekrets über die Bilderverehrung," *Theologische Quartalschrift* 116 (1935) 143–88, 404–29, and here esp. 143–44.
25. *G.K.T.*; Zweiter Halbband, 164–89, 228–92.
26. *C.T.*, Tomus 9, Actorum Pars 6, 1079. For the discussion of these two decrees in the general congregation of December 2, ibid., 1070–71. See also: *G.K.T.*; Zweiter Halbband, 181, 183.

27. *G.K.T.*, 185.
28. Ibid., 187.
29. Ibid. See too: *C.T.*, 9:1107.
30. For high praise of at least some of the committee work done at Trent, cf. A. G. Dickens, *The Counter Reformation*, 133, with regard to the Decree on Justification (n. 8 above).
31. For references see n. 18 above.
32. *C.T.*, 9:1076.
33. See n. 24 above.
34. *G.K.T.*, 185.
35. *C.O.D.* 750. Translation mine. According to the wording of the text, Trent had already taught something about purgatory. This it had done in the context of justification and with regard to the sacrifice of the Mass; DS 1580, 1743, 1753.
36. *C.O.D.* 750. Translation mine.
37. Ibid.
38. Jedin, *Crisis*, 145 (n. 5 above).
39. *C.O.D.* 750–52.
40. *LG* 50.
41. See Carl J. Peter, "The Church's Treasure (*Thesauri Ecclesiae*) Then and Now," *Theological Studies* 47 (1986) 251–72, and here esp. 254–68.
42. DS 1448.
43. *Historia del concilio Tridentino* . . . (London: G. Billio, Regio Stampatore, 1619) 783–85.
44. *C.O.D.* 772–73.
45. Jacques Le Goff, *The Birth of Purgatory* (trans. A. Goldhammer; Chicago: University of Chicago Press, 1984) 357.
46. Cf. *A.V.S.*, vol. 3, Periodus 3, Pars 5., 60, 64.
47. *LG* 51.
48. *AAS* 59 (1967) 20. Translation mine.
49. Ibid., 11–12.

8. Gritsch

1. Luther preached about eighty sermons on Mary, all based on biblical texts. An exhaustive collection of Luther's statements on Mary has been offered by Walter Tappolet and Albert Ebneter (eds.), *Das Marienlob der Reformatoren* (Tübingen: Katzmann, 1962) 17–218, 357–64. Two studies have analyzed the chronological development of Luther's views in conjunction with his basic theological views: Hans Düfel, *Luthers Stellung zur Marienverehrung* (Kirche und Konfession, Veröffentlichungen des konfessionskundlichen Instituts des Evangelischen Bundes 13; Göttingen: Vandenhoeck & Ruprecht, 1968) and William J. Cole, "Was Luther a Devotee of Mary?" *Marian Studies* 21 (1970) 94–202. The contemporary significance for the Lutheran-Catholic dialogue of Luther's reflections on Mary has been stressed by Horst Gorski, *Die Niedrigkeit seiner Magd. Darstellung und theologische Analyse der Marientheologie Luthers als Beitrag zum gegenwärtigen lutherisch/römisch-katholischen Gespräch* (Europäische Hochschulschriften 23; Berlin and New York: Lanning, 1987).
2. Table Talk dated November 30, 1531, §119. *WA TR* 1:46.24; *LW* 54:14–15.

3. Table Talk dated July 15–16, 1539, §4707. *WA TR* 4:440.9–10. For an analysis see Eric W. Gritsch, *Martin—God's Court Jester, Luther in Retrospect* (Philadelphia: Fortress, 1983) 6–7.
4. Sermon of December 22, 1532. *WA* 36:388.28–29.
5. Paltz advocated his Mariology in a 1507 Collection of Torgau sermons entitled *Coelifodina* or *Himmlische Fundgrube*. For a summary of his views, see Düfel, 39–45 (n. 1 above).
6. Ibid., 43. On the relationship between Luther and Paltz and the latter's dependence on Gerson and others, see Reinhold Weijenborg, "Doctrina de immaculata conceptio apud Johannem de Paltz, O.E.S.A., Magistrum Lutheri novitii" in *Virgo Immaculata* (Acta congressus mariologici-mariani Romae anno 1954 celebrati; Rome: Academia Mariana Internationalis, 1957) 14:160–83.
7. Sermon on the Feast of the Assumption of Mary, August 15, 1516. *WA* 1:79.6–7.
8. First Lectures on the Psalms, 1513–15. *WA* 3:454.24–25; *LW* 10:397. See also Lectures on Romans, 1515–16, Rom 3:4, "Let God be true," where Luther quotes Luke 1:51 as proof that God alone works faith in human life (*WA* 56:212–13; *LW* 25:197–98). Luther used Mary to oppose the abusive cult of Mary by portraying her as the model of humble faith; see, for example, the 1516 sermon on the Feast of the Assumption of Mary, *WA* 1:78.31–37; 79.6–7, and the Sermon on the Decalogue, 1518. *WA* 1:422.30–35.
9. Explanations of the Ninety-five Theses, 1518. *WA* 1:622.5–7; *LW* 31:240.
10. Conrad Wimpina defended Tetzel's assertion. See Walter Köhler, ed., *Dokumente zum Ablasstreit von 1517* (2d ed.; Tübingen: Mohr, 1934) 139. Even Sylvester Prierias, the Dominican churchman in Rome, agreed with Tetzel's assertion. See Düfel, 89–90 (n. 1 above).
11. Sermon on Christmas Day, 1520. *WA* 7:189.1–20. See also the sermon preached in Erfurt during his journey to Worms, April 7, 1521. *WA* 7:809.10–13. There is a growing consensus among Luther scholars that Luther's reflections on Mary were grounded in a christocentric theology from the beginning. Major Catholic studies making this point: Thomas A. O'Meara, *Mary in Protestant and Catholic Theology* (New York: Sheed & Ward, 1966) 123, states: "Christocentric is the key word"; Brunnero Gherardini, *La Madonna in Lutero* (Roma: Citta Nuova Editrice, 1967) 23, claims that Luther's doctrine is defective because it does not anticipate Pius IX's definition of the Immaculate Conception (1854), as argued by Reintraud Schimmelpfennig, *Die Geschichte der Marienverehrung im deutschen Protestantismus* (Paderborn: Schöningh, 1952) 14, but Gherardini implies that Luther's christocentric theology made his Mariology defective. Major Lutheran studies on this point: Düfel, 273 (n. 1 above), states that Luther moved from Mariology to Christology; Horst-Dietrich Preuss, *Maria bei Luther* (Schriften des Vereins für Reformationsgeschichte 172; Gütersloh: Gerd Mohn, 1954) 22: "To Luther Mary is the embodied doctrine of grace (*verkörperte Gnadenlehre*)." Other studies include Walter Delius, "Luther und die Marienverehrung," *Theologische Literaturzeitung* 79 (1954) 409–14; K. Algermissen, "Mariologie und Marienverehrung der Reformatoren," *Theologie und Glaube* 49 (1959) 1–24; Heiko A. Oberman, "The Virgin Mary in Evangelical Perspective," *Journal of Ecumenical Studies* 1 (1964) 271–98 (reprinted Philadelphia: Fortress Press, Facet Book, 1971; on Luther, 20–22); Eduard Stakemeier, "De Beata Maria Virgine eiusque cultu iuxta reformatores" in *De Mariologia et oecumenismo* (Rome: Pontificia Academia Mariana Internationalis, 1962) 423–77; Arthur C. Piepkorn,

"Mary's Place Within the People of God According to Non-Roman Catholics," *Marian Studies* 18 (1967) 46–83, especially 73–78; Franz Courth, "Das Marienlob bei Luther. Eine katholische Würdigung," *Münchener Theologische Zeitschrift* 34 (1983) 279–92. See also Eric W. Gritsch, "Embodiment of Unmerited Grace. The Virgin Mary According to Martin Luther and Lutheranism" in *Mary's Place in Christian Dialogue* (ed. Alberic Stacpoole; Wilton CN: Morehouse-Barlow, 1983) 133–41.

12. For the historical context, see Jaroslav Pelikan in *LW* 21: xvii–xix. The original German text is in *WA* 7:538–604, the English translation in *LW* 21:297–358.
13. *WA* 7:555.33–35; *LW* 21:308.
14. *WA* 7:568.4; *LW* 21:321. Italics added.
15. *WA* 7:577.30–33; *LW* 21:331.
16. *WA* 7:573.22–27; *LW* 21:327.
17. *WA* 7:574–75.3; *LW* 21:328–29. This text has sometimes been labeled a "medieval remnant" in Luther's piety. But it is quite consistent with his view of the praise of God by the saints on earth and the saints in heaven. The emphasis is on the work of salvation done "in every way [by] God alone." How Luther linked the "invocation" of Mary with his view of the church as the communion of saints has been shown by Vilmos Vajta, "Die Kirche als geistlich-sakramentale communio mit Christus und seinen Heiligen bei Luther," *Lutherjahrbuch* 54 (1984) 10–62; on the invocation of Mary and the controversial text cited, ibid., 53–54.
18. *WA* 10/2:408.10–13; *LW* 43:39–40.
19. *WA* 10/2:408.4–8; *LW* 43:39. That is perhaps why Luther did not deal with the phrase "Pray for us."
20. This shift in translation occurred between 1522 and 1544. For a detailed analysis of Luther's translation of the Vulgate's *plena gratia*, see Heinz Bluhm, "Luther's Translation and Interpretation of the Ave Maria," *Journal of English and German Philology* 51 (1952) 196–211.
21. Personal Prayer Book, 1522. *WA* 10/2:409.9–12; *LW* 43:40–41.
22. Sermon on the Feast of the Immaculate Conception (December 8?) 1527. Festival Postil (*Festpostille*). *WA* 17/2:288.17–34. In another version of the sermon from 1528 Luther declared that Scripture did not say anything about the conception of Mary. Accordingly, various ideas can be advanced, as long as none of them becomes an article of faith. For an analysis of the two versions, see Düfel, 169–170 (n. 1 above).
23. Disputation on the Divinity and Humanity of Christ, February 28, 1540. *WA* 39/2:107.8–13.
24. That Jesus Christ Was Born a Jew, 1523. *WA* 11:320.1–6; *LW* 45:206. More evidence cited by Cole, 119 (n. 1 above).
25. *WA* 11:324.15–18; *LW* 45:212.
26. Sermons on the Gospel of John, 1537. *WA* 46:723.30–33; *LW* 22:214–15.
27. On the Schem Hamphoras and the Genealogy of Christ (*Vom Schem Hamphoras und vom Geschlecht Christi*), 1543. *WA* 53:640.18–22.
28. *WA* 53:634.22–24.
29. See Luther D. Reed, *The Lutheran Liturgy* (Philadelphia: Fortress, 1947) 439–40.
30. See, for example, the choral motets by Albert Dietrich, Karl Hassler, Melchior Vulpius, John Crüger; or the elaborate five-part setting by Johann Sebastian Bach. See Reed, 440.
31. *WA* 35:462–63; *LW* 53:292–94.

32. *WA* 35:424; *LW* 53:220.
33. Third stanza of "All Praise to Thee, O Jesus Christ" (*Gelobet seist Du Jesus Christ*). *WA* 35:434; *LW* 53:241.
34. Third stanza of "Come the Heathens' Healing Light" (*Nun komm der Heiden Heiland*). *WA* 35:430; *LW* 53:236.
35. Third stanza of "Jesus Now We Must Laud and Sing" (*Christum wir sollen loben schon*). *WA* 35:433; *LW* 53:239.
36. Thirty-six hymns are listed in *WA* 35:411–73; English translations in *LW* 53:211–309.
37. Table Talk, dated August 18–22, 1532, §1755. *WA TR* 2:207.22. However, the painting has not been found. See Josef Lieball, *Martin Luthers Madonnenbild* (Stein am Rhein, Switzerland: Christiana, 1981) 14–15. "Marienbilder" texts in Tappolet, 145–52 (n. 1 above).
38. Sermons on the Gospel of John, 1537. *WA* 46:663.34–36. *LW* 22:146.
39. Sermon on the Festival of the Visitation (July 2?) 1544. *WA* 52:682.11–32.
40. See Delius, 414 (n. 11 above).
41. Luther spoke of the persecution of the church but insisted that, like Mary, the church would never be "destroyed (*vertilgt*)." Sermon on the Sunday after Christmas on Luke 3:23–40. Church Postil (*Kirchenpostille*), 1522. *WA* 10/1/1:405.13–16. Oberman used the phrase *typus ecclesiae* in his discussion of the differences between Roman Catholic and Protestant views on Mary (13 [n. 11 above]).
42. "Only the 'Word made flesh' helps and saves me." Epiphany sermon of January 6, 1539. *WA* 47:644.28–32. Both the theological and the liturgical use of the phrase *mater misericordiae* have been traced to the time of Bernard of Clairvaux (1090–1153). See Heiko A. Oberman, *The Harvest of Medieval Theology* (3d ed.; Durham NC: Labyrinth Press, 1983) 311.
43. "Haec pia cogitatio et placet." Exposition of the Ninth Chapter of Isaiah, 1543/44. *WA* 40/3:680.31–32. Two scholars doubt whether Luther affirmed the doctrine of the Immaculate Conception of Mary: Preuss (n. 11 above) came to the conclusion that Luther rejected the doctrine after 1528; O'Meara states that "it is likely, but not certain" that Luther rejected the doctrine (118 [n. 11 above]). But Tappolet (32 [n. 1 above]) demonstrated with the use of texts that Luther did not change his mind. The literary evidence from Luther's works clearly supports the view that Luther affirmed the doctrine, but did not consider it necessary to impose it.
44. Sermon on the Festival of the Assumption, August 15, 1522. *WA* 10/3:269.12–13. Sermon on the Festival of the Visitation (preached on the same date), August 15, 1522. *WA* 52:681.27–31.
45. Luther continued to preach on these festivals, but stopped preaching on the other three festivals after 1523. See Tappolet, 160 (n. 1 above).
46. Sermon on the Afternoon of Christmas Day on Luke 2:1–14, December 25, 1530. *WA* 32:264.4–8; *LW* 51:213.
47. CA 21:2; *BS* 83b, c; *BC* 47.
48. Melanchthon's source was Gabriel Biel's *Exposition of the Canon of the Mass* as well as contemporary worship handbooks. Ap 21:23, 25–26; *BS* 321–22; *BC* 232.
49. Ap 21:27, 29, 32; *BS* 322–23; *BC* 223, 233.
50. SA 1:4; *BS* 414.
51. FC SD 8:24; *BS* 1024; *BC* 595.
52. CA 21:1; Ap 21:4–6; *BS* 83b, 317–18; *BC* 46, 229–30.

53. Ap 21:28, 34; *BS* 322, 324; *BC* 232, 234.
54. Ap 21:27; *BS* 322; *BC* 232.
55. See Piepkorn, 74 (n. 11 above).
56. In his massive *Examination of the Council of Trent* (1565–73) (trans. Fred Kramer; St. Louis: Concordia, 1986) 2:353–507.
57. Gottfried Maron, "Mary in Protestant Theology" in: *Mary in the Churches* (Concilium, Religion in the Eighties, 168; ed., Hans Küng and Jürgen Moltmann; Marcus Lefebure [English ed.]; Edinburgh: Clark; New York: Seabury, 1986) 42.
58. Ibid.
59. In this section I draw on the research of Karlfried Froehlich in his essay "Modern Liturgical Movements, the Saints, and Mary in Protestantism (Germany Only)" (unpublished; February 1986).
60. Quoted ibid., 3. Translation mine.
61. *Maria die Mutter Gottes* (Stuttgart: Evangelisches Verlagswerk, 1950) 61. Translation mine.
62. *Maria: der Weg der Mutter des Herrn* (4th ed.; Darmstadt: Evangelische Marienschwesterschaft, 1960).
63. Baumann's publications on Mary are: *Evangelisches Marienlob heute* (Rottweil/Neckar: Actuelle Texte, 1969); *Kennen wir Maria*? (Rottweil/Neckar: Actuelle Texte, 1973); *Die Retterin: Gedanken eines evangelischen Christen über die Mutter Jesu* (Leutesdorf [am Rhein]: Johannes-Verlag, 1973); *Marias Stunde kommt: das 3 Wort vom Kreuz* (Aschaffenburg: Pattloch, 1974); *Mit Maria in die Zukunft* (Leutesdorf [am Rhein]: Johannes-Verlag, 1975).
64. Wickert has argued his mariocentric view of the salvation history in several essays dealing with "Mary and the church."
65. Max Thurian, *Mary, Mother of All Christians* (trans. N. B. Cryer; New York: Herder and Herder, 1963).
66. "Nachrichten aus Rom. November 1854," *Evangelische Kirchenzeitung*, No. 103 (December 27, 1854) 1027–30.
67. The events of the years 1849 to 1855 are chronicled by Siegfried Gruber, *Mariologie und katholisches Selbstbewusstsein; ein Beitrag zur Vorgeschichte des Dogmas von 1854 in Deutschland* (Beiträge zur neueren Geschichte der Katholischen Theologie 12: Essen: Ludgerus, 1970), according to Eamon Carroll, "Papal Infallibility and the Marian Definitions, Some Considerations," *Carmelus* 26 (1979) 222, n. 11.
68. *Handbuch der protestantischen Polemik gegen die römisch-katholische Kirche* (7th ed.; Leipzig: Breitkopf und Härtel, 1900) 330–35.
69. *Die römische Lehre von der unbefleckten Empfängnis aus den Quellen dargestellt und aus Gottes Wort widerlegt* (Berlin: Schlawitz, 1865).
70. Ibid., v. Translation mine.
71. See Augustino de Roskovány, *Beata virgo Maria in suo concepta Immaculata ex Monumentis omnium seculorum* (9 vols.; Budapest: Athanae, 1879–81) 9:692.
72. *Evangelisches Ave Maria. Ein Beitrag zur Lehre von der selig zu preisenden Jungfrau* (Halle: Fricke, 1863). I have relied on the summary of Dietlein's work in Delius, 303–304 (n. 11 above).
73. Ibid., 303.
74. Ibid., 304.
75. Walther von Loewenich, *Modern Catholicism* (trans. Reginald H. Fuller; New York: St. Martin's, 1959) 198, 201.

76. *The Encyclopedia of the Lutheran Church* (ed. J. Bodensieck; Minneapolis: Augsburg, 1965) 2:1495–96.
77. *The Riddle of Roman Catholicism* (New York and Nashville: Abingdon, 1959) 131–32.
78. Ibid., 137.
79. Piepkorn, 83 (n. 11 above).
80. Ibid., 79.
81. The reactions are collected in Friedrich Heiler, "*Assumptio*. Zur Dogmatisierung der leiblichen Himmelfahrt Marias," *Theologische Literaturzeitung* 79 (1954) 1–2. For a complete list of German Protestant publications, cf. Heinrich M. Köster, "de novo Dogmate Mariano quid Protestantes Germaniae sentiant," *Marianum* 17 (1955) 37–75.
82. *Evangelisches Gutachten zur Dogmatisierung der leiblichen Himmelfahrt Mariens* (Munich: Kaiser, 1950). See also the summary and discussion of this "Opinion" in "Zur Dogmatisierung der Assumptio Mariae. Ein Gutachten evangelischer Theologen," *Theologische Literaturzeitung* 75 (1950) 578–85.
83. *Gutachten*, 21.
84. The letter was signed by Bishop Hans Meiser of Bavaria. I could find only the English translation, in F. E. Mayer, "German Lutheran Bishops Denounce Rome's New Dogma," *Concordia Theological Monthly* 22 (1950) 144–46.
85. Heiler, "*Assumptio*," 39 (n. 81 above).
86. Walter Künneth, *Christus oder Maria? Ein evangelisches Wort zum Mariendogma* (Berlin: Wichern, 1950) 10.
87. Fritz Viering, *Römisch-katholischer Marienglaube und die Botschaft der Reformation* (Gladbeck: Schriftensmissions-Verlag, 1955). I have used the summary of Viering's book in Albert Brandenburg, *Maria in der evangelischen Theologie der Gegenwart* (Paderborn: Bonifacius, 1955) 61–63; quotation, ibid., 62.
88. "Das neue Mariendogma im Lichte der Geschichte und im Urteil der Ökumene," *Ökumenische Einheit* 2 (1950), fascicles 2 and 3. See the summary in Heiler, "*Assumptio*," 45 (n. 81 above). On the Catholic use of the Transitus legend, see Thomas A. O'Meara, *Mary in Protestant and Catholic Theology* (New York: Sheed and Ward, 1966) 102, n. 57.
89. Ibid., 107. Quoted in O'Meara, 263.
90. F. E. Mayer, "The Dogma of Mary's Assumption. A Symptom of Anti-Christian Theology," *Concordia Theological Monthly* 21 (1950) 181–89, especially 181.
91. "Mariologie," *Religion in Geschichte und Gegenwart* (3d ed.; Tübingen: Mohr) 4 (1960) 767–70.
92. Gerhard Ebeling, "Zur Frage nach dem Sinn des mariologischen Dogmas," *Zeitschrift für Theologie und Kirche* 47 (1950) 383–91; quotation, 391. See also Harding Meyer, "The Ecumenical Unburdening of the Mariological Problem: A Lutheran Perspective," *Taproots* 4 (Summer 1988) 2–20 (this is the journal of Lutheran Theological Southern Seminary). The essay views the Lutheran-Catholic consensus on the *Theotokos* as a protection against a church-dividing Marian dogma.

9. Bertram

1. *WA* 17/2:460.
2. *WA* 16:209.
3. *WA* 40/1:495–507; *LW* 26:319–27.

4. *WA* 40/1:78–79; *LW* 26:30.
5. *WA* 40/1:78; *LW* 26:29.
6. Ap 21:4–5; *BC* 229; *BS* 317.
7. Small Catechism 2, 4; *BC* 345; *BS* 511.
8. *WA* 40/1:435, 438; *LW* 26:278, 280. Much of what follows appeared earlier and in greater detail in my *How Theology Is About Man: Luther Since Barth* (unpublished doctoral dissertation; The University of Chicago, 1963) 195–221.
9. *WA* 40/1:432–46; *LW* 26:279–86.
10. *WA* 40/1:435; *LW* 26:278.
11. *WA* 40/1:432–36, 448; *LW* 26:276–79, 287.
12. *WA* 40/1:434; *LW* 26:277–78.
13. *WA* 40/1:96–97; *LW* 26:41–42.
14. *WA* 40/1:94–95; *LW* 26:39–40.
15. *WA* 40/1:434–40, 451; *LW* 26:278–81, 290.
16. *WA* 40/1:261; *LW* 26:151.
17. *WA* 40/1:438, 443; *LW* 26:281, 284.
18. *WA* 40/1:433; *LW* 26:277.
19. *WA* 40/1:86–87; *LW* 26:34–35.
20. *WA* 40/1:261; *LW* 26:151.
21. *WA* 40/1:437; *LW* 26:280.
22. *WA* 40/1:449; *LW* 26:288. Italics added.
23. *WA* 40/1:448; *LW* 26:288.
24. *WA* 40/1:452; *LW* 26:290.
25. *WA* 40/1:433; *LW* 26:277.
26. *WA* 40/1:554, 565, 567; *LW* 26:363, 370, 372.
27. *WA* 40/1:449; *LW* 26:288.
28. *WA* 40/1:449; *LW* 26:288–89.
29. *WA* 40/1:440; *LW* 26:282.
30. *WA* 40/1:273; *LW* 26:160.
31. *WA* 40/1:443; *LW* 26:284.
32. *WA* 40/1:565; *LW* 26:370.
33. *WA* 40/1:447; *LW* 26:287. Italics added.
34. See how, in connection with Gal 2:20, Luther understands *persona* (*WA* 40/1:281–82; *LW* 26:166) as inseparable from being "present in the flesh, living your familiar life, having five senses, and doing everything in this physical life that any other man does." *WA* 40/1:288; *LW* 26:170.
35. *WA* 40/1:45; *LW* 26:7.
36. John Osborne, *Luther* (New York: The New American Library of American Literature, 1963) 50.
37. *WA* 40/1:443; *LW* 26:284.
38. H. W. Bartsch (ed.), *Kerygma and Myth* (trans. R. H. Fuller; London: SPCK, 1957) 6.
39. *WA* 40/1:402–403; *LW* 26:256.
40. *WA* 40/1:434, 436; *LW* 26:277–79. Italics added.
41. *WA* 40/1:435; *LW* 26:278.
42. *WA* 40/1:279; *LW* 26:164.
43. *WA* 40/1:238; *LW* 26:136.
44. *WA* 40/1:434; *LW* 26:278.
45. *WA* 40/1:238; *LW* 26:135.
46. *WA* 40/1:438; *LW* 26:280–81.

47. "For if the blessing in Christ could be conquered, then God himself would be conquered. But this is impossible." *WA* 40/1:440; *LW* 26:282.
48. *WA* 40/1:440; *LW* 26:282.
49. *WA* 40/1:451; *LW* 26:290. Italics added.
50. *WA* 40/1:560; *LW* 26:367.
51. *WA* 40/1:440; *LW* 26:282.
52. *WA* 40/1:448; *LW* 26:287–88.
53. *WA* 40/1:297; *LW* 26:177.
54. *WA* 40/1:298–99; *LW* 26:178–79.
55. *WA* 40/1:437, 434; *LW* 26:280, 278. Italics added.
56. *WA* 40/1:99; *LW* 26:42.
57. *WA* 40/1:455; *LW* 26:292.

10. Jelly

1. *Papal Teachings: Our Lady* (Boston: St. Paul Editions, 1961) No. 62.
2. *Decree on Ecumenism* 11.
3. See R. Laurentin, "The Role of the Papal Magisterium in the Development of the Dogma of the Immaculate Conception" in: *The Dogma of the Immaculate Conception—History and Significance* (ed. E. D. O'Connor, C.S.C.; Notre Dame IN: Notre Dame Press, 1958) 271–324. Cf. E. R. Carroll, O. Carm., "Papal Infallibility and the Marian Definitions—Some Considerations," *Carmelus* 26 (1979) 213–50.
4. DS 2015.
5. Cf. W. Sebastian, O.F.M., "The Controversy over the Immaculate Conception from after Scotus to the End of the Eighteenth Century" in O'Connor, 232 (n. 3 above).
6. DS 1516.
7. Cf. Roger Aubert, *The Christian Centuries, Vol. Five, The Church in a Secularized Society* (New York: Paulist Press, 1978) 57, 119–20.
8. See F. M. Jelly, O.P., *Madonna: Mary in the Catholic Tradition* (Huntington IN: Our Sunday Visitor, 1986) 103–15.
9. *DV* 8.
10. *DV* 10.
11. See J. M. R. Tillard, O.P., "Sensus Fidelium," *One in Christ* 11 (1975) 2–29.
12. Cf. E. Schillebeeckx, O.P., "Exegesis, Dogmatics and the Development of Dogma" in: *Dogmatic Vs. Biblical Theology* (ed. H. Vorgrimler; Baltimore/Dublin: Helicon, 1964) 140.
13. *LG* 56.
14. *LG* 55.
15. Cf. R. H. Fuller, *Preaching the New Lectionary: The Word of God for the Church Today* (Collegeville MN: The Liturgical Press, 1971) xxvi– xxxi; *The Use of the Bible in Preaching* (Philadelphia: Fortress Press, 1981) 35–41.
16. Cf. Schillebeeckx, 115–45 (n. 12 above).
17. Cf. C. Journet, "Scripture and the Immaculate Conception: A Problem in the Evolution of Dogma" in O'Connor, 3–48 (n. 3 above).
18. Cf. *Behold Your Mother: Woman of Faith*, A Pastoral Letter on the Blessed Virgin Mary from the American Bishops (Washington DC: United States Catholic Conference, 1973) 40.

19. Cf. L. Deiss, C.S.Sp., *Daughter of Sion* (Collegeville MN: The Liturgical Press, 1972) 204.
20. Cf. J. H. Newman, *The New Eve* (Westminster MD: Newman Press, 1952) 62.
21. Hymn 27, v. 8; *CSCO* 219:76.
22. *PG* 98:292–309.
23. Cf. J. Ford, C.S.C., "Newman on Sensus Fidelium and Mariology," *Marian Studies* 28 (1977) 120–45.
24. Cf. C. Balić, O.F.M., "The Medieval Controversy over the Immaculate Conception up to the Death of Scotus" in O'Connor, 161–212 (n. 3 above).
25. Ibid., 207.
26. Cf. J. Pelikan, *Development of Christian Doctrine: Some Historical Prolegomena* (New Haven & London: Yale University Press, 1969) 112–13.
27. Cf. G. Wainwright, *Doxology: The Praise of God in Worship, Doctrine and Life* (New York: Oxford University Press, 1980) 218–83.
28. *Papal Teachings: Our Lady*, No. 32 (n. 1 above).
29. See F. M. Jelly, O.P., "Marian Dogmas within Vatican II's 'Hierarchy of Truths,' " *Marian Studies* 27 (1976) 17–40.
30. Karl Rahner, S.J., "The Immaculate Conception" in: *Theological Investigations* (Baltimore: Helicon, 1961) 1:202.
31. Cf. K. Rahner, S.J., "The Dogma of the Immaculate Conception in Our Spiritual Life" in: *Theological Investigations* (Baltimore: Helicon, 1967) 3:140.
32. Cf. Carroll, O. Carm., 236–50 (n. 3 above).
33. Cf. John Macquarrie, *Christian Unity and Christian Diversity* (London: SCM Press, 1975) 90–96.
34. Ibid., 93.
35. Ibid., 95–96.
36. See William Henn, O.F.M. Cap., "The Hierarchy of Truths Twenty Years Later," *Theological Studies* 48 (1987) 439–71, esp. 457–59; "Interpreting Marian Doctrine," *Gregorianum* 70 (1989) 413–37, esp. 429–36; F. M. Jelly, O.P., "St. Thomas' Theological Interpretation of the 'Theotokos' and Vatican II's Hierarchy of Truths of Catholic Doctrine," *Tomasso d'Aquino nel suo settimo centenario* (Atti del congresso internationale 4; Naples: D'Auria, 1976) 221–30.

11. Dulles

1. Clément Dillenschneider, *Le sens de la foi et le progrès dogmatique du mystère marial* (Rome: Academia Mariana Internationalis, 1954) 351.
2. *Sacrorum conciliorum nova et amplissima collectio* (ed. J. D. Mansi; reissued J. B. Martin and L. Petit; Paris: H. Welter, 1927) 53:418–519.
3. On this theme see H. E. Cardinale, "Pope Pius XII and the Blessed Virgin Mary," *Mary's Place in Christian Dialogue* (ed. A. Stacpoole; Middlegreen, England: St. Paul Publications, 1982) 248–60.
4. G. Hentrich and R. G. de Moos (eds.), *Petitiones de Assumptione corporea B. V. Mariae in Caelum Definienda ad Sanctam Sedem delatae* (2 vols.; Rome: Vatican Polyglot Press, 1942).
5. *AAS* 42 (1950) 782–83.
6. These figures are immediately taken from Dominic J. Unger (ed.), *Mary All-Glorious: The Apostolic Constitution "Munificentissimus Deus" Translated and Annotated* (Patterson NJ: St. Anthony Guild Press, 1956) 37, n. 8. Similar figures are given by many other authors.

7. Giovanni Caprile, "Pio XII e un nuovo progetto di concilio ecumenico," *Civiltà Cattolica* 117:3 (1966) 208–27.
8. *AAS* 42 (1950) 775. Unger, in *Mary All-Glorious*, 37, n. 6, reproduces the list of members of the commission from *Osservatore Romano*, December 9–10, 1950 (n. 6 above).
9. Martin Jugie, *La Mort et l'Assomption de la Sainte Vierge: Etude Historico-Doctrinale* (Vatican City: Biblioteca Apostolica Vaticana, 1944).
10. Walter J. Burghardt, *The Testimony of the Patristic Age Concerning Mary's Death* (Westminster MD: Newman, 1957) concludes that Jugie's doubts about whether Mary died are not well supported by the patristic witnesses.
11. Carlo Balić, "De definibilitate Assumptionis B. Virginis Mariae in caelum," *Antonianum* 21 (1946) 3–67. On the death of Mary, see esp. 44–65.
12. Berthold Altaner, "Zur Frage der Definibilität der Assumptio B.V.M.," *Theologische Revue* 44:3 (1948) 129–40; 45:3 (1949) 129–42; 46:1 (1950) 5–20.
13. Altaner cites in this connection the statement of Thomas Aquinas in *S.T.* 1.1.10 ad 1 that no dogmatic argument can be drawn from senses other than the literal. In *S.T.* 3.27.1 Aquinas notes in passing that Scripture does not state that Mary's body was assumed into heaven.
14. Joseph Coppens, "La définibilité de l'Assomption," *Ephemerides theologicae lovanienses* 23 (1947) 5–35.
15. Gérard Philips, "Autour de la définibilité d'un dogme," *Marianum* 10 (1948) 81–111. A similar line of argumentation is pursued by Bernard Lonergan in his "The Assumption and Theology," *Vers le dogme de l'Assomption de la Sainte Vierge* (Montreal, 1948), reprinted in B. Lonergan, *Collection* (New York: Herder and Herder, 1967) 68–83.
16. I. Filograssi, "De definibilitate Assumptionis Beatae Mariae Virginis," *Gregorianum* 29 (1948) 7–41.
17. I. Filograssi, "Theologia catholica et Assumptio B.V.M.," *Gregorianum* 31 (1950) 323–60.
18. An English translation may be found in William J. Doheny and Joseph P. Kelly, *Papal Documents on Mary* (Boston: St. Paul Editions, 1981).
19. In a later encyclical, *Fulgens Corona* (September 8, 1953), announcing the Marian Year of 1954, Pius XII further developed the intrinsic links between these two privileges of Mary.
20. DS 3886.
21. See Jugie, *La Mort*, 424–30 (n. 9 above); Dillenschneider, *Le Sens de la foi*, 152–55 (n. 1 above).
22. The work of Pseudo-Augustine is discussed in Jugie, *La Mort*, 285–91 (n. 9 above) and by Dillenschneider, *Le sens de la foi*, 106–16 (n. 1 above).
23. The most useful collection of texts is Carolus Balić, *Testimonia de Assumptione Beatae Virginis Mariae ex omnibus saeculis* (2 vols.; Rome: Academia Mariana, 1948, 1950). The early Scholastic period is treated in 1:175–220.
24. Balić, *Testimonia*, 1:222–389; 2:5–280.
25. See Jugie, *La Mort*, 414 (n. 9 above); cf. Balić, *Testimonia*, 2:151.
26. Jugie, *La Mort*, 458; cf. Balić, *Testimonia*, 2:260.
27. Cf. Thomas Aquinas, *S.T.* 2–2.5.3c.
28. An excellent survey of the various positions is given in Jan Walgrave, *Unfolding Revelation* (Philadelphia: Westminster, 1972) 164–78.
29. Francisco Marin-Sola, *L'Evolution homogène du dogme catholique* (2 vols.; Fribourg, Switzerland: Imprimerie de l'oeuvre de S. Paul, 1924).

30. On Reginald Schultes see Walgrave, *Unfolding Revelation*, 165–67 (n. 28 above).
31. Walgrave calls this third position the "theological theory of development" and explains it with references to contemporary Catholic theologians in his *Unfolding Revelation*, 332–47.
32. K. Rahner, "The Development of Dogma," *Theological Investigations* (Baltimore: Helicon, 1961) 1:39–77.
33. "The Interpretation of the Dogma of the Assumption," *Theological Investigations* 1:215–27.
34. *Mary the Mother of the Lord* (New York: Herder and Herder, 1963 [German original, 1956]).
35. *Mariologie* (multilithed notes for theology students), Innsbruck, 1951; rev. ed., 1959.
36. Ibid., 424–66.
37. *Mary the Mother of the Lord*, 91 (n. 34 above).
38. E.g., "The Intermediate State," *Theological Investigations* (New York: Crossroad, 1981) 17:114–24, esp. 120.
39. "Pseudo-Problems in Ecumenical Discussion," *Theological Investigations* (New York: Crossroad, 1983) 18:51.
40. "The Intermediate State," 122 (n. 38 above).
41. Text in *Origins* 9 (August 9, 1979) 131–33; quotation from 133. Notwithstanding this admonition, the Rahnerian thesis on immediate entrance into bodily life after death permeates several articles in the issue of the *Ephemerides Mariologicae* 35:1–2 (1985) dealing with the Assumption of Mary in the light of contemporary anthropology and eschatology.
42. *Eschatology* (Washington DC: Catholic University of America Press, 1988 [German original, 1977] 107–11).
43. Ibid., 111.
44. *Daughter Zion* (San Francisco: Ignatius Press, 1983) 74.
45. Ibid., 73–81.
46. "Glorious Assumption," Assumption Day Lecture; lithographed by F. H. Brown, Burnley, England, 1981; no pagination.

12. Peter

1. *A.V.S.*, vol. 2, *Periodus Secunda*, Pars 3, (1972) 338–45.
2. This was on November 23, 1962. Cf. *A.V.S.*, vol. 1, *Periodus Prima*, Pars 4 (1971) 11, 92–120. During the Council's second period that same schema would be discussed at length but under a different title: *De Beata Maria Virgine Matre Ecclesiae*. Cf. *A.V.S.*, vol. 2, *Periodus Secunda*, Pars 3 (1972) 300.
3. *A.V.S.*, vol. 2, *Periodus Secunda*, Pars 3 (1972) 300.
4. In his "Editorial: Mary in the Churches" Hans Küng alludes to the importance of this debate but mistakenly identifies Santos as Archbishop of Colombo rather than Manila. Cf. *Mary in the Churches* (Concilium: Religion in the Eighties 168; ed. H. Küng and J. Moltmann; New York: Seabury, 1983) vii.
5. *A.V.S.*, vol. 2, *Periodus Secunda*, Pars III (1972) 340.
6. Ibid., 339.
7. Ibid., 342–45.
8. Ibid., 343: "Et ne dicas tale schema vel caput redintegratum exhibere posse tantum mariologiam ad modum alicujus sic dictae mariologiae ecclesiotypicae,

in qua scilicet Beata Virgo non exhibetur nisi ut membrum inter caetera membra Ecclesiae passive recipiens beneficia Redemptoris."

9. Ibid., 343–44: "Cum Ecclesia non sit merus fructus redemptionis sed instrumentum redemptionis in manu Christi ad salutem active cooperans."
10. Ibid., 344: "Beata Maria Virgo potest in tali capite vel schemate integrato optime proponi tamquam sublimissima Christi ex ejus gratia cooperatrix in opere salutis et perficiendo et propagando."
11. Ibid., 345.
12. Ibid., 627.
13. The teaching on Mary became the final chapter of the Dogmatic Constitution *Lumen Gentium;* it was given the title *De Beata Maria Virgine Deipara in Mysterio Christi et Ecclesiae.*
14. Paulo Molinari, S.J., *Saints: Their Place in the Church* (trans. D. Maruca, S.J.; New York: Sheed and Ward, 1965) 162. This book was published in Italian in 1962. The author later added an Appendix: "The Saints in the Church according to the Recent Dogmatic Constitution *Lumen Gentium* of the Second Vatican Council," 160–75.
15. This gave a new perspective to the whole chapter. Previously it was the cult of the saints that was highlighted. The introduction of eschatology led to featuring the solidarity of the living and dead members of God's people because of Christ.
16. *A.V.S.*, vol. 3, *Periodus Tertia*, Pars 5 (1975) 75, 96.
17. Ibid., 115.
18. *A.V.S.*, vol. 3, *Periodus Tertia*, Pars 8 (1976) 374.
19. Section 48 includes four significant additions recommended by the Doctrinal Commission and reported by Cardinal Santos on October 19, 1964. Those additions, made in direct response to criticism and requests from Council participants, involve: (a) expressing more clearly the role of the Holy Spirit in bringing the church to its promised future, (b) putting more stress on the collective, ecclesial, and cosmic dimensions of that future, (c) making explicit mention of hell when speaking of that future, and (d) calling attention to the importance of human efforts to anticipate in this world at least in some limited way the final state to which the Trinity is directing history. Cf. *A.V.S.*, vol. 3, *Periodus Tertia*, Pars 5 (1975) 58, 63–64.
20. In reference to the beatific vision, the formulation of the Council of Florence is employed; cf. DS 1305.
21. The biblical citation was added as a result of a request to indicate more clearly the relation of the church on earth to those in purgatory and not as a proof text. At the same time a request was denied that would have spoken of aid coming to the church on earth from those in purgatory. The reason given by the Doctrinal Commission for the failure to adopt this amendment was that it would resolve an issue that was freely disputed among theologians. Cf. *A.V.S.*, vol. 3, *Periodus Tertia*, Pars 5 (1975) 60, 64.
22. DS 1821; see also CS §§31–37.
23. *LG* 53.
24. Ibid.: "Simul autem cum omnibus hominibus salvandis in stirpe Adam invenitur conjuncta. . . ."
25. Ibid.
26. Ibid. There had been a discussion as to whether the title of this chapter should refer to Mary as Mother of the church. The decision was in the negative. The

Preface, however, says equivalently what the title does not. This was noted in the conciliar discussion. Cf. *A.V.S.*, vol. 3, *Periodus Tertia*, Pars 6 (1975) 24. When Paul VI approved *Lumen Gentium* on November 21, 1964, he took the occasion to deliver an allocution. In the latter he declared with considerable emphasis that Mary is the Mother of the church. Cf. *A.V.S.*, vol. 3, *Periodus Tertia*, Pars 8 (1976) 916.

27. Ibid., 54. The Preface ends by saying that what follows is not intended: (a) to be a complete statement of the church's teaching; or (b) to resolve differences of opinion on matters that are freely disputed in Catholic theology.
28. *LG* 55–59.
29. Ibid., 55. This specification regarding hermeneutics and exegesis seems to have been prompted by awareness that historical criticism may not lead to such readings of the two texts cited from the Old Testament. In general the way Scripture functions in chapters 7 and 8 of *Lumen Gentium* rests on a confidence born of faith; namely, that the whole Bible as God's word consigned to writing is a unity and may be legitimately read that way by the church.
30. Ibid., 56.
31. Ibid., 58–59.
32. Ibid., 62. On October 29, 1964, this text was proposed to the Council; it resulted from revision of an earlier version which had read: "Propterea Beata Maria Virgo in Ecclesia, praeterquam aliis, etiam titulo Mediatricis condecorari consuevit." Cf. *A.V.S.*, vol. 3, *Periodus Tertia*, Pars 6 (1975) 16, 30–32, 35–37. That prior text had drawn three kinds of reactions. The first was to retain the title *Mediatrix* in that it does correspond to the piety of the faithful and to drop it might create scandal. The second wished to eliminate the title; noted its relatively recent origin; said it introduced a whole theological system into doctrine—something the Council would do well to avoid—and declared it had no desire to increase ecumenical problems. Further, the New Testament as well as the Councils of Florence and Trent use the term Mediator for Christ only. The third urged retaining the title while disarming it theologically by introducing others that are also popular in Catholic piety but lacking in the connotations rightly objected to by the second group. It was the third proposal that won out—the vote on the entire chapter being 1,159 *Placet;* 10 *Non Placet;* 521 *Placet juxta Modum;* and 1 invalid ballot. Cf. *A.V.S.*, vol. 3, *Periodus Tertia*, Pars 6 (1975) 49. The *modi* were then evaluated. Although the same three tendencies occurred again in the amendments proposed regarding the term *mediatrix*, no change was made; *A.V.S.*, vol. 3, *Periodus Tertia*, Pars 8 (1976) 163–64. The final vote on the eighth chapter was: 2,096 *Placet;* 23 *Non Placet;* 1 invalid ballot. For the importance and significance of the conciliar understanding of cooperation in relation to Christ's mediation (*LG* 62), see also CS §§57–60.
33. *LG* 64.
34. Ibid., 65.
35. Ibid., 67.
36. Ibid., 68.

13. J. F. Johnson

1. This is subtitled: Die Gestalten des evangelischen Namenkalenders (Kassel: Johannes Stauda-Verlag, 1965). Interestingly enough, February 2 commemorates Burkhard von Würzburg. August 15 commemorates Johann der Beständige and concludes with a reference to Luther's sermon at the occasion of John's death.

2. *Lutherisches Gesangbuch* (St. Louis: Concordia Publishing House, 1892), used for German language services in congregations of the Lutheran Church–Missouri Synod, contains hymns to commemorate the three Marian festivals. Each refers to Christ. One hymn of seventeen verses commemorates the Holy Apostles, but the entire hymn invokes Christ. Three hymns refer to the Nativity of Saint John the Baptizer. Each points the worshiper to Jesus the Redeemer.
3. *LBW*, 9–12.
4. *LWp*, 8–9.
5. *The Lutheran Hymnal* (St. Louis: Concordia Publishing House, 1941).
6. *LBW* 177/178; *LWp* 193/194.
7. *LBW* 184; *LWp* 186.

14. E. A. Johnson

1. Possible candidates: Ephraem the Syrian, Romanos the Singer, Basil of Seleucia, Andrew of Crete, or Germanus of Constantinople. See Armand Robichaud, "Mary, Dispensatrix of All Graces," in: *Mariology* (ed. Juniper B. Carol; Milwaukee: Bruce, 1957) 2:444; Michael O'Carroll, *Theotokos: A Theological Encyclopedia of the Blessed Virgin Mary* (Wilmington DE: Glazier, 1982) 240.
2. Hilda Graef, *Mary: A History of Doctrine and Devotion* (New York: Sheed and Ward, 1963) 1:146.
3. See Jaroslav Pelikan, *The Growth of Medieval Theology (600–1300)* (Chicago: University of Chicago Press, 1978) 158–74; Walter Delius, *Geschichte der Marienverehrung* (Munich: Reinhardt Verlag, 1963) 149–70; Heiko Oberman, *The Harvest of Medieval Theology* (Cambridge MA: Harvard University Press, 1963) 281–322.
4. *PL* 144:761.
5. Hermann of Tournai, *PL* 180:30.
6. "Sermo in Nativitate B.V. Mariae (De aqueductu)," *PL* 183:441 (complete sermon, cols. 437–48). This line was quoted by later popes and became a classic axiom in the literature of Mariology.
7. *PL* 183:429–38.
8. "Omnis gratia, quae huic saeculo communicatur, triplicem habet processum. Nam a Deo in Christum, a Christo in Virginem, a Virgine in nos ordinatissime dispensatur. . . ." "Sermo 5 de nativitate B.M.V.," *Opera Omnia* (Florence: Ad Claras Aquas ex typ. Collegii S. Bonaventurae, 1650) 4:96.
9. Louis Grignon de Montfort, *True Devotion to the Blessed Virgin Mary* (trans. F. Faber; London: Burns & Oates, 1904) 12–13.
10. Alphonsus Liguori, *The Glories of Mary* (ed. E. Grimm; Brooklyn, NY: Redemptorist Fathers, 1931) 162.
11. The excerpts from all encyclicals are taken from *The Papal Encyclicals: 1740–1981* (5 vols.; ed. Claudia Carlen; Wilmington NC: McGrath, 1981). Pius IX, *Ubi Primum* §4; Carlen 1:292.
12. Ibid., *Octobri Mense* §4; Carlen 2:272–73.
13. Ibid., *Iucunda Semper*, §5; Carlen 2:356–57.
14. Ibid., *Ad Diem Illum Laetissimum* §13–14; Carlen 3:14.
15. *Cognitum Sane*, *AAS* 18 (1926) 213.
16. *Mediator Dei* §169, quoting Bernard; Carlen 4:146 (n. 11 above).
17. Overview in E. Dublanchy, "Marie Mediatrice," *Dictionnaire de Théologie Catholique* IX/2 (Paris: Librairie Letouzey et Ané, 1927) cols. 2389–2405. A survey

of the state of the Catholic question was made for Protestants by Cornelis de Ridder, *Maria als Miterlöserin?* (Göttingen: Vandenhoeck & Ruprecht, 1965).

18. Juniper B. Carol, *De corredemptione B.V.M.; Disquisitio positiva* (Vatican City: Typis Polyglottis Vaticanis, 1950) 9.
19. Reginald Garrigou-Lagrange, *The Mother of the Savior and Our Interior Life* (trans. B. J. Kelly; St. Louis: B. Herder, 1959) 176–77.
20. *Alma Socia Christi* (Proceedings of the International Mariological Congress; Rome: Academia Mariana, 1950) 1:234.
21. René Laurentin, *La Vierge au Concile* (Paris: Lethielleux, 1965) 186, n. 26.
22. Text in *Marian Studies* 12 (1961) 16–18.
23. See René Laurentin, "Le chapitre De Beata Virgine devant les exigences de la renovation conciliare," *Ephemerides Mariologicae* 16 (1966) 5–32.
24. Karl Rahner, "Zur konziliaren Mariologie," *Stimmen der Zeit* 174 (1964) 87–101; and René Laurentin, *La Vierge au Concile*, 20–21 (n. 21 above).
25. *Schema constitutionis de beata Maria Virgine Matre Dei et Matre Hominum (1962), Acta et Documenta Concilio Oecumenico Vaticano II Apparando*, Series 2 Praeparatoria III:1 (Rome: Typis Polyglottis Vaticanis, 1969) 206–207.
26. *Relatio* of Cardinal Roy and the relevant speeches are in *A.V.S.*, III:1 (1973) 435–544.
27. *Animadversiones scripto exhibitae quoad cap. VIII Schematis de Ecclesia, A.V.S.*, III:2 (1974) 99–188.
28. *LG* 60.
29. *LG* 62, with the Latin *in* translated as "in" rather than as "by," which is done in Abbott.
30. *LG* 62.
31. See observation by Eamon Carroll, *Understanding the Mother of Jesus* (Wilmington, DE: Michael Glazier, 1979) 92–96.
32. *Redemptoris Mater, Origins* 16:43 (April 9, 1987) 745–66.
33. Yves Congar, *Christ, Our Lady and the Church* (trans. H. St. John; London: Longmans, Green & Co., 1956) 68–77.
34. Elsie Gibson, "Mary and the Protestant Mind," *Review for Religious* 24 (1965) 397.
35. René Laurentin, "Esprit Saint et théologie mariale," *Nouvelle Revue Théologique* 89 (1967) 26–42. See also his "Bulletin sur Marie," *Revue des sciences philosophique et théologique* 60 (1976) 452–56; and 70 (1986) 119 n. 122, with bibliography.
36. Congar, *I Believe in the Holy Spirit* (trans. D. Smith; New York: Seabury, 1983) 1:159–66 and 3:155–64. For other insights see also H. Mühlen, *L'Esprit dans l'Eglise* (Paris: Editions du Cerf, 1969) 134–37; L. J. Suenens, "The Relation That Exists between the Holy Spirit and Mary," *Mary's Place in Christian Dialogue* (ed. Alberic Stacpoole; Wilton CN: Morehouse-Barlow Co., 1982) 69–78; and Elizabeth Johnson, "Mary and the Female Face of God," *Theological Studies* 50 (1989) 500–526.
37. Garrigou–Lagrange, *The Mother of the Savior and Our Interior Life*, 206 (n. 19 above).
38. Laurentin, *La Vierge au Concile*, 122 (n. 21 above).
39. Michael Schmaus, *Der Glaube der Kirche: Handbuch katholischer Dogmatik* II (Munich: Max Hueber Verlag, 1970) 693.
40. K. Rahner, "One Mediator and Many Mediations," *Theological Investigations* (trans. G. Harrison; New York: Seabury Press, 1972) 9:172–73 and n. 24 above.

41. See Elizabeth Johnson, "May We Invoke the Saints?" *Theology Today* 44 (1987) 32–52.
42. E.g., Otto Semmelroth, "Dogmatic Constitution on the Church," chapter 8, *Commentary on the Documents of Vatican II* (ed. Herbert Vorgrimler; New York: Herder & Herder, 1967) 5:291.

15. Forde

1. So, apparently, the Cynics and Stoics. See Bernard J. Verkamp, "The Limits Upon Adiaphoristic Freedom: Luther and Melanchthon," *Theological Studies* 36 (1975) 55.
2. Ibid., 56.
3. Eric W. Gritsch and Robert W. Jenson, *Lutheranism. The Theological Movement and Its Confessional Writings* (Philadelphia: Fortress Press, 1976) 201. Gritsch and Jenson work from the question of what is necessary. Since nothing is necessary once one is justified by faith alone, one must go on to ask: Necessary for what? The only answer can be: Necessary to the preaching of the gospel and the contingent commands involved therewith. This specifies more carefully a Lutheran understanding of what is commanded and forbidden because a mere biblicistic answer to that question would be inadequate.
4. *CR* 7:259.
5. Clyde L. Manschrek, "The Role of Melanchthon in the Adiaphoristic Controversy," *Archiv für Reformationsgeschichte* 49 (1957) 170.
6. FC Ep 10; *BC* 492–94; *BS* 813–16; FC SD 10; *BC* 610–16; *BS* 1053–63.
7. Manschrek, "Adiaphoristic Controversy," 180 (n. 5 above). See also Oliver K. Olson, "Politics, Liturgics, and Integritas Sacramenti," in: *Discord, Dialogue, and Concord* (ed. L. W. Spitz and W. Lohff; Philadelphia: Fortress Press, 1977) 74–75.
8. Manschrek, "Adiaphoristic Controversy," 166 (n. 5 above).
9. *CR* 7:259 f. Not all of these rites and practices, of course, were newly forced upon them by the Interims. Many were standard or carry-overs from previous practice.
10. *BC* 229, n. 9; *BS* 316, n. 4.
11. *BC* 229; *BS* 316.
12. *BC* 230; *BS* 319.
13. Ap 21:10–11; *BC* 230; *BS* 318.
14. *BC* 231; *BS* 319.
15. *BC* 297; *BS* 425.
16. Ap 21:14; *BC* 230; *BS* 319.
17. *WA* 28:177 f.
18. *WA* 32:91 f.
19. *WA* 12:262; *LW* 30:7.
20. *WA* 10, 3:407 f.
21. *WA* 17, 2:255.
22. SA 2:3:28; *BC* 297; *BS* 425.
23. Carl J. Peter, "A Moment of Truth for Lutheran-Catholic Dialogue," *Origins* 17, n. 31 (1988) 541.

List of Participants

CATHOLICS

The Most Rev. T. Austin Murphy (until September 1984)
Auxiliary Bishop of Baltimore, Maryland
The Most Rev. J. Francis Stafford (beginning February 1985)
Archbishop of Denver, Colorado
The Rev. Avery Dulles, S.J.
Laurence J. McGinley Chair of Theology, Fordham University, Bronx, New York
The Rev. Robert B. Eno, S.S.
Catholic University of America, Washington DC
The Rev. Joseph A. Fitzmyer, S.J.
Catholic University of America, Washington DC
The Rev. John F. Hotchkin
Director, Bishops' Committee for Ecumenical and Interreligious Affairs, Washington DC
The Rev. Frederick M. Jelly, O.P. (beginning February 1984)
Mount St. Mary's Seminary, Emmitsburg, Maryland (consultant)
Sr. Elizabeth A. Johnson, C.S.J.
Catholic University of America, Washington DC
The Rev. Kilian McDonnell, O.S.B.
Institute for Ecumenical and Cultural Research, Collegeville, Minnesota

The Rev. Carl J. Peter
Catholic University of America, Washington DC

The Rev. Walter Principe, C.S.B. (beginning September 1988)
Institute Professor of the Pontifical Institute of Mediaeval Studies and Professor at the University of Toronto, Ontario, Canada

The Rev. Msgr. Jerome D. Quinn (until February 1984)
The St. Paul Seminary, St. Paul, Minnesota

Dr. Jill Raitt (until September 1987)
Department of Religious Studies, University of Missouri-Columbia, Columbia, Missouri

The Rev. George H. Tavard, A.A.
Methodist Theological School, Delaware, Ohio

LUTHERANS

Dr. H. George Anderson
President, Luther College, Decorah, Iowa

Dr. Robert W. Bertram
Christ Seminary-Seminex Professor of Historical and Systematic Theology, Lutheran School of Theology at Chicago, Chicago, Illinois

Dr. David G. Burke
Director, Office of Studies, USA National Committee of the Lutheran World Federation, New York, New York (until September 1987)

Dr. Joseph A. Burgess
St. Paul, Minnesota

Dr. Gerhard O. Forde
Professor of Systematic Theology, Luther Northwestern Theological Seminary, St. Paul, Minnesota

Dr. Karlfried Froehlich
Professor of Ecclesiastical History, Princeton Theological Seminary, Princeton, New Jersey

Dr. Eric W. Gritsch
Professor of Church History, Lutheran Theological Seminary, Gettysburg, Pennsylvania

Dr. Kenneth Hagen
Professor of Theology, Department of Theology, Marquette University, Milwaukee, Wisconsin

Dr. Horace Hummel (beginning September 1984)
Professor of Old Testament, Concordia Seminary, St. Louis, Missouri

Dr. John Frederick Johnson
Inter-Lutheran Council for Continuing Education, St. Petersburg, Florida

Dr. George A. Lindbeck
Pitkin Professor of Historical Theology, Yale University Divinity School, New Haven, Connecticut (advisor)

Dr. Daniel F. Martensen
Associate Director, Office of Ecumenical Affairs, Evangelical Lutheran Church in America, Chicago, Illinois (beginning February 1988)

Dr. John Reumann
Professor of New Testament, Lutheran Theological Seminary, Philadelphia, Pennsylvania